To the Mountaintop

Also by Stewart Burns

Social Movements of the 1960s: Searching for Democracy (1990)

A People's Charter: The Pursuit of Rights in America (1991, coauthor)

Birth of a New Age: The Papers of Martin Luther King Jr.,
volume 3 (1997, coeditor)

Daybreak of Freedom: The Montgomery Bus Boycott (1997)

Martin Luther King Jr.'s

Sacred Mission to

Save America: 1955–1968

To the Mountaintop

Stewart Burns

 HarperSanFrancisco

A Division of HarperCollins*Publishers*

TO THE MOUNTAINTOP: *Martin Luther King Jr.'s Sacred Mission to Save America: 1955–1968.*
Copyright © 2004 by Stewart Burns. All rights reserved. Printed in the United States of
America. No part of this book may be used or reproduced in any manner whatsoever
without written permission except in the case of brief quotations embodied in critical
articles and reviews. For information address HarperCollins Publishers, Inc., 10 East
53rd Street, New York, NY 10022.

HarperCollins books may be purchased for educational, business, or sales promotional
use. For information please write: Special Markets Department, HarperCollins Publishers, Inc., 10 East 53rd Street, New York, NY 10022.

HarperCollins Web site: http://www.harpercollins.com

HarperCollins®, 📖 ®, and HarperSanFrancisco™ are trademarks of HarperCollins
Publishers, Inc.

FIRST EDITION

Library of Congress Cataloging-in-Publication Data is available upon request.

ISBN 0–06–054245–4

04 05 06 07 08   RRD(H)   10 9 8 7 6 5 4 3 2 1

Dedicated to Rev. Dr. Robert McAfee Brown (1920–2001),
friend, mentor, saint

Contents

Preface

I met Dr. Martin Luther King Jr., when I was twelve and he was thirty-two, in a house of worship in my hometown. It was April 1961, a month before the freedom rides that desegregated southern bus terminals. Dr. King was spending a week in residence at Williams College in western Massachusetts. That Sunday evening he was preaching at the tall Gothic chapel up the street from my home. His sermon was called "Three Dimensions of a Complete Life." As I marched down the left-hand aisle to find a seat, I found myself walking right next to the heroic preacher, awash in brightly colored robes. He looked holy. His chocolate face was glowing.

Two summers later, during the Negro Revolution of 1963, I took a month-long train trip around my country. In cosmopolitan Chicago, my first stop, a middle-aged man tripped over my feet and fell into the busy street, breaking his glasses. Despite my earnest apology, he screamed at me: "I'd expect that from a nigger, but not from a boy like you!" Shaken, I forged on. On my return from the West Coast, I tested desegregation of Atlanta's train station, quietly sitting in the "colored" waiting room.

In late August, I rode a chartered bus all night from New England down to the March on Washington. Standing under a shady elm tree by the reflecting pool below the Lincoln Memorial, I encountered King again, this time from a distance. His voice boomed into history on that hot afternoon.

As a civil rights historian years later, I was privileged to serve as an editor of Dr. King's papers at Stanford University. Learning about his life and leadership has transformed my own.

. . .

ON THE EVE OF THAT HISTORIC March on Washington, the great African-American scholar and activist W. E. B. Du Bois died in his adopted country of Ghana. "One ever feels his twoness," Du Bois wrote a hundred years ago at the height of Jim Crow repression and brutality, "an American, a Negro; two souls, two thoughts, two unreconciled strivings; two warring ideals in one dark body."

To the Mountaintop explores how on his climb toward freedom, a divided Martin King battled for his soul, struggled to make peace between his unreconciled strivings. There was King the black man, the American, the global citizen; the fighter for black emancipation alongside the fighter for American renewal and redemption, for the redemption and salvation of humanity. There was King the lofty idealist at odds with King the rooted realist; the rock of faith beset by the sands of doubt.

Even more consequential, for his time, our time, and times to come, stood King the fiery warrior for justice and right striving to reconcile with the increasingly devout apostle of nonviolence or "soul force." Like his spiritual mentor Saint Paul, he fought his way to the revelation that militant faith, however essential, would remain blind without the morning light of compassion.

"Though I have the gift of prophecy," Paul confessed to the Corinthians, in words King took to heart, "and understand all mysteries and all knowledge, and though I have all faith, so that I could remove mountains, but have not love, I am nothing.

"And now abide faith, hope, love, these three; but the greatest of these is love."

Book One

A Mighty Stream

1955–1957

Prologue:

Lamb of God

Strange fruit.

Jeremiah Reeves, seventeen years old, was a popular student at Booker T. Washington High School in Montgomery, Alabama. He played drums in a rhythm-and-blues band. Like his father he drove a delivery truck. One of his stops was a house in a white neighborhood. The housewife, attracted to the handsome, dark-skinned boy, invited him in one day. They began having an affair. Neighbors took notice. Someone peeked in the window, saw them undressing, called the police. Reeves was accused of rape. He spent the rest of his short life behind bars.

Despite diligent efforts by the National Association for the Advancement of Colored People (NAACP), Reeves was convicted of sexual assault and sentenced to death. Upon turning twenty-one, he was electrocuted. Reeves was one of countless black men murdered by law or lynching for the most grievous sin against white supremacy: sex with a white woman.

During his trial a young friend of his, ninth-grader Claudette Colvin, took up collections and showed movies to raise money for his defense. His conviction made her bitter. She grieved about his wasting away on death row. "I knew I had to do something," she recalled. "I just didn't know where or when."[1] She wanted to become a lawyer to help her people who were being railroaded in the racist courts.

The smart young girl lived in the rundown King Hill neighborhood surrounded by railroad yard, stockyard, and junkyards. Her mother worked as a maid. Her father mowed lawns. She had hated segregation for as long as she could remember. Her first memory of anger, when she was nine or ten, "was when I wanted to go to the rodeo. Daddy bought my sister boots and bought us both cowboy hats. That's as much of the rodeo as we got. The show was at the Coliseum, and it was only for white kids."

Her mind "got pricked" by a ninth-grade history teacher, Geraldine Nesbitt, who impressed on her the importance of self-worth, and to "think for ourselves" about what rights they had. Colvin tried to get her classmates to talk about how they could change things, but they "looked at me like I was from another planet."[2]

Nesbitt, tall and the color of dark chocolate, took pride in her blackness. "Do you feel good about yourselves?" she asked her students. "You feel good inside?" She insisted that "you won't let anything stop you, regardless of your complexion."

She assigned essays about how her students felt about being black. Colvin wrote about the indignities of segregation. "I felt clean," she wrote, "and I didn't see why we couldn't try on clothes in the store. Furthermore, why do we have to press our hair and straighten our hair to look good?"

Nesbitt read her essay to the class. "Oh, Claudette! You're crazy," her friends said. Showing the courage of her convictions, she refused to straighten her hair from that day on and wore kinky braids. Friends taunted her. Her boyfriend broke up with her. She felt it important to set an example.[3]

Two years later, on March 2, 1955, Colvin's yen for simple justice caused Montgomery's racial cauldron to overflow. As usual, the fifteen-year-old eleventh-grader rode city buses home from school. Carrying a heavy load of schoolbooks to prepare for tests, the straight-A student waited for her transfer on Dexter Avenue. Before it came she did something out of the ordinary. While her friends were shopping, she walked into Dexter Avenue Baptist Church, where her teachers worshiped, and prayed.

"Something spiritual just came over me. I said, 'How is it You don't love Your children?' I said it again: 'How is it the Lord doesn't love the black children?' "[4]

She boarded the bus. It stopped at Court Square, where during slave auctions girls as young as she had been shown off bare breasted to rapacious buyers. Several white passengers got on, filling up the bus. The driver demanded that Colvin and her schoolmates give up their seats. They were sitting in the unreserved middle section near the back door. Her friends got up. Colvin did not move. A black girl said, "She knows she has to get up." Another said, "She doesn't have to. Only one thing you have to do is stay black and die."

The driver walked back to her seat. "If you are not going to get up I will get a policeman." He came back with a traffic cop.

"Why are you not going to get up?" the cop asked her. "It is against the law here." Still she did not move.

"I didn't know," she replied, "that it was a law that a colored person had to get up and give a white person a seat when there were not any more vacant seats and colored people were standing up. I said I was just as good as any white person and I wasn't going to get up." The cop left to get reinforcements to deal with the skinny schoolgirl weighing under a hundred pounds.

Two patrolmen pulled up in a squad car, lights flashing. As they approached Colvin, a white girl told them she was right "because there is no room for them in the back." Another white girl disagreed: "Make them stand up because after a while they will try to take over."[5]

One of the cops asked Colvin, who was crying, "Aren't you going to get up?"

"No, sir," she said, and explained her defiance in a storm of words. "That was worse than stealing," she recalled, "talking back to a white person." Her mother liked to say that "she can out-talk forty lawyers."

The cop was unpersuaded. "I will have to take you off." He kicked her with his heavy boots and knocked the books out of her arms.

"One got on one side of me and one got the other arm and they just drug me out." As they pulled her roughly from the bus she called out in her high-pitched voice, "It's my constitutional right to sit here! You have no right to do this." She had learned about the Constitution and the Bill of Rights from Mrs. Nesbitt. Her constitutional understanding was correct in light of the Supreme Court's nine-month-old *Brown* decision, although it applied to school segregation. She must have known too about the city's "separate but equal" bus law, which required a Negro to give up a seat only if a vacant one was available.

"It really hurt me," she recalled, "to see that I have to give a person a seat, when all those colored people were standing and there were not any more vacant seats."

They shoved her in the back of the patrol car and handcuffed her through the window. A motorcycle cop said he was sorry.[6] She was interrogated at the police station.

"What happened to this black bitch?" one cop asked. "This is a black whore. Take her to Atmore [state prison] and get rid of her." The desk sergeant warned her: "I am going to make it hot for you in the morning."[7] She was taken to the city jail, locked in a small cell. Her pastor at Hutchinson Street Baptist Church bailed her out. Police threw the book at the traumatized girl, charging her with violating the segregation code, disorderly conduct, and assault and battery on a police officer.

To defend their daughter Colvin's parents called a family friend, Fred Gray, twenty-four, one of Montgomery's two black lawyers, who had grown up in the city, graduated from Alabama State College, and just earned his law degree from Case in Cleveland. An ordained minister, Gray had decided to pursue law because he was determined to help destroy segregation. Colvin's arrest might be the case he was looking for to upset its constitutionality in public transportation. He knew her already because she was involved in Young Alabama Democrats, a group he had started.

Gray persuaded Colvin to attend the local NAACP Youth Council, run by Rosa Parks, forty-two, a longtime NAACP activist who as a young girl had played with Colvin's mother. Parks organized a legal defense fund for Colvin.

Her arrest galvanized the black community like nothing else in recent memory. It occurred amid a city election in which black concerns, and black assertiveness, were central for the first time. In late February E. D. Nixon, NAACP activist and union leader, had organized an unprecedented meeting at the black-owned Ben Moore Hotel where black leaders quizzed the white candidates about pressing issues, including the bus situation. On March 5 the Citizens Coordinating Committee, formed by undertaker and ex–Alabama State football coach Rufus Lewis to speak for all black organizations, issued an appeal to the "Friends of Justice and Human Rights." It denounced injustices on city buses and presented the Colvin case as "an opportunity, in the spirit of democracy, and in the spirit of Christ, to deal courageously with these problems."[8]

As the March election neared, the Women's Political Council brought a small delegation to meet with the bus manager and a racially moderate city commissioner. The WPC, comprising black professional women, had been fighting to improve bus treatment for several years. The delegation, led by WPC president Jo Ann Robinson, an English professor at Alabama State, included Parks, Nixon, Lewis, and twenty-six-year-old Rev. Martin Luther King Jr., who had arrived in town six months earlier to take over Dexter Avenue Baptist Church. The white officials appeased the indignant blacks; the commissioner was counting on black votes for reelection. The bus manager admitted that the driver had violated regulations by ordering Colvin to give up her seat and promised to investigate. Responding to the group's demand to get rid of reserved sections, the commissioner said he would have the city attorney determine its legality. He assured the group that justice would be done, Robinson recalled, "and that Claudette would be given every fair chance to clear her name."[9] The leaders left cautiously optimistic.

Their momentary hope was dashed when Colvin's trial took place in mid-March before Juvenile Court judge Wiley Hill Jr., cousin of Alabama senator J. Lister Hill. Although several people had been convicted of violating bus segregation, no one had ever before pleaded not guilty. Judge Hill denied Gray's motion to acquit because the city bus segregation law was unconstitutional, flouting the Fourteenth Amendment. When Gray then moved for acquittal because no vacant seat was available, the prosecutor abruptly switched the charge to disobeying the state law, which had no such provision. Gray objected that the state law did not apply to city buses, but Hill found Colvin guilty. He dismissed the disorderly conduct charge, but convicted her also of assault and battery. Although his partner did not back him up, one of the arresting officers testified that, handcuffed in the police car, Colvin had "kicked and scratched me on the hand, also kicked me in the stomach."[10]

Judge Hill put Colvin on indefinite probation and, declaring her a juvenile delinquent, made her a ward of the state. Gray appealed her conviction to Montgomery Circuit Court, hoping to challenge the segregation violation.

Although her supporters in the courtroom had no illusions about Jim Crow justice, even for a juvenile, the verdict came as a shock. Despite her distress Colvin had remained calm, Robinson remembered, but when convicted, "Claudette's agonized sobs penetrated the atmosphere of the courthouse. Many people brushed away their own tears."[11]

Robinson reported that "blacks were as near a breaking point as they had ever been. Resentment, rebellion, and unrest were evident in all Negro circles. For a few days, large numbers refused to use the buses" in a spontaneous boycott.[12]

Rev. King, many of whose congregants were shaken by Colvin's plight, wrote that "the long repressed feelings of resentment on the part of the Negroes had begun to stir. The fear and apathy which had for so long cast a shadow on the life of the Negro community were gradually fading before a new spirit of courage and self-respect."[13]

In this supercharged atmosphere, black leaders held a second meeting with bus and city officials. The bus manager could have defused the crisis if he had carried out his promise to investigate Colvin's arrest and clarify the seating policy. But at this follow-up meeting, lawyers were marched in and the white stand hardened. Mayor W. A. Gayle, who did not need black votes for reelection, and the city attorney represented the city. The bus company lawyer, Harvard Law graduate and racial moderate Jack Crenshaw, expressed certitude that neither the city nor state segregation law would permit a "first come, first serve" seating arrangement without reserved sections. In fact the bus line in Mobile, Alabama, owned by the same company, had done this since 1917.

Frustrated by the official intransigence, the black leaders found their tempers flaring. Robinson threatened a boycott of the buses, which the WPC had almost started right after Colvin's arrest. Several days later, following a campaign more racially polarized than ever, the moderate commissioner was defeated by exterminator Clyde Sellers, ex-chief of the state highway patrol, who had race-baited his way to victory.

Gray's appeal of Colvin's conviction was heard in May by Circuit Court Judge Eugene Carter, who denied Gray's challenge to the Alabama bus segregation law. But the prosecutor dropped the segregation charge, preventing Gray from pursuing his constitutional battle in a higher state court. Despite flimsy evidence, Carter affirmed Colvin's conviction for assault and battery on the police officer.

Gray explored options with his mentor, prominent white lawyer Clifford Durr, a Montgomery native who had served Roosevelt's New Deal as a member of the Federal Communications Commission. Gray decided he would file a lawsuit in federal court with Colvin as plaintiff. Gray, Durr, his wife Virginia Foster Durr, an anti-segregation activist, and E. D. Nixon drove to Colvin's home to discuss the lawsuit with Mary Ann and Quintus Publius Colvin. Mrs. Colvin revealed to them that their daughter "done took a tumble." She had just found out that she was pregnant. The couple were devastated.[14] They did not want their daughter to be publicly shamed in another courtroom. The meeting convinced Nixon that even if Claudette could handle the pressure, her parents might not. That was the end of the lawsuit—for the time being.

Colvin had gotten pregnant by a married man two or three months after her arrest. "I didn't know what to do," she recalled. "I couldn't marry him, I didn't have the money to run away, my mother wouldn't hear of an abortion. It was so hard on my nerves."[15]

The arrest and trials had ravaged her emotionally. She dropped out of school in the fall, abandoning her dream of college and law school. Humiliated, shunned by former friends, she struggled to regain the self-worth that the ordeal had stolen from her. Jim Crow had sullied, then wrecked her childhood, dragging her into an unforgiving adulthood. She gave birth to her son, Raymond, in the winter—she had turned sixteen—and raised him with her family.

"The only thing I am still angry about," she confided forty years later, "is that I should have seen a psychiatrist. I needed help. I didn't get any support. I had to get well on my own."[16]

Colvin lost her childhood and her last illusions about justice. In neighboring Mississippi a boy barely fourteen had his young life crushed out of him. In August 1955 Emmett Till, who lived in Chicago, was visiting his cousins in the flat, fertile cotton-rich Delta his parents had come from. He had a speech defect caused by polio. Buying candy at a country store in Money, the high-spirited kid whistled to the white proprietress, out of nervousness or jest. This was an intolerable affront to Deep South racial order.

Three days later, after midnight, the woman's husband and his brother took Till from the shack where he was staying to a plantation barn, where they found a white girl's photo in his wallet. Unfamiliar with southern rules, he admitted she was his girlfriend. The men beat him savagely, shot him through the head, cut off his testicles, and dumped him in the Tallahatchie River with a heavy cotton gin fan wired to his neck. His body somehow floated to the surface and was discovered by a white teenager fishing. His mother, Mamie Till, insisted that her son's mutilated corpse, his monstrous crushed face, be displayed at his funeral for the world to see. The killers were caught. Despite gripping testimony by Mrs. Till, an all-white jury set them free. Paid by *Look* magazine for their story, they confessed to the crime but were never punished.

The murder and trial drew a surprising amount of national publicity. Why all this fuss over a dead nigger in the Tallahatchie? asked a white Mississippian. "That river's full of niggers."[17] Throughout the country African Americans were horrified by the brutality of the child lynching and the killers' acquittal. For many it washed out the optimism they had felt with the *Brown* decision a year before.

Till's slaying was a barbaric example of a customary practice of white repression that grew out of slavery. More than four thousand black citizens, almost all male, had been lynched since Reconstruction. Nearly a century after slavery's abolition, lynching was still the core of a violent system of social control that terrorized African Americans in the Deep South.

Back in Montgomery, where the Till horror hit black people hard, official promises proved hollow as usual. Bus riders continued to be mistreated and forced out of seats they had a right to. Mary Louise Smith was an eighteen-year-old housemaid making two dollars a day. She had toiled all week for a white woman who had not paid her. Now she had to give up a morning and two bus fares to ride across town to collect the eleven dollars, which she and her family depended on.

When she knocked at the middle-class home no one came to the door. Furious, fighting back tears, she took the bus home. Her day got worse.

"I was sitting behind the sign that said for colored," she later testified in federal court about this October day. "A white lady got on the bus and she asked the bus driver to tell me to move out of my seat for her to sit there. He asked me to move three times, and I refused. So he got up and said he would call the cops."

She told the driver: "I am not going to move out of my seat. I got the privilege to sit here like anybody else."[18] Police took her to jail. Her father, a widower working two jobs to raise six children, got a ride from a friend to bail her out. She was tried in city court and fined, not for violating the segregation law but for refusing to obey an officer. Like Colvin she did not believe she had broken the law.

As winter swept into Montgomery, black citizens felt beleaguered and betrayed. Would they resign themselves to their subjugation, dig in their heels, and wait for a better day? Or would they walk an untraveled path into the future?

I

First Baptist Church, Montgomery, Alabama
January 30, 1956

"Onward Christian soldiers," the spirited assembly belted out, "marching as to war." The hymn had been written to inspire Union forces during the Civil War. Prayer followed, then another hymn, "Plant My Feet on Higher Ground." A short, somber minister rose to the pulpit for that evening's pep talk.

"Some of our good white citizens told me today that the relationships between white and colored used to be good," he said softly, "that the whites have never let us down and that the outsiders came in and upset this relationship. But I want you to know," his voice building volume, "that if M. L. King had never been born, this movement would have taken place. I just happened to be here.

"There comes a time," his words now a resonating shout, "when time itself is ready for change. That time has come in Montgomery and I had nothing to do with it.

"Our opponents—I hate to think of our governmental officers as opponents, but they are—have tried all sorts of things to break us, but we still hold steadfast. Their first strategy was to negotiate into a compromise and that failed. Secondly, they tried to conquer by dividing and that failed. Now they are trying to intimidate us by a get-tough policy and that's going to fail too, because a man's language is courage when his back is against the wall." The assembly erupted in thunderclaps.

"When we are right, we don't mind going to jail!" More ear-splitting applause. "If all I have to pay is going to jail a few times and getting about twenty threatening phone calls a day, I think that is a very small price to pay for what we are fighting for. We are a chain. We are linked together, and I cannot be what I ought to be unless you are what you ought to be."[19] More thunderous clapping as he sat down.

Following him at the pulpit was Solomon S. Seay, former head of the national African Methodist Episcopal (AME) church.

"You know," Rev. Seay started out, "if a man doesn't want to sit besides me because I'm dirty, that's my fault. If he doesn't want to sit besides me because I'm loud, that's my fault too, but if he doesn't want to sit besides me because I'm *black*, that's not my fault because God made me black and my white brother is discriminating against God and His will. But even though they are, we must love them. We must love Mr. Sellers and Mr. Gayle for God said that we must love our enemies as ourselves. Let's not hate them, for with love in our hearts and God on our side, there are no forces in hell or on earth that can mow us down.

"I had a book which was so interesting," he continued, "that I gave it to the city officials to read. It's a book on great powers, the stories of men who ruled and conquered by force only to lose. Men like Alexander the Great, Napoleon and Hitler were discussed, men who lived by the sword. Their empires are no longer, but have perished.

"But there was a man who taught that love and faith could move mountains and more mountains. And unto this day that empire which was built by a man who said while dying on the cross, 'Forgive them O Lord, for they know not what they do.' That is the empire of Jesus Christ! He was asking forgiveness for the men who crucified him, drove nails through his hands and put thorns on his head. So we forgive Sellers and Gayle, but we do not give up."[20]

Back at the King parsonage on South Jackson Street, a small one-story clapboard house, Coretta Scott King was watching television, still a novelty, in the front parlor, a church friend keeping her company. She heard the thud of something landing on the concrete porch and footsteps scurrying away. Alert to what it might be, she grabbed her friend and they dashed to the back of the house, where tiny, two-month-old Yolanda was sleeping in her crib. Then came the explosion, the loudest noise she had ever heard. She held her screaming friend. The baby cried. The dynamite sticks had blown a hole in the concrete floor, wrecked porch columns and the front wall, and smashed several windows. It would have injured anyone sitting in the parlor. It would likely have killed Coretta King had she looked out the window to investigate the thud.

Over at First Baptist on the other side of the statehouse, Rev. King was supervising the collection. A member of his church walked briskly down the aisle and whispered to Rev. Ralph Abernathy, King's closest friend, whose church this was. Out of the corner of his eye King saw ministers conferring urgently. Agitated, he turned to Abernathy and asked what the hell was going on.

"Your house has been bombed."

He asked about his wife and baby.

"We are checking on that now."[21]

He returned to the pulpit, told the people what happened. Several shouted out in shock and alarm. A few women screamed. King urged calm, which he somehow embodied, advising them to go home directly and hold to nonviolent principles.

"Let us keep moving," he said firmly but wearily, "with the faith that what we are doing is right, and with the even greater faith that God is with us in the struggle."[22]

Staring straight ahead, he marched out of the church and drove home. The parsonage was surrounded by a furious sea of several hundred black people, who "came to do battle," Coretta King recalled.[23] New waves were arriving every minute. Densely packed, they closed in around the house. Making his way through the strangely silent crowd, King saw many handguns in belts and pockets, a few hunting rifles, scores of knives and baseball bats. He heard a black man defy a white cop.

"Move back, boy. What's the matter, you can't understand plain English?"

"I ain't gonna move nowhere," the black fellow burst out. "That's the trouble now. You white folks is always pushin' us around. Now you got your .38 and I got mine. So let's battle it out."[24]

Stunned by the sight of the bombed-out porch, lit by police searchlights, King strode into the house past police, reporters, cameras, Mayor W. A. Gayle, and Police Commissioner Clyde Sellers. He found his wife and baby unhurt. Gayle and Sellers tried to reassure him that such behavior would not be tolerated. King did not reply, but C. T. Smiley, head of the Dexter church trustees and principal of segregated Booker T. Washington High School, where Claudette Colvin had gone, could not hold back:

"Regrets are all very well," he said sternly, "but you are responsible. It is you who created the climate for this."[25]

The phone rang nonstop, mostly supporters. A white woman said she was sorry, but the Negroes were responsible; the boycott had made the white people lose all respect for them. Another white woman claimed that she had thrown the bomb, that she was sorry she did such a poor job, but she wanted to teach Rev. King a lesson. She hung up before a detective grabbed the extension. The Kings made statements for the TV cameras aimed at calming the furor.[26]

Hapless police efforts to disperse the still growing crowd had the opposite effect, provoking them into belligerent defiance. They jeered the beet-red mayor and police boss when the arch-segregationists tried to pacify them. The officials retreated into the house, where they beseeched King to stop a full-scale race riot. The pastor walked grimly out on the mangled porch and the huge throng cheered lustfully. He raised one hand and silence broke out.

"Everything is all right," he reassured the crowd. "It is best for all of you to go home.[27]

"We believe in law and order," he continued. "Don't get panicky. Don't get your weapons. He who lives by the sword will perish by the sword. Remember that is what God said.

"We are not advocating violence. We want to love our enemies. I want you to love our enemies. Be good to them. Love them and let them know you love them.

"I did not start this boycott. I was asked by you to serve as your spokesman. I want it to be known the length and breadth of this land that if I am stopped this movement will not stop. If I am stopped our work will not stop. For what we are doing is right. What we are doing is just.

"And God is with us.[28] With love in our hearts, with faith and with God in front we cannot lose."[29]

Many of the people were crying. Coretta King "could see the shine of tears on their faces, in the strong lights. They were moved, as by a holy exaltation." Some shouted "Amen" and "God bless you, Reverend."[30]

The multitude of over a thousand started to drift away but then swayed ominously back toward the parsonage. Standing in the dark night like solid granite, they solemnly sang, "My country 'tis of Thee, sweet land of liberty." Then "Amazing Grace," composed as an act of repentance by John Newton, an English slave ship captain. Softly hymning, "I once was blind but now I see," the black mass, moving as one body, disappeared into the darkness.

A relieved policeman had the final word: "If it hadn't been for that nigger preacher," he said to a fellow cop, "we'd all be dead."[31]

"This could well have been the darkest night in Montgomery's history," King wrote in his memoir. "But something happened to avert it: The spirit of God was in our hearts."[32]

Forty years later Coretta King reflected that this moment was "a turning point in the movement, in terms of injecting the nonviolent philosophy into the struggle. It could have been a riot, a very bloody riot. If that had happened the whole cause could have been lost."[33]

2

Two months before:
Early Thursday evening, December 1, 1955

Rosa Parks was eager to get home after a long, hot day of tailoring in the pre-Christmas rush at Montgomery Fair department store. She earned fifty cents an hour, below minimum wage, in a steamy, claustrophobic sweatshop, where she handled a heavy pressing iron that worsened the painful bursitis in her shoulder.

After work, hefting a full bag of groceries, the light-skinned Negro woman climbed on a city bus at historic Court Square, once the center of slave auctions and the first capital of the Confederacy. In February 1861, ex-Mississippi senator Jefferson Davis chaired a meeting here of white leaders from six Deep South states that had decided to secede from the Union. These slaveholders drafted a constitution for the new Confederacy and elected Davis president. He was inaugurated a few blocks away near the statehouse.

Now a century later, Court Square sparkled with Christmas lights. A bright banner declared, "Peace on Earth, Goodwill to Men." Parks sat down in a row between the "whites only" section up front and the rear seats reserved for "colored." By custom blacks always sat in the midsection if the back was filled. A white man got on the crowded bus and the driver—who a decade before had ejected Parks for refusing to enter through the back door—ordered her and three other black riders to stand so the white man could sit alone. The others reluctantly got up, but she did not budge. She was put off by the driver's command, since she believed she was sitting where she belonged. Certainly she wasn't violating the law. He stopped at the Empire Theater and called the police. She felt no fear. Police arrested her and took her to jail.

Parks had not planned her calm, resolute protest but had prepared well for it. Like Claudette Colvin, Mary Louise Smith, and other black women in past years, her cup of forbearance had cracked open.

"I had almost a life history of being rebellious against being mistreated because of my color," she recalled. On this occasion more than others—did her bursitis hurt more that day?—"I felt that I was not being treated right and that I had a right to retain the seat that I had taken." The time had come "when I had been pushed as far as I could stand to be pushed. I had decided that I would have to know once and for all what rights I had as a human being and a citizen."[34]

Reflecting later on her motives, she said that she refused to obey the driver "because I was so involved with the attempt to bring about freedom from this kind of thing." She felt determined "to give what I could to protest against the way I was being treated, and felt that all of our meetings, trying to negotiate, bring about petitions before the authorities, really hadn't done any good at all."[35] A civil rights activist of long standing, Parks had served as secretary of both the Montgomery and Alabama state NAACP. For years she had advised the local NAACP Youth Council, which she had helped found in the 1940s. Colvin had joined the activist youth group after her March arrest for the exact same "crime" that Parks herself had just committed.

Since childhood in the rural outskirts of Montgomery, when on her own she learned Bible passages by heart, Parks had been an ardent worker in the African Methodist Episcopal Church—known as the "Freedom Church," she was proud to say, during the abolitionist movement. Founded in 1816 in Philadelphia, the AME church had broken away from the white Methodist mainstream that condoned slavery. The AME, less patriarchal than black Baptists, had always had a majority of female members, who like Parks were its informal leaders. Women AME preachers had been prominent for a century, although not ordained until 1948.

"God is everything to me," she once confessed. Civil rights leader

James Farmer later remarked of her "biblical quality"—"a strange religious glow" about her, a "humming Christian light."[36]

BY THE EARLY 1950s ill treatment on city buses, which replaced the half-century-old electric streetcars during the Depression, had emerged as the most acute problem in the black community, since so many thousands, especially women and schoolchildren, depended on the bus every day. Inflicting the injustice of Jim Crow apartheid, it proved the impossibility of "separate but equal" accommodations.[37] Resentment and anger grew, fueled by expectations of better race relations in the postwar era. The black community felt most aggrieved when, during the Korean War, young army vet Hilliard Brooks, wearing his uniform the day after discharge, was shot dead by a cop after arguing with the bus driver over his dime fare.

Leaders of the Women's Political Council converted the pain of abusive treatment on buses into a glaring public issue. Mary Fair Burks, chair of the English department at all-black Alabama State College in Montgomery, founded the council in 1949 after experiencing racial harassment by local police. As a teenager growing up in Montgomery during the 1930s, she had defied the Jim Crow system by insisting on using white-only elevators, rest rooms, and other public facilities in "my own private guerrilla warfare."[38] Burks, her Alabama State colleague Jo Ann Robinson, and other active members of Dexter Avenue Baptist Church made up the core of the group's membership of middle-class professional women, many being teachers. The WPC's initial purposes were to foster black women's involvement in civic affairs, to promote voting through citizenship education, and to help victims of rape.

Robinson was born in 1912 on a small cotton farm in southern Georgia, youngest of twelve. After her father died and the farm failed, she graduated from Georgia State College and earned her master's degree at Atlanta University. She got married, but the death of her infant child embittered her and the marriage collapsed. She joined the newly formed Montgomery women's group in fall 1949, having just begun teaching English at Alabama State. Upon completing her first semester, happier than she'd ever been, she boarded a bus to the airport to spend the Christmas holidays with family in Cleveland, Ohio. Not habituated to seating rules because she usually drove, the young professor absent-mindedly sat down in the front white section of the almost empty bus. The driver yelled at her and raised his arm to strike her. Fleeing in terror, she cried for days—so shaken that she vowed to remedy such racial abuse.

After she succeeded Burks as WPC president in the early 1950s, the group focused more on bus treatment and other everyday concerns like police brutality. Robinson persuaded Mayor Gayle to permit WPC leaders to attend all city meetings that affected black residents. They learned how to lobby white officials face-to-face, but with little success.

The WPC was the largest, best-organized, and most assertive black civic organization in the Alabama capital. It worked with other community groups like the NAACP that had been organizing longer but had made voter registration and electoral politics their priority, particularly after the Supreme Court in 1944 abolished the "white only" southern primaries.

Tall, stately, and ebony black, E. D. Nixon, in his mid-fifties, had been a Pullman train porter for thirty years and for nearly that long head of the Alabama region of A. Philip Randolph's Brotherhood of Sleeping Car Porters. He once spoke of the Pullman porters' role as heralds of black freedom.

"Everybody listened because they knowed the porter been everywhere," he explained, "and they never been anywhere themselves. In cafés where they ate or hotels where they stayed, they'd bring in the papers they picked up—white papers, Negro papers. We'd put 'em in our locker and distribute 'em to black communities all over the country. Along the road, where a lot of people couldn't get to town, we used to roll up the papers and tie a string around 'em. We'd throw these papers off to these people. We were able to let people know what was happening."[39]

In June 1941, the month of a threatened black march on Washington against racial discrimination, Nixon led several hundred aspiring voters to the Montgomery courthouse in an attempt to register, which was blocked by county officials. Two years later he founded the Montgomery Voters League to promote black registration and voting. Registration efforts gathered steam after World War II, when black combat veterans like Hilliard Brooks came home with boosted confidence and self-esteem. They expected to be rewarded for fighting for freedom overseas with more freedom at home.

Nixon hammered away at a host of civil rights issues as president of both the Montgomery NAACP branch, which he helped found in the 1920s, and the state NAACP conference. Rufus Lewis, a mortician who had coached a championship Alabama State football team in the 1930s, made voter registration a single-minded crusade. In the late 1940s he established a night club called the Citizens Club to promote registering and voting among vets and other young people. No one could enter the club without proof of registration.

A handful of ministers too had battled racial injustice. In 1949 Solomon Seay sought redress without success for a young black woman raped by two white police officers—a common outrage in the segregationist South. After the Supreme Court's 1954 decision in *Brown v. Board of Education* he led a campaign to desegregate local schools. For several years, through 1952, Vernon Johns railed against segregation from the pulpit of Dexter Avenue Baptist Church. One of his brash sermons helped inspire Burks to start the Women's Political Council.

Owing to friction among Negro leaders, like that between middle-class Lewis and working-class Nixon, and to resignation in the black community, but more because of monolithic resistance by the white elite, none of these reform efforts made much headway by the mid-1950s. Black leaders faced a sobering dilemma that would bedevil the freedom movement for years to come. They lacked political power and knew that they could not really change their circumstances until they were fully enfranchised. But electoral initiatives toward this end, vital for long-term progress, did not offer immediate solutions to their pressing problems.

Then came the lightning flash of Rosa Parks's auspicious "no."

Nixon, whom Parks had worked with for a dozen years in the NAACP and as his secretary in his union office, bailed her out of jail. To make sure there would be no problem, two liberal whites accompanied him: attorney Clifford Durr and his wife, Virginia Foster Durr, a well-known activist, a leader of the antisegregation Southern Conference Educational Fund (SCEF), a crusader against the discriminatory poll tax, and sister-in-law of Supreme Court justice and ex-Alabama senator Hugo Black, who had been an active member of the Ku Klux Klan during its heyday in the 1920s.

Virginia Durr, then fifty-two, had become close friends with Parks, who had sewn dresses for her four daughters when she had no money to buy new ones. In August 1955, the month of Emmett Till's killing, Durr had arranged a scholarship for Parks to attend a two-week workshop on school desegregation at the Highlander Folk School, in the Appalachian mountains of Tennessee. Union Theological Seminary graduate Myles Horton, born and bred in the region's poverty, started the school in 1932, the Depression bottom. He burned with desire to help poor people gain power to improve their lives. For twenty years Highlander had served as a training center for community activists and CIO labor organizers. Recently it had begun schooling southern activists for the civil rights struggle. Like a modern-day Socrates, Horton fired questions to workshop participants to help them find answers to social problems from their own experience, then taught them how to apply this method to develop grassroots leadership.

At the close of the August workshop, Horton asked participants what changes they hoped for in their far-flung southern communities. Parks said that she did not expect things to improve in Montgomery, where the Negroes were "timid and would not act" and "wouldn't stand together." Still, she was deeply stirred by her sojourn at the mountain retreat, experiencing Highlander, where whites and blacks talked, ate, square-danced, swam, and played volley ball together, as a microcosm of a racially integrated society.

"I found out for the first time in my adult life that this could be a unified society," she recalled, "that there was such a thing as people of differing races and backgrounds meeting together in workshops and living together in peace and harmony. I gained there strength to persevere in my work for freedom."[40]

Now four months later Nixon and the Durrs returned with Parks from jail to her small apartment in a housing development on Cleveland Avenue, eventually renamed Rosa Parks Avenue. Rosa Parks shared it with her husband, Raymond, and her ailing mother, a former schoolteacher who had wanted Rosa to teach. As they drank coffee, Nixon persuaded her, over her husband's diehard resistance, to use her arrest as the long-hoped-for test case to challenge the constitutionality of bus segregation. Raymond Parks, whose skin was so light he could pass for white, cut airmen's hair at integrated Maxwell Field Air Force base outside town. He was no stranger to activism, a longtime NAACP member who had served during the 1930s on the National Committee to Defend the Scottsboro Boys, nine youngsters falsely accused of raping two white women on a freight train in northern Alabama. Virginia Durr recalled his panic: "He kept saying over and over again, 'Rosa, the white folks will kill you.' "[41]

Her quiet resolve prevailed. Having worked with her closely for a long time, Nixon was sure that—although he would never have foreseen it—she was the right person to serve as public symbol. She was well known and esteemed in the black community as activist and church worker, she was educated and articulate, and her character was unblemished—the ideal representative of black grievances and hopes. And it helped that she had a light complexion. "If ever there was a woman who was dedicated to the cause," Nixon recalled, "it was Rosa Parks."[42]

Later that night, attorney and part-time pastor Fred Gray, two weeks shy of twenty-five, told Jo Ann Robinson about Parks's arrest. They agreed that if they were ever to boycott the buses, this was the time. Robinson then talked with Nixon on the phone. They concurred that pursuing the slow-moving constitutional challenge should be reinforced by a boycott, initially for one day, that the Women's Political Council had long been mulling over and others had tried to start more than once. They set the boycott for Monday, December 5, the date of Parks's trial, to dramatize their grievance and demonstrate newfound black unity and determination.

Nixon placed a sheet of paper on his kitchen table, drew a rough sketch of the city, measuring distances with a slide rule. "I discovered nowhere in Montgomery at that time a man couldn't walk to work if he wanted to." He said to his wife: "We can beat this thing."[43] While Nixon, knowing how things got done in the black world, wanted first to enlist the backing of black ministers, Robinson and her WPC colleagues kicked off the bus boycott on their own. This time they would not let it be held back by more cautious leaders. She quickly typed up a half-page flyer on a stencil and around midnight drove to the Alabama State campus. She and a business professor stayed up the night covertly mimeographing thousands of copies. Next day, between and after classes, she and two trusted students delivered bundles to black neighborhoods, schools, and businesses.

Before he left on his Pullman run that morning, Nixon called the preachers. According to his recollection, activist Ralph Abernathy was enthusiastic but Martin King, one of the newest pastors in town, was hesitant.

"Brother Nixon," he replied slowly, "let me think about it a while, and call me back." When Nixon did so, he was supportive.

"I'm glad you agreed," Nixon chuckled, "because I already set the meeting up to meet at your church," which was also Robinson's.[44] Later that day at Dexter Avenue Baptist, ministers joined with the WPC ladies, the Citizens Coordinating Committee, Progressive Democrats, and other black groups to prepare the Monday protest. On Sunday morning preachers pushed participation from their pulpits. The best publicity came from a front-page article in Sunday's *Montgomery Advertiser*, intended to alert the white community.

Scarcely any African Americans rode the buses on Monday, December 5. Most walked to work or school, carpooled with friends, hitchhiked. Some rode farm tractors, mule wagons. Hundreds took taxis as black cabdrivers cut fares to the price of a bus ride. In the morning Parks appeared in Recorder's Court with her supporters. Judge John B. Scott convicted her of violating the state (not city) segregation law and fined her fourteen dollars. Gray appealed the verdict as planned.

Awestruck by the boycott's stunning success, eighteen leaders met in the afternoon at Mount Zion AME Zion Church, Parks's church, and created a new organization, the Montgomery Improvement Association, to direct the protest. They elected officers, set up committees, and drew up an agenda for a preannounced mass meeting at Holt Street Baptist Church that night. Rufus Lewis nominated King, his pastor, for MIA president, and—getting over their surprise—participants elected him without opposition. They chose him because he was known as a strong social gospel preacher—and because as a newcomer he was unencumbered by long-running quarrels and rivalries among his peers.

S EVERAL THOUSAND SOULS converged on spacious, newly restored Holt Street Baptist Church in a black working-class area, filling the sanctuary and basement two hours before the 7 P.M. starting time, tightly packing the aisles and entryway. Four or five thousand stood silently outside, listening to the meeting by loudspeakers. Those who found seats sang hymns and spirituals and prayed until the meeting began with singing of "Onward Christian Soldiers" and "Leaning on the Everlasting Arms." When the mammoth audience stood to sing, King recalled, "the voices outside swelling the chorus in the church, there was a mighty ring like the glad echo of heaven itself."[45] Then a rousing prayer by Rev. W. F. Alford, and a Scripture reading by U. J. Fields, a mid-twenties Korean War vet and pastor of Bell Street Baptist Church.

Fields read Psalm 34, David's hymn of praise and thanksgiving to the Lord, in which, as the Old Testament put it, he "pretended madness" before Abimelech, murderous king of Shechem, who expelled him. But what appeared as madness to the king was for David possession by the Spirit of God, which gave him an unearthly glow.

"I sought the Lord, and He heard me, and delivered me from all my fears. The angel of the Lord encamps all around those who fear Him, and delivers them. Many are the afflictions of the righteous, but the Lord delivers him out of them all."[46]

This was the radiant courage, Fields was saying, that black people had to wear before their white rulers. But what did it mean to fear God, in order to be delivered from all fears? It did not mean to cower before God but rather to feel reverential awe, to feel God's presence within through the power of the holy spirit. This was the source of David's radiance, as for all those whose light within was moving them to leave the buses. To many in the white community, black folks were acting crazy. Rather, in their own minds they were being glorified by their inner light. Fear of God removed human fear.

The featured speaker was the MIA's new president, a stranger to most people there. In this whirlwind day he'd had less than half an hour to prepare his address. His anxiety nearly paralyzing him, he had prayed for help.

"How could I make a speech," he had asked himself, glaring at blank note paper, "that would be militant enough to keep my people aroused to positive action, and yet moderate enough to keep this fervor within controllable and Christian bounds? I knew that many of the Negro people were victims of bitterness that could rise to flood proportions. What could I say to keep them courageous and prepared for positive action and yet devoid of hate and resentment? Could the militant and the moderate be combined in a single speech?"[47] The resolution of this dilemma, making this "the most decisive speech of my life," prefigured the moral quest that would define his ministry from that moment on.[48]

After reviewing Rosa Parks's arrest and the black community's history of abuse on the buses, and sketching the national and global context in which they were acting, he declared baldly that "we are not wrong in what we are doing." If they were wrong, he insisted, the Supreme Court and the Constitution were wrong. Justice would be a lie and love have no meaning. If we are wrong, "God Almighty is wrong. If we are wrong, Jesus of Nazareth was merely a utopian dreamer that never came down to earth."

This last claim was the most absolute of all. If they were wrong, in other words, Jesus was no more than a naïve idealist, pontificator of lofty beatitudes—but not God's anointed messiah who took earthly form to redeem humanity from its wickedness. Jesus would be a fake. For black Baptists in particular this would be blasphemy. King was stepping out on the first of many trembling moral limbs. If their protest was wrong, he might as well give up not only the MIA presidency but his Baptist ministry, his whole faith. That's how sure he was, or convinced himself to be.

"We are determined here in Montgomery," he went on, "to work and fight until justice runs down like water (*Yes, applause*), and righteousness like a mighty stream (*Keep talking, applause*).

"We must keep God in the forefront. (*Yeah*) Let us be Christian in all of our actions. (*That's right*) But I want to tell you this evening that it is not enough for us to talk about love. Love is one of the pivotal points of the Christian faith. There is another side called justice. And justice is really love in calculation. (*All right*) Justice is love correcting that which revolts against love. (*Well*)" He borrowed this formulation from theologian Paul Tillich, the subject of his doctoral dissertation. Then he upped the ante to cosmic heights.

"The Almighty God himself is not the God just standing out saying through Hosea, 'I love you, Israel.' He's also the God that stands up before the nations and said: 'Be still and know that I am God (*Yeah*), that if you don't obey me I will break the backbone of your power (*Yeah*) and slap you out of the orbits of your international and national relationships.' (*That's right*) Standing besides love is always justice, and we are only using the tools of justice. Not only are we using the tools of persuasion, but we've come to see that we've got to use the tools of coercion."

After Rev. Abernathy read the boycott resolutions from the pulpit, the vast audience rose as one and with great cheering called out their resolve to continue the boycott "until some arrangement has been worked out" with the bus company.

When King returned to the pulpit after Parks was introduced and the resolutions ratified, he sharpened his words. They will face any consequences, he bellowed, as long as they get justice. As they struggle for their rights, some might die. But "if a man doesn't have something that he'll die for, he isn't fit to live. (*enthusiastic applause*)"[49] Not only might some in this new crusade lose their lives, but if they weren't willing to do so, they were not worthy of life.

Thus, as much as he might have intended to balance the absolute demand for justice with the tempering force of Christian love, and as much as he sought to subdue his rhetoric in his reconstruction of the speech in his memoir *Stride Toward Freedom*, in fact he failed to "combine the militant and the moderate." It was, despite evocations of forbearance and compassion, an unabashed call for moral militancy, for unbridled moral courage, to attain God's Truth. He did not utter the words *nonviolent* or *passive resistance*. He did not say the "weapon of love," but the "weapon of protest." He deployed violent imagery, speaking of an angry God slapping peoples around and breaking their earthly power. He set no limits on how far justice might go in "correcting that which revolts against love."

But the thirty-fourth Psalm Fields had recited promised that God would not harm those who were righteous, even as the divinity smashed to oblivion those who did evil, to the unforgiving extreme of cutting off "remembrance of them from the earth." Like most black preaching through the ages, King's sermon was inspired by the prophetic fire of the Hebrew Scriptures. The Jesus he invoked in this instance was not the beatific rabbi of the Sermon on the Mount, but the militant Christ of Revelation, fury overflowing.

What then was the "new meaning" that the morally courageous black people of Montgomery would inject into "the veins of history and of civilization"?[50] Above all, it was the power of unity in faith. Beginning on December 5, the participants in this saga learned that true democracy cannot bloom without deep community. The bus boycott exemplified an unparalleled solidarity across class and gender lines, the schooled and unschooled, literate and illiterate, Ph.D.s and "no D's." The driving force of it all was thousands of African-American women, middle class and working class, active in churches, clubs, and sororities. They transplanted democracy from their sheltered sanctuaries to public streets and squares. They turned faith and friendship from the healing balm of survival into the fire of defiance and transformation.

Montgomery's black citizens understood, as did their nineteenth-century forebears who conquered slavery, that democracy meant that they "must themselves strike the blow." They must act as their own agents of change. They would learn in the coming months that democracy was more than a right, more than a responsibility, but a pantheon of hope and faith. These citizens' reach for democracy was rooted in the churches, scriptures, and spirituals that tied them to their divinity and to generations past and not yet born. They would make Montgomery a praying movement, a testament to their faith in God and, through God, faith in themselves. A testament to God's grace.

Their Bibles and preachers taught them that they were God's chosen people, like the children of Israel. The bus boycott consummated this faith, made it surge alive in mass meetings, car pools, and weary soulful walking. Every day, in their minds, they were moving toward the promised land. The mass church-based protest exalted them as makers of history, vehicles of the holy spirit. The sense of divine calling catapulted their self-esteem, their dignity, their collective self-confidence. They came to believe that they were building, through toil, sacrifice, and sharing, a "new Jerusalem" in Montgomery and "a new heaven and a new earth" in the dispirited South. Black people of Montgomery believed that they were breaking a new day.

3

The boycott leaders agreed upon three demands to the bus company: courteous treatment; a "first-come, first-serve" seating arrangement that would preserve segregation but without reserved sections (the Women's Political Council had been pushing this proposal for two years); and hiring black bus drivers on predominantly Negro routes. Some leaders were willing to give up the last demand if they won the first two, but all thought the three demands were fair and reasonable—if anything, too accommodating. They expected a settlement within a few days.

The biracial Alabama Council on Human Relations (ACHR), which worked to improve race relations, arranged the first negotiating session between the MIA and city and bus company officials. On Thursday, December 8, the opposing sides met at Montgomery City Hall. King, Abernathy, Jo Ann Robinson, and eight others negotiated for the MIA. Mayor Gayle and commissioners Clyde Sellers and Frank Parks represented the city. Manager J. H. Bagley and counsel Jack Crenshaw spoke for Montgomery City Lines. The icy meeting was stiffened further by acts of violence: four buses had been fired on, and two black homes, including that of a Negro cop, were hit by shotgun blasts; no one was hurt. The meeting quickly deadlocked over the seating demand, which the officials insisted would be illegal—even though the parent bus company, based in Chicago, used that seating arrangement in Mobile and other Deep South cities.

Because press coverage might have contributed to the impasse,

Gayle convened a smaller group to talk in private. Still the four whites in the group were unyielding. From their perspective, of course, the black delegates were no less unyielding on the seating policy. The difference was that the black leaders, in their own eyes, had gone to the limit of compromise; any further and their constituents would likely have considered them to be selling out in the familiar tradition of "Uncle Tom" capitulation. They were already catching flak from Nixon and the NAACP for not opposing segregation outright. But the white officials probably felt the same about their constituents. Most white citizens were in no mood to compromise. Each side misread the other, partly out of mutual ignorance.

According to King's account Crenshaw, "our most stubborn opponent," admitted at the smaller meeting: "If we granted the Negroes these demands, they would go about boasting of a victory that they had won over the white people; and this we will not stand for."[51] The whites' rigid stance stunned the MIA leaders and dashed their expectation that the protest would be short.

Not all of white Montgomery opposed the bus boycott, and many of those who did were impressed by the black community's resolve. "They know after this," Virginia Durr wrote a friend, "that they have a united group to deal with."[52] Montgomery native Juliette Morgan, librarian at the public library, was the fifth generation of female college graduates in her family; her great-great-grandmother had graduated in 1822, when women rarely attended college. Morgan, in her early forties, had written her first letter to the *Montgomery Advertiser* opposing segregation in June 1952, titled " 'White Supremacy' Is Evil." Now, one week into the boycott, she published an even more subversive letter to the editor. At a time when no one in the mass protest was thinking seriously about Mahatma Gandhi or nonviolence, she wrote about the 1930 boycott of the British salt monopoly that the Indian leader launched with his famous Salt March, and about the American boycott of British tea "that this nation was founded upon." Montgomery's black people "seem to have taken a lesson from Gandhi—and our own Thoreau, who influenced Gandhi. Their own task is greater than Gandhi's, however, for they have greater prejudice to overcome.

"It is hard to imagine a soul so dead, a heart so hard, a vision so blinded and provincial as not to be moved with admiration at the quiet dignity, discipline, and dedication with which the Negroes have conducted their boycott. Their cause and their conduct have filled me with great sympathy, pride, humility and envy. I envy their unity, their good humor, their fortitude, and their willingness to suffer for great Christian and democratic principles." She called for an end to segregation.[53] Of course such verbal dynamite could not go unpunished. For months white people harassed her, even former friends. School kids threw rocks through her windows. The relentless hate campaign drove her to kill herself by an overdose of sleeping pills, the bus boycott's only known death.

To provide alternative transportation, most of Montgomery's hundred-plus black cab drivers cut rates to a dime, the bus fare. At the first negotiating session, Police Commissioner Sellers mentioned a city law requiring cab drivers to charge a minimum fare of forty-five cents, making it unaffordable—round-trip fare would cost two hours' labor. Black cabs offered the bus fare until the police started citing them. Some circumvented the law by charging a group of riders the minimum fare. But even if all black cabs were commandeered for the cause, they could not have met the demand. Ten times as many workers and schoolchildren needed rides as the cabs could handle. They needed something on a grander scale.

The MIA transportation committee, led by Rufus Lewis and women activists, set in motion a car-pool system modeled on one used during a brief bus boycott in Baton Rouge, Louisiana, in June 1953 that had won its modest demand (to enforce a new city law improving segregation) in ten days. For hands-on advice, King phoned an old family friend, noted Baptist preacher T. J. Jemison of Baton Rouge, an official of the National Baptist Convention, who had led the earlier boycott. The small army of drivers in Montgomery included ministers, shop owners, teachers, laborers, students, homemakers. Sedans, pickup trucks, and then a fleet of shiny, church-bought station wagons—1956 was the first big year for Detroit's mass-marketed family wagon—collected passengers patiently lined up at forty-eight "dispatch stations." Most of these were churches, where passengers could stay warm at dawn. Drivers returned them from forty-two "pick-up stations" after work or school. Hymns wafted lustily out car windows as these "rolling churches" crisscrossed the city with what the segregationist White Citizens Council admitted was "military precision."

Many preferred to walk, as much as twelve miles a day, to pound out their determination and hope. "I'm not walking for myself," an elderly woman explained, turning down a ride, "I'm walking for my children and my grandchildren." Another old woman, Mother Pollard, vowed to King that she would walk until it was over.

"But aren't your feet tired?" he asked.

"Yes," she said, "my feets is tired, but my soul is rested."[54]

January 1956 opened a critical new phase of the bus boycott. As the new year dawned, MIA leaders and white officials held a fourth and final fruitless meeting. Heated debate flared in the *Montgomery Advertiser*, on the street, and in meeting rooms about whether a compromise was achievable, of what it might consist, and whether the protest was justified. The civic temper grew more and more polarized. A black cook complained in a letter to the editor: "Why is it a sin to ride the bus?" A white supporter wrote: "Here is one white ex-bus rider who would like to declare that as long as the boycott is on, it will be a dreary, rainy day, when I have a sprained ankle, and less than 45c cab fare, before I board one of those yellow rolling cell blocks again."

Hill Lindsay bemoaned the Negroes' ingratitude. His letter claimed that whites were responsible for every civilized advance they enjoyed. "You are indebted to the white people of Montgomery for life itself," he hectored.

A white housewife declared it was time to stop pussyfooting around: "We housewives must quit being so lazy, get together and tell the help to either ride the buses and get to work on time or quit. We white people have tried to be understanding of our servants for years and I feel we were understanding until some outside influence put fear in them.

"We have been good to our Negroes," her letter concluded, "but now is the time to make them understand a few things. We should quit paying taxi fare, quit going for them or taking them home, quit paying their Social Security tax, quit lending them money."

Rev. U. J. Fields, MIA recording secretary, inflamed the climate and rankled his coworkers by telling the editor: "We have no intention of compromising. Such unwarranted delay in granting our request may very well result in a demand for the annihilation of segregation which will result in complete integration."[55]

Day in and day out through the winter chill and rain, thousands of black citizens of all ages trod miles to work or school or rode in car pools along slippery streets.

Around 9 P.M. on Saturday, January 21, *Minneapolis Tribune* reporter Carl Rowan phoned King long-distance to ask about a wire-service teletype he had just received announcing that the bus dispute had been settled. That afternoon city commissioners had met with three black ministers not associated with the MIA. The meeting might have been initiated by the ministers, rankled at how the bus boycott had alienated them from the black community. Although they denied it later, the ministers apparently agreed to a compromise keeping reserved seats, even though they had no authority to do so. And while King and the MIA may have believed that a "settlement" had in fact been reached, they denounced it as a hoax by the commissioners. It proved to be a hoax only in the sense that it was illegitimate and patently unrepresentative of, and unaccountable to, the black community's general will.

Rowan recalled of his phone call that King "was startled to hear of the phony announcement. He came to the same conclusion that I did: the whites had bought, cajoled, or threatened three blacks, the assumption being that if the mass of blacks could be tricked into going back aboard the buses, it would be almost impossible to get the boycott going again." King and other leaders frantically called dozens of volunteers, who ran all over town crying out, "No matter what you hear or read, the boycott is not over. Please do not go back onto the buses."[56]

Late into the cold Saturday night King and Abernathy visited bars, poolrooms, and nightclubs—new to King but not to his worldly pal—to deny the bogus settlement. King delighted the drunk patrons, many his own age, by his pool-playing finesse. In one dark club someone shouted, "Just let us know who they were, we'll hang 'em." King smiled in recounting this at the next executive board meeting. It seemed to be the common mood they encountered in darker black Montgomery.

"We can't hurt Uncle Toms by violence," he admonished his colleagues, "but only by mass action."[57] At this meeting he defended himself against scurrilous white accusations. His fellows gave him a vote of confidence. The three apostate preachers publicly repudiated the settlement. The boycott did not lose a beat.

Leaders knew that humiliated city officials would have to strike back—hard. The commissioners announced a "get tough" policy to end the boycott. It included pressuring housewives not to chauffeur their servants, and stepped up harassment of car-pool drivers, stopped by police for contrived or trivial offenses. And no further talks with the MIA until the protest ended. Mayor Gayle stressed that this boycott led by "Negro radicals" was about much more than bus seating: "What they are after," he warned, "is the destruction of our social fabric."[58] To underscore their resolve, all three commissioners joined the Montgomery chapter of the White Citizens Council.

On January 26 police arrested King, driving in the car pool that afternoon, for alleged speeding (30 m.p.h. in a 25 m.p.h. zone) and jailed him for the first time. On the long, circuitous ride to the city jail, the handcuffed preacher was terrified that the cops were delivering him to a waiting lynch mob. He had lived in the city for a year and a half and didn't yet know where the jail was located, notwithstanding Jesus' directive to visit those behind bars.

"I found myself trembling within and without," he recalled. "Silently, I asked God to give me the strength to endure whatever came.

"We turned into a dark and dingy street that I had never seen and headed under a desolate old bridge. I was sure now that I was going to meet my fateful hour on the other side." He found himself relieved to arrive at the jail, where he was placed in a smelly overcrowded cell with several other blacks. He was appalled: "men lying on hard wood slats, and others resting on cots with torn-up mattresses. The toilet was in one corner of the cell without a semblance of an enclosure."[59] His jailers were unwilling to release him, but finally relented when a furious black crowd gathered outside; they couldn't get him out the door fast enough. In the darkness he saw a radiant star of unity.[60] That night the MIA ran several mass meetings out of concern for their leader.

Next afternoon a neatly dressed store maid in her mid-thirties, wearing a cap and jacket, was interviewed by Willie Lee, a young black researcher from Fisk University in Nashville who was giving her a ride home.

"I'm so mad I don't know what to do," the dark-skinned protester burst out. "Do you know those bastards put Reveren' King in jail last night. They think they bad 'cause they got guns, but I sho hope they know how to use 'em, 'cause if they don't, I'll eat 'em up with my razor. If they can use 'em, they bet not come up on me and hit me, 'cause he'll never use it then 'cause he'll be in pieces so fast he won't know what hit 'em."

"Before the people stopped riding the buses," Lee asked her, "did you ever have to get up and stand so white people could sit down?"

"Yeah, that happen almost every day," she answered. "But let me tell you about this. One morning I got on the bus and I had a nickel and five pennies. I put the nickel in and showed him the five pennies. You know how they do you. You put five pennies in there, and they say you didn't. And do you know that bastard cussed me out. He called me bastards, whores, and when he called me motherfucker, I got mad and I put my hand on my razor. I looked at him and told him, 'Your mammy was a son-of-a-bitch, that's why she had you a bitch. And if you so bad, git up outta that seat.' I rode four blocks, then I went to the front door and backed off the bus, and I was jest hoping he'd git up. I was going to cut his head slamp off, but he didn't sey nothing.

"Dey started this thang, and now they can't finish it. They didn't have a bitter need to 'rest Miss Park. All they had to do was talk to 'er lack she was a lady, but they had to be so big and take her to jail. Dey bit the lump off and us making 'em chew it. I know ole Sellers, ole dog, wish he could spit.

"But God fix 'em," she rapped on, "all colored folks ain't like they use to be. They ain't scared no more. Guns don't scare us. These white folks jest keep messing up. Dey gona have a war if they keep on. We be jest forced to kill 'em all 'cause if they hurt Rev. King, I don't mine dying, but I sho Lord am taking a white bastard with 'em. If I don't have my razor with me, I'll use a stick.

"You can do anything for 'em, but jest don't set beside 'em. Now you know it ain't no harm in that. I don't wont they no good men 'cause a white man can't do nothing fur me. Give me a black man any day. And I never worry 'bout any no good white bitch taking a man o' mine. She ain't woman 'nough to take 'em."

If the bus boycott ended, she told Lee, "I'm gona walk that mile still. If they git another dime from me, I won't know it. Well this is my stop. Let's hold out and pray, and I know we'll get what we wont."

Lee recorded similar angry sentiments at a car-pool dispatch station where protesters were waiting for rides to work.

"I'll crawl on my knees 'fo I git back on dem buses," a domestic worker exclaimed to a friend. "Look at dem red bastards over der watching us"—she pointed to the cops—"Ain't nobody scared of dem."

"I ain't 'bout to get on dem buses," another woman said. "Des white folks gona mess right 'round here and git killed. I don't mind dying but I sho take one of dem with me. God done got fed up wid des white folks. We kin stand hard time betterin dey kin 'cause us use to it and dey ain't."

If "dat son-of-a-bitch I work fur" threatened to fire her for not riding the bus, the first domestic said sternly, furrowing her brow, "I beat her skinny ass and tell 'er keep de money 'cause I ain't hongry. Did you see 'em when they put dat boy in jail?" referring to King.

"Dey jest trying to skere us back on dem buses," the other replied, "but I'll be damn if I get on one. I'll walk twenty miles 'fo I ride 'em. Dey trying to be smart, but if dey beat dat boy dere is going to be hell to pay."

The researcher picked up other random comments at the dispatch station: "Dey got dem guns but us ain't skered," one woman said. Another woman: "Dey bet not come in our neighborhood by de self." A third protester: "Some of 'em gona mess right 'round here and get killed." A fourth woman said somberly, "I ain't got but one time to die and I may as well die fur somethin'."[61]

That night, after a day fraught with chilling phone calls—a white friend warned him about a plot to kill him—King spoke at a mass meeting to reassure the black community that he was all right, that he had not been mistreated in jail. "I attempted to convey an overt impression of strength and courage," he recalled, "although I was inwardly depressed and fear-stricken."[62] His off-the-cuff words betrayed his thinly veiled terror:

"If one day you find me sprawled out dead, I do not want you to retaliate with a single act of violence."[63] The audience froze in silent dread. After the meeting, seventy-two-year-old Mother Pollard, the tire-less walker, called him over. He hugged her warmly.

"Son, what's wrong with you? You didn't talk strong tonight."

"Oh, no, Sister Pollard, nothing is wrong," he lied. "I am feeling as fine as ever."

"You can't fool me," she replied. "I knows something is wrong. Is it that we ain't doing things to please you? Or is it that the white folks is bothering you?"

"Everything is going to be all right, Sister Pollard."

She looked straight into his chocolate eyes. "Now, I don told you we is with you all the way." Her face radiated serenity. "Now, even if we ain't with you, the Lord is with you. God's gonna take care of you." As she spoke these comforting words, King later wrote, "everything in me quivered and quickened with the pulsing tremor of raw energy."[64] The Spirit was warming his bones.

Around midnight, as he struggled to sleep, the phone rang one more time. "Listen, nigger," an ugly voice crackled over the wire, "we're tired of you and your mess now. If you aren't out of this town in three days, we're going to blow your brains out and blow up your house." He paced the bedroom floor in angry fear, then walked across the hall to the kitchen and heated some coffee. He tried to find solace in what philosophy and theology had taught him about the meaning of evil. Could there be good without evil? Could there be redemption without sin? No answer came to shake his despair. Nothing relieved the fear in his gut. He was ready to give up.

"I got to the point that I couldn't take it any longer," he recalled in a sermon the summer before his death. "I was weak. Something said to me you can't call on Daddy now," as he had in past troubles. "You can't even call on Mama now. (*My Lord*) You've got to call on that something in that person that your daddy used to tell you about. (*Yes*) That power that can make a way out of no way. (*Yes*)" He had to call on the holy spirit's power to help him through. The church had been so much his home all of his young life that he had never stepped outside of it far enough, or boldly enough, to forge his own relationship with God, with Jesus, with the Spirit—not that of his father or mother or Ebenezer Baptist in Atlanta.

He discovered at this midnight hour that "religion had to become real to me"—not merely the hand-me-down family business—"and I had to know God for myself. (*Yes, sir*) With my head in my hands, I bowed down over that cup of coffee. Oh yes, I prayed a prayer. I prayed out loud that night. (*Yes*) The words I spoke to God that midnight are still vivid in my memory:

"Lord, I'm down here trying to do what's right. (*Yes*) I think I'm right. I think the cause that we represent is right. (*Yes*) But Lord, I must confess that I'm weak now. I'm faltering. I'm losing my courage. (*Yes*) I am afraid. The people are looking to me for leadership. I can't let the people see me like this because if they see me weak and losing my courage, they will begin to get weak. (*Yes*) I am at the end of my powers. I have nothing left. I've come to the point where I can't face it alone."

"At that moment," he continued, "I experienced the presence of the Divine as I had never experienced Him before. I could hear an inner voice saying to me, (*Yes*) Martin Luther, (*Yes*) stand up for righteousness, (*Yes*) stand up for justice, (*Yes*) stand up for truth. (*Yes*) And lo, I will be with you, (*Yes*) even until the end of the world. I heard the voice of Jesus saying still to fight on. He promised never to leave me, never to leave me alone. No, never alone. No, never alone. He promised never to leave me, (*Never*) never to leave me alone."[65]

A branch shall grow out of his roots, spoke Isaiah. The Spirit of the Lord shall rest upon him, the Spirit of Wisdom and understanding, the Spirit of counsel and might, the Spirit of knowledge and of the fear of the Lord.

I have put My Spirit upon him. He will bring forth justice to the Gentiles. He will bring forth justice for truth. He will not fail nor be discouraged, till he has established justice in the earth.

Then Jesus, when he had been baptized, came up from the water. And behold, the heavens were opened to him, and he saw the Spirit of God descending like a dove and alighting upon him. And suddenly a voice came from heaven.[66]

4

Birmingham civil rights activist Pinkie Franklin heard about the bombing of King's home, three days later, the morning after. She couldn't sleep that night. Like many supporters far and wide, she wrote King a letter to help strengthen him. Forty years old, the Alabama State College graduate, born in Selma, had been a schoolteacher and for ten years had owned a Birmingham grocery store with her husband.

"For years," she wrote him, "we Negro Mothers of the Southland have prayed that God would send us a leader such as you are. Now that the Almighty has regarded our lowly estate and has raised you up among us, I am indeed grateful.

"Be assured that day and night without ceasing I shall be praying for your safety and that of your family's. The Arm of God is everlastingly strong and Sufficient to keep you and yours. There shall no harm come to you, and the Comforting Spirit of God shall guide you."

She closed her letter, "A fellow Suffer, (Mrs.) Pinkie S. Franklin of the Sixteenth Street Baptist Church."[67] Her own church would be bombed on a Sunday morning seven and a half years later, killing four young girls dressing up for the Lord.

Birmingham, the big industrial city a hundred miles north of Montgomery, had already racked up such a fearsome record of bombings by the Ku Klux Klan that it had earned the nickname "Bombingham." A frequently targeted middle-class black neighborhood was called "Dynamite Hill" because so many black homes had been blown up. The "Big Mules," iron and steel magnates who dominated this American Johannesburg, were determined to preserve Jim Crow by any means necessary in order to keep the industrial work force divided and weakened.

Their man in city hall, ambitious police commissioner Eugene "Bull" Connor, gave the green light to Robert "Dynamite Bob" Chambliss and other Ku Klux Klan members who had mastered the use of dynamite in northern Alabama mines and quarries they had labored in. They were not apprehended for the rash of bombings. Was a similar pattern taking hold in Montgomery? Evidence later showed that city officials might have known in advance about some bombings of churches and parsonages. Montgomery was the first place where ministers were bombed.

Just before the attack on King's home, MIA leaders had secretly shifted course, a move that would change the course of history. Among many reasons black Montgomerians hated segregation was the conviction, reaffirmed daily, that it could never be equitable or fair. In December and January they had experienced publicly, as a unified community, what most already knew in their bones: legalized segregation could never be but white supremacy, naked or veiled. It could not be fixed by cosmetic touch-ups.

The authorities "did not do what we wanted done," attorney Fred Gray later reflected. "When that became apparent, then the question is, 'how long are we gonna stay off the buses?' People have to look forward to something. And the logical thing is to stay off the buses until we can return to them on an integrated basis. Because they wouldn't give us the smaller things, we go for the larger and the only way we can go for that, and I knew it, was a federal suit."[68]

The dynamics of the mass protest taught participants that they finally had no recourse but to challenge the constitutionality of bus segregation—encouraged, of course, by the Supreme Court's recent *Brown* decisions overturning the *Plessy v. Ferguson* doctrine of "separate but equal." Officials subverted their own segregation laws when they refused to enforce them fairly yet hid behind and manipulated them to preserve the unsustainable status quo. The movement spawned an efficient carpool operation that might have grown into a full-fledged system of public transport. But when the city commission refused to bend on reserved sections (partly to preserve the fiction of equal treatment), renewed the bus company's franchise, and denied the MIA proposal for its own jitney service, they closed off any possibility of a "separate but equal" solution and made bus desegregation inescapable.

Toward the end of January Gray spent a few days in New York conferring with Thurgood Marshall and other top NAACP lawyers to prepare the ground for a federal lawsuit. It was a delicate situation for the MIA. While they needed NAACP expertise and money, over which tension had already surfaced, the NAACP's name and reputation in the white South were mud—only slightly less sullied than those of the Communist Party. Many white southerners saw them as one and the same, the way black people conflated the White Citizens Council and the Ku Klux Klan.

The pivotal meeting of the MIA executive board took place on Monday, January 30—the afternoon before the bombing attack on King's home. It was the eighth anniversary of Mahatma Gandhi's assassination in New Delhi. While remotely possible that a spy's report on the meeting triggered the bombing, most likely the attack had already been planned for that night with no link to this meeting. The midnight January 27 phone call had given King three days to leave town. The three days were up.

Participants were sworn to secrecy at this meeting. "It is *very* important," King stressed, "that this information does not leak out about the NAACP and the court action until it's printed in the newspaper. We want to surprise the whites." Surprise was a key element of nonviolent combat, like every other kind.

Opening with prayer, the specially called meeting dealt first with a proposal by Rev. Alford to accept a compromise tendered by the city that would keep a smaller number of reserved seats. The general feeling was that it didn't come close. But many ministers were tired and frustrated—though they had not been walking—and sought a graceful way out. King was ambivalent but swayed by the foot soldiers' fervency.

"I've seen along the way," King commented, "where some of the ministers are getting weary"; he said he wouldn't mention any names.

If you think that Negroes "should go back under the same conditions, we won't ostracize you. We should iron it out here."

Alford took up the challenge. "There's a time in the life of any crisis," he argued, "when you ought to be reasonable." The leaders would have been willing to give up, for now, the demand for black bus drivers. It was the fairer seating arrangement, a more civil if not quite civilized segregation, that they would not budge on. Nothing could have been more "reasonable."

"From my limited contact," King countered, "if we went tonight and asked the people to get back on the bus, we would be ostracized. They wouldn't get back. I believe to the bottom of my heart that the majority of Negroes would ostracize us. They are willing to walk."

What did he mean by "ostracize"? He worried that the aroused mass following might repudiate the current leaders, replace them with others more militant, more responsive to the people's will, perhaps advocates of violent tactics.

He then turned to the federal lawsuit about to be filed. This constitutional challenge to city and state bus segregation laws would not be brought formally by NAACP lawyers, he explained, but rather by five female plaintiffs, including Claudette Colvin, now sixteen, who had just given birth to her baby son, Raymond. The lawyers estimated that the lawsuit would be decided by the Montgomery federal court within three weeks.

"We need to train people to go back to the bus," the Reverend Seay urged. "We would disgrace ourselves before the world if we give up now." Feeling strong pressure from below, the leaders resolved to continue the boycott. They hoped that the daily civic disruption and media spotlight would penetrate the minds and hearts of the federal judges holding court in the boycott's epicenter.

"By the way," King disclosed, "I've found out that the Negro lady who was beat up by a Negro man a few days ago is the cook for the mayor. She attends the mass meetings and tells the mayor what happened the next morning. We also found out that Sellers has let three Negro prisoners attend the mass meetings so that they can tell him what has happened."

Gray pitched for one or two respected gentlemen to join the five women as plaintiffs.

"I think it is very important in throwing sentiment our way," King pleaded, "if we have a minister as a plaintiff. Who will volunteer?" he asked the two dozen men of cloth. We cannot know whether he or Abernathy would have been willing to sign up, but it was evident to all that they were too central as leaders. No one raised his hand. A few ministers claimed that they were acting for their parishioners but were not personally aggrieved. Many like King had never ridden the bus. The meeting ended with prayer—and only women as plaintiffs.[69] The men of cloth had feet of clay.

Two nights after King's home was bombed, dynamite thrown from a passing car exploded in E. D. Nixon's yard, causing little damage but sending a strong message. His wife told him about it when his train from Chicago pulled into Birmingham the next morning.

King had gone to the sheriff's office to request firearm permits for himself and his bodyguards, but the application was rejected. On February 2, King, Abernathy, Gray, and Jo Ann Robinson met with the Alabama governor in his capitol office a block from King's church. A populist politician in the mold of Louisiana's fabled Huey Long, "Big Jim" Folsom was the most racially liberal governor in the South. He had set off a brouhaha three months before (and probably wrecked his career) when he drank Scotch in his governor's mansion with New York's black congressman, Adam Clayton Powell Jr.—and had him chauffeured around town in his limousine. He was noncommittal when King asked for state police protection from white violence. What King wanted most was what the sheriff had just denied him.

"What we would like to have is to have you issue a permit to keep a gun in my car."[70] He deemed armed protection worth a private meeting with the governor. Supportive of the protest in principle, its ends if not its means, Folsom declined to help him with his personal need. The parley revealed the naked fear King felt—his nascent premonition of death.

We are not of those who shrink back from destruction, the writer of Hebrews declared, *but of those who believe to the preservation of the Spirit.*[71]

. . .

THERE WAS NO ATTACK on Fort Sumter or outright secession, but southerners both black and white saw signs of a second Civil War. Even official vocabulary reprised the rhetoric that led to the War Between the States. On January 24, the day after Gayle announced the city's get-tough policy, the governors of Virginia, South Carolina, Georgia, and Mississippi vowed to resist the Supreme Court's *Brown* decision through "interposition." The Alabama legislature, like others, enacted a statute of "nullification." There was no Lincoln in the White House, only a southern-born war hero who personally opposed *Brown*. No Jefferson Davis conspiring with fellow secessionists in Montgomery, "Cradle of the Confederacy," but another Mississippi senator of far lesser stature, James Eastland, exhorting his followers to hold the line against "mongrelization" of the races.

The 1956 equivalent of Fort Sumter—less destructive but no less menacing—broke out on Monday, February 6, in Tuscaloosa, Alabama, an hour and a half's drive northwest of the capital. Autherine Lucy, twenty-six, was the tenth child of tenant farmers in Shiloh, in Alabama's fertile Black Belt, where she had helped her family grow cotton, watermelon, sweet potatoes, and peanuts. Ever since getting her undergraduate degree from all-black Miles College in 1952, the Birmingham secretary had fought to be admitted to the University of Alabama as its first openly black student. NAACP lawyers took up her case a year before the *Brown* decision; in June 1955 a federal judge forced her admission. A month prior, the Supreme Court's delayed enforcement decree had mandated school desegregation "by all deliberate speed." The university stalled with an unsuccessful appeal, then announced on January 30, the day King's house was bombed, that Lucy could register for spring semester. Next week she enrolled for graduate study in library science.

As school officials escorted her to class the first two days, she encountered angry protests. Fiery crosses burned on campus three nights in a row. On Friday and Saturday evening a thousand protesters marched on the home of the university's president, Oliver Cromwell Carmichael. His wife was hit by a flying egg. On Monday, February 6, the growing mob of incensed students and townspeople were joined by a large phalanx of rubber workers from the nearby Goodrich tire factory. Heading to her first morning class, Lucy, together with the dean of women and a male administrator, were pelted by eggs, rocks, and mud balls. The protesters called the officials "nigger-lovin' bastards" and screamed "Keep 'Bama White!" Several tried to break into her classroom. When Lucy and her escorts escaped by the back door, they were ambushed by the vicious mob, shrieking, "Let's kill her! Let's kill her!" Miraculously, they managed to drive away, rocks smashing the back window. The police were lying low; they made three arrests.

The rioting crowd multiplied during the day. By nightfall they were joined by high school students and rubber workers from the day shift. A mob estimated at three thousand marauded around campus and again besieged the president's house. State police repulsed them, firing tear gas, never before used on a college campus. It was the first organized violence on an American campus in two decades; the first time that school desegregation had brought rioting anywhere in the South. A report to Governor Folsom revealed that rioters intended to kill Lucy. Many of the militant rubber workers were members of the Klan, which drew its shock troops, like "Dynamite Bob" Chambliss, from the exploited white working class.

During the Monday rioting the university board of trustees met in emergency session. Dismissing entreaties by moderate faculty and students against "mob rule," the trustees suspended Lucy. "They did it because the mob forced them to," a student leader told *Time*. "The mob won."[72] Three weeks later the trustees expelled her, a move applauded by the White Citizens Council and whites generally. 'Bama stayed white for seven more years, until another governor, a protégé of Big Jim Folsom, made a last stand at the schoolhouse door in Tuscaloosa.

5

The Oconee River wound southward, cutting a valley through pine-forested hills of central Georgia, seventy miles east of Atlanta, then widened into Lake Oconee. In this pine river valley, in the village of Penfield, in November 1846, Willis Williams, thirty-six, joined Shiloh Baptist Church, a racially mixed congregation of fifty whites and twenty-eight slaves founded in 1795. He was owned by another Willis Williams, one of the county's most prosperous slaveholders, who joined the church later, perhaps through his namesake's influence.

Two years after joining up, slave Williams was convicted of theft by a biracial church committee and expelled. Two months later, in October 1848, church minutes reported that "Willis, servant to Bro. W. N. Williams, came forward and made himself confession of his guilt and said that the Lord had forgiven him for his error. He was therefore unanimously received into fellowship with us."[73] His redemption augured his conversion into a zealous slave preacher, or "exhorter." He devoted himself to preaching the Word among Greene County slaves and brought many families into the Baptist fold, which after the Civil War split into segregated congregations.

By turn of the century his son Adam Daniel Williams, endowed with a double dose of Old Testament namesake—and his twin sister was Eve—had emerged as a prominent black Baptist preacher in Atlanta. His daddy had taught him his calling as a young boy, growing up in the wake of the Civil War, when he reveled in preaching the funerals of "snakes, cats, dogs, horses or any thing that died. The children of the community would call him to preach the funeral and they would have a big shout."[74] His daughter, Alberta Christine, married a young backwoods Georgia preacher, like he himself had started out. Michael and Alberta King's first son, namesake of Martin Luther, entered the earthly kingdom on January 15, 1929.[75]

When Willis Williams preached the gospel in the mid–nineteenth century, black Christianity was only two or three generations removed from its African roots. Many older slaves, perhaps Williams's parents or grandparents, had grown up in the African Spirit world of ancestor worship and nature gods, whether in their homeland or transplanted in the New World. They heard and passed on tales of African spirits and saints, both good and evil. Stories were sung and danced as well as spoken. A favorite sacred ritual was the "ring shout"—slaves danced and called out in a circle to embody the ties between past, present, and future.

Mixing up African beliefs and practices with Christian language and ritual, slave spirituality served as the driving force of all aspects of the slave community. Slaves shaped it anew to meet their needs and ensure their survival and salvation.

The gift of African-American Christianity to the Christian religion, and ultimately to all the world's faiths, was the magic of intimate interplay with the divine. This was not to imply that mainstream Christianity (as well as Judaism and Islam) did not already worship a personal God, but that black Christians, perhaps most like Muslims, staked their faith on divine intimacy. Other believers tended to keep God at arm's length, as a general rule, despite lip service to the contrary (or, like many Catholics, saved their intimate devotion for the Virgin Mary or a personal saint).

Black people's divine intimacy varied in form. It was often intensely emotional. It was a felt connection with a God not only of emotion, but at times of raw passion and physicality. Just as their West African ancestors had conversed directly with their nature gods and ancestral spirits, so did enslaved African Americans commune with their divinity on a horizontal as much as a vertical basis.

As one slave put it, "Gwine to argue with de father and chatter wid the son." Another said simply, "Our God talks to his children."[76]

From slavery time to twentieth-century gospel singing, African Americans have nourished a special intimacy with Jesus, or with God through Jesus, God as Jesus—both called Lord without distinction. Spirituals, and later on gospel and blues, expressed the connection with Jesus in ways that words alone could not.

> Sometimes I hangs my head an' cries,
> But Jesus goin' to wipe my weep'n eyes.
> He pluck my feet out'n de miry clay,
> He set dem on de firm rock of ages.[77]

No song conveyed this intimate relationship with more feeling than Thomas Dorsey's gospel classic, "Precious Lord, Take My Hand"—Martin King's favorite song, sung at his funeral in Atlanta's Ebenezer Baptist Church.

W. E. B. Du Bois's encounter as a young man with the "frenzy" of Deep South black religion left a searing imprint on his consciousness. It was the core event around which he constructed his 1903 masterpiece, *The Souls of Black Folk.*

A "suppressed terror hung in the air and seemed to seize us," he recalled, "a pythian madness, a demoniac possession, that lent terrible reality to song and word. The people moaned and fluttered, and then the gaunt-cheeked brown woman beside me suddenly leaped straight in the air and shrieked like a lost soul, while round about came wail and groan and outcry, and a scene of human passion such as I had never conceived before."

The frenzy, or shouting, "when the Spirit of the Lord passed by, and, seizing the devotee, made him mad with supernatural joy" varied from "the silent rapt countenance or the low murmur and moan to the mad abandon of physical fervor—the stamping, shrieking, and shouting, the rushing to and fro and wild waving of arms, the weeping and laughing, the vision and the trance."

So solid a hold did it have on the rural Negro, the scholar activist concluded, "that many generations firmly believed that without this visible manifestation of God there could be no true communion with the Invisible."[78]

The term *spirit possession* pinpointed the physical, forceful quality of the divine interaction in African-American Christianity. The divine spirit invaded the human bodysoul, but only when it opened itself. The human vessel, male or female, was not a passive receptacle. It passionately clutched the spirit force with its whole physical and emotional being, possessing the spirit from within just as it was being seized from without.

"All night long I've been feelin' 'im," Georgia slave Mary Gladdys described an all-night prayer meeting. "Jest befo' day, I feels 'im. Jest befo' day, I feels 'im. The sperit, I feels 'im. The sperit, I feels 'im!"[79] Another testified: "I got Him! I hold him here all the time!"

That this spiritual intercourse corresponded, more than symbolically, with female worshipers' experience of sexual intercourse, and that Christians believed that God impregnated a flesh-and-blood woman, often lent women's spiritual expressions an erotic undertone—as, for example, gospel singers' cry to Jesus or the holy spirit to "fill me up!" Communicating one-to-one with divine force through prayer, song, rapture, or frenzy opened the gateway between the profane and sacred worlds.

For the slaves and for generations of descendants, the omnipresent Spirit world translated into the experience of what Christians called the holy spirit. If God was the transcendental Supreme Being and Jesus the incarnate personality who sacralized the cosmos, the Word becoming flesh, the Spirit was the divine force itself manifested on earth, and thus the spark of divinity, or "inner light," that glorified each creature. Of course the three persons of the Trinity were really One, viewed from different angles on earth.

Holy spirit, breath of God, wind of the cosmos was the life energy that flowed through beings either as acts of grace or as invoked or conjured by believers. The Spirit, which generated and protected sacred time and space amid the travails of ordinary life, was the force that simultaneously emancipated and unified those who embodied it. Liberated them from sin, evil, forces of darkness, mortality itself. Unified them into a chain, a cosmic arc of relationship and interdependence, an "inescapable network of mutuality." Above all, the Spirit expressed the content of the relationship between humans and God, the substance of things unseen—the relationship, as Jewish theologian Martin Buber put it, between I and Thou. This relationship was made of love.

For people in traditional societies, religious historian Mircea Eliade explained, religion was a means of extending the world spatially upward "so that communication with the other world becomes ritually possible, and extending it temporally backward so that the paradigmatic acts of the gods and mythical ancestors can be continually re-enacted and indefinitely recoverable. By creating sacred time and space, Man can perpetually live in the presence of his gods, can hold on to the certainty that within one's own lifetime 'rebirth' is continually possible, and can impose order on the chaos of the universe.

"Life is lived on a twofold plane; it takes its course as human existence and, at the same time, shares in a trans-human life, that of the cosmos or the gods."[80]

Historian Gayraud Wilmore pointed out that the religions of West and Central Africa had a single dominating quality that endured among African Americans: "a profound belief that both the individual and the community had a continuous involvement with the spirit world in the practical affairs of daily life. African religions know of no rigid demarcation between the natural and the supernatural, the sacred and the profane. All of life is permeated with forces or powers which exist in some relationship to man's weal or woe. Man is, therefore, required—for his own sake and that of the community—to understand and appreciate this spirit world which merges imperceptibly with immediate, tangible reality."[81]

LITTLE OF THIS SPIRIT awareness seemed to have imbued young Martin King, even though as a child he considered the church his "second home" and was ordained a Baptist minister at nineteen.

"My call to the ministry," he wrote two years later at Crozer Seminary in Pennsylvania, "was not a miraculous or supernatural something, on the contrary it was an inner urge calling me to serve humanity." It was the "noble moral and ethical ideals" conveyed by the church, by his father and other preachers of black social gospel that swayed his vocational doubts, in his view a more secular than spiritual springboard.

"Even though I have never had an abrupt conversion experience," he concluded his 1950 autobiographical essay—he knew this was obligatory for a truly called Baptist—"religion has been real to me and closely knit-ted to life. In fact the two cannot be separated; religion for me is life."[82]

But how deep did it run? How deep had he drunk? Religion was so completely life for him, such an all-consuming everyday reality—his hot dates were Sunday worship services—that it came to be mundane, taken for granted. The Spirit world had boundaries, however porous. His religious world, undifferentiated, had none.

His parents pushed him so hard to pursue the path of ministry—he sang church solos at six—that he never made a real choice. He con-fessed that he joined his father's church impulsively at age seven out of a competitive desire "to keep up with my sister."[83] He was so condi-tioned by outward forms and rituals that he found little room to absorb the sacred substance—the abiding if elusive Spirit itself—which many he preached to had experienced firsthand. He was so caught up in the appearances, sights, sounds, and smells that he came to reject the inner core of emotionalism, of "soul"—the experience of an intimate rela-tionship with God. Whether he was rebelling against his patriarchal father, whether it embarrassed his middle-class striving, or whether it cut against the grain of who he thought he was or would be, the great-grandson of Shiloh's Willis Williams scorned the God of emotion at the heart of black faith.

King may have preached earnestly about the personal God central to the black church, but it was an intellectual and formal God. By all accounts he did not yet have a relationship with this divinity, however flowery his lip, his outward projection. By the time he graduated from Crozer Seminary in May 1951, he was determined to find an orderly, rational God to undergird his faith, a God of ideas rather than emo-tions, a thinking man's personal God befitting a suave, modern Negro intellectual. A doctorate in theology from an elite northern university might be just the ticket he needed to escape what he considered the primitive religiosity of the backward black South.

In September 1951, at the height of the Korean War and the anticom-munist witch hunt led by Wisconsin senator Joseph McCarthy, twenty-two-year-old Martin King had just finished a fourth summer of preaching in Atlanta as Ebenezer's assistant pastor. Upon his graduating as Crozer's award-winning valedictorian, and giving the valedictory address, his parents bought him a shiny green Chevy. Now he drove it from his boyhood home on "Sweet Auburn" Avenue through the Jim Crow states of the Carolinas, Virginia, and Maryland, over the Mason-Dixon line into eastern Pennsylvania, where he had attended Crozer near Philadelphia, into the burst of early fall's fiery foliage across New York and New England. Searching for housing in Boston, he faced overt discrimination for the second time in the North. The first had been in a New Jersey restaurant the year before; the owner had fired a pistol when King and friends insisted on being served. That he largely escaped such humiliations in Atlanta showed how sheltered was his middle-class southern boyhood.

Securing an apartment on St. Botolph Street, he readied himself for a rigorous doctoral program in systematic theology at Boston University. He was drawn to B.U. to search out the philosophical and theological basis for belief in a personal divinity. This would be the philosophy of personalism that his liberal evangelical Baptist professor, George W. Davis, had introduced him to at Crozer.

Boston and personalism met his intellectual needs. For half a century the university's school of theology had been the wellspring of American personalism. A term that Walt Whitman coined in the 1860s in *Democratic Vistas* to express his vision of cosmic self, personalism congealed in the twentieth century as a school of thought holding that all reality was personal, of a personal nature, and that God was the ultimate personality, a personal divinity in the most literal sense. Influenced by the German idealism of Kant and Hegel and by the New England transcendentalism of Emerson and Thoreau, resonating with the slave religion that King thought he had left behind, personalists contended that valid spiritual communion came through a direct, unmediated relationship between autonomous personalities—between an individual and their personal deity.

Some personalist theologians, such as King's teacher Edgar Brightman, stressed the invisibility of personality to human beings. Bodies could be seen and touched, but not personalities or souls. All outward things were manifestations of invisible personality, cosmic or human. Personality was the divine inner light inside each individual. King came to accept on a rational theological basis what had troubled him in raw experience.

Personalism's rationalistic depiction of a personal God, however, did not take him far enough from the unruliness of the black Baptist church. He raised his doubts about a personal divinity to even higher scrutiny in his doctoral dissertation. He spent only a year writing it, starting in spring 1954 and finishing during his first six months pastoring Dexter Avenue Baptist Church in Montgomery, writing in longhand early in the morning and late at night. In the heavily plagiarized thesis he not only weighed and tested his own God concept, but sought to expand the conception of divine personality to encompass views that appeared to deny a personal God. He focused on the theologies of Paul Tillich and Henry Nelson Wieman, two perspectives that strongly challenged personalism without addressing it directly. Flawed though his dissertation proved to be in its wholesale borrowing and shoddy attribution of sources—partly the result of his hectic ministry in Montgomery—it nevertheless provided the theoretical groundwork for him to reconcile personalism with its critics, not least himself.

He tried to show that neither Tillich nor Wieman accepted the idea of an impersonal divinity, that their God concepts not only were not antithetical to personalist philosophy, but affirmed its premises and corrected some of its problems. Experimenting with the dialectical method that would loom large in his later life, he posed the thesis of personalism against the challenges of Tillich and Wieman in order to move toward a synthesis that reconciled the strengths of each side.

What was at stake here? King sought to supplant the anthropomorphic concept of a personal God that he found distasteful—a divinity created, in effect, as a reflection of sinful human beings—with the notion of personality originating as a divine essence, that human beings laid claim to personality and personhood because God created these in the divine image. Personality was not a given, but a gift of grace. Thus King redefined personality in its human incarnation as the divine presence within, the holy spirit internal.

Tillich, a refugee from Nazi Germany, rivaled Reinhold Niebuhr as the preeminent American theologian of the postwar era. Both luminaries taught at Union Theological Seminary in New York while King was studying in Boston. Tillich believed that God was not a being in the usual sense (thus could not be a personal being) because he was "being-itself," the ground and depth of all being, of all meaning. As ground of being, so King interpreted Tillich, God was the creative force of the universe—immanent in his own creation. As depth, or "abyss," God was transcendent not spatially above or outside, but deep within creation. God was simultaneously visible and invisible, manifest and latent—visible as ground of being, invisible as depth, as darkness. Tillich turned the traditional model of a transcendent God upside down and inside out. It would take only a small further step to suggest that if conscious human personalities could relate to God as ground of being, their subconscious minds might communicate with God in the dark abyss inside their souls.

Unlike Tillich, Wieman was not a well-known American theologian. He "stresses the fact that men must worship the actuality of God and not their ideas about God," King wrote. "It is imperative that men not allow their wishes and needs to shape their ideas of God," but that their ideas be "shaped solely in the light of objective evidence." One can imagine his relief; this was the problem with the faith of his fathers. He employed Wieman's "scientific" frame of reference to comprehend divine personality as it might be viewed from the "objective" standpoint of the cosmos, of "ultimate reality," rather than from the subjective vantage point of a fragmented individual or of sinful humanity.

Wieman suggested that God was a dynamic, interactive process, not a static object—energy, not matter; a verb, not a noun. God was the "creative event" (grace of God)—here foreshadowing physicists' discoveries that subatomic particles were events, process, not objects, and that the universe was not only expanding but unifying. Wieman defined God as the integrating process that "works through all the world not only to bring human lives into fellowship with one another but also to maintain and develop organic interdependence and mutual support between all parts and aspects of the cosmos."

God was the "integrating behavior" of the universe, the "growth of meaning and value in the world," the nurturing of organic connections to bring about a "new structure of interrelatedness." This evolving structure of interrelatedness called for transformation of meanings such that (as King paraphrased Wieman), "the individual sees what he could not see before. Events as they happen to him now are so connected with other events that his appreciable world takes on an expanded meaning unimaginable before." According to Wieman this integrating process of communication, support, and learning "must be not only between contemporaries but also between successive generations, ages, and cultures."[84]

As much as Tillich's, Wieman's theology was basic to King's expanding conception of divinity and a key to his budding cosmology.

He returned to the Deep South with his new bride, Coretta Scott, a native of rural Alabama, who had attended Antioch College and Boston's New England Conservatory of Music. She regretfully gave up a promising career as a classical singer to return to her Black Belt roots as a preacher's wife, an unwanted fate that was not easy for her to accept. Her love for Martin and her sense of spiritual duty warred with her personal ambition.

Nor was her husband entirely happy about moving to Montgomery, a city still steeped in white supremacy and with few pretensions of New South modernity. But wearing the armor of his elite northern education, he seized the opportunity to share his newfound knowledge of a rational God and a scientific theology with an educated, middle-class Baptist congregation, a thinking fellowship. They would listen to his logos and not lose themselves in frenzy. The first year was consumed by taking charge of the church and completing his dissertation a world apart from Boston.

All of a sudden his comfortable world took a tumble. On the night of December 5, 1955, he was thrust into presiding over a church mass meeting that was a supercharged melting pot of black spirituality of all shades. His Dexter Avenue flock was out in force, but a far larger number were poor working people who, unlike King, talked to God every day and lived their toilsome lives in an elevated world of Spirit. He stood face-to-face with the fierce raw emotionality of black church culture, a volcanic congregation believing itself in the presence of the Lord. As many participants later testified, the holy spirit was alive that night, and in a hundred such nights to come, with a palpable power and crystal clarity that overwhelmed the freshly minted doctor of theology.

Yet by some uncanny act of grace, the breath of Spirit that he drew in that evening burst out of him in a jeweled torrent of unscripted words, a Lincoln-like synthesis of the rational and emotional, the secular and sacred. The faithful, King now among them, had conjured the kingdom of God in that place.

6

Two months later:
Early February 1956

Anna Holden, a white woman in her mid-twenties, walked into the law office of Luther Ingalls, general counsel and chief organizer of the Central Alabama White Citizens Council. She felt like she was living a hundred years in the past, walking into Confederate headquarters, which Montgomery had once been—just a few blocks away. Although she hailed from the Deep South, it felt like enemy territory. She introduced herself to Ingalls, with whom she had an appointment, as a social scientist researching the Montgomery situation. Late thirties, crew cut, he wore a tweed jacket without tie over a gabardine sport shirt. He came from an old-line Montgomery family and commanded respect in the white community. His great-grandfathers had owned many slaves.

Ever since the Supreme Court's *Brown* decision of May 1954, arch-segregationists had been leading a grassroots campaign of "massive resistance" to desegregation and "race mixing." While the Ku Klux Klan reignited its tactics of terror, a militant organization arose to draw the white mainstream to the cause. It began when Mississippi judge Tom Brady warned the Sons of the American Revolution in his state that desegregation, which he blamed on communists, would lead to extinction of the white race. Brady's speech spurred thirty-three-year-old Robert Patterson, manager of a Mississippi Delta cotton plantation and former Mississippi State football star, to organize a town meeting in Indianola on July 11, 1954. The seventy-five participants, led by business and civic leaders, founded the White Citizens Council.

Chapters instantly proliferated across the Magnolia State. In October delegates from 250 chapters with 60,000 members in half of the state's counties gathered to create a state association. Publicly they vowed to fight integration through education and propaganda. Less visibly they promoted their real strategy: boycotts and other methods of economic strangulation of black agitators and their white sympathizers. Mississippi Council leaders spread the gospel to Alabama.

"Come on inside the office and we can talk there," Ingalls said to Holden. "Senator Engelhardt is in my office now and you can talk to him too." The two white supremacists were hard at work organizing a mammoth rally at the state Coliseum two days hence, fielding a flurry of phone calls.

"Sam, there is a young lady here from Fisk University in Nashville who wants to talk to me, and I told her she could come in here and talk to both of us. Miss Holden, this is Senator Engelhardt." Sam Engelhardt, mid-to-late fifties, was state senator from nearby Macon County and president of the recently formed Central Alabama WCC. Conservatively dressed, he projected a somber mood that contrasted with Ingalls's upbeat spirit.

Engelhardt: Fisk University? That's a colored school, isn't it?

Holden: Yes it is. I am a researcher on staff there.

Engelhardt: You take white students there now, don't you?

Holden: Yes. It has been opened to white students since the Supreme Court decision.

He demanded to know what she was doing at a "nigra" college.

"Now, Sam," Ingalls jumped in. "Let's let Miss Holden ask her questions. We don't want to be disrespectful to the young lady." He chuckled. "Well, Miss Holden, you aren't gonna like anything I'm gonna say but I don't really mind talking to you."

"It doesn't really matter, does it? Say what you please and I will write it down. That's what I'm here for, to get everybody's view." She asked him how the bus boycott started.

"Well," he explained, "you probably know by now that it was started by NAACP agitators. Ninety-five percent of the nigras here were happy with things the way they were and are now the victims of their exploitation. They didn't want this. NAACP leaders like King and Nixon forced it on them. It was a plant to get a case. The Parks woman tried five or six times to create an incident before they finally arrested her. I got that from the drivers. You know, she used the white toilet at Montgomery Fair. You can see what she is after.

"The mayor's committee was picked to meet with them and work out a compromise, but we couldn't get anywhere." King had wanted him booted off the committee. Black delegates came "with a mimeographed sheet with their stand printed on it and they never departed from it. We came in willing to compromise, but they wouldn't give an inch. They wanted first come, first serve without any regard to the state segregation law and that was it. We offered them the whole bus except for one seat in the back and one in the front, but they wouldn't take that."

For Ingalls and the other whites it made no difference how reasonable the blacks' demands had been. What mattered was that they were making demands at all, that they were setting the terms. From the white point of view, the concession to negotiate was a major compromise, all that they could afford.

"So that's what the committee did—wasted a lot of time. Has anybody called to your attention the statute making a boycott illegal?" He pulled down a big dusty law book, the Alabama Code of 1940. "See here," he showed her, "misdemeanor for two or more persons to enter into any conspiracy to deprive . . ."

"I knew there was such a law," she replied, "but I hadn't heard anything about anyone trying to enforce it."

"You'll hear plenty about it," Ingalls countered, "when Monday rolls around. The grand jury goes into session Monday and you'll hear plenty about it then. They'll be indicting all the nigras who are pullin' the thing."

"There were other demands besides the seating arrangements, weren't there?"

"Two others—courtesy and nigra drivers. The committee held no brief on courtesy. That's the southern way. All races are entitled to that." He laughed. "We don't hate the nigras or want to be mean to them or anything like that. Certainly bus drivers should be polite to them, and the bus company wants them to be. After all, they are in business."

"I wondered if there was any evidence that the drivers had been discourteous to them?"

"I don't ride the bus myself, but I hadn't heard anything about it. Our own girl never said anything about being treated discourteously. She did come to work late all the time and when I said something to her about it, she told me that the bus wouldn't stop and pick her up—that it would go on by and leave her. I went down to the bus company to find out about it and they said that they couldn't run so many buses during peak hours and that the buses would only hold so many people. What they said seemed logical to me and I took their word that that was the reason they would pass people by sometimes and not stop. I don't know what she's doing about getting to work now, I haven't even asked her. But she's been on time since the boycott started.

"I don't doubt that some of the drivers were rude at times," he admitted, "but I don't think they were any ruder to the nigras than to the whites."

"I want to be clear on the seating demand," Holden said. "Did the first come, first serve basis they asked for mean they would want that on a nonsegregated basis?"

"What they are out for is full integration. Hell, we don't care whether they have two seats or ten seats. This bus boycott is piddlin' stuff. Everybody knows what the NAACP is after—complete integration, even to intermarriage."

"How do most white people feel about the bus situation?"

"They're scared to death, Miss Holden. Most of them are afraid there will be riot and havoc if this thing keeps on. They feel sorry for the nigras who are walking and suffering and are afraid to do anything to end it. You know how they have kept them off the buses, don't you? They have goon squads take them out and work them over. I don't mean they work everybody over—most of them can be kept in line by threats and intimidation. I know of two cases where they worked on two of them—beat them up. One was the cook of a personal friend of mine," the incident King had reported at the MIA executive board meeting. "Those are exceptions, of course. But that keeps the rest of them afraid."

"What about your organization, Mr. Ingalls, the Citizens Council? Are you doing anything on the bus boycott?"

"We ran some ads, that's all we've done, asking all citizens to ride the buses. We asked nigras as well as whites to support the buses."

"Have you done anything else?"

"No, that's all. We've been building up our membership. Nearly 10,000 in the Central Alabama Council. Most of them in Montgomery. We had less than 200 in November," before the boycott.

"I heard that you have tried to get people to take economic sanctions against Negroes who are taking part in the boycott."

Engelhardt had stepped back in. "The White Citizens Council doesn't work through economic sanctions," he said.

"I had the impression that you did, Senator."

"Where did you hear that?"

"I had the impression from the papers . . ."

"Well we don't. The papers have given people a false picture of the Citizens Council. Don't believe anything about the Citizens Council you read in the newspaper. We definitely don't use economic sanctions." Ingalls handed her a copy of the WCC constitution.

"Did you come here to talk about the Citizens Council or the bus boycott?" he asked with annoyance.

"I am interested in the relationship between the two."

"We are an educational organization, and a charitable organization," he told her. "Members try to persuade people in talking to them personally. I have talked it over with my yardman, for instance. I haven't discussed it with our girl yet, but I did talk to the yardman and told him why he should ride the bus. He said he is afraid to ride, and I can't talk him into riding it. But we work like that."

"I heard that you are asking people to fire their maids until they went back to the buses."

"Hell," Ingalls replied, "you can't get people to do anything like that. I told you, I haven't even discussed this with our girl. I'm still paying her the same salary and I gave her a better Christmas present than I gave my wife." He laughed. "You see how bad we treat them?"

"You have been very generous with your time, and I appreciate it."

"Have I been courteous to you? Have I been kind?"

"Oh, yes indeed. No complaints on that score."

"I don't want you to go away from here saying that you weren't well received. Well, if you are through asking me questions, there is one I would like to ask you. Miss Holden, would you marry a nigra?"

"I haven't married anybody so far, white or black."

"That's not what I asked you. Would you be willing to marry a nigra?"

"Why don't you ask me whether I would be willing to marry a soldier or a farmer? I am not under the impression that people marry on the basis of these large categories."

"Now, you still aren't answering my question. Would you marry a nigra?"

"I am answering you by saying that is not the kind of question a person can answer 'yes' or 'no.' How do you know who you would marry and who you wouldn't until the situation comes up? People marry individuals. They don't marry because a person is a teacher or a member of some large group like that."

"You're young, honey, but you're off on the wrong road. You'd better think about this. Here you are working in a nigra college. You'd better ask yourself that question and answer it. If you can't answer it now, you'd better hurry and make up your mind, because intermarriage is what is at the heart of the whole thing. Tell me this. If you let your children go to school with nigras and eat with 'em and play with 'em and go to the same social functions and work with them, how can you teach them that it's wrong to marry them?

"Well, I see that you aren't going to answer any of my questions, so you might as well be on your way. Now I meant that. You'd better think about whether you'd marry a nigra, because that is the whole thing in a nutshell."[85]

Two days later, Friday evening, February 10, the Central Alabama Citizens Council held the "largest segregation gathering in the recent history of the South," as one speaker called it, overflowing the state Coliseum with a record-setting crowd. Arriving from Montgomery and nearby counties in "shiny new Cadillacs, pickup trucks, rattletrap old

Fords, and atomic age Jaguars," the zealous assembly was one in its purpose: to "rededicate themselves to the southern way of life." Reporter Joe Azbell described it as a mix of pep rally, political convention, and old-fashioned revival. The crowd wildly cheered, rebel yells ricocheting, when Mayor Gayle, standing with commissioners Sellers and Parks, promised to "hold the line against Negro integration."[86]

But it was Mississippi's senior senator, James Eastland, a driving force behind the Citizens Council movement born in his state in June 1954, that the crowd had come to hear. Owner of a six-thousand-acre cotton plantation in the Mississippi Delta, Eastland had built his political life on white supremacy. His first Senate speech in 1942 denounced black soldiers as lazy, ignorant, and prone to rape. Soon after the war, Virginia Durr brought a small group of high-society Methodist ladies from Mississippi, wearing white dresses, white gloves, and white flowered hats, to talk to their senator. All was cordial until one lily-white lady mentioned repeal of the poll tax. Eastland jumped out of his chair. "I know what you women want," he screamed, "black men laying on you!"[87]

In 1954 Eastland had called Durr before a hearing of his McCarthyite Senate subcommittee in New Orleans to testify about her alleged communist ties. When another witness accused her of passing war secrets from her friend Eleanor Roosevelt to a Soviet spy ring, Clifford Durr blew up. Vaulting over the jury rail, he yelled, "You goddam son of a bitch, lying about my wife that way—I'm going to kill you!"[88] Marshals grabbed him. He collapsed with a heart attack and was hospitalized for a week.

"There is only one course open for the South to take," Eastland yelled to the vast white sea at the Montgomery Coliseum two years later, "and that is stern resistance. We must fight them with every legal weapon at every step of the way. Southern people are right both legally and morally" and to win must "organize and be militant." Condemning the *Brown* decision that sparked the WCC as "illegal, immoral, dishonest, and a disgrace," he warned that the South faced an "era of judicial tyranny." But "the Anglo-Saxon people have held steadfast to the belief that resistance to tyranny is obedience to God."[89] The crowd's roars echoed eerily through the hall.

A handbill floated around the Coliseum that declared war on black people, in the spirit of 1776.

"When in the course of human events it becomes necessary to abolish the Negro race, proper methods should be used. Among these are guns, bows and arrows, sling shots and knives.

"We hold these truths to be self-evident," the handbill proclaimed, "that all whites are created equal with certain rights; among these are life, liberty and the pursuit of dead niggers.

"In every stage of the bus boycott we have been oppressed and degraded because of black slimy, juicy, unbearably stinking niggers. The conduct should not be dwelt upon because behind them they have an ancestral background of Pigmies, head hunters and snot suckers.

"My friends it is time we wised up to these black devils. I tell you they are a group of two legged agitators who persist in walking up and down our streets protruding their black lips. If we don't stop helping these African flesh eaters, we will soon wake up and find Rev. King in the White House. LET'S GET ON THE BALL WHITE CITIZENS."

"It is rather difficult right now to take a stand in favor of the preservation of the Union," the Durrs wrote to a friend up north. "Our old pal, Eastland, has become the leader of the crusade for righteousness and racial purity and as he got an audience of between ten and fifteen thousand to hear him when he spoke here last week, I don't think he can be laughed off, as irresponsible as he has proved himself to be. Black rather than red seems to be the incendiary color here, but they are rapidly beginning to identify them as one in the Southern Spectrum. Things are getting pretty rough."[90]

7

The tall, stately men greeted each other with a warm handshake. Asa Philip Randolph, sixty-six, had convened a meeting in his Harlem office on West 125th Street, headquarters of the Brotherhood of Sleeping Car Porters, which he had founded and led for thirty years. A. J. Muste, four years older, had shepherded the Fellowship of Reconciliation (FOR), an international Christian-based pacifist organization born with the First World War. They had been allies for years in campaigns for social justice. Both men came from Protestant religious backgrounds—Randolph's father a Baptist preacher in Jacksonville, Florida, ministering to poor blacks. Randolph's parents were children of slaves. Muste, who immigrated from Holland with his parents at age six, was an ordained minister of the Dutch Reformed Church, graduate of Union Theological Seminary. He had been forced out as pastor of a Congregational church near Boston because he opposed World War I.

Muste and Randolph were longtime democratic socialists with decades of labor leadership. Muste had led a nonviolent strike of textile workers in Lawrence, Massachusetts, in 1918, served as general secretary of the Amalgamated Textile Workers of America, then directed Brockwood Labor College, where many future CIO organizers learned the ropes. As a Trotskyite labor leader during the 1930s he played a key role in strikes and helped popularize the sit-down strike invented by the Congress of Industrial Organizations (CIO) auto workers. During the

Depression decade his pacifism solidified; he resigned from the Old Left and took the helm of FOR. Under his leadership FOR put civil rights on the front burner and in 1942 cooked up the Congress of Racial Equality (CORE), which conducted the first sit-ins to desegregate restaurants (and an ice-skating rink) in Chicago and other northern cities.

Randolph's hard-earned success in winning recognition of his union in 1937, two years after passage of the New Deal's National Labor Relations Act, made him the nation's preeminent black labor leader. Four years later he mounted a massive march on Washington by black workers against job discrimination. Tens of thousands of his followers were readying a nonviolent confrontation on July 1, 1941, when President Roosevelt buckled. Prodded by his wife, Eleanor, the conscience of the White House, he issued an executive order banning racial discrimination in war industry. Although she opposed the march, the first lady had attended meetings with Randolph and other black leaders and sympathized with their cause.

The threat of thousands of black working men invading the segregated capital on the eve of global war proved to be the single most effective protest by African Americans, thus far. The outcome was largely symbolic, however, because the fair employment committee FDR set up had little enforcement power. Soon after the war ended, Randolph's threat of nationwide civil disobedience to the first peacetime draft pressured President Truman to desegregate the armed forces in 1948. Some called Randolph the "American Gandhi."

Randolph, the most influential black American, and Muste, dean of American pacifists, were the architects of the two main schools of nonviolent direct action in the United States. Randolph's March on Washington Movement, which had moved on to organize wartime rallies and "Negro mass parliaments" to fight racism, combined Gandhian methods with mass direct-action techniques that CIO unions had employed in the 1930s. Muste's FOR tradition stressed nonviolent solutions to war and racial conflict aiming at reconciliation. The FOR tradition was largely white and middle class, shaped explicitly by Gandhian practice, rigorously pacifist. It focused on small-group actions, was committed to interracialism, anchored in the Christian faith. By contrast, what Randolph called "nonviolent goodwill direct action" was shaped as much by the labor movement as by the Gandhian independence struggle. It featured mass action, aimed at mobilizing African Americans as an autonomous force, was working-class, democratic socialist, and secular. It placed racial justice ahead of peacemaking. Yet the two traditions, like Randolph and Muste, had more in common than not.

This February 20 meeting in Randolph's book-lined office concerned a personal relationship the two men shared. They had been mentors to Bayard Rustin, who more than anyone else bridged these nonviolent traditions. His experience and skill in nonviolent direct action were unequaled among American pacifists; he had "an extraordinary way of pulling people into political action."[91] Muste had guided him more in personal, ethical, and spiritual ways, Randolph more in politics, ideology, and strategy. They were father figures to this forty-three-year-old man with no father of his own.

If Ingalls and Engelhardt were obsessed with the horror of black men's sexuality as an overarching principle, Randolph, Muste, and their mostly white colleagues from FOR, CORE, and the War Resisters League, along with socialist leader Norman Thomas, worried about the sexuality of one black man in flesh and blood. Apart from his homosexual lifestyle, however, they held Rustin in high esteem. But three years earlier he had been arrested and jailed in Pasadena, California, for homosexual activity in a parked car, right after he had given an FOR public lecture. Muste had forced him to resign his FOR position as race-relations director.

The radicals had gathered to discuss how they as northern civil rights activists could support the Montgomery struggle, in light of the bombings of King's and Nixon's homes and the tightening noose of repression. But their urgent business was to pass judgment on the suggestion of white Georgia novelist and CORE activist Lillian Smith that Rustin go to Montgomery to help the beleaguered movement. Most of those present were adamantly opposed. Only Igal Roodenko of the War Resisters League, which Rustin served as executive secretary, backed the mission without reservation. Charles Lawrence, the black sociologist who chaired FOR, spoke sharply:

"It would be too easy for the police to frame him with his arrest in L.A. and his police record generally, and set back the whole cause there."

FOR executive secretary John Swomley Jr. chimed in: "Whether or not there's a frame-up, there could be an actual incident or something dramatic in which Bayard in his usual fashion becomes the focal point."

Listening carefully to each side, Randolph and Muste made up their minds. Randolph believed that his protégé could help to make Montgomery a springboard for a Negro mass movement across the South, his dream for half his life. He offered to pay Rustin's expenses. Muste concurred with Randolph's OK. If a vote had been taken, the two elder statesmen would have lost. But none of the distinguished activists, not even five-time socialist presidential candidate Thomas, had the gall to challenge their judgment. Rustin left by car in the morning.

Businessman Ben Moore had built Montgomery's only black-owned hotel after World War II, a showpiece of black uplift. After Rustin checked in, the clerk warned him to keep his window blinds tightly drawn. "This is like war," he said, urging the tall lanky Yankee not to go out alone after dark. "If you find it necessary to do so, by all means leave in the hotel everything that identifies you as an outsider. They are trying to make out that Communist agitators and New Yorkers are running our protest."[92]

As usual Rustin took the risk. The street-smart New Yorker headed toward Court Square, the first capital of the Confederacy. He passed a car-pool lot where a team of disheveled winos camped out in station wagons, guarding the "rolling churches" against saboteurs.

What was strikingly different from everything he'd done—sitting down in segregated white restaurants in the North, defying Jim Crow seating on buses and trains, refusing to serve in the military during the war, threatening mass draft resistance to desegregate the military, leading FOR's interracial Journey of Reconciliation in April 1947 to desegregate interstate bus transportation, and witnessing Gandhian protest in India—was that Parks's action was unplanned, almost accidental. No tactical wizard like himself could have conjured a more suitable person to contest the bus segregation law and to rally around for a mass protest. He could never have organized such a perfect direct action. Quakers like Rustin didn't usually think about God having a plan, but maybe God worked differently in the Deep South.

He walked up Dexter Avenue past King's church, turned right on South Jackson Street below the brightly lit statehouse flying Alabama's

Confederate flag. He passed by the King parsonage, lit up with flood-lights and strings of lightbulbs. Rifle-toting guards patrolled the perimeter. Heading deeper into Montgomery's black west side, he found the home of Jeanetta Reese, two police cars parked in front. One of five plaintiffs in the *Browder* federal lawsuit that Fred Gray filed on February 1, she had told the press next day: "You know I don't want nothing to do with that mess."[93] She accused Gray of tricking her into signing the complaint. The county grand jury charged him with fraud and "unlawful appearance as an attorney." If convicted, he could be disbarred. Rustin wanted her to withdraw the charges. First he had to get past the burly cops who were guarding her house.

"I am Bayard Rustin," he said in the clipped British accent he had assumed as a young man. "I am here as a journalist working for *Le Figaro* and the *Manchester Guardian*."[94] Whether it was persistence, tact, or the cops' bewilderment, they let him approach her door. All she said was, "I had to do what I did or I wouldn't be alive today."[95] She was the cook for the mayor's mother-in-law. She had earlier told a black reporter that her boss had threatened to fire her, as had her husband's boss threatened to fire him. Menacing phone calls from White Citizens Council members threatened foreclosure of their home.[96] Rustin walked briskly back to the Ben Moore Hotel.

ON TUESDAY, FEBRUARY 21, the foreman of the Montgomery County Grand Jury, standing next to the county solicitor, announced to the press that they had indicted eighty-nine bus boycott leaders for violating a 1921 state law prohibiting conspiracies to interfere with a lawful business. Legislators had made the law, aimed at suppressing labor unrest, at the tail end of the nation's Red Scare, after a bloody coal miners' strike had shut down the state's core industry. The Durrs were right. Black and red had bled into each other, become one.

The authorities, though woefully ignorant of the black community, understood that the protest had many leaders. "These indictments should not come as a surprise," county solicitor William Thetford declared. "We are committed to segregation by custom and by law"—cameras flashing around him—"and we intend to maintain it."[97]

King was out of town at Fisk University on his first speaking tour. Cutting short his Nashville lectures, he flew to Atlanta to pick up Coretta and their baby daughter Yolanda at his parents' home.

Emotions soaring, the indicted leaders gathered for an emergency meeting at Abernathy's First Baptist Church. Abernathy had invited Rustin to attend and introduced him. He didn't hesitate to offer advice. The leaders knew that the grand jury had been deliberating and heard rumors of the verdict, but they were staggered by the sweep of the dragnet. It was by far the largest mass indictment in Alabama history; the only larger indictment in the nation had been the roundup of 173 Wobbly (Industrial Workers of the World) organizers in Chicago during the First World War. They had expected King and a handful of others to be prosecuted. But two dozen ministers? Twenty-eight drivers? Doctors and dentists, hairdressers and schoolteachers? Would this doom the movement, or rescue it? Was it the death knell, or a disguised gift of grace giving new life? Hand the whites enough rope, some hoped, and they might hang themselves.

Leaders believed that the move to prosecute came as reply to the movement's spurning of a proposal by the Men of Montgomery, a white businessmen's group promoting industrial development. The group was alarmed that the prolonged protest was giving Montgomery a black eye, especially to northern investors. At the mass meeting the night before, the protesters voted to turn down the proposal that was apparently OK'd by officials. Rev. Roy Bennett and another pastor cast the only votes in favor. The offer did not differ from minor concessions the MIA had rejected before. A leader commented afterward that "the morale of the masses, once again, revived the morale of the leaders."[98]

After this mass meeting Abernathy had explained to the press, whom they did not allow inside, that they would gain little by accepting the proposal and "would have to return to the buses with increased rates besides. We have walked for eleven weeks in the cold and rain. Now the weather is warming up. Therefore," he announced, "we will walk on until some better proposals are forthcoming from our city fathers."[99]

Now at their emergency meeting next day MIA leaders tossed around every option. Rustin goaded his Alabama friends to face their fear of jail. Discussion turned to whether they would wait to be arrested at home or work. Rev. H. H. Hubbard suggested they dress up like they were going to church and all go down to the courthouse together, showing their unity, the pastors up front. They would carry their churchly spirit to the courthouse.

"Let's all go to jail!" the Reverend Seay hollered.[100] After a tense silence someone called for a vote. Half the ministers voted nay, but the lay people voted yea. The proposal carried. They closed with prayer.

NEXT MORNING, WEDNESDAY, Martin King was greeted at the Atlanta airport by his parents, wife, and baby daughter. Coretta appeared calm as usual, but his parents' faces were chiseled with anguish. His parents would never be the same.

"My father, so unafraid for himself," he recalled, "had fallen into a constant state of terror for me and my family. Many times he had sat in on our board meetings and never shown any doubt about the justice of our actions. Yet this stern and courageous man had reached the point where he could scarcely mention the protest without tears. My mother too had suffered. After the bombing she had had to take to bed under doctor's orders and she was often ill later."[101]

They were barely in the black Cadillac when Daddy King began preaching on the dangers of returning to Montgomery. "Although many others have been indicted," he declared, "their main concern is to get you. They might even put you in jail without a bond." He explained that a pair of Montgomery gumshoes had showed up at the Atlanta police station searching for a police record that would enable them to banish him from Alabama. The cops were dejected, Daddy King said with a strained chuckle, when his friend Chief Jenkins told them that King junior had never even been arrested. "All of this shows that they are out to get you." He could spend the rest of his life rotting in Atmore prison, or be dead before thirty.

King was alarmed by his parents' fragile emotional state. He knew that if he resumed battle in Montgomery the pain he caused them would plague him. "But if I eased out now," he recalled, "I would be plagued by my own conscience, reminding me that I lacked the moral courage to stand by a cause to the end."[102] Above all, he had made a solemn vow to his divinity on the hallowed, harrowing night of January 27 that he would never give up the fight for righteousness. The divine voice had promised to stay with him forever—never to leave him alone, no never alone. He could not now, not ever, turn tail on such a sacred covenant. But how could he release his parents' torment, the mother and father he loved to the depth of his soul, who loved him even more? As the older and younger couple hashed it out in the home that Martin knew so well, he found his anger rising at his father.

While Martin tried to explain why he could not abandon his coworkers, Coretta retreated upstairs with the baby. His blood pressure surged. He may have flashed back on childhood face-offs with his father; he may have remembered the sting of the lash. Now fully grown, a father himself, he was more afraid of his father's tears than his rage.

A phone call from Abernathy broke the funereal mood, telling King of the march on the courthouse the next morning. But Daddy King persuaded his son to stay another day. Despairing of his own ability to change his son's mind—his emotional whip only springing back on his own heart—he called for reinforcements.

THE OLD MONTGOMERY COUNTY Courthouse had always been a place of terror for the black community. Hardly a black family had a member or friend who had not been beaten, framed, or railroaded. How many untold victims had been imprisoned for crimes they had not committed? How many black men had been convicted on false charges of rape? Raw in the guts of many was the conviction of young Jeremiah Reeves, Claudette Colvin's friend, for rape of a married white woman he was having a fling with. He awaited electrocution on Atmore's death row. White cops were notorious for raping black women with impunity like their slave-owning forebears. The courthouse was a voracious machine for locking up black citizens on the slightest pretense. But when these citizens sought to register to vote, or serve on a jury, courthouse doors shut in their face.

Nixon, dressed to the nines, was the first to go in on Wednesday morning, a crowd cheering him as he proudly climbed the steps.

"You are looking for me?" he asked a stunned deputy in the sheriff's office. "Here I am."[103] They took a mug shot and fingerprints, then released him on three hundred dollars bail.

MIA leaders had sent out an emergency call for people to show up at the courthouse that morning for a prayer vigil and be willing to stay all day. The nearly one hundred defendants arrived at the courthouse, some marching in groups from their homes or churches. The mass turn-in "had a startling effect in both the Negro and the white communities," Rustin wrote in his diary. "White community leaders, politicians, and police were flabbergasted. Negroes were thrilled to see their leaders surrender without being hunted down."[104]

As the sun grew warmer, the black assembly ballooned. A white reporter wrote that the triumphant feeling was like "old home week."[105] By early afternoon gaggles of schoolkids had discovered the courthouse fair. Colvin may have come by with her just-born baby to show support; it was nearing the anniversary of her own arrest. Jokes flew back and forth, laughter blended with cheering the parade of heroes. The deputies' stiff demeanor loosened; by lunchtime they were joining in the merriment. The Klan would have been apoplectic. For a sunny moment Montgomery's civic life had been desegregated.

Sheriff Mac Butler walked out red-faced. "This is no vaudeville show!" he barked at his men.[106] The crowd exploded in laughter.

By midafternoon, when more than four score had been booked and bailed out, the defendants and several hundred supporters marched solemnly up Dexter Avenue and gathered in King's church for a prayer meeting.

Without knowing quite what they were doing, the leaders had flawlessly conducted the first mass civil disobedience of the civil rights era. But it was disobedience turned into its opposite, mass civil obedience—an imaginative leap of collective action, contrived in grassroots spontaneity, that even Gandhi had never tried. Outdoing the Mahatma, they had marched to the courthouse to submit freely to arrest—showing the world, not least their own children and grandchildren, that they were no longer terrified of the white man's jail. They were cleansing the forbidding gray courthouse of its corrosive evil, if only for a day, discharging its demonic spirits, freeing its ghosts from suffering. Those who were there that day would never again see the courthouse, or themselves, in the same way.

A LESS LOYAL SON might have considered it a trap. That same afternoon Daddy King assembled the black elite of Atlanta in his parlor: the leading black attorney, two prominent businessmen, editor of the *Atlanta Daily World*, bishop of the AME church, president of Atlanta University; and one whose advice it would be hardest for Martin to ignore: Benjamin Mays, president of Morehouse College, King's alma mater. Rev. Mays, his first and most influential mentor, had shaped his growth nearly as much as his father had. Every Tuesday morning for four teenage years, the young man had listened to the president's weekly sermon in the Morehouse chapel, drinking in the black social gospel that would drive his own life.

With undisguised emotion Daddy King told his longtime friends how fear for his son had caused him and his wife sleepless nights and great distress. He laid out his reasons for Martin to stay in Atlanta, with a fervent prayer to spare his son's life. Martin listened soberly to his father's plea. His parents had raised him to hold these elders in reverence. They were the giants of the Atlanta black community. One after another they backed up his father. But Martin stood his ground, following the commands of the divine and the needs of his flock.

"I must go back to Montgomery," he told them. "My friends and associates are being arrested. It would be the height of cowardice for me to stay away. I would rather be in jail ten years than desert my people now. I have begun the struggle, and I can't turn back. I have reached the point of no return."[107] His father sobbed. Martin looked at his mentor.

"You're right, son," Mays said quietly.[108] *Daily World* editor C. A. Scott concurred. Others followed.

The Atlanta attorney called Thurgood Marshall in New York, who promised that King would get the best legal help from NAACP lawyers. The visitors embraced Martin and Coretta and his parents, then walked out the door. From that hour on, the father knew that his son would be taken from him.

As before—about his son going to Boston, marrying Coretta, pastoring Dexter—once Daddy King had been forced to change his mind, he acted like a zealous convert. He drove with his son and daughter-in-law back to Montgomery at dawn.

When they arrived at the Kings' home, Martin was mobbed by TV cameras. Abernathy drove King junior and senior to the courthouse, where a crowd of supporters greeted them. Abernathy had recounted with glee the exhilarating drama of the day before, saying with a laugh that some MIA people were upset to find their names not on the list. The three pastors, wearing white crosses on their lapels, fended off more cameras and microphones and mounted the courthouse steps. Just like his eighty-eight fellow conspirators, Martin was photographed, fingerprinted, and released on bond, offered by a Dexter church friend.

King had come far from his admonition to Dexter members when he took charge of their church that leadership never flowed up to the pulpit, but only from the pulpit down. He had learned that some rivers flowed upstream.

THE WEEK OF THE INDICTMENTS was the first week of Lent, the forty-day Christian season of praying, fasting, and servanthood—cleansing the soul, reconciling with sinners, and preparing for redemption, for the kingdom of God. As Lent encouraged ardent prayer, MIA leaders voted to turn the mass meetings into prayer meetings to magnify the spiritual nature of the struggle. The coming Friday would be a "Double P-Day" of prayer and pilgrimage: everyone would walk in solidarity, giving the drivers a holiday.

Adoption of prayer meetings dramatized the movement's religious currents. For devout African Americans, especially in the Deep South, praying was central to everyday life. They believed that, just as they actually ate Jesus' flesh and drank his blood in Holy Communion (like Catholics), prayer was a real-life conversation with Jesus, God, or holy spirit. Praying opened the channel that dissolved the boundary between the spirit world and ordinary life, much as meditation was understood by Hindus and Buddhists, inviting the Spirit in to enrapture one's soul.

People filled up Abernathy's First Baptist Church on Thursday, the day of King's return, by midafternoon. They sang and prayed out loud till darkness fell. At 7 P.M. the eighty-nine heroes, a mix of class and gender, clergy and laity, the "classes" and the "masses," strode down the aisle with sublime dignity. They were dressed brightly as if Easter had come early. Everyone in the pews stood and cheered; the clapping, stomping, whooping, and whistling rattled the stained-glass windows. Lights for TV cameras eerily lit the nave. It was the first mass meeting that network television covered, the first time the bus boycott was featured on page one of the *New York Times*.

"Overnight these leaders had become symbols of courage," Rustin jotted in his diary. "Women held their babies to touch them."[109] They stood arm to arm across the altar and circling back around the pews. King stood smiling at the pulpit, looking as though lifted up by the semicircle of light arcing around him. He managed to quiet the happy tumult. The show began, as usual, with the singing of "Onward Christian Soldiers," the movement's anthem, then a prayer to God "not to leave us in this hour." Rev. U. J. Fields brought a message from Saint Paul:

"Though I speak with the tongues of men and of angels," he recited, "but have not love, I have become as sounding brass or a clanging cymbal.

"And though I have the gift of prophecy, and understand all mysteries and all knowledge, and though I have all faith, so that I could remove mountains, but have not love, I am nothing.

"And though I bestow all my goods to feed the poor, and though I give my body to be burned, but have not love, it profits me nothing.

"Love suffers long and is kind; love does not envy; love does not parade itself, is not puffed up; does not behave rudely, does not seek its own, is not provoked, thinks no evil; does not rejoice in iniquity, but rejoices in the truth; bears all things, believes all things, hopes all things, endures all things.

"Love never fails. And now abide faith, hope, love, these three; but the greatest of these is love."[110]

All stood and sang lustily, "O lift me up and let me stand on higher ground."

King gave that night's pep talk. He declared that the long winter protest was about an unceasing stream of injustices that "go deep down into the archives of history," three centuries of white supremacy.

"It is one of the greatest glories of America that we have the right of protest, the right to protest for right." Loud clapping, cheering, and whistling. "Tell it doctor!" "That's all right!" "We can't stop now."

"There are those who would try to make of this a hate campaign," he warned. "This is not war between the white and the Negro but a conflict between justice and injustice. This is bigger than the Negro race revolting against the white. We are seeking to improve not the Negro of Montgomery but the whole of Montgomery. We are not struggling merely for the rights of Negroes but for all the people of Montgomery, black and white. We are determined to make America a better place for all people. Ours is a nonviolent protest. We pray God that no man shall use arms.

"If we are arrested every day, if we are exploited every day, if we are trampled over every day, don't ever let anyone pull you so low as to hate them. We must use the weapon of love. We must have compassion and understanding for those who hate us. We must realize so many people are taught to hate us that they are not totally responsible for their hate. But we stand in life at midnight, and we are always on the threshold of a new dawn."[111]

Ministers took turns leading prayers for success of the meeting, strength of spirit to carry on nonviolently, strength of body to walk for freedom, and for all people to live in justice and equality. The Reverend Seay led the assembly in "a prayer for those who oppose us," the toughest of the prayers.[112] By forgiving their adversaries, protesters sought to convert them in their hearts, turning enemies into friends, moving toward reconciliation and a new relationship. Loving their enemy would loosen the grip of fear, fortifying their courage when faith might falter.

BECAUSE KING WAS OUT OF TOWN when he had arrived in Montgomery, Rustin sought out Abernathy, who invited him to strategy meetings and put him to work drafting a position paper and composing a song. On Friday, February 24, he walked up the front stoop of the King parsonage. Coretta King greeted him with an excited smile.

"I know you, Mr. Rustin." She told him that he had lectured about nonviolent resistance to segregation at her high school in Marion, then later she heard him at Antioch College in Ohio.

"Bayard told me how strongly he felt about our work," she recalled, and his desire to turn it into a nonviolent movement all over the country.[113] When Martin got home, he greeted the visitor he had heard so much about with warm respect. We can imagine Rustin telling the young couple his life story: how he had been born out of wedlock to a caring Quaker family in West Chester, Pennsylvania; about the deep Quaker faith instilled in him; about his days as a popular New York folksinger and as a youth organizer for the Young Communist League, then as race relations secretary for the Fellowship of Reconciliation during the 1940s; about his constant travels lecturing about nonviolent methods, his twenty-eight months in federal prisons for resisting the draft during the war. Then working with Randolph to integrate the military, and leading the first freedom ride, the Journey of Reconciliation in spring 1947, to desegregate interstate buses in the upper South. For seeking to enforce a Supreme Court ruling, he was sentenced to thirty days in a wretched North Carolina prison camp. His *New York Post* articles about the black chain gang he worked on—in which he forged a mutually respectful relationship with the white gang boss—led to reform of North Carolina's prison system.

The next morning, Saturday, undertaker Rufus Lewis invited Rustin to attend a meeting of car-pool drivers, women and men from all walks of life. These were the twenty-eight-plus full-time drivers who had submitted to arrest three days before, charged with conspiracy to shut down the bus company.

"The success of the car pool is at the heart of the movement," Lewis opened the meeting. "It must not be stopped."[114] Rustin had predicted that some drivers, fearing jail, would back out. He was astonished when, one after another, these Christian soldiers pledged that they would be arrested again and again if necessary. The problem wasn't with the drivers, though a few had pocketed money meant for tires or repairs, but an alarming shortage of cars.

After the meeting Rustin grabbed the nearest phone and called New York.

"Mr. Randolph, there's a need for automobiles. Do you think we can get enough middle-class blacks to give up their automobiles?"

"I don't think so, Bayard," he replied. "But I'll tell you what to do. Go up to Birmingham, where the steelworkers are making enough money to afford two cars. Ask them to donate their second car."[115]

That afternoon, MIA leaders turned down a proposal that people be asked to stop work for an hour in late March to show support for the boycott, an idea floated nationally by Congressman Adam Clayton Powell Jr. They endorsed an alternative proposal for a nationwide day of prayer at the end of Lent spearheaded by black Baptist and AME church leaders and sympathetic white clergy.

"We do not want to place too much of a burden upon white housewives," King put in, "nor to give them the impression that we are pushing them against the wall." Rustin was heartened by the MIA's attitude, which he felt "adhered to the Gandhian principle of consideration for one's opponents."[116] He was struck by the movement's split personality: adhering to Gandhian precepts by day, flagrantly violating them with armed guards at night.

In the evening several leaders gathered with Rustin, upon his suggestion, to brainstorm ideas for another basic Gandhian element: a "constructive program" that would help spread the meaning of nonviolent struggle in the wider community, especially to moderate whites. Nothing as grandiose as a South-wide campaign of cotton spinning or other home industry to build economic self-sufficiency, as Gandhi might have suggested. They came up with ideas for a national high school essay contest on "Why We Should Use Nonviolence in Our Struggle," and to promote preaching of nonviolent principles in all churches, white and black. They considered Rustin's proposal for a workshop on nonviolent skills to train people to lead resistance campaigns in other southern cities. He felt sure that this was the time to take the movement on the road. They would fail in Montgomery, he warned, if they didn't grow a broader movement against segregated transportation. He would hit the road sooner than he had imagined.

8

Rustin recalled that he and King "hit it off immediately," but the protest leader "had very limited notions about how a nonviolent protest should be carried out. When I first got there, the leadership were carrying guns, had Dr. King's home, and the homes of others, protected day and night by men, not only with shotguns, but with pistols. In fact two days after I got down there, CORE activist Bill Worthy"—a reporter for the *Baltimore Afro-American* who at the height of McCarthyism had defied the government by traveling to Communist China—"walked into Dr. King's house, and was about to sit down, and I said, 'Oh, Bill, wait, wait, Bill. Couple of guns in that chair. You don't want to shoot yourself.'

"I do not believe," Rustin asserted two decades after King's death, "that one does honor to Dr. King by assuming that, somehow, he had been prepared for this job. He had not been prepared for it: either tactically, strategically, or his understanding of nonviolence. The glorious thing is that he came to a profoundly deep understanding of nonviolence through the struggle itself, and through reading and discussions which he had in the process of carrying on the protest.

"It was as he began to discuss nonviolence," Rustin contended, "as the newspapers throughout the country began to describe him as one who believed in nonviolence, he automatically took himself seriously because other people were taking him seriously."

He remembered a vital dialogue about the Indian revolution, which fascinated King. Rustin explained to him that "the great masses of Indians who were followers of Gandhi did not believe in nonviolence. They believed in nonviolence as a tactic: the British can, in fact, be won over without violence. But it was precisely what I discussed with Dr. King that, because the followers will seldom, in the mass, be dedicated to nonviolence in principle, that the leadership must be dedicated to it in principle, to keep those who believe in it as a tactic operating correctly. But if, in the flow and the heat of battle, a leader's house is bombed, and he shoots back, that is an encouragement to his followers to pick up guns. If, on the other hand, he has no guns around him, and they all know it, they will rise to the nonviolent occasion."[117]

On Sunday night, February 26, Rustin relaxed with Martin and Coretta King in their parlor. Rustin told King that he and his movement were sowing the seeds of Gandhi in the soil of the South. People felt in his presence what one had felt around Gandhi. Nevertheless, he was betraying nonviolent principles. Having guns in his home and armed guards outside not only was hypocritical but would invite more violence than it would repel.

The movement "*is* nonviolent," King replied stiffly. "We're not going to harm anybody unless they harm us."[118] If the whites don't attack us, he said, we won't attack them. But he believed that black people had the right to defend their homes and families. Rustin responded that in this historic situation such rights were trumped by a greater moral responsibility. A commitment to Gandhian nonviolence called for unconditional rejection of retaliation, even in self-defense.

"I'm for peaceful evolution rather than damaging revolution," King insisted, but he was a practical man, and this was Alabama. "When a chicken's head is cut off," he said, "it struggles most when it's about to die. A whale puts up its biggest fight after it has been harpooned. It's the same thing with the southern white man. Maybe it's good to shed a little blood. What needs to be done is for a couple of those white men to lose some blood. Then the federal government will step in."[119]

Give us until Easter, he said. "The spirit of nonviolence may so have permeated our community by that time that the whole Negro community will react nonviolently."[120]

"Dr. King, I have a feeling that you had better prepare yourself for martyrdom, because I don't see how you can make the challenge that you are making here without a very real possibility of your being murdered. I wonder if you have made your peace with that."

The preacher replied that he and Coretta had long talks about his death, and her death, lying in bed late at night, steadying each other. They had prayed over it together, knowing that it would be a lot easier without a child. But they had come to accept the inevitable.

"I have the feeling," Rustin said softly, "the Lord has laid his hands on you and that is a dangerous, dangerous thing."[121]

Rustin reported to WRL colleagues that the boycott leaders "are clear that they will have no part in starting violence. There is, however, considerable confusion on the question as to whether violence is justified in retaliation to violence directed against the Negro community. At present," he understated, "there is no careful, nonviolent preparation for any such extreme situation."[122]

THE NEXT NIGHT another prayer meeting took place, this time at Holt Street Baptist Church, where it had all started three months before.

"Direct us, Lord God," Rev. J. W. Barnes called out. "Tell us what you want us to do. We know that no harm can come over us with your hand over us."

"Even those who oppose us," Abernathy began his pep talk, "must agree that this is a spiritual movement. It gives us just room for giving thanks to God. We are not trying to put any firm out of business. This is not a matter of economic reprisal. The buses can run the streets as long as they please, but we're going to continue to walk. Thanks must go to fifty thousand Montgomery Negroes. This is your movement. We don't have any leaders in this movement. You are the leaders." Wild cheers. "That's right!" "You know it, Rev!" "Lord have mercy!"

"Someone asked me yesterday," he continued, " 'Who are the leaders?' "

"We are!" many cried out. "There ain't no leaders!" one yelled. People shouted back and forth, arguing whether all were leaders, or none were. Or was God their leader?

"There are too many people to talk at once," Abernathy broke into the cacophony, setting off laughter. "Since we can't all talk at once, we talk through one unified voice. We tell Reverend King what to say and he says what we want him to say. He is our mouthpiece, the mouthpiece of fifty thousand Negroes of Montgomery."

"Make us strong," Rev. Smith prayed, "to walk the sea of time."

Rev. Hubbard preached: "For the past eighty-four days many of us have sacrificed, suffered, and have been put in jail. The end is not here yet. The novelty has worn away, and we're down to the deep roots of the situation. We've emptied ourselves of pent-up emotions. Something will fill that vacuum—what it is remains up to you.

"This is not local," he continued. "It did not begin in Montgomery. But it was in Montgomery that God chose us to play this all-important role. We must accomplish the will of God. The white church does not practice what it preaches—the Brotherhood of man and the Fatherhood of God. We must grab the whites with a spiritual hand"—he clasped his hands firmly and brought them to his chest—"and tell them, 'We love you as though you were our very own.' We must not fail God in this hour.

"It used to be," he said in closing, "that the white man could toe us along. The white man has discovered that Negroes are no longer afraid to go to jail. I spent Wednesday night in jail. Remember this day, the year of our Lord, 1956. I stayed home all day waiting on them." Finally he walked down to the courthouse. "They tried to fingerprint me and were all thumbs. When they finished they couldn't tell what it was. They tried to do it again and I said, 'Don't bother, mister, I'll do it myself.'" The crowd howled. "We don't mind going to jail, giving our lives."[123]

Seeing the people slowly leave the church, a sparkling sea of smiles and embraces, Rustin scribbled in his diary: "I had a feeling that no force on earth can stop this movement." It had all the elements, he believed, to transform the human heart.[124]

The visitor knew that he was being watched. He minimized phone calls because he assumed they were tapped. Montgomery police awkwardly followed him. Twice when two northern white reporters questioned him in public, two cops "stood over us with the most menacing expressions," he wrote WRL colleagues. "When I called one of the girls to ask her not to contact me publicly, she told me to be careful, that every move I made was being watched; that I should be prepared to leave town by car at a moment's notice; that the rumor was being spread by a reporter on *The Advertiser,* the local paper, that I was a communist NAACP organizer; and that the Rev. Abernathy, trained in Moscow, and I were planning a violent uprising. So I must be prepared if necessary to leave here."[125] Rumors swirled that he was about to be arrested for fraud, or inciting a riot.

It wasn't only the FBI, white police, and reporters who were alarmed by Rustin's presence. Emory Jackson, *Birmingham World* editor and moderate activist, warned Nixon and other MIA leaders that he would expose Rustin's leftwing baggage if they didn't send him packing. Meanwhile across the Atlantic, the *Manchester Guardian* and *Le Figaro* were investigating the alleged impostor posing as a correspondent—the *Guardian* reportedly offering a reward. Later, he cleared up the problem with the European journals, to which he submitted articles about the protest but denied he had identified himself as a correspondent.[126]

Although they valued his advice and loved to hear him sing, some MIA leaders resented Rustin's arrogant style. They felt the sophisticated New Yorker was patronizing to his less educated southern brethren.

White Lutheran minister Robert Graetz, who pastored a black congregation, recalled that "we had almost a paranoia about anybody getting involved who was related to any kind of a subversive or questionable organization." Indeed the national NAACP, to which many in the MIA belonged, was conducting its own purge of alleged Communists. It was determined to ward off repression that might destroy the half-century-old organization, in which liberals like Roy Wilkins and radicals like W. E. B. Du Bois had long battled.

"We were just on our guard constantly," Graetz stated. So anxious were they that he and other leaders talked frequently with an air force intelligence officer from nearby Maxwell Field keeping tabs on the movement. On a regular basis Graetz reported to a local FBI agent. "If you don't mind," the agent had introduced himself, "I'll be checking in with you occasionally."[127] It is possible that Graetz told the FBI agent about Rustin's arrival. During the early civil rights movement, despite the FBI's anticommunist obsession, activists believed that the agency was a neutral force if not benign, being an arm of the Department of Justice. They had no idea of the extent of FBI collusion with southern cops, with whom they were often pals.

Nixon called Randolph, his boss in the railroad porters' union, on Monday night, February 27. He asked why Rustin had been sent, whether he could be trusted. Randolph vouched for his longtime associate. But he knew the moment had come to get him out of there. Yet he believed, from reports he had heard, that Rustin's intervention had done far more good than harm.

Next morning he made urgent calls to the same leaders who had reluctantly signed off on his and Muste's plea to approve Rustin's mission. An even bigger group than two weeks earlier gathered in his Harlem office, which as before included Muste, Norman Thomas, James Farmer, and John Swomley Jr., who had recently taken the helm of FOR when seventy-year-old Muste retired. A key concern, knowing Rustin's talent for self-embroidery, was that he was taking credit for more than he prudently should. He was not known for humility.

"Should we recall Bayard from Montgomery?" Randolph somberly asked the two dozen seasoned activists. Only strong-willed Igal Roodenko of WRL pushed for him to stay. A printer and World War II draft resister, Roodenko had served time in federal prison with Rustin. Later, arrested in the 1947 freedom ride Rustin led, Roodenko was given the longest jail sentence. The North Carolina judge berated him: "It's about time you Jews from New York learned that you can't come down here bringing your nigras with you to upset the customs of the South. Just to teach you a lesson, I gave your black boy thirty days, and I now give you ninety." Rustin, said black boy, had kidded Roodenko, "See, there are certain advantages to being black."[128]

Now nearly a decade later, Randolph and his colleagues concluded that "there were very serious elements of danger to the movement there for Bayard to be present," Swomley noted. Randolph reported that "influential leaders down there had phoned him to find out whether Bayard was the genuine article, and whether they should cooperate with him. He is obviously being watched, in view of the fact that he has been accused of being a Communist and coming down from the North."

The meeting reached consensus, Swomley summed up, "that we should not try from the North to train or otherwise run the nonviolent campaign in Montgomery, as Bayard had hoped to do, but rather to expect them to indicate ways in which we could be of help." This realization transcended the issue of Rustin's role. Many in the room had hoped that they would lead the civil rights crusade they had long awaited. Now they were shifting to a role of backup support. Rustin had been the lightning rod.

Randolph closed the meeting by observing that "the Montgomery leaders have managed a mass resistance campaign thus far more successfully than any of our so-called nonviolence experts." He referred not only to Rustin. "We should learn from them, rather than assume that we know it all."[129] They were not just pulling Rustin from the battlefield. Reluctantly, they were removing themselves.

Rustin's critics in New York fretted that he might not leave. "There are some here," Swomley wrote to an FOR organizer just arrived in Montgomery, "who feel the local leaders ought to know about Bayard's personal problem but dare not mention it over the phone. They ought to know the risks that are being taken and if they are prepared to accept those risks then it is not our responsibility."[130] This was the first time that the prospect of exposing Rustin's homosexuality—"outing" him, in later parlance—had been broached. Among sympathizers it would have been dynamite. What would enemies do if they got wind of this bombshell?

Rustin did not dally. On the last day of February, three black sedans pulled up in the Ben Moore's back parking lot. Rustin and Bill Worthy were waiting for them. Rustin folded his tall body into the trunk of one car, hugging his luggage. Worthy lay down on the backseat. Rustin assumed the drivers were armed. The three sedans, their contraband cargo in the middle car, drove off in the black night. Minutes later they crossed the Alabama River, heading north to Birmingham.

9

John Swomley and Charles Lawrence, the FOR leaders who attended the meetings in Randolph's office, were making their own plans to assist the suddenly exploding movement. After the approval of Rustin's mission, they decided to send their own organizer, Glenn Smiley, into the Montgomery cauldron—"not to compete or collaborate with Bayard," their former race relations director, but to carve out their own niche.[131] When Rustin was compelled to leave Montgomery, the field was clear. Rustin was too eager to take charge, they felt. They would tread more lightly, more attuned to southern rhythms. Their determination to upstage him showed the extent to which FOR had ostracized their star performer of the postwar era.

Smiley, forty-five, was a white Methodist minister raised in Texas who had pastored churches in the Southwest and joined the FOR staff in 1942. Like Rustin, whom he considered "my guru" in nonviolence, he had been imprisoned as a draft resister during the war. He was teaching nonviolent methods and fostering interracial links in southern hot spots when he was sent to Montgomery. He did not share his superiors' umbrage toward Rustin; he admired his mentor. FOR wanted him to set the stage for effective negotiations to resolve the bus dispute. But King, who was expecting him, had bigger plans.

Rustin's last act before hastily leaving Montgomery had been to introduce his former colleague to King on February 28. King knew what he wanted from the warm-hearted white southerner. Having just been upbraided by Rustin for his shortcomings, he asked Smiley to "teach me all you know about nonviolence," and to teach nonviolent methods in Montgomery and across the South. He asked him to assist other protests and to organize support groups of white ministers. "I would try to build bridges with the white community in Montgomery, as well as serve as an open and above-board intelligence by which Dr. King could be kept informed about white thinking." He would keep watch on the White Citizens Council, even the Klan. Smiley asked King what he knew about Gandhi.

"I know very little about the man," King replied, "although I've always admired him."[132] Smiley was taken aback. He handed him an armful of books on Gandhi and nonviolence, including works by Richard Gregg, Krishnalal Shridharani, and Aldous Huxley. Smiley was impressed that King borrowed from these writers at the next mass meeting.

The minister told him about the bombing of his family.

"Dr. King," Smiley cut in, echoing Rustin's concern, "I'm afraid that I have to say that I think they will kill you."

"I know," he replied softly. "Coretta and I have already settled this in many a dark and sleepless night."[133] Many a dark and sleepless night— Smiley remembered those words forty years later. When he mentioned "the committee," nickname for the armed bodyguards, King mused, "You know, I feel like a hypocrite because I talk about nonviolence yet I have a gun."[134]

Smiley cautioned that "the law of retaliation is the law of the multiplication of evil," a notion that intrigued King; he would make it his own. He asked his guest to accompany him to a press conference with reporters from as far away as Bombay.

"Dr. King," a journalist queried, "downtown they say you are a communist. What do you reply to this?"

He laughed his baritone laugh.

"Well, I am Negro, I am a Baptist minister, and if after saying that you would believe that I were a communist, you would believe most anything." Everyone laughed. But he didn't leave it there. He gave a thumbnail lecture on Marx and Hegel and where he differed, concluding that

Marx got the problem right but the solution wrong. And how could he believe in a godless religion?[135]

In a letter to FOR colleagues Smiley wrote that King told him he "had Gandhi in mind when this thing started," that he was "aware of the dangers to him inwardly, wants to do it right, but is too young and some of his close help is violent. King accepts, as an example, a body guard, and asked for a permit for them to carry guns. This was denied by the police, but nevertheless, the place is an arsenal. King sees the inconsistency, but not enough. He believes and yet he doesn't believe. The whole movement is armed in a sense, and this is what I must convince him to see as the greatest evil. If he can *really* be won to a faith in nonviolence there is no end to what he can do."[136]

"The die has been cast," Smiley reported to fellow clergy around the country. "There is a crisis of terrifying intensity, and I believe that God has called Martin Luther King to lead a great movement here and in the South. But why does God lay such a burden on one so young, so inexperienced, so good? King can be a Negro Gandhi, or he can be made into an unfortunate demagogue destined to swing from a lynch mob's tree. That is why I am writing more than two dozen people of prayer across the nation, asking that they hold Martin Luther King in the light."[137]

He delivered a note to King telling of his appeal to clergy to pray for him. He quoted Gandhi: "'If one man could achieve the perfect love it is enough to neutralize the hatred of millions.' Who knows? Maybe in Montgomery someone may achieve this perfect love! I am at your service."[138]

On Thursday night, March 1, King and Abernathy entered the packed church amid rousing cadences of "When the Saints Go Marching In." Lewis pleaded for more car owners to drive in the car pool and for people to walk shorter distances. At the peak of an emotional prayer a woman shook and shrieked in hysterics. When the Reverend Lambert gave a long-winded "singing prayer," many grew impatient. King's discomfort made him squirm. He covered his face, first one hand, then the other, to keep from cracking up. An observer noted: "It was comical to me to see him fighting with himself and to note his definite relief once the prayer had ended."[139]

Smiley, introduced by King, was stunned by the power of the gathering, gratified by the applause he got for his talk on Gandhi's work in India. "Religious fervor is high and they are trying to keep it spiritual," he reported to FOR. "They are sure this is the will of God. We can learn from their courage and plain earthy devices for building morale." But, he added pointedly, "they can learn more from us."[140]

Unlike most of his fellow leaders and followers, King joined the bus boycott committed to a qualified Christian nonviolence. If his grasp of it had been rooted mainly in the New Testament, it might have looked more like the Gandhian nonviolence espoused by Rustin and Smiley. But King's faith-based nonviolence was anchored in the Hebrew Scriptures and had been tempered by Reinhold Niebuhr's compelling conception of evil. The young preacher's makeshift philosophy differed from that of Gandhi and his radical pacifist disciples in that he faced sin squarely, without illusion, like the Hebrew prophets. He believed that love could not endure without the power to defeat evil that revolted against love—and that this power of justice and righteousness required coercion as well as suasion.

Thus in his own mind he was not being inconsistent when to Rustin he defended guns in his house and asserted that his concept of nonviolence might allow armed self-defense as a last resort—when attackers came to his own door. The gun might be needed still as an instrument of justice, if it was the only way to keep love alive. But in a matter of weeks, through patient tutoring by Rustin, Smiley, and others, King came to reject all use of violence. When he picked up Smiley at the airport in April, he told him that he had put down the sword. It had gotten too heavy. Another time at another airport he said to Smiley that what mattered to him more than tactics was, "Can I apply nonviolence to my heart?"[141]

His developing ideas shaped by the two American Gandhian traditions imported by Rustin and Smiley respectively, during 1956 King forged an amalgam of Gandhian nonviolence and black Christian faith, in oratory and mass action. This was fifty years after Gandhi invented satyagraha—"truth force" or "soul force"—in a South African protest against white racism. If, as King later wrote, "Christ furnished the spirit and motivation, while Gandhi furnished the method," black Protestant practice provided much of the method as well, particularly mobilizing rituals like call-and-response preaching, praying, and singing hymns and spirituals.[142]

Although refined by FOR's faith-based pacifism, which itself blended Gandhian with Christian motifs, King's resolutely Christian nonviolence did not derive so much from the moral reform tradition of evangelical Protestantism, of which FOR was an offshoot, with its accent on moral perfectibility. He fashioned it more from values, themes, rituals, and other resources of the African-American religious experience rooted in slavery—despite his reservations about the slave-based religion's wildness, which he sought to tame, to rationalize, to modernize. His philosophy centered on the black social gospel tradition he had picked up from his father, grandfather, and other activist preachers. His signal contribution to nonviolent protest was to incorporate Gandhian principles and techniques into the black church culture that had nurtured him, and to do so in ways that enabled the church culture to manifest powerfully its latent legacy of resistance.

King would bring together Randolph's Gandhian mass action with black social gospel to create a synthesis of visionary but pragmatic nonviolent politics. If Randolph's goodwill direct action was more strategic and operational, applied social gospel unleashed prophetic fire.

Unlike its better-known white counterpart, the black social gospel tradition was driven more by the Old Testament than by the New. It sought to merge the two Bibles in ways that much of white Christianity shied away from. One reason that King was so drawn to Niebuhr's neoorthodox theology was that in his reclaiming of Hebrew Scriptures Niebuhr began in roughly the same place as did the black Christian belief system: with the problem of evil, its omnipresence in human life, and prophetic resistance to it. The basis of the white social gospel of Walter Rauschenbusch and others was that people were naturally good, original sin notwithstanding, and were corrupted by sinful social structures.

The basis of black social gospel was that, from the time of Adam and Eve and Cain and Abel, evil had overtaken the world and its peoples. Black spirituality took the Devil for real, which was a defining theme of African-American literature. It was presently Satan's world as much as

God's. Every person, though created in God's image, was cleaved by a jagged fault line between contending forces of good and evil. God was commanding humankind, especially black people, to pursue a messianic mission to fight the Devil and win the world back for God and goodness, which included cleansing each soul from inside out.

Human fighters for good and justice must wield prodigious power, as channels or proxies of God, to vanquish the evil Goliath, within and without. This power must be equivalent to the power God wielded to part the Egyptian sea, which brought "the death of evil upon the seashore," the theme of a sermon King gave in May; power on a par with lightning and thunder, storms and floods. Mere moral witness, useful, necessary, and mandated by Jesus, was hardly sufficient as a weapon against evil. Nonviolent methods had to be more powerful than violent ones, applications of greater mass and energy. Mass nonviolent power fused physical with psychological, moral, and spiritual force: the Godlike power of moral absolutes, certitudes, and commandments, fueled by fervent faith.

Such mighty sacred force had to be tempered and bounded by compassion, sensitive understanding, and humility—qualities compressed in what King called goodwill, the love that Paul honored in his first letter to the Corinthians. The grace of goodwill—"the love of God working in the lives of men"—not only rendered righteousness a power that could be wielded safely by mortal beings. It also deepened this power by making it simultaneously a force for personal conversion and transformation, for releasing one's inner evil, for realizing one's higher self—the "better angels of our nature," as Lincoln put it. This difficult alchemy of justice and love was the only way to avert psychological legacies of hatred and bitterness, and to bring about long-term social healing, the mending of broken community.

Traditional pacifism and Gandhian nonviolence, especially that reflected by FOR, stressed the power of love alone to effect change. The nonviolent philosophy King synthesized aspired to be more dynamic and dialectical. It would combine two divinely originated forces, as he interpreted them, into one—the power of justice and righteousness and the power of *agape,* or creative goodwill. If the power of love could transform individual hearts and minds, righteousness grappled with collective, structural evil. King sought to merge these two powers, incompatible on the surface, into a seamless union more potent than the sum of its parts; in philosophy and rhetoric, if not easily in action—or in one's heart. The moral passion for justice would be even stronger, more irresistible, could truly part waters, move mountains, make ways out of no way, when leavened by the unifying force of compassion.

"Love must be at the forefront of our movement if it is to be a successful movement," he told Smiley at their first meeting. "When we speak of love, we speak of understanding goodwill toward *all* men. We speak of a redemptive, a creative sort of love." Then he shifted accent marks.

"We see that the real tension is not between the Negro citizens of Montgomery and the white citizens," he said to his new white friend, "but it is a conflict between justice and injustice, between the forces of light and the forces of darkness. If there is a victory—and there will be a victory—the victory will not be merely for the Negro citizens and a defeat for the white citizens. It will be a victory for justice and a defeat of injustice. It will be a victory for goodness in its long struggle with the forces of evil. This is a spiritual movement."[143]

Love or compassion necessitated justice and vice versa. The bus protest served as crucible for the faith that good would ultimately triumph over evil.

ACTIVIST WRITER LILLIAN SMITH, fifty-eight, who had first proposed that Rustin go to Montgomery, had grown up in an affluent Georgia family and sparked controversy with her 1944 novel, *Strange Fruit*, about a steamy interracial romance in the Deep South. It was banned in Boston and Detroit, sold 3 million copies, and was translated into fifteen languages. She had been fighting breast cancer for three years. Her Georgia home had just been burned to the ground by white teenagers aroused by her threatening creed. All of her manuscripts, her current work, library, records, and seven thousand letters were destroyed. Notwithstanding her own struggles, she was thrilled by the Montgomery protest, which embodied the values she held dear. She wrote King that at the end of World War II she had suggested to Morehouse president Benjamin Mays (when King was a sophomore) that "the Negroes begin a nonviolent religious movement. But the time had not come for it." She had no money to send right now, but rather "a spoonful of advice: don't let outsiders come in and ruin your movement. You know the fury a northern accent arouses in the confused South. The white South is irrational about this business of 'outsiders.' "[144]

"Irrational" was putting it mildly. The white South was still traumatized by the Civil War and Reconstruction, sharing a collective posttraumatic stress disorder. Despite Lincoln's prophetic words, there had been no reconciliation. Yankees were still the enemy. They had ravaged the southern way of life in the exceedingly bloody war. In the aftermath they had imposed a regime of conquer and plunder whose "carpetbaggers" bamboozled Negroes to be their political pawns in remaking the South according to northern designs. This was the version of southern history still taught North and South: the narrative of southern defeat and redemption popularized by D. W. Griffith's breathtaking 1915 film, *The Birth of a Nation,* which made the Ku Klux Klan heroic and helped inspire the Klan's rebirth in the 1920s.

The white southern mind believed in 1956 as doggedly as in 1866 that indolent, illiterate Negroes were incapable of mounting effective resistance to white supremacy—and had no desire to. Challenges to the southern way of life could be orchestrated only by northerners. Anything else was unimaginable—or imagined only in that most diabolical of nightmares, slave rebel Nat Turner's return. Everywhere they looked, both respectable and extremist whites (often one and the same) saw evidence of Yankee conspiracy.

The two-year-old *Brown* decision was the tip of the iceberg. A new army of carpetbaggers was infiltrating the Southland. King might have grown up in Atlanta, but he had been brainwashed in elite northern schools. Bayard Rustin, Glenn Smiley—the old familiar pattern was repeating itself. No wonder the Montgomery-area White Citizens Council had mushroomed in a few months to be the largest in the South. Segregationists were fighting not only the "second Reconstruction," but a second Civil War—and this time, by God, they would prevail. Slavery might have proved ultimately untenable, but the Jim Crow system, they convinced themselves, had matured into a viable and reliable protector of racial peace. Separate but equal had been the national rule for sixty years, until a northern cabal led by communist dupe Earl Warren had thrown it out in a judicial coup d'état.

A rift opened up among northern activists over whether they should be involved in the South's new awakening and if so, how. King and MIA leaders were torn because, in their darker days, they doubted whether they could succeed without northern help. Yet they had to show the world and themselves that they could manage on their own. After visiting Montgomery, Unitarian minister and FOR leader Homer Jack, from suburban Chicago, suggested that northern activists, white and black, had a valuable role to play. Socialist leader Norman Thomas wrote back: "I do not think it good to send Northerners into that Montgomery situation," especially someone with dark skin. He warned about Rustin, toeing the line of Swomley and James Farmer: "He is entirely too vulnerable on his record—and I do not mean his record as a c.o. [conscientious objector]."[145]

Jack replied to Thomas that northerners should help out if asked. As for Rustin, "I can attest that he did a necessary job which nobody else apparently had the foresight to do: to help indoctrinate the Negro leadership into some of the techniques of Gandhism."[146] *Indoctrinate* was a telling word.

To iron out this dilemma, Rustin and William Worthy sneaked back to Montgomery to meet with King on March 7. Rustin was still hotly pursued by Montgomery police. He awoke in his Ben Moore hotel room to find his face gracing the front page of the *Montgomery Advertiser*, headline screaming: "Who is this man? He is wanted for inciting to riot."[147] In their meeting the trio spelled out three areas in which outsiders could play a role: mentoring leaders, as they were doing with King; literature, logistics, and fund-raising; and nonviolent education to spread the protest.

Rustin left fired up to marshal northern support and stimulate further protests. Returning to New York, he joined Muste and Farmer to create the Committee for Nonviolent Integration, which held workshops on nonviolent resistance for southern black leaders. This short-lived support committee complemented In Friendship, a group just founded by NAACP leader Ella Baker to "provide economic assistance to those suffering economic reprisals" in the civil rights struggle.[148] Besides giving financial, technical, and intellectual aid, Rustin, Baker, and other figures in the boycott's expanding support network helped convey King's ideas to likely allies among liberals, labor, and the religious left.

IO

The Montgomery movement was more spiritual than Gandhi's but not as principled. In his March 1956 conspiracy trial King and his lawyers put bus segregation on trial, somewhat in Gandhian fashion. Yet while Gandhi insisted on truth telling in the courtroom and a willingness to go to prison, asking judges for the maximum sentence, King's and his fellow leaders' sworn testimony was riddled with evasions and prevarications, approaching perjury. Gandhi, a British-trained lawyer, put his faith in direct action to topple the British Empire. King and the American movement relied upon legal protections afforded by the Constitution and its First and Fourteenth amendments, which Britain lacked, to reinforce mass protest and to defend themselves against what they perceived to be unconstitutional legal assaults. This legal realpolitik, which kept nonviolent principles out of the courtroom, owed partly to the mind-set of NAACP lawyers, partly to King's realistic dread of southern jails. Gandhi would not have been lynched.

Although King's timorous handling of his 1956 trial did not square with his later advocacy of open civil disobedience, the difference was that, like Rosa Parks and Claudette Colvin, King and colleagues did not believe they had broken the law.

MIA leaders and lawyers turned the crisis of the conspiracy indictments into an opportunity to bolster the movement just when it had begun to falter. Judge Eugene Carter and prosecutors agreed to the defense motion to try the eighty-nine defendants individually, without juries. While the defense lawyers did not expect to win over the segregationist judge, he probably would not have allowed separate trials if they had all demanded juries. The decision to try King first and alone meant that media coverage would magnify his leadership mystique and emerging role as preeminent national symbol of black advance. The trial marked the second fateful step in his journey toward martyrdom, the first being the terror bombing and his Christlike response to it.

Boycott participants felt blessed by the string of blunders made by white officials, encouraging their belief that God must be with them. Officials refused to accept a reasonable, face-saving settlement that would have ended the protest in a jiffy. Then they adopted their self-defeating "get tough" policy of harassment followed by mass indictments that even the prosecutor felt skeptical about and moderate white leaders like *Montgomery Advertiser* editor Grover Hall publicly opposed. Now they had agreed to eighty-nine separate trials, which might tie up the court for months and give steady publicity to the protest. The prospect of trying King first, with its windfall of national sympathy for David fighting Goliath, felt like pure grace.

The four-day trial began on Monday, March 19, with exuberant crowds ringing the courthouse. The handful of white prosecutors and witnesses in the segregated courtroom found themselves engulfed by a black sea: defendants, defense witnesses, a six-man legal team headed by Fred Gray, supporters, and distinguished visitors including Congressman Charles Diggs Jr. of Detroit. Spectators wore white cloth crosses on their lapels saying "Father, forgive them." The trial was covered by scores of journalists from all over the world, showed up on network news, and won a front-page berth in the *New York Times*.

The prosecutors were no match for the heavyweight defense team, which included Alabama's most prominent black lawyer, Arthur Shores from Birmingham, and savvy NAACP attorney Robert Carter from New York, an associate of Thurgood Marshall's and a veteran of the *Brown* case. Rather than aim at the illegality of the protest, prosecutors sought to prove that King was its prime mover. But that claim was dubious on its face. Their actions spoke louder than their words. They had indicted close to a hundred boycott leaders, thus acknowledging that

King was one leader among many. Prosecutors were stymied by the movement's underlying paradox, one that even a crew of black spies on work release from jail and two detectives could not unravel. King was both leader and follower. He could hide behind his follower mask whenever convenient or necessary. Despite meeting minutes, signed checks, and other hard evidence, the movement's informality and dispersed responsibility made it difficult for prosecutors to pin specific acts, like formulating the demands, on the MIA president. The vagueness, evasiveness, and half truths of hostile witnesses added to the white man's burden.

Rev. Fields's testimony was evasive to the point of comedy. As recording secretary, he had written the telltale minutes of the MIA's founding meeting.

> Q. Do you remember who called the mass meeting for that night?
> A. Since I promised to tell the truth, the whole truth, and nothing but the truth, I don't know. I am not sure of that. I couldn't say.
> Q. Were these minutes made by you?
> A. They were.
> Q. Do they reflect what went on at the meeting on the afternoon of December the 5th, to the best of your judgment?
> A. They do. However, I don't profess to be an adequate secretary.
> Q. Are you now the secretary of the organization?
> A. I am secretary in name, sure.
> Q. What do you mean by secretary in name, sure? Somebody else doing the work with your name signed to it?
> A. I am secretary, but my multiplicity of duties makes it impossible for me to be an efficient secretary.
> Q. Do you mean you are secretary but you are just not efficient?
> A. That is right.
> Q. What are your multiplicity of duties at the present time?
> A. I have to keep in touch with my Creator. It takes a lot of prayer through times like this.

Fields could recall little about the historic mass meeting that night, or any discussion of the bus boycott.

"All the time," he stated, "we were trying to inform our people to go with their Master, keep God before them in these trying times. Regardless of what conditions might be they must always keep God before them." It was just "a happily singing group" that had gathered for "spiritual edification," hardly more than a church service, free expression of religion protected by the First Amendment.[149] This response echoed an age-old black strategy of dissembling that had helped slaves survive slavery.

Fields's curious testimony exposed another paradox that disadvantaged the prosecution. No legal or constitutional hairsplitting could have defined the boundary between the movement as church, as spiritual expression, and the movement as secular political action. Only poetry could have articulated the relationship. Although Fields and other witnesses hid behind religion and used the language of Spirit to obfuscate the "truth," on a deeper level this language was as truthful as any other. Ultimately if subliminally, defense lawyers were implying that if there was a single "leader," God or Jesus was the culprit, the hidden cause of all the commotion.

Defense testimony began on the third day. The strategy was to show that, though he led the MIA, King was not the leader of the mass protest; that the boycott was started spontaneously by the black community; and that the protesters had "just cause" for their actions, a loophole in the 1921 law that may have been a leftover from turn-of-the-century Alabama populism. In particular King's lawyers sought to disprove the prosecutors' contention that he had urged people to boycott the buses.

"My exposition has always been," King testified, "to 'let your conscience be your guide, if you want to ride that is all right.'" Under cross-examination he denied that he had "anything to do with calling" the boycott, or that he knew who did. "It was a spontaneous beginning," he claimed, "one of those things which just had been smoldering."[150] While these sworn statements were technically correct, they were misleading and incomplete. In a narrow legal sense he did not specifically incite or instruct his followers to refuse to ride. But in countless mass meetings from the very first he had given inspirational talks in which there could be no doubt that he was encouraging his listeners to boycott, if not in so many words. Of course, each participant decided for herself; but for how many was King's exhorting the decisive motivating factor? It proved impossible for the white man's law to translate the dialect of moral and spiritual protest, which they could not even comprehend, into the discourse of legal accountability. But that would prove a moot point.

KING'S TESTIMONY was the culmination of the four-day trial, but anticlimactic because it was all about minimizing his role. His lawyers' tack was to shift the spotlight off him and shine it on the evils of segregation. Most of the two days devoted to the defense was taken up by thirty-one women, ranging in age from their twenties to their sixties, speaking with bristling honesty about how they had been abused on the buses.

Gladys Moore testified that drivers treated her and other black riders "just as rough as could be. I mean not like we are human, but like we was some kind of animal." She recalled an instance in 1950, the same year that a cop killed army veteran Hilliard Brooks for no reason but that he was an uppity Negro. Although Moore's bus was fairly quiet, the driver yelled: "You niggers there. Don't you upset me with the racket." He stopped the bus and turned to the back: "You niggers, come on and get your fare and get off." Moore stayed put. She had to get home. Black passengers commonly ignored such commands. "When the driver tells you to move," she said, "you look the other way."

Two years later Moore was riding on a South Jackson Street bus and the driver "closed the door on my foot getting off the bus. I had on a coat, it was a heavy coat, and landed on the highway. It throwed me clean off the bus when the door caught my foot."

The bus driver called out: "The next time you catch your foot, I ought to drag you all the way up South Jackson hill." He didn't stop to see if she was hurt. "I didn't report the injury," she said, "because I didn't think it would do any good."[151]

For years, middle-aged Henrietta Brinson had labored as a maid in the upscale neighborhood of Cloverdale, riding the trolley cars—Montgomery was the first city in the Americas with electric streetcars—then motor buses when they replaced trolleys in the mid-1930s. Because she worked in two homes, she rode the bus four times daily. One day in 1953 she got on a bus and squeezed by a swarm of white private-school kids. She put her transfer ticket on the meter box and stood up in the back. The driver, "the meanest man I ever saw," called her an "awful name" and accused her of giving him a used transfer.

"There it is," she said, pointing to the ticket.

"Who are you talking to?" he asked gruffly.

"I am talking to you," she replied. "Every time I catch the South Cloverdale I always have to worry with you about something. I don't see why you always keep on griping about something. The other bus driver that carries me on the South Cloverdale bus, you don't have no trouble with him."

Startled, the driver glared at her angrily. "Who do you think you are talking to? You are just getting off this bus, all you niggers behaving like a parcel of cows."

"Well, that is all right," she told him. "Just as long as I get to work."[152]

Martha Walker was married to a World War II vet who had been blinded fighting against Germany. One afternoon in 1954 they were returning home from the Veterans Administration hospital in Tuskegee, where he had been hospitalized. They got on a bus downtown going home. She pulled the cord several times before the driver finally stopped; then she led her husband to the exit.

"When I got ready to get off," she testified, "he didn't stop, he slowed up. I stepped down on the side of the step there, and he opened the door. I got out, ready for my husband to step down. Just as my husband put his left foot down, the driver started on out with his right foot still on the bus. I screamed. A white lady said, 'Wait a moment!' Finally I jiggled his foot free. He couldn't get loose by himself. With me helping him he did, and he got his foot out." She ran into a store at the corner, crying, and said to the white proprietor: "I just had some trouble with a bus operator." The woman gave her the name of the manager.

Walker left her husband at the store and crossed the street, waiting for the bus to return. She flagged it down.

"Look yourself what you just done to my husband," she said angrily.

"I don't remember seeing you niggers on the bus," the driver retorted.

"My husband and I got off that bus there. He caught his foot in the door and broke the skin here on his ankle."

"I didn't do no such damn thing."

"He is over there on the corner to prove it. If you cannot give me any consideration," she said, "I am afraid I will have to take further steps." He pulled away. She called the bus company but never heard back from the manager. "They promised me I would, but I never did."[153]

Georgia Jordan, cook, nurse, and midwife, a city resident since 1920, grew so enraged by unrelenting abuse that she decided to boycott the buses on her own. The cruel name-calling tore her up. She was sick of ugliness like "Back up, nigger, you ain't got no damn business up here, get back where you belong."

What galled her the most was the humiliation of paying her fare at the front, then having to get off and enter through the back door, no matter how cold or rainy or heavy her load. A painful experience with her mother stuck in her craw.

"She was an old person," Jordan told the court, "and it was hard for her to get in and out of the bus except the front door. The bus was crowded that evening with everybody coming home from work. This bus driver was mean and surly, and when she asked him if she could get in the front door, he said she would have to go around and get in the back door. She said she couldn't get in, the steps were too high." He refused to let the old woman enter in the front.

"You damn niggers are all alike," he barked. "You don't want to do what you are told. If I had my way I would kill off every nigger person."

Mother told daughter they were "riding among maniacs."

Another time, Jordan paid her fare in front, and the driver snapped: "Nigger, get out that door and go around to the back door." Holding her anger, not wanting trouble, she got off. The driver then closed the back door in her face and pulled away, leaving her fuming. "So I decided right then and there I wasn't going to ride the buses anymore." She assuaged her rage by taking a stand against any more hurt.[154]

Like many of their enslaved forebears, these women resisted being dehumanized. They confronted and scolded abusive drivers, ignored or defied commands, reported drivers to the manager, occasionally engaged in physical self-defense. More and more often they refused to give up their seats to white people. Once in a while they held their ground even if a driver called the cops. And like Georgia Jordan, well before December people had voted with their feet and stopped riding the buses. The protest that began as a trickle soon swelled into a mighty stream.

The women's soul-stirring testimony, producing the longest trial transcript in Alabama history, spoke deeper truths than white lawyers and judges could fathom. It answered who started the protest, why they felt compelled to do so, why they were persisting with such passion, why jailing ninety of its leaders would only magnify their fire. It explained why the protesters did not need King or anyone else to urge them to act; why more often it was they who had to buck up their leaders, keep them on course. Their testimony explained how it could happen that, far from being ignorant Negroes manipulated by Yankees, local people were leading the movement every step of the way, giving new meaning to democracy.

"Wasn't no one man started it," Gladys Moore summed up. "We all started it over night." Over a long dark night of captivity.

ANY DECENT JUDGE or jury would have had to conclude that the protesters had just cause for their actions, and thus the boycott was not illegal. The prosecution had not proved its case, certainly not beyond a reasonable doubt. But Judge Carter was oblivious to the deeper or higher truths dramatized in his courtroom. After closing arguments, he swiftly convicted King of conspiring to disrupt the bus system and sentenced him to a five-hundred-dollar fine plus court costs. He gave him the minimum sentence, he said, because of King's advocacy of nonviolence. When the defendant indicated that he would not pay the fine, Carter converted it to a year in county jail at hard labor. Defense lawyers announced that they would appeal, sentence was stayed, and King remained free on bond. The judge postponed all the other cases pending resolution of the appeal.

King sauntered out of the courthouse with a brimming smile, cheered by hundreds of supporters. That night a raucous meeting shook Holt Street Baptist Church, full and rocking since the verdict. "It ain't hardly fair," a woman complained to researcher Anna Holden. "Folks who works and needs to sit down can't be coming in time to get a seat. Those that don't work and don't need to sit gets here and takes up all the seats." Another woman turned to Holden: "We all wanted to be here together tonight, because this is where we started."

A minister stood at the podium and gestured to the sea of people to cease singing. "He who was nailed to the cross for us this afternoon approaches," he called out.

King walked down the center aisle in flowing black robes, milk chocolate face glowing as if lit from within. "He's next to Jesus himself," a woman muttered. "He's my darling," another cooed. "He's right there by God," a third exclaimed. A woman in the balcony's front row burst into wanton soprano wailing, head bobbing up and down, banging on the railing, tears dripping on heads below. The audience sang heartily, "I Want to Be Near the Cross Where They Crucified My Lord," after which Dr. Moses Jones introduced the MIA president: "He is a part of us. Whatever happens to him, happens to us. Today he was crucified in the courts."

"We don't mind the cross," King declared to the still assembly, "because we know that beyond the tragedy of Good Friday"—a week away—"is the breathlessness of Easter. We know that Easter is coming through the suffering of Good Friday. Easter is coming to Montgomery.

"Almost since the beginning of his existence," he kept on, "man has recognized the struggle between the forces of good and evil. A philosopher named Plato saw it, and later on, a man called Thoreau. Christianity has always insisted that in the persistent struggle between good and evil, in the long battle between dark and light, the forces of light emerge as victor. This is our hope, that we will know the day God will stand supreme over the forces of evil, when the forces of light will blot out the forces of dark.

"You don't get to the promised land," he concluded, "without going through the wilderness. You don't get there without crossing over hills and mountains, but if you keep on keeping on, you can't help but reach it. We won't all see it, but it's coming, and it's coming because God is for it.

"There can never be growth without growing pains. There is no birth without birth pains. Like the mother suffering when she gives birth to new life, we know there is glory beyond the pain.

"I believe that God is using Montgomery as his proving ground."

At the end of the long gathering Dr. Jones put into words what most everyone must have felt in their gut: "The fellowship is like an electric charge to us. We can't give it up." The black souls walked out of the church singing "God Be with Us."[155]

II

Easter is the holiest of Christian holy days, commemorating Jesus' resurrection three days after his crucifixion. Piling on more cruelty, the Romans executed Jesus on Passover, the Jewish holy day marking the miracle of Pharaoh's "passing over" the Hebrew slave children he sought to slay, which came to symbolize the Hebrews' earthly resurrection in escaping from Egypt over the Red Sea. But Easter as a celebration of fertility, of birth and rebirth, was as old as humankind. The name came from Eastre or Esther, a Teutonic/Scandinavian goddess, whose festival was celebrated on the spring equinox, the first day of spring.

Easter's glorification of rebirth was Christianity's most important transfiguring of pagan spirituality. Easter echoed Greek and Roman myths of rebirth, such as the earth princess Persephone's return from the underworld. Easter encouraged black Christians to recover, if subconsciously, the fertility and reawakening of African nature spirits. The "drums of Easter," in King's words, resurrected African spirit worship like nothing else in Christian liturgy.

So black Christians even more than white experienced Easter as the holy of holies. Black women and girls paraded colorful new dresses and hats to express with their bodies spiritual cleansing and the bright light of spring. Like evangelicals of old, they shone as "new lights."

While Jews observed Passover as collective deliverance, mass rebirth, and Africans worshiped the reemergence of the natural world from winter death (including in their own being), Christians glorified the resurrection of the individual soul, as represented by Jesus, and of the body containing it. As a boy King shocked his Sunday school class by denying the bodily resurrection of Jesus.

The Christian concept of the soul stemmed from Greek influences, especially Plato and Aristotle. Unlike in Judaism, the Christian faith's primary source, which treated the human body and soul as a unit—thus encouraging the body to be savored, not reviled—Greeks following Plato considered the soul to be individual, a revolutionary idea, but also imprisoned within bodily matter just as ideas were shackled by earthly distortion. So Christianity arose as a double-edged sword: the individual soul was discrete, independent, and equal to every other, but it was polluted by the flesh in which it was trapped. Body was dirty and sinful, soul was (potentially) good and virtuous. Yet soul and body, if saved, would ultimately be resurrected together—King's childhood heresy to the contrary notwithstanding.

For each soul to be reborn in the spring, and later for eternity, it was essential that it cleanse itself from the evils of flesh, that it repent for sins flowing mainly from bodily needs and lusts. Of course as theologians from Augustine to Niebuhr stressed, sin (especially pride) issued from the corrupted soul as well. Thus Christians had Lent: forty days of repentance and purification to empty the soul into a womb for its own rebirth. Saving each soul from one spring to the next would prepare the way for immortality, the eternal spring of heavenly life. Saving souls in the here and now might also, with grace, bring the kingdom of God on earth.

So Martin King was speaking to each person as an individual, and to his flock as a whole, when he called for transforming the Good Friday of pain and sacrifice into the Easter of triumphant regeneration. As a Christian and especially a southern Baptist, he took on a pastoral responsibility that was all about personal redemption, personal salvation. His faith in a personal God, and in a one-to-one personal relationship between each believer and their divinity, was buttressed by his personalist philosophy, which redefined personality as the inner light within each person, the divine presence within. Every personality was sacred without exception.

Christianity being a religion of paradox, the individual soul was independent and yet dependent; dependent not only upon God but also on other souls. If its separate nature owed to Greek rationality, its interdependence owed to Jewish origin, interdependence articulated fervently by Christianity's founding genius, the Greek Jew Paul of Tarsus. To figure out how individual souls were related to each other, King turned as much to Jewish teaching as to Christian. He learned from theologian Martin Buber that true divinity was not found inside, or only inside, each personality but more fundamentally in the relationship among personalities. It was in the ether of connection between persons that God's presence was strongest. This relationship could not be between objects—I and it—but only among beings made sacred by their interconnection—I and Thou.[156]

Thus in King's preaching, Easter signified the rebirth of each human soul not in isolation, but embedded in relationship with other souls, together constituting the beloved community.

The new meaning he brought to personal rebirth was to make it transformative not only of the individual but of the whole society. Social gospel preachers spoke of restructuring institutions through which persons, already good, would be bettered. In a sense King was being a traditional Baptist evangelist by focusing on individual redemption, individual salvation. In fact he was turning social gospel theology inside out. Harking back to abolitionists of the Second Great Awakening such as David Walker, William Lloyd Garrison, and Henry Highland Garnet, he claimed that renewing, reforming, indeed revolutionizing individuals would reform and revolutionize society, more than the other way around. Like evangelical abolitionists he took on white sinners, but during the bus boycott he dwelt as much on remaking black souls as the route to the whole society's deliverance.

"The tragedy of physical slavery," King exhorted a gala New York NAACP dinner marking the second anniversary of the *Brown* decision, "was that it gradually led to the paralysis of mental slavery. The Negro's mind and soul became enslaved.

"Then something happened to the Negro," he asserted. "The Negro masses began to reevaluate themselves. They came to feel that they were somebody.

"With this new self-respect and new sense of dignity on the part of the Negro, the South's negative peace was rapidly undermined. The tension which we are witnessing in race relations in the South today is to be explained in part by the revolutionary change in the Negro's evaluation of himself.

"This is at bottom the meaning of what is happening in Montgomery. There is a new Negro in the South, with a new sense of dignity and destiny."

As he wrote in his first published essay, which appeared in the April issue of *Liberation*: "We Negroes have replaced self-pity with self-respect and self-depreciation with dignity. In Montgomery we walk in a new way. We hold our heads in a new way."[157]

For black Americans to see themselves in a new way, they had not only to defy three centuries of crippling white supremacy; they had to challenge reigning social norms of conformity and adjustment. While King acknowledged some forms of maladjustment as harmful, he urged black people to be creatively and courageously maladjusted to the evils of racism and injustice. In a Dexter sermon he quoted Saint Paul's admonition: "Be not conformed to this world, but be ye transformed by the renewing of your mind."[158]

The scarring of the soul by slavery and segregation had eventually brought the soul's awareness of its psychic wounds and its determination to heal them. King's designation of "the Negro" (singular) as subject of transformation converted a patronizing and disparaging reference to African Americans (as in "What does the Negro want?") into a shorthand for his philosophy of self-liberation. The freeing of each Negro soul would be the means of freeing the souls of all black folk. The Negro as full individual would save the Negro as a full people. Each Negro was a potential messiah just as black people, like the Hebrew chosen people, were a collective messiah.

King made it clear that the Negro's self-renewal was not occurring in a vacuum of time. It was prepared by a century of social struggle during which African Americans slowly but surely threw off their shackles, first physical, now psychological. The self-renewal, the new birth of freedom, was inconceivable outside the flowing tide of social protest, and diehard resistance to it, of the 1950s—in Africa and Asia as much as in the American South.

The Negro in Montgomery was transforming herself in the cauldron of her community's white-hot battle to be free. Her rebirth was bound to that of her sisters and brothers like links on a chain. As the singer-activist Bernice Johnson Reagan pointed out, when black men and women sang for freedom in the first person singular—"This Little Light of Mine," "I've Got the Light of Freedom"—they included in "I" and "mine" the "we" of their people.[159]

Just as the Negro's revolution in self-image and self-assertion was embedded in large-scale historical forces as well as in the storms of everyday struggle, so too this revolution soul by soul was giving birth, painful but necessary birth, to a new world of freedom and justice. Not only individuals but the whole world, it seemed, was being reborn in the middle of the twentieth century.

Around the globe, 1956 gave birth to new beginnings, fresh bursts of freedom sprouting from withered husks of the preatomic order. The triumphant nonviolent movement in Ghana would render irreversible the overthrow of European colonialism in Africa, its last frontier. Poor nations of the Southern Hemisphere banded together in Bandung, Indonesia, to create the nonaligned movement as an independent third force between the rival American and Soviet empires. In Moscow the new Communist Party leader, Nikita Khrushchev, denounced Stalinist crimes at a February party congress, sparking disaffection among communists worldwide and a democratic revolt in Hungary that Soviet tanks crushed in the fall. In the United States the demise of Senator Joseph McCarthy diminished the anticommunist witch-hunt bearing his name, opening up breathing room in the constricted veins of American political culture for nonconforming ideas and initiatives.

"We stand today between two worlds, the dying old and the emerging new," King told the fiftieth-anniversary gathering of Alpha Phi Alpha, his college fraternity. "The tensions which we witness in the world today are indicative of the fact that a new world is being born and an old world is passing away."[160] In King's eye the key evidence for this global turning was that two-thirds of the world's population was freeing itself from the yoke of white dominion. He saw that people of color more than whites, at home and abroad, were straddling the boundary of old world and new, wandering in the twilight between darkness and daybreak, navigating the complex ambiguities of a transition time from winter to spring, Good Friday to Easter. Between two worlds—a familiar stance for dark-skinned peoples. To prepare for entering the new world, he felt, black people needed to adopt a spirit of interdependence free from bitterness, open to forgiveness.

This identity of personal and social rebirth was not an idea that King came up with out of thin air. He was interpreting what he was witnessing, doing what he did best, translating into eternal diction what the people were teaching him—leadership rising from the pews.

THIS EMBRYONIC SPIRITUAL POLITICS that synthesized personal and social rebirth coincided with, and was shaped by, a more secular vision being fashioned by radical pacifists. Like King they were striving to create a third way between authoritarian socialism and Cold War liberalism, the dominant ideologies of the age.

From the right came rival efforts to rethink freedom and democracy, notably the philosophers of a new conservatism who also saw individual liberation as the engine of social freedom. Ayn Rand's best selling *Atlas Shrugged*, published in 1957, became the bible of an acquisitive generation for whom unchaining the (white middle-class) individual became an ideal: secular redemption through unfettered free-market capitalism. Critics on the left averred that Rand's "objectivism" would move society backward, not forward. Nor would people's souls be renewed, only defrauded.

The manifesto of the new radical pacifism was written by Rustin, A. J. Muste, Dave Dellinger, and Paul Goodman, editors of the new magazine *Liberation,* which featured their "Tract for the Times" in its founding issue, March 1956. Rustin sent a copy of the first issue of *Liberation* to King, explaining the journal's significance. *Liberation*'s editors suggested in their manifesto that the crisis problems of racism, poverty, and nuclear weapons had to be attacked on a fundamental level, requiring "changes in our deepest modes of thought." Grounding their thinking in four traditions—Judeo-Christian prophesy, American egalitarianism, libertarian socialism, and Gandhian nonviolence—the editors put forth a new political sensibility that stressed personal ethics and honesty, dwelt more in "concrete situations than in rhetorical blueprints, in individual lives than in 'global historical forces' which remain merely abstract. What matters to us is what happens to the individual human being— here and now." Unlike liberals they would go to the roots of social problems. Unlike Marxists they would refuse to sacrifice the present for the future, to treat persons as pawns for "a tomorrow that never comes."

For their "politics of the future," Rustin and his New York colleagues sought to forge a radical pragmatism, a pragmatic radicalism, that would fuse politics and ethics. Means and ends would condition each other reciprocally, the ends built into the means, the basis of Gandhian philosophy. Rather than put down idealistic thinking as did tough-minded liberals and Marxists, the new politics would be inspired by utopian visions, which expressed "the growing edge of society and the creative imagination of a culture." Above all, "the very presuppositions on which human relationships are based must be revolutionized."

This dynamic politics aspired to be an American moral equivalent of the Third World's nonaligned movement (born in 1955) and of fledgling democratic dissent behind the Iron Curtain. It would stand for "refusal to run away or to conform, concrete resistance in the communities in which we live to all the ways in which human beings are regimented and corrupted, dehumanized and deprived of their freedom."[161]

We can see the revolt of the bus boycott, and the precepts King drew from it, as a living out of this manifesto. To an extent the boycott's collective leadership was shaped by this new thinking that Rustin brought to Montgomery in February and continued to promote in his advising and ghostwriting for the MIA president. To a greater extent the boycott movement was the shaping force—not only grounding this new philosophy, transmuting ideas into flesh, but deepening the ideas themselves that struggled to birth a new world.

NOT ONLY IN MONTGOMERY was spring blowing in new births of freedom. Students at South Carolina State College in Orangeburg boycotted classes after the arch-segregationist governor sent in police to stop a civil rights rally. It grew into a full-fledged student strike against police spying and White Citizens Council harassment. Several thousand black people commenced a bus boycott in Capetown, South Africa, against imposition of segregated seating. In Washington, D.C., seventy-five black leaders gathered for the State of the Race conference in late April, headed by Randolph. They responded to southern Congress members' shrill denunciation of the *Brown* decision by calling for a South-wide school-desegregation campaign. In Tallahassee in May, two Florida A&M students, Wilhelmina Jakes and Carrie Patterson, were arrested for sitting in the white section of a bus (the only vacant seats, again), sparking a seven-month bus boycott that applied lessons from Montgomery.

After tea with Rosa Parks in her New York apartment, Eleanor Roosevelt wrote in her syndicated column that "human beings reach a point when they say: 'This is as far as I can go.'

"That is what seems to have happened in Montgomery, and perhaps it will happen all over our country wherever we have citizens who do not enjoy complete equality. It may be that this attitude will save us from war and bloodshed and teach those of us who have to learn that there is a point beyond which human beings will not continue to bear injustice."[162]

Among mountains of support letters King received in the wake of his trial, most of which he or his secretary answered, came one from Juanita Moore of Baltimore. She praised his successful work that "comes only through God & good leadership an followers. i my self is a widow with a 4 yeairs old Sun to support is why i am writing this letter without a donation. Keep the good work up and ask God for what you wont for I no he is able he said he will fight your battle if you just keep still just trust him for his Word and dont get empatience."[163]

As spring turned to summer in Montgomery, the bus boycott's legal offensive heated up along with the air, pavement, and car-pool car radiators. For several surreal days it looked like the boycott might have won, with news of a Supreme Court ruling on a South Carolina bus case. Alas, reporters missed the fine print. In 1954 soon after the *Brown* decision, a young woman in Columbia, South Carolina, Sarah Mae Flemming, sued the bus company for violating her right to equal protection by forcing her to sit in the black section. A federal district judge, father of the segregationist governor, rejected her lawsuit. But the

Fourth Circuit Court of Appeals, upholding her appeal, declared in-state bus segregation unconstitutional. The Supreme Court's ruling in late April 1956 did not affirm the Fourth Circuit decision but merely dismissed the bus company's appeal as premature.

Nonetheless, the narrow technical ruling was widely perceived as striking down bus segregation. The *New York Times* headlined: HIGH COURT VOIDS LAST COLOR LINES IN PUBLIC TRANSIT. IMPACT OF RULING IS EXPECTED TO BE AS WIDE AS DECISION AGAINST SEPARATE SCHOOLS.

The hyperbole spurred thirteen southern bus lines to desegregate. The Montgomery parent company in Chicago, eager to save the local franchise from collapse, instructed Montgomery drivers to end Jim Crow seating. But Mayor Gayle and Police Commissioner Sellers resolved to maintain the status quo. Sellers threatened to arrest drivers who disobeyed their higher law.

The split between commissioners and bus company tore wide open in early May, when the city obtained an injunction from Judge Walter B. Jones making the bus company cancel its desegregation order. Jones quoted an 1899 Alabama Supreme Court finding that it was reasonable to seat passengers so as "to prevent contacts and collisions arising from natural or well known customary repugnances which are likely to breed disturbances by a promiscuous sitting." He appealed to the Tenth Amendment, which arguably authorized states' rights, thus putting that amendment on a collision course with the Fourteenth, which restricted them.[164] Before year's end, as in 1954, the latter would prevail over the former. This constitutional conflict foreshadowed the South's social drama of the next decade.

Now the movement's hopes rested foursquare on the *Browder v. Gayle* lawsuit, which looked promising. But the unpredictability of a federal panel of three southern whites ranging from solid segregationist to racially moderate made a strikeout seem possible. If they lost in this federal court, an appeal to the Supreme Court would take months, maybe a year or more.

With so much at stake, tensions ran high when plaintiffs Aurelia Browder, Claudette Colvin, Susie McDonald, and Mary Louise Smith testified on May 11 in the old federal courthouse two blocks from the bus stop where Rosa Parks had been arrested. The bus boycott played a lead role in the courtroom drama. The defendants' attorneys put the boycott on trial, but less credibly than King's lawyers had done with bus segregation in March. When a defense lawyer tried to show that the boycott aimed strictly at making segregation fairer, thus indirectly accepting Jim Crow, Aurelia Browder cut him off at the pass: "It is the segregation laws of Alabama that caused all of it."

During Colvin's last appearances in Montgomery courtrooms, she had been traumatized by the judges' vindictive verdicts. Her wails careened off the courtroom walls. Now a year later, the tables had turned, in no small measure because of her brave defiance. The sixteen-year-old who had aspired to be a lawyer, but now was a struggling unwed mom with an infant son, was getting her calm revenge. This time in federal court, the sudden adult told the tale of her arrest and jailing in cinematic prose, then immortalized her saga in one pithy sentence. When asked by the opposing lawyer who was the leader of the bus protest, she replied sternly: "Our leaders is just *we ourself!*"[165]

On June 5, the federal judges ruled two-to-one for the *Browder* lawsuit. The court declared unconstitutional the Montgomery and Alabama bus-segregation statutes as violations of the Fourteenth Amendment. The decision hinged on how the judges interpreted the Supreme Court's two-year-old school-desegregation verdict. Federal appeals judge Richard T. Rives's majority opinion, with which new local district judge Frank M. Johnson Jr., concurred, found that the *Brown* decision's rejection of the 1896 "separate but equal" doctrine "impliedly" reached beyond public schools to other forms of legal segregation. District judge Seybourn H. Lynne's dissent argued that it did not.

The court panel suspended enforcement of its decree until the Supreme Court could rule on the city's appeal. With renewed spirit the boycott carried on through summer and fall. Foot soldiers believed that the arc of the moral universe had bent, and that justice was rolling down.

On the surface it seemed, as the *Montgomery Advertiser* later editorialized, that the *Browder* decision was "achieved in absolute independence" of the bus boycott.[166] A deeper look showed that not to be the case. In the first place, a likely motive in the minds of Rives and Johnson was to halt the growing disorder on the streets of Montgomery and the potential for mass violence. Confirmed by Congress the day before *Browder* was filed, Johnson was a Republican from northern Alabama whose three-month tenure in Montgomery was dominated by the boycott disruption that had put Montgomery on the national and global map. Were it not for the ongoing protest, he might not have pressed the chief appeals court judge to create the special panel required for constitutional challenges; and the latter, very reluctant as it was, might not have agreed. Historically, nonviolent direct action has achieved its goals most often by forcing authorities to give in to preserve social order. This was certainly true seven years later in Birmingham.

While there was little doubt that Rives and Johnson would have voted for *Browder* without the boycott, on the strength of *Brown*, it was less likely that they would have faced the decision had the mass protest not put the case before them. MIA lawyers would not have initiated the lawsuit until black leaders had learned the hard way that bus segregation was brittle; it could not bend without breaking. Other than a cosmetic touchup, it could not have been modified easily—especially by black demand. They would not have learned about this irrational rigidity, largely a result of the commissioners' electoral needs, without the boycott. Thus they would have been unlikely to take the dangerous step of suing to end segregation.[167]

As King explained the dynamic to a radical pacifist later that year, "We had negotiated for several weeks to no avail. The City Commission insisted that what we were asking for could not be done on the basis of the present law; so we had no other alternative but to attack the structure of the law itself."[168]

Nor did they know anything about who would hear the case. Johnson, the brand-new Montgomery judge, was a stranger. To MIA leaders all southern judges looked as white as snow. Even with *Brown* to buttress them they thought the prospects looked dicey.

It was also unlikely they would have filed such an incendiary lawsuit without the protection afforded by the MIA and the organized black community, and the shield of the media presence that kept a spotlight on the city. Fear of physical or economic retaliation might have deterred them and the brave plaintiffs, like it did Jeanetta Reese. Furthermore, without the disorder and threat of worse, the federal judges might have sidetracked or defused the *Browder* suit as happened to the *Flemming* case that the NAACP had been betting on.

While it would be overstating to claim that the bus boycott directly produced the *Browder* decision, it would be wrong to conclude that it had little or no impact. Weighing all factors, it looked probable that the mass protest had an important indirect influence.

THE FELICITOUS *Browder* ruling made victory unstoppable, but its immediate fruit was bitter. King's most severe test of leadership came not from outside—bombings, White Citizens Council intimidation, intransigent city officials—but inside, from the threat to the MIA's carefully manicured unity posed by Rev. Uriah J. Fields. He would have hesitated to challenge the MIA leadership so brazenly had the *Browder* outcome not made the movement less vulnerable.

The young pastor of Bell Street Baptist had been elected MIA recording secretary at the founding meeting. As we have seen, he testified in King's trial that he was a lousy secretary. At the end of May the MIA was incorporated with a constitution and bylaws and its structure reorganized. Rev. W. J. Powell replaced Fields as secretary. This was partly because the latter had not been attending meetings faithfully—he was absent from this one—and partly because King's inner circle did not trust him. Having a tendency to act with impulsive independence, he had angered his colleagues in January when he published his *Advertiser* letter scorning compromise and threatening "annihilation" of segregation. His rogue letter had spurred the MIA executive board to require its approval for all public statements except King's.

Fields angrily denounced his removal at a mass meeting on June 11, but the assembly reaffirmed his ouster. Livid, he stormed out and announced to the press he was resigning from the MIA because of "misappropriation of funds" by leaders who were "misusing money sent from all over the nation." He said: "I can no longer identify myself with a movement in which the many are exploited by the few." The leaders had become "too egotistical and interested in perpetuating themselves." The MIA "no longer represents what I stand for."[169]

When Fields made his public charges, King and Abernathy were in California, taking a rare vacation with their families, hosted by a Los Angeles black church, and promoting the boycott. King's chronic fatigue and sleep deficit, his doctors warned, made rest vital. Realizing that the allegations threatened the MIA's reputation, fund-raising, and cohesion, he flew back to Montgomery and met with the apostate, whom the black community was treating as a traitor, a "black Judas." According to King's account of their conversation, Fields withdrew the allegations and admitted they had been motivated by his feeling of mistreatment by two executive board members.

"I want you to know," Fields told him, "that I was not referring to you in my accusations. I have always had the greatest respect for your integrity and I still do. All of those things I made up in a moment of anger. This was my way of retaliating."

He agreed to publicly recant and apologize at the next mass meeting. In the sweltering heat of overflowing Beulah Baptist Church, an "unaccustomed atmosphere of bitterness," Fields joined the MIA president at the pulpit. "Look at that devil!" someone shouted. King denied that the MIA had mishandled any money. He asked the agitated assembly to forgive the young pastor in a spirit of Christian love.

"We must meet this situation with the same dignity and discipline with which we have met so many difficult situations in the past. Let us never forget that we have committed ourselves to a way of nonviolence, avoiding not only external physical violence but also internal violence of spirit. You not only refuse to shoot a man, but you refuse to hate him.

"We are all aware of the weaknesses of human nature," he proceeded. "We have all made mistakes along the way of life. We have all had moments when our emotions overpowered us. Now some of us are here this evening to stone one of our brothers because he has made a mistake.

"Let him who is without sin cast the first stone." People were still. Fields prayed out loud, got an *Amen!*, and asked for forgiveness. His retraction was equivocal, referring to statements "attributed to me as having said." The assembly nonetheless applauded him as he walked down from the altar.[170]

Although the young preacher acted out of resentment and his allegations were overblown, they were not entirely untrue. On some occasions, possibly on a regular basis, King and other leaders who spoke and raised funds for the MIA out of town received honoraria that they kept.

"We had a whole lot of money at that time and some of it we handled unwisely," MIA treasurer E. D. Nixon later stated. "There wasn't nobody stealing much of anything, but we just handled it unwisely." It might have been Nixon's grousing that prompted his protégé Fields to let loose. Nixon was even more alienated from the MIA inner circle than was Fields; later he too resigned in anger. Not willing to disagree with Fields's charges, he said: "A lot of times a minister would go and make a speech and he'd think that he's entitled to some of it." He admitted that he once kept a six-hundred-dollar fee.[171]

When Fields publicly atoned, he sidestepped the issue of speaking fees. "Money sent to the organization" was not misused, he said. He was silent about cash given to individuals.[172]

Not all speakers accepted personal fees. Rosa Parks, despite her penury and family illness, and white Lutheran minister Robert Graetz were among those who didn't. Graetz later recalled that Fields's charges "reignited my own concerns about the way money was handled. I had raised several thousand dollars through speeches at fund-raisers, and each time, after paying for my travel expenses, I turned everything else over to the MIA. After one of those trips, however, when I brought the money in to be deposited, someone asked, 'Did you keep enough out for yourself?'

"I balked. 'I never keep any for personal use,' I replied. 'This money was raised for the movement.'

" 'I know, but the other speakers normally keep an honorarium for themselves out of the money they raise.' I was shocked. I had no idea others were doing that. But I never changed my policy."[173] Fields, however, had little opportunity to earn such fees, had he been so inclined, since the speakers' bureau rarely if ever asked him to represent the MIA. That might have contributed to his jealousy.

Fields and Nixon might have been more upset about a different excess. Funds were routinely spent on things unrelated to the car pool or community organizing, especially relief to families in need, an off-the-cuff welfare program. This largesse resulted from the MIA's fund-raising prowess, especially after King's trial. The MIA took in more money every month than the boycott needed; some of the overflow was sent to an Atlanta savings bank. Financial secretary Erna Dungee remembered:

"We paid rent. We paid gas bills. We paid water bills. We bought food. We paid people's doctor bills. We even buried somebody. Those were free rides as far as I was concerned. But they seemed to think this is what we had to do. We even bought washing machines. We did everything trying to get along with the people," to maintain morale and unity at whatever cost. She recalled that it was "usually the poorest ones" who came for help. King was "real sympathetic" to these people's needs. Though "he was against some of that," she stated, "he felt he had to go along with most of it."[174] Daddy King's son was such a fastidious financial overlord that not much of anything dollar-wise escaped his notice.

12

In his memoir King concluded that "nonviolence triumphed again" in the Fields blowup "and a situation that many had predicted would be the end of the MIA left it more united than ever in the spirit of tolerance."[175] Within two weeks of the *Browder* victory, King had directed a morality play on the boycott's stage that illustrated the power of nonviolent action *within* the movement. He faced the problem head-on; communicated directly, forcefully, but compassionately with Fields; shamed him into a public act of contrition; persuaded the mass meeting, the jury of the people, to forgive him; finessed Fields's reconciliation (at least in appearance); and transformed a setback into a step forward, repairing the broken community into restored wholeness. As with any show, however, the performers returned to their real selves after the curtain fell. Fields was not pacified for long.

Still, like many things about the bus boycott, this experience was a new departure, a new way of dealing with internal conflict. Other radical or revolutionary movements dealt with dissidents or apostates by censoring, suppressing, ostracizing or, like the Soviet Union, sending them to Gulags. Committed both to free speech and to challenging untruths, the Montgomery movement conducted a public display of redemption and reconciliation. Even though Fields's staged apology was not fully sincere, what mattered was the "spirit of tolerance" and the reunifying of the movement.

Within the fold and against the walls of injustice, King pioneered the first self-consciously nonviolent movement in U.S. history. It did not avoid, appease, or stifle conflict but faced and fostered it. The movement did not constrain or inhibit force but marshaled it creatively for transformative ends. Like martial artists, activists took the force of the adversary and turned it against itself. The nonviolent theorist Richard Gregg, who influenced King, called this force "moral jujitsu."

Guided by Gandhi, Gregg, Rustin, Smiley, and other teachers—above all by the Montgomery foot soldiers—King crafted a coherent philosophy of nonviolent conflict. It incorporated others' ideas about strategy, tactics, and technique into a wider ethical and spiritual framework. In Montgomery he tested the philosophy in the raw experience and uncharted terrain out of which he articulated it. He staked his moral authority and prestige on the daunting task of winning support for it, at least on a tactical level, from activists and the black community.

Rarely has a leader melded theory and practice so successfully as King did during the bus boycott; better than he did later on. For this new public philosophy, which until his death he retooled to fit historical shifts, he owed much to circumstance and locale, more to experienced organizers who tutored him, more still to the black church culture and social gospel that he refashioned to serve his nonviolent ideal.

Initially he called the method "passive resistance," but this was misunderstood as passivity. He stressed how it was spiritually aggressive while physically nonthreatening, in the first place toward its own practitioners—an inward scouring that supplanted the "normal" internalized aggression of anger turned into powerless depression. It "does something to the hearts and souls of those committed to it. It gives them new self-respect; it calls up resources of strength and courage that they did not know they had."[176] It converted the energy of anger and fear into the sinews of inner strength. It helped to heal one's own pain and trauma.

In its outward projection the spiritual aggression grasped the adversary's conscience, awakening his moral sense by shaming, or by appealing to his higher values. Just as no physical harm would be inflicted, there would be no internal violence of spirit—no derogatory language or gestures, for example. Any emotional hurt—from shame, let's say—

would be the pain of growth, not dehumanization, and ultimately healing. (We must distinguish between healthy shaming and guilt-laying,
the latter harmful because it mired one deeper into sin rather than
opening a door out. MLK was never clear about this distinction, especially in his own soul.)

The aim was not to defeat or humiliate the adversary but to humanize him or her. To plant seeds of eventual friendship or alliance—to
communicate, to forge a relationship against the grain. The person's
humanity would be respected at all times, even while their actions were
interrupted.

While aimed at redeeming the adversary, the spiritual force sought
to eliminate the evil structure that the adversary served, often against
his better judgment, or feeling trapped in it. The spiritual force would
give the adversary a choice, a way out. It would do away with the evil
structure not by destroying its physical form, but by dismantling it
from within: releasing the human energy that kept it going. No lives or
limbs would be lost—on the opposing side, anyway. The evil structure
would be no less dead than if physically destroyed—and much harder
to rebuild.

Again and again King rang out his Christian mantra that unearned
suffering was redemptive. Black Christians took to this New Testament
platitude without much persuasion, but it did not sit well with everyone. The idea was that suffering educated, transformed, and ennobled
the sufferer and those who witnessed it. The model was Jesus on the
cross and the martyrs who followed his path. The pain of Good Friday
would give way to the glory of Easter. Suffering brought rebirth, of the
soul and of the community.

"The cross," King wrote, "is the eternal expression of the length to
which God will go in order to restore broken community. The resurrection is a symbol of God's triumph over all the forces that seek to block
community."[177]

In extolling Christ's crucifixion was King glorifying violence and
masochism and making a fetish of victimization? He would have
argued, like Hindus who followed Gandhi and Buddhists he got to
know toward the end of his life, that suffering was omnipresent in
human life. Whether pain and hardship were inflicted by Roman

soldiers in Jerusalem, by remorseless plagues, by agonizing poverty, by the whip of injustice, suffering was the raw material of mortality that humans had to work with. The question was not whether but how one dealt with suffering, and whether suffering ennobled oneself.

The Christian faith evoked by King said that suffering was fertile, not futile; mutable, not immobilizing. That the divine force looked kindly upon the human passion to overcome suffering. When people pushed against suffering, the immanent God would pull from the other side. Jesus modeled this: "Take this cup from me." But if people were passive God would remain transcendent, "wholly other." He would hear but not answer their prayers, listen but not act.

The moral universe was on the side of justice and healing. People had cosmic companionship in their struggles to transform mortal suffering into personal and social rebirth. But this did not mean that the kingdom of God would roll in on "wheels of inevitability." People had to activate the Spirit within them, turn on their inner light, in order to connect their soul's transfiguration with the bending of the universe toward wholeness.

The real struggle, King asserted, was between justice and injustice, "between the forces of light and the forces of darkness." If there was a victory, "and there *will* be a victory," it would be a victory for justice and a defeat of injustice. "It will be a victory for goodness in its long struggle with the forces of evil."[178]

What kept this cosmic struggle between light and darkness, good and evil, from turning into a modern-day crusade against infidels, and an inquisition against heretics? If this was, in some sense, a holy war, what would prevent it from wreaking havoc upon bodies and souls, leading to an endless future of bitterness and revenge, a ceaseless reign of chaos? What would prevent the holy war for justice and wholeness from being consumed by its own fire of certitude and self-righteousness?

Justice was not the highest good—certainly not absolute justice, if such a thing existed. The highest good, the summum bonum, was love or compassion, the "most durable power" in the world. Justice, as King declared on the first night of the bus boycott, was "love in calculation. Justice is love correcting that which revolts against love."[179] Justice would not be true justice if allowed to escape the bounds of love.

Although King, being a Christian preacher, might have found it impossible to do otherwise, it may have been a strategic error for him to put so much weight on the tender word *love*. He tried to distinguish his concept of love, or *agape*, from other forms of love expressed in Greek as *eros*, romantic or erotic love, and *philia*, affection between friends. (He did not consider a fourth type of love, *storge*, maternal or parental love, or pastoral caring.) He made it clear that agape had nothing to do with liking someone, fondness or affection. Agape was tough love—tough as a lion, yet gentle as a lamb.

He defined agape as "understanding, creative, redeeming goodwill." It was not a feeling or emotion but a relationship—between I and Thou. It was a way of seeing and approaching the Other, a way of communicating. Goodwill meant suspension of judgment ("judge not, that you be not judged") and prejudice (pre-judging).[180] It meant refusal to communicate with the Other's lower self (I-it), which was the human norm; insistence on communicating with his or her higher self, even if invisible or repressed. It meant making a leap of faith to see the Other as a fellow child of God, a fellow sinner whose essence was good even if his existence was evil.

A stance of empathic goodwill toward another flawed being was not possible without compassionate understanding. One had to comprehend that the other person's sinfulness and evil doing were the result of suffering (this as much a Buddhist as a Christian notion); that on a fundamental level—King called it the "fundamentum"—everyone's suffering was equal or commensurate. Suffering caused some people to be better, others to be bitter, some almost irredeemable. But just as Jesus would not give up on one lost sheep, even at the risk of losing the flock, so one who truly understood the human condition would never give up on a single soul, no matter how depraved. This meant at least not taking his life.

The creative aspect of agape was the commitment to figure out how to save the soul of the sinner who oppressed you, while at the same time throwing off the oppression and turning over the temples of injustice. How to bring about your adversary's rebirth while nurturing your own and that of society as a whole.

Since King sought not only to revive the nonviolent tradition but to reshape it, he tried to find a more robust term. *Passive resistance,* equated with nonresistance, perpetuated the false stereotype of nonviolence as weak and submissive. *Creative goodwill direct action,* from Randolph, was a mouthful. He chose *soul force,* Gandhi's term, but it never caught on. Such an imaginative communicator, he was nonetheless stuck with the word *nonviolence,* which became an easy target for his militant critics on the left and for watering down by the right. He made the most of the term. Toward the end of his life it meant for him what he wanted it to mean.

Perhaps King should have worked harder to make *soul force* stick. Gandhi coined the compound *satyagraha* from two Sanskrit words, *satya* ("truth" or "love") and *graha* ("to grasp or cling"), to mean "clinging to the truth." He translated it into English as "truth force" or "soul force." A practitioner of soul force called herself a *satyagrahi.*

King's conception of the commingling of personal and social rebirth resonated as much with Hindu faith as Christianity. The satyagrahi achieved self-purification and self-realization through social struggle—in India, fighting for independence, for peace between Hindus and Muslims, for land reform. Through struggle (inward and outward) her individual soul, "atman," would move toward merger with the universal Soul, or "Brahman." The unity of the self with the "Oversoul" was a basic tenet of the transcendental philosophy that King had absorbed, itself influenced by Hinduism. But transcendentalism did not require a life of action or commitment.

Soul force was a good name for King's method because, like the satyagrahi, the soul-force activist in the American context sought to remold her personality in the course of struggle in such a way that her transformation and that of others would lead to society-wide transformation. What Hindus called the universal Soul and transcendentalists the Oversoul, King called the beloved community, a termed coined by Harvard philosopher Josiah Royce after the Civil War.

The "new Negro in the South" could not begin to exercise soul force until social circumstances had brought a measure of self-respect and self-confidence. But once she had claimed her new dignity and destiny, she was ready for the next step of risky activism. As both Gandhi and King stressed, soul force was a weapon for the self-assured, for the strong and brave. Gandhi said famously that he preferred violence to cowardice. So did King, who unlike Gandhi knew he had a cowardly streak. One's exercise of soul force would further enhance self-esteem and self-empowerment, leading in turn to more powerful expression of soul force. The born-again black and the technology of soul force would make an irresistible synthesis to change history.

So when King preached that the means must be as pure as the end, representing the end in process, "the ideal in the making," when he preached that the end was "preexistent in the means," he referred above all to people as means and as ends.[181] A movement, he came to believe, was "finally judged by its effect on the human beings associated with it."[182] Only new selves could give birth to a new world. Only such a new world could sustain the new human beings who constituted it, who would sustain it in turn.

Soul force would tap into the cosmic force forging universal wholeness. "Whether we call it an unconscious process, an impersonal Brahman, or a Personal Being of matchless power and infinite love," King said, "there is a creative force in this universe that works to bring the disconnected aspects of reality into a harmonious whole."[183]

13

Summer 1956 was a season of ripening for civil rights forces in Alabama and beyond. Rustin's urging to King that he go national with the movement was bearing fruit. As the national and international symbol of the newly empowered Negro, darling of black and white media alike, King grew in stature in tandem with the growth of the nascent movement he led. A big part of his attraction for both races was his aura of responsibility and reasonableness. His persona was closer to conservative educator-politician Booker T. Washington than to radical nationalist Marcus Garvey. If King was a safe bet for white Americans, he was also safe for most blacks, who dared to ruffle feathers only if real progress could be made. But for black Americans King stood for implacable resistance to the racial status quo, unlike Washington, more like Garvey. It was thus in the interest of both communities to enhance his prestige, and to prevent the rise of a black messiah who might accentuate race hatred.

As King and the Montgomery movement reached a national audience, so did the movement's philosophy of nonviolent conflict. King's forthright advocacy of mass protest at home and of anticolonial struggles abroad flew in the teeth of America's Cold War hysteria and ideology of consensus.

The spectacle of King's conspiracy trial as David beaten by Goliath enabled King to tap existing black leadership networks, in both the

North and the South, along with northern-based white and biracial civil rights groups. While his main purpose in cultivating this spreading web was to get backing and funds for the MIA, he drew upon these diverse allies during the boycott's aftermath, when southern leaders utilized the Montgomery victory to launch a South-wide organization to combat segregation.

Support for the bus boycott in the white world came mostly from its progressive fringes, but backing among blacks was pervasive, centered in mainstream black institutions. During the 1950s as in the prior half century, African-American leadership was sheltered in a professional subculture of black-run institutions: churches, businesses, colleges, newspapers, fraternities, sororities, social clubs, and civic groups such as the NAACP. Because he had grown up in this middle-class milieu in Atlanta and his parents had close links to ministers, educators, and journalists all over, King was well positioned to get allegiance from the black elite, many of whom were acquaintances and several his mentors. Most were eager to help. He pulled them in quickly, methodically, and respectfully.

He began closest to home, with the black Baptist church. He had grown up not only in Atlanta's flagship Ebenezer Baptist, but also in the nation's largest black organization, National Baptist Convention, USA, with its thousands of preachers, several million lay members, myriad missions, services, ministers' and Sunday school training programs, seminaries, and colleges like Morehouse, his alma mater. His leadership of the bus boycott propelled his rise in this religious empire in which his father and grandfather had been players. As in Montgomery, the new kid had not been around long enough to make enemies. During 1956 two senior ministers promoted the candidacy of the twenty-seven-year-old boy wonder to challenge autocratic J. H. Jackson of Chicago, an old family friend, for the NBC presidency. Imagine the effect on your self-image of dozens of esteemed elders writing or wiring that you were the prophet or messiah they had long been waiting for.

Adulation of the prodigy peaked when he preached "Paul's Letter to American Christians" to the NBC's annual gathering in Denver in early September. Daddy King was so agitated with pride that he couldn't sit down. King's mentor J. Pius Barbour wrote in the national Baptist journal that the boy he had guided in his Crozer Seminary days had grown into "the greatest orator on the American platform," the "first Ph.D. I have heard that can make uneducated people throw their hats in the air over philosophy.

"The center of attraction was THE KING," Barbour oozed. "Never in the history of the Baptist denomination has a young Baptist preacher captured the hearts and minds of the people as has young King. He just wrapped the convention up in a napkin and carried it away in his pocket." When the young pastor said, "'I must close now,' the sea of black Baptists arose as one and protested."[184]

Praising his "masterpiece," a retired Tuskegee preacher wrote him: "You spoke as a prophet and seer which you are," his sermon "as vivid and real as any of the Pauline Epistles. The preachers will be talking about it always." Perhaps it was his "calm, dispassionate" style that won over these bourgeois black Baptists to what was in part an anticapitalist diatribe excoriating consumerism.

Leading lights of the NBC were moved to tears, unashamed. "You may not have known it, but many, myself and others, wept like babies, and couldn't help ourselves," the Tuskegee elder confessed. "Like Joseph, God is with you, because *you* are with God."[185]

While his boycott leadership had lifted him to this mount of admiration, he used his growing popularity in the NBC ranks to further the civil rights cause in the black religious world. He aspired to be a black Billy Graham for earthly emancipation.

If one looked over *Jet, Ebony,* and venerable papers like the *Pittsburgh Courier, Chicago Defender, Baltimore Afro-American,* and *Amsterdam News* during 1956, one might have concluded that the black print media almost single-handedly made King black America's new hero. One reason that ministers, journalists, and other black opinion leaders rushed to King like moths to flame was to fill the abyss of African-American leadership, ravaged by McCarthyism. By the mid-1950s other political heroes like W. E. B. Du Bois, Paul Robeson, and Richard Wright, or budding ones like Bayard Rustin, had been soiled by the un-American mix of black and red. King's instantaneous rise must be explained in large part because of deep-seated black hunger for a political savior, especially one of the rising generation.

The older generation of progressive, noncommunist leaders were publicly pleased but privately uneasy about King's threat to their status and stature. The two most prominent elder statesmen, both men of King's father's age whom he had not known before, took different tacks with the upstart. Randolph, whose prestige in the black world was beyond question, sought to draw the young minister under his wing, with Rustin his emissary. Roy Wilkins, combative new chief of the NAACP, waved an iron fist in a velvet glove to show him who was boss.

King's roots sunk deep in the NAACP. His maternal grandfather, A. D. Williams, headed the NAACP branch in Atlanta after World War I. His father was active in it during the 1930s and 1940s. He himself had served on the Montgomery NAACP executive committee, invited by branch secretary Rosa Parks before the bus boycott; he had decided against being branch president. But King had little contact with the national NAACP. Wilkins's national office refused to back the bus boycott because MIA demands did not include eliminating segregation. After MIA lawyers Fred Gray and Charles Langford filed the *Browder* lawsuit with much NAACP help, Wilkins covered most legal costs for the lawsuit and the conspiracy trial. But the national NAACP never formally endorsed the bus boycott. Friction arose over King's concern that the NAACP might exploit the boycott for fund-raising, and Wilkins's fear that the MIA would capture his own funding sources. Daddy King's son, child of the Depression, always worried about money for his organizations, though not—to his wife's chagrin—for his own family.

His need to stand abreast with established civil rights figures showed also in his first contacts with Randolph, who had been battling for black people's rights, especially on the labor front, well before King's birth. He valued Randolph's support and guidance, which opened the door to backing by progressive groups and several national labor unions. Randolph served as the first black vice president of the AFL-CIO, which had just been formed from the merger of the AFL and CIO under George Meany's heavy hand. But King did not always reciprocate: He respected but rarely deferred to his elders. Despite Randolph's repeated appeals, he did not take part in the State of the Race Conference, nor did he speak at a major civil rights rally in New York's Madison Square

Garden in May 1956 that featured the Montgomery struggle. Parks and Nixon represented the MIA at the latter.

White media rivaled black in celebrating King's emergence, though stressing his respectability over his militancy. *Look* and *Redbook* featured him. King's June address to the national NAACP convention appeared in *U.S. News & World Report*. *Newsweek* and *Time* covered the bus boycott favorably. *Time* put King on its cover in March 1957. He appeared on television interview shows such as *Meet the Press* and began to master the powerful new medium that blessed his voice and image.

King baptized himself in the rituals of national party politics at the August Democratic convention in Chicago, where he prodded the platform committee to support a strong civil rights plank. Starting off with a prayer, he urged the party to endorse federal enforcement of the *Brown* decision, even withholding federal funds.

"The question of civil rights is one of the supreme moral issues of our time," the neglect of which "would mean committing both political and moral suicide." He warned that the doctrine of states' rights "must not be made an excuse for insurrection," which had brought the Civil War. "Whenever human rights are trampled over by states' rights, the federal government is obligated to intervene.

"If democracy is to live, segregation must die." Because of stiff resistance from southern delegates, the party platform failed to endorse the *Brown* decision but opposed use of force to block federal court rulings.

In the half year following King's conspiracy conviction, he and his associates planted bulbs of connection, alliance, and shared thinking in fields black and white, marginal and mainstream, that would mature underground for several years until bursting forth as the most powerful grassroots movement in American history.

14

For Montgomery's black community, buoyed by the *Browder* ruling, boycotting buses had become a way of life. When King came home from Chicago and from heralding "The Birth of a New Age" to his fraternity jubilee, a new season of white repression was setting in to break the boycott. Taking his cue from Louisiana, Alabama's attorney general, John Patterson, had secured a court order shutting down the state NAACP. This led to Rev. Fred Shuttlesworth's founding of the Alabama Christian Movement for Human Rights (ACMHR), powered by his evangelist followers, to fill the gap with a militancy foreign to the legalistic NAACP. Patterson contended falsely that the NAACP had orchestrated the illegal bus boycott and thus should be outlawed.

During the summer, insurance for car-pool station wagons was mysteriously canceled—WCC fingerprints. Drivers continued to be harassed and fined. Police brutality against black citizens mounted, even while black crime rates plummeted to record lows because of the community's new solidarity. Threats by mail and phone proliferated against librarian Juliette Morgan and the coterie of whites who dared to publicly back the boycott or oppose segregation. As we saw, the harassment got to be too much for Morgan: She took her life the next summer.

In late August Rev. Robert Graetz's home was bombed. Fortunately he, his wife, and children were visiting Highlander Folk School in

Tennessee, accompanying Rosa Parks. Graetz had invited fellow white pastors to attend an interracial meeting the day before to hear King speak; none showed up. Mayor Gayle called the bombing a publicity stunt to beef up fund-raising. "It is a strange coincidence," he told the press, "that when interest appears lagging in the bus boycott, something like this happens."[186]

A week later in Clinton, Tennessee, segregationists rioted against the admission of twelve black kids to the high school, prompting the governor to send in the highway patrol and national guard to enroll them. Rioting against school desegregation took place later that week in another Tennessee town. En route to speak at Hampton Institute in Virginia, King was denied service at the Atlanta airport restaurant, despite being an interstate passenger. He refused to be hidden in a "dingy" section behind a screen. He sued for damages with NAACP help.

The grip of white supremacy and Cold War conformity loosening, fall 1956 saw surprising breakthroughs around the globe. In mid-September, after a long nonviolent struggle, Britain granted independence to Ghana, the first African nation freed from colonial rule. After Egypt nationalized the Suez Canal, pressure from President Eisenhower and other world leaders prevented England and France from retaking the strategic waterway, a major blow to European dominance of the Middle East. In October, after a surge of anti-Soviet protest by students and workers, the reformist leader Imre Nagy withdrew Hungary from the Warsaw Pact. Khrushchev sent Soviet tanks to suppress the spreading revolt; fierce resistance left thirty thousand Hungarians and seven thousand Soviet troops dead. In the United States, the liberal National Committee for a Sane Nuclear Policy was founded, while radical pacifists led by A. J. Muste engaged in civil disobedience against air-raid drills and nuclear missile sites.

Cold War conformity was also under siege in the arena of art and entertainment. Poet Allen Ginsberg's "Howl," an inflammatory indictment of corrupted American values, became so notorious that police banned it in California and publisher Lawrence Ferlinghetti was tried for obscenity. Enlightened by jazz, blues, and urban black culture, Beat writers and their "beatnik" following were determined to give America rhythm and "beatification" as the remedy for its spiritual depression.

Just as the Deep South–bred black freedom struggle was getting national exposure, so earth-rich black southern rhythm-and-blues was going mainstream by means of an unlikely white boy from Tupelo, Mississippi, raised in gospel music and Pentecostal preaching. In September 1956, Elvis Presley sang to 54 million Americans on *The Ed Sullivan Show,* shown from waist up to hide his Afro-dance-influenced pelvic thrusts. His hit songs, launching the era of rock and roll, thrilled teenagers, especially girls, and shook up complacent parents. For middle-class white America the veiled menace of black deviance was reaching ominous proportions.

KING AND OTHER MIA LEADERS repeatedly appealed to President Dwight Eisenhower and his attorney general to investigate violence and civil rights violations by segregationists, including city officials, but to no avail. An assistant attorney general replied to King that because there did not appear to be violations of federal law, the violent incidents were immaterial. In September supremacists formed a Klan klavern in Montgomery, which had not had one since the earlier klavern collapsed in the 1930s. Luther Ingalls of the local White Citizens Council warned of a conspiracy to give white nursery school kids black and white dolls to condition them to integration.[187] Confidential word came to the MIA—probably through Graetz's trusted local FBI contact—that Citizens Council outside agitators who considered the Montgomery-based WCC weak-kneed (battling children's dolls?) were plotting a vigilante mission to stop Montgomery's civil war. And rumors flew that a phalanx of white trade unionists would swoop into town and round up car-pool drivers by citizen's arrest.

Troubled by the tightening repression, expectant that the boycott would end before long, King and colleagues decided they must prepare not only blacks but the white community for desegregated buses. White leaders would not lift a finger to ease the passage. King appointed a special committee to try to "change the bitterness" of whites toward blacks. This committee met in late September "to consider ways of creating the most wholesome attitude possible among the mass of whites." King stated that "we must make friends with those who oppose us, we should make our motives clearly understood, and we must move from protest to reconciliation."[188] They adopted a plan that included *Advertiser* articles, direct dialogue with middle-class white citizens, and utilizing local radio and TV to spread their message of reconciliation. Would their efforts make a dent in the armor of white hatred?

How could they expect to ride buses sharing seats with whites when, according to Judge Walter Jones and the Alabama Supreme Court, the "customary repugnances" of "promiscuous sitting," especially between black males and white females, would "breed disturbances"? There might be physical contact, accidental or not—God knew where that might lead. From the segregationist standpoint it was the worst thing besides racial mixing of schoolchildren. If hostility was thick now, before the change, what meanness might be uncorked when judgment day arrived?

As part of their tutoring of the MIA president, Glenn Smiley and Bayard Rustin taught him how to conduct nonviolent training workshops, which had been practiced by FOR and CORE activists for over a decade, but only with small teams like Rustin's 1947 freedom riders. Never before had there been a training of hundreds, thousands. Could it be done? In early October King tried his hand.

"Even though our hopes must not be raised too high," he told a packed mass meeting, "it is nevertheless important to consider how we are to manage ourselves on integrated buses, because it is only to integrated buses that we plan to return." Crashing applause.

"There will be some people who will not like this change, and they will not hesitate to express themselves to you. There will possibly be some unpleasant experiences for us at the hands of people who will not immediately accept the idea of sitting with us on the bus. It is important that we begin to think seriously about how we are going to face up to these possibilities of abuse, slander, and embarrassment." Thus began the first workshop for the multitude.

"Now I want just two persons to stand up," King instructed from the pulpit, "and tell us how they plan to act on the buses. Suppose you sat down next to a white person on a bus. Suppose this person begin to make a fuss, calling you names, or even going so far as to shove you? What would you do?"

Emotions were electric. A pair of middle-aged women rose.

"All right, sister," King called on one.

"Well," she said, nervously at first, "if someone was to start calling me names, I guess I would be kinda upset. But mind you, I don't intend to move. I think I would just sit there and ignore her and let folks see how ignorant she was. But if she were to start pushin' me, maybe I would give her just a little shove."

Many shouted, "No! No!"

"Thank you for your candid opinion," King replied to the woman. "Now let me ask you this. If you were to shove this white person back, what would you achieve?"

"Nothing!" others called out.

"Now do you agree with the opinion expressed here," he asked her, "that nothing would be achieved by treating the white person in question the same way you were treated?" She nodded.

"Then why would you push that person back?"

"Well, I guess I wouldn't."

The second woman was more astute. "Now, I think most of us know the white folks pretty well," she said. "We have to remember that they are not used to us, but we're used to them. It isn't going to do us any good to get mad and strike back, 'cause that's just what some of them *want* us to do."

"That's right!" people shouted.

"Now we've got this freedom," she continued. "It is something they can't take away from us. But we will *lose* it if we get mad and show them we are incapable of acting like good Christian ladies and gentlemen." Great clapping answered her.

"This is good," King concluded. "Now you can see the seriousness of our task here. We are going to be doing some more of this in the meetings to come. Let's discuss and think this through together, for this is serious business. I want you to feel free to discuss and express your opinions about this. But I also want you to see what our Christian responsibility is to each other when we return to the buses of Montgomery."[189]

Meanwhile, events in Florida's capital were impinging on the boycott's resolution in Alabama. The Tallahassee bus boycott had copied the MIA's car-pool system, but Tallahassee officials were cannier than the Montgomery commissioners. When talks fell apart in July, the city moved to disable the alternative transportation. Authorities insisted that drivers have chauffeur licenses and proper license plates. They got a local judge to impose a hefty fine on the Inter-Civic Council and its leaders for operating an illegal business without permit, bond, or tax. In late October the legal and financial pressure compelled leaders to shut down the Tallahassee car pool, weakening the boycott.

Montgomery's extreme white leaders paid close attention. Printers' union chief Jack Brock, former head of the Alabama AFL (his brother had been a Klan grand dragon), was spearheading an effort to secede from the new AFL-CIO because of its national leaders' tilt toward civil rights. Not only was the bus boycott an outrage in itself, he and associates felt, but its harmful publicity made it harder for them to promote the interests of the white working class. This cabal nudged the county attorney, who got advice from Tallahassee's prosecutor. A delegation led by Brock then persuaded the city commission to apply the Tallahassee tactic. Despite public opposition from *Advertiser* editor Grover Hall (who had also objected to King's prosecution) that the problem should be left to the Supreme Court, the commissioners announced they would seek an injunction to end the MIA car pool.[190] City attorney Walter Knabe filed the petition on the same day the MIA petitioned federal judge Frank Johnson to block the city's maneuver.

On November 13, Judge Carter heard testimony from both sides and ordered the car pool to cease and desist. Next day Judge Johnson refused to stay the state court's ruling.

15

As King and MIA lawyers sat through the daylong hearing in Judge Carter's courtroom, crestfallen about the foregone result, "I was faltering in my faith and my courage," he recalled.[191] During a noontime break, after King noticed the commissioners scurrying about, an Associated Press reporter handed him a teletype. In one terse sentence the Supreme Court that morning had unanimously upheld the lower court's *Browder* ruling: "The motion to affirm is granted and the judgment is affirmed."[192] Despite its brevity the high court had done explicitly what the *Brown* decision had done only implicitly—overturned the 1896 *Plessy v. Ferguson* ruling that had given constitutional sanction to segregated public transportation, and by extension a segregated society, for sixty years.

When the good word bounced through the courtroom a black spectator exulted, "God Almighty has spoken from Washington, D.C." King wrote that the "darkest hour of our struggle had indeed proved to be the first hour of victory."[193] Many black people felt that the simultaneity of the twin decisions could not have been coincidence, but the intercession of the holy spirit.

That evening Montgomery's new Klan klavern made its public debut. Preceded by bomb threats, forty carloads of white-robed racists invaded black neighborhoods. In the past residents would have pulled down shades and locked doors, rifles at hand. This time they refused to be intimidated. They turned on porch lights, opened their doors, and sat on stoops watching the Klan pass by like a holiday parade. Some waved to the masqueraders. Flummoxed, the Klan caravan cut short its tour and drove off into the dark.

Although Judge Johnson had refused to block the car-pool injunction, MIA leaders expected the Supreme Court's ruling to be enforced in a matter of days. King called an executive board meeting to make recommendations to dual mass meetings that evening for the people to decide whether, and when, to end the boycott.

"If there is anything about this Christian faith that means anything to us," he preached to the executive board, "it says to us that lives can be changed! (*Yes*) There is a Nicodemus standing before Jesus asking about it. (*Yeah*) Jesus cries out, 'You must be born again,' but he implies that you *can* be born again. We must live by that and we must believe it."[194]

That night, to eight thousand souls gathered at Holt Street Baptist and Hutchinson Street Baptist, King interpreted their triumph as a reliving of the Jews' liberation from Egypt. In a powerful exposition on the meaning of freedom and the danger of misunderstanding it, he asserted that it meant not only freedom from oppression.

"It is not only breaking aloose from some evil force, but it is reaching up for a higher force. Freedom from evil is slavery to goodness." More important than their right was their duty to be free. Freedom meant a responsibility to respect everyone as a sacred personality, even those who despised you—believing that they can be better.

Like the parable of the prodigal son, "strayed away to some far country of sin and evil, I must still believe that there is something within them that can cause them one day to come to themselves (*That's right, Yes*) and rise up and walk back up the dusty road to the father's house.

"I want to tell you this evening that I believe that Senator Engelhardt's heart can be changed. (*Yes*) I believe that Senator Eastland's heart can be changed! (*Yes*) I believe that the Ku Klux Klan can be changed into a clan for God's kingdom. (*Yes*) That's the essence of the gospel."

Everyone must be born again. "The fact that you must means you can." They had to live by the faith that rebirth was possible.

"And we must go back to the buses with that faith. (*Yes*) I'll tell you, if we will go back to that faith, we will be able to stagger and astound the imagination of those who would oppress us. (*That's right*) We will be able to astound the world.

"Tonight as we go home," he concluded, "let us pray (*Yes*) that God will touch the hearts of some of these people. (*We will, Amen*) And that through the constraining and compelling power of the holy spirit," the opposition, and the silent middle, would be forced to be true to the Spirit within.[195]

Without a single nay both assemblies voted to cease the boycott as soon as the enforcement order arrived from Washington.

But the order did not come. The city commissioners waited three weeks to file a last-ditch appeal for a rehearing by the high court. The MIA replaced the car pool with a neighborhood ride-sharing operation, but it carried a fraction of the former traffic. As a second winter set in, most of the multi-thousand protesters, unbent, walked the last leg of their crusade along the city's cold, slick streets.

WCC leader Luther Ingalls warned the press that "any attempt to enforce this decision will inevitably lead to riot and bloodshed." Another segregationist announced: "We are prepared for a century of litigation."[196] King knew that the most difficult stage of the struggle lay ahead.[197]

While the foot soldiers were still walking, the MIA was busily preparing the centerpiece of its effort to train participants for reconciliation with the hostile white majority. In early December, commemorating the movement's first birthday, King opened the MIA's weeklong Institute on Nonviolence and Social Change with an address before several thousand townspeople and visitors at Holt Street Baptist Church.

"God decided to use Montgomery as the proving ground," he declared to the assembly, "for the struggle and triumph of freedom and justice in America. It is one of the ironies of our day that Montgomery, the Cradle of the Confederacy, is being transformed into Montgomery, the cradle of freedom and justice.

"All of the loud noises that you hear today from the legislative halls of the South in terms of 'interposition' and 'nullification,' and of outlawing the NAACP, are merely the death groans from a dying system. The old older is passing away, and the new order is coming into being. We are witnessing in our day the birth of a new age." He called for reconciliation, redemption, creation of the beloved community. "It is this type of understanding goodwill that will transform the deep gloom of the old age into the exuberant gladness of the new age."[198]

The educational marathon featured workshops and mass meetings led by distinguished guests on the dynamics of the "new and powerful weapon" of soul force. It culminated in a huge Sunday prayer service with Rev. J. H. Jackson, president of the National Baptist Convention. On its second night Smiley moderated a forum on nonviolent change at Bethel Baptist Church, including ministers T. J. Jemison, architect of the 1953 Baton Rouge bus boycott; C. K. Steele, leader of the current boycott in Tallahassee; and Fred Shuttlesworth, organizer of Birmingham bus protests.

Next evening, the anniversary of the boycott's heroic opening day, Baptist educator Nannie Burroughs enthralled her listeners by likening the protest to the American Revolution. "Work as if all depended upon you," she exhorted, "and pray as if all depended upon God."[199]

THE SPIRITUAL PARADOX that the darkest night preceded the dawn derived from pagan, Celtic, and Christian worship of the winter solstice—for Christians in the guise of evergreens, St. Nicholas, stars guiding the Magi, and a heaven-gifted birth. Through cosmic force alone, the darkest midnight turned magically into the return of the light, days of rising brightness.

Of all poets Robert Frost perhaps best captured the moment of transition, of soul stopping, between dark and light, death and rebirth. On the "darkest evening of the year," his snowy woods comprised a dark night of the soul, a pregnant womb in which one prepared for the soul's rebirth. "The woods are lovely, dark, and deep,"—one might wish to lose oneself in the seductive fertile darkness, even to die—"but I have promises to keep, and miles to go before I sleep." The new light of redemption, leading to the promised land, could emerge only out of the deepest depth of darkness.

As November fell into December, five long weeks passed before the Supreme Court rejected the city's groundless appeal, a ploy to postpone the inevitable. With the advent of Christmas, "bus classes" continued apace, folding chairs lined up on the altar to simulate buses in which protesters role-played as black and white riders and bus drivers. Despite MIA urging and Smiley's gentle persuasion, the white community steadfastly refused to prepare for "promiscuous sitting." Its leaders took the opposite stance of defiance.

When the Supreme Court put out its final word, the commissioners publicly reviled its unconstitutional "usurpation." Foreseeing bloodshed and "the curse of tragedy," they asserted that the city commission, backed by the white citizenry, "will not yield one inch, and will forever stand like a rock against social equality, intermarriage, and mixing of the races in the schools. There must continue the separation of the races under God's creation and plan. In so doing, we know that the best interest of both races will be served."[200]

The enforcement order arrived in Montgomery on December 20 and took effect. At a spirited mass meeting that night at St. John AME Church, the people reaffirmed their decision to return.

"We have lived under the agony and darkness of Good Friday," King called out, "with the conviction that one day the heightened glow of Easter would emerge on the horizon." Along with exaltation, people were anxious with worry about what would come, some semiconsciously afraid of life without the now familiar comfort of shared sacrifice. "Like many consummations," King commented, "this one left a slight aftertaste of sadness."[201]

A code of nonviolent conduct, drafted by Smiley, was handed out to the foot soldiers, and published in the *Advertiser*. Among the seventeen guidelines was to "be loving enough to absorb evil and understanding enough to turn an enemy into a friend."[202]

Just before dawn on the winter solstice, Abernathy, Nixon, Smiley, and Rosa Parks arrived at the King parsonage. When the first bus pulled up on South Jackson Street at 6 A.M., King was greeted politely by the driver and sat in the front next to Smiley, behind Abernathy.

The first two days of desegregation stirred little resistance. But late Saturday night, December 22, someone fired a shotgun through King's front door. On Christmas Eve, five white men savagely assaulted a fifteen-year-old black girl at a bus stop. Right after Christmas half a dozen buses were shot up at night. One blast hit laundress Rosa Jordan, eight months pregnant, inches from her unborn child, shattering her leg. Doctors were afraid to operate until after her baby was born. When the city commissioners suspended night service, snipers fired by day. Sellers blamed black people for the attacks as a tactic to win white sympathy.[203] The new day of bus desegregation came to a city mired more than ever in the bleak darkness of racial division.

Would the world turn forward with the return of the light?

DURING THE IMMEDIATE AFTERMATH, in which participants' heady feeling of triumph and vindication mingled with fear and foreboding, King barely paused to take a deep breath. He turned his attention to how his acclaimed leadership might catalyze a broad civil rights structure to support local struggles across the South. It was needed as much for protection of fragile gains as for further progress. This goal had been central for Rustin from the outset. When he first arrived in Montgomery he had suggested to Coretta King the need for a coordinating agency.[204] Smiley too had felt the necessity of a South-wide vehicle for communication, coordination, and the teaching of nonviolent methods to local leaders and had done some spadework through FOR.

King conferred often during the bus boycott with leaders of sister movements, sharing tales and counsel and arranging mutual aid, particularly with fellow Alabama preachers Fred Shuttlesworth of Birmingham and Joseph Lowery in Mobile. The state's June 1956 court injunction barring Alabama NAACP operations made such interchange all the more urgent since the state NAACP had provided what little coordination had previously linked Alabama activists. He also kept in touch with Baptist ministers C. K. Steele, leader of the Tallahassee bus protest, and T. J. Jemison in Baton Rouge. Lowery recalled that he, King, and Shuttlesworth "saw this need to get together and then we just talked about how we ought to broaden it to include Steele, Jemison, and the other guys."[205]

Having nudged King's thinking all year about the need for a regional organization, Rustin began active planning in the second half of

November with two New York colleagues, NAACP leader Ella Baker and Stanley Levison, a white leftwing attorney, businessman, and civil rights fund-raiser with ties to the Communist Party. In a letter to King just before Christmas Rustin suggested: "Regional groups of leaders should be brought together and encouraged to develop forms of local organization leading to an alliance of groups capable of creating a Congress of organizations."[206] The same idea had been urged on King by others such as Rev. Doug Moore of Durham, North Carolina, a friend from Boston University days.[207]

On the last Sunday of the year King spoke to a convention banquet of the black Omega Psi Phi fraternity in Baltimore. Afterward he and his wife were driven to Washington by Harris and Clare Wofford, authors of a firsthand account of the Indian independence struggle, *India Afire*. Harris Wofford, a Washington attorney, was one of King's tutors in Gandhian nonviolence and later became President Kennedy's special assistant for civil rights. The two couples were joined in the crowded sedan by Rustin and Levison, who met King for the first time. Along the Maryland highway—where the racially mixed group would have been barred from sitting together in a roadside restaurant—the six discussed Rustin's and Levison's ideas for a new civil rights organization. Rustin fired up the dialogue.

"I believe that you have got to have a South-wide organization, which I think you must now head up, made up of key boycott leaders across the South, not involving Urban League or NAACP, because if you bring all those organizations together, you will have to compromise to their needs. But you're in a very strong position now, to set up an organization, but to set it up so that you are the key, and to set it up in a way where your board is only advisory."

Although Rustin had decisively parted company with the Communist Party long before, and was an ardent rhetorical advocate of grassroots democracy, his blueprint sounded curiously redolent of Leninist democratic centralism.

"You can't set up an organization like that!" King replied testily—despite his longtime fealty to the democratic centralism of the black Baptist church.

"I can show you how to do it," Rustin shot back. As usual King did not want to argue.

"OK," he said, "draw up the plans."[208]

As they rode through the wintry Maryland countryside, Levison was struck by King's frank doubts about his leadership. The New York socialist would soon become King's trusted adviser and confidant, his closest white friend. King pierced the tension by opening up.

"If anybody had asked me a year ago to head this movement," he said quietly, "I tell you very honestly, that I would have run a mile to get away from it. I had no intention of being involved in this way. As I became involved, and as people began to derive inspiration from their involvement, I realized that the choice leaves your own hands. The people expect you to give them leadership. You see them growing as they move into action, and then you know you no longer have a choice. You can't decide whether to stay in it or get out of it. You must stay in it."

Levison was seized by the sense that he "didn't seem to be the type to be a mass leader. There was nothing flamboyant, nothing even charismatic about him as he sat in an ordinary discussion. He looked like a typical scholarly kind of person—very thoughtful, quiet, and shy—very shy. The shyness was accented, I felt, with white people.

"There was a certain politeness," he observed, "a certain arm's length approach, and you could feel the absence of relaxation. As the years went on this vanished. But it was as if Dr. King's southern background, largely with the black community, had its effect on him as far as thinking comfortably and easily in the company of white people."[209]

The MIA announced an "emergency conference call" sent out by King, Steele, and Shuttlesworth on New Year's—known to black America as Emancipation Day—to about a hundred southern leaders in a dozen states. It asked them to gather in Atlanta on January 10 and 11.

Despite legal victories in Montgomery and Tallahassee, the Southern Negro Leaders Conference on Transportation and Nonviolent Integration convened in a crisis mood. In the Florida capital leaders had just suspended the seven-month boycott after a federal judge, at the bus company's behest, restrained the city from enforcing bus segregation. But after a week of desegregated riding, the Florida governor declared a state of emergency and halted bus service.

On Christmas night in Birmingham, Klan dynamite destroyed Shuttlesworth's home, but he and his family miraculously escaped death. The next morning, as planned, he led 250 black citizens to defy

Jim Crow seating on Birmingham buses, backed by King. He and twenty others were arrested. This represented an escalation of tactics, a new departure; the MIA never did civil disobedience as such. The Birmingham leader was not only a more rhetorically radical preacher than King. He and his spirited evangelist followers were more militant in action. At the same time bus desegregation campaigns were taking place in Atlanta, Miami, Mobile, New Orleans, and other cities.

King Sr. hosted the two-day conference at Ebenezer. Martin and Coretta King stayed at his parents' home along with Abernathy. At 2 A.M. the night before the meeting began, Juanita Abernathy phoned to tell her husband that their home and church had just been bombed, along with the Graetz parsonage, again, and three other black churches. King and Abernathy rushed home to Montgomery. In their absence Coretta King, Steele, and Shuttlesworth chaired the conference. Rustin and Ella Baker orchestrated in the wings.

Sixty representatives from twenty-nine communities in ten southern states spent the first day discussing several working papers Rustin had drafted. A large majority were black clergy, only a handful were women, and only one was a paleface, Rev. Will Campbell of Mississippi. Besides Coretta King none of the boycott's women leaders, not even Jo Ann Robinson, attended the Atlanta parley.

Rustin's seven mimeographed handouts addressed issues such as responding to violence, the role of nonviolence and law, and the relationship of voting-rights organizing to direct action. His first paper asked the key questions: "Do we need a coordinating group for advice and council among the present protest groups?" "Should such a council try to stimulate bus protests in other areas of the South?"[210] The gathering answered the first affirmatively by constituting themselves a continuing group and choosing King chairman when he returned on the second afternoon. They did not resolve the second, thornier question. The consensus seemed more to press for federal intervention against violence and violation of court rulings than to launch new protests. For the time being they wanted to forestall terrorist reprisals sparked by more confrontational efforts.

Upon adjourning, the leaders called for national protest and prayer decrying the dynamite and TNT bombings of churches and parsonages in Montgomery. They issued a wide-ranging "Statement to the South and Nation," appealing to Christian principles of love and reconcilia-tion. They addressed the white majority, particularly "white southern-ers of goodwill" and white churches and clergy.

"We advocate nonviolence in words, thought and deed, we believe this spirit and this spirit alone can overcome the decades of mutual fear and suspicion that have infested and poisoned our southern culture." Through this spirit "a miracle will be wrought from this period of intense social conflict."

They called for federal action to stop the "reign of terror": for Presi-dent Eisenhower, resoundingly reelected over Adlai Stevenson, to speak in a southern city urging citizens to abide by Supreme Court decisions, stressing the moral justice of civil rights; for Vice President Richard Nixon to make a fact-finding tour of the South like his European trip for Hungarian refugees after the Soviet invasion; and for the attorney general to meet with their representatives about the Justice Depart-ment's responsibility to preserve law and order in the Deep South.[211] They got only a polite nonresponse.

Back in Montgomery, the strain on King from violence, exhaustion, MIA quarreling, and others' jealousy of his stardom—he felt guilty for all that was amiss—caused him one night to lose himself in the emo-tional preaching he had always disdained. During the first mass meet-ing after the bombings, he led a prayer at Bethel Baptist that pumped up "an emotion I could not control" in the crowd and in himself. Beseeching God about the dangers they faced, he cried out, "If anyone should be killed, let it be me!"[212] The assembly's pandemonium pushed him over the edge. He collapsed behind the lectern, kept from falling by fellow ministers holding him up.

Supremacist violence struck again later in January. A powerful bomb, a dozen dynamite sticks with smoldering fuse, was found out-side King's front door. The home of a hospital orderly was blown up down the street, probably as a diversion. Police believed that the neigh-boring blast was timed to bring King or his wife to the door just as the bomb exploded at their feet. A few days earlier the Klansmen who car-ried out the attacks forced a black man to jump to his death in the Alabama River for allegedly going out with a white woman. It was a case of mistaken identity, like so many others. All black men looked alike; all were guilty of the desire if not the act. Negroes were interchangeable. The Klan made their point.

The Saturday night that King's parsonage was nearly blown to kingdom come happened to be the anniversary of his midnight vision. In his sermon at Dexter next morning he revealed how much this assassination try had shaken him by recalling, for the first time publicly, the holy spirit's visitation in his kitchen, which had given him the strength to persevere.[213]

"I went to bed many nights scared to death," he said to his congregation, but "early on a sleepless morning in January 1956, rationality left me. Almost out of nowhere I heard a voice that morning saying to me, 'Preach the gospel, stand up for truth, stand up for righteousness.' Since that morning I can stand up without fear.

"So I'm not afraid of anybody this morning. Tell Montgomery they can keep shooting and I'm going to stand up to them. Tell Montgomery they can keep bombing and I'm going to stand up to them. If I had to die tomorrow morning I would die happy because I've been to the mountaintop and I've seen the promised land and it's going to be here in Montgomery."[214]

MODERATE WHITE BUSINESSMEN prodded the city to track down the bombers—a class fracture in the fortress of white supremacy. The trail led to the city's new klavern, dominated by union activists. Seven Klan members, local laborers, were apprehended. But when the first two defendants were tried in May 1957, after an energetic public campaign on their behalf, an all-white jury acquitted them easily. The prosecutor announced that further convictions were impossible; he let the others go free. The fact that a ringleader had been editor of the White Citizens Council newspaper and that others were associated with the WCC gave the lie to the council's claim that its tactics were peaceful and lawful.[215] For quite a few it was Citizens Council by day, Klan after dark.

Due in part to the climate of intimidation surrounding the Klan trial, white moderates who had rarely opened their mouths before were now chilled into frozen silence. Supremacists believed that their success in stemming further black advances in Montgomery resulted from their silencing of racial moderates. Actually the glacial racial progress, slower even than before the bus boycott, had much to do with acrimony among black leaders, not able to preserve the fragile unity of the bus boycott. King's frequent absences did not help matters. Race relations reached a low ebb with the failure of school desegregation around the time he moved back to Atlanta at the end of the 1950s.

Although supremacists succeeded after the boycott in unifying the white community in cowardly quiescence, they never hardened them behind everlasting segregation—though in the early months of 1956 it looked like they were making headway. Why did their momentum stall? For one thing, despite its ability to induce mass hysteria, the fast-growing Citizens Council movement did not have leadership comparable to the MIA's at either top or grass roots. During the boycott King and his colleagues managed—barely, at times—to keep egos and ambitions under control and harnessed toward common aims. The WCC, and its Klan underground, revealed itself as a muscular front without a strong back to hold it up and keep it accountable to an anxious constituency. Jealousies, rivalries, and turf battles, and the lack of any but a rear vision, tore holes in supremacist armor and kept it from sustaining its mobilization.

Did the black movement's empowerment by black church culture have a lot to do with this contrast? Was white resistance too secular, despite pious platitudes obligatory in a highly religious culture, for its own good? Fuller use of fundamentalist Christian symbols, done with integrity, might have inhibited its means and undermined its ends. To be sure, the Klan made mileage with cross burnings and other rituals that condemned black Christians as the Antichrist; to bomb a heathenish black church was a blow for the avenging white Christ.

During the bus boycott both racial communities mobilized with fierce determination, blacks fueled more by anger, whites by fear. But only the black community effectively organized. For these organizing miracles, to which white blunders contributed, the women leaders and black churches deserved the lion's share of credit.

IN EARLY FEBRUARY 1957 King wired the Atlanta conferees asking them to reconvene on Valentine's Day in New Orleans at New Zion

Baptist Church. Its pastor, A. L. Davis, helped lead the New Orleans bus desegregation campaign. Ninety-seven activists from thirty-four cities created the Southern Leaders Conference and elected King president. More than a coordinating body, the new association emerged as a regionwide equivalent to the MIA: a top-down organization of black leaders, mostly ministers, to link church-based movements sprouting across the South. The mass base of the black church, with grassroots activists in each city, was incorporated into the organization through its preacher leaders.

A clergy-led association composed of affiliates like the MIA, Birmingham ACMHR, and Tallahassee Inter-Civic Council could not only foster leaders' collaboration but enhance their ability to mobilize their own communities behind shared goals. The leaders opted not to make it a mass-membership organization, so as not to compete with the NAACP, but this would affect organizing choices and fund-raising down the road.

Smiley had tried to set up something different: a biracial group of southern activists, including white and black clergy, educators, and college students, more explicitly grounded in nonviolent principles. Although King trusted Smiley and FOR and appreciated their help, his Baptist orientation combined with the success of the MIA model drew him toward a more indigenous, all-black formation in which preachers centering around himself would run the show. He and his colleagues christened it the Southern Christian Leadership Conference (SCLC) at a third gathering in Montgomery in August 1957. Thus movement leaders chose for their strategic vehicle the nonviolent tradition of A. Philip Randolph, which called for a black-led organization and mass action, rather than FOR's pacifist tradition that was oriented more toward moral witness than mass organization.[216]

As it took shape SCLC opted not to further bus boycotts or other direct action against segregation. That would come later. In the next few years, even in Montgomery, black citizens made scant progress in desegregating schools, parks, other public facilities, or in voter registration. Local activists were divided by strategic choices, especially between voting and desegregation.

SCLC leaders decided to concentrate on voting-rights education and organizing, hoping to launch a South-wide movement to secure the ballot. This strategy was idealistic in that achieving universal suffrage would require not only changes in official practices but also in black attitudes and customs. The betterment promised by black voting power would take time. The voting strategy was practical in that, being less of an immediate threat to white supremacy, it would not provoke as much violent opposition, outside of Mississippi; nor would it be impeded by the mythology of separate but equal. And for what it was worth, the hallowed Constitution mandated their right to vote.

At the New Orleans meeting on Valentine's Day, King and his colleagues made plans for a "Prayer Pilgrimage" to Washington on May 17, third anniversary of the *Brown* decision. Randolph helped negotiate cosponsorship with the NAACP. King's speech to the rally of twenty-five thousand at the Lincoln Memorial culminated in his resounding call to "Give us the ballot!" Foreshadowing his famous address six years later at the same spot, his hit performance solidified his symbolic leadership of the rising black movement.

Despite this dramatic start, SCLC floundered in carrying out its voting-right campaign. Although it faced daunting obstacles, failure to build a southern mass movement in the late 1950s was rooted in its identity crisis. Was SCLC to center around and capitalize on King's fame and prestige? Or was it to be the congress of local organizations that would nurture and coordinate grassroots activism? Was its priority to build up King, or to build up the affiliates and their indigenous leadership, dynamic organizers such as Jo Ann Robinson, E. D. Nixon, and Shuttlesworth? It could not do both; centralism clashed with autonomy. The growing gulf between King and the local groups not only hindered the latter's efforts but held back SCLC.

An astute recruiter of leadership, King had the good sense to hire seasoned organizer Ella Baker to manage SCLC's operations. With her organizing prowess, three decades full, she ran in a league of her own. But as in the bus boycott, he could not keep from micromanaging at whim, delegating responsibility without authority. He erred in not backing her efforts to grow the grassroots movement that he rhetorically advocated. In early 1958 SCLC launched the Crusade for Citizenship, aimed at doubling the number of southern black voters by 1960, but it failed to adopt Baker's blueprint. By the end of the first year the crusade had run aground.

If SCLC had forged firmer ties with affiliate "movement centers"—in Nashville, for example—it might have realized that, as Montgomery had presaged, building protest against the everyday evil of segregation, rather than pushing for suffrage, was the strategy needed at this historical moment to ignite and fuel a sustained large-scale movement. The unanticipated explosion of southern student activism in early 1960 compelled King's organization to downplay voting and pursue the path of mass protest not taken at its founding meetings.

Even so, SCLC stumbled before finding its footing. But the brilliant Birmingham campaign and the "Negro Revolution of 1963" led to achievement of civil rights reforms that abolished legal segregation and enforced voting rights. All across the South, as Montgomery had heralded, ordinary citizens proved themselves the motors of change, the leaders of their leaders, the shapers of history.

Bringing into being SCLC, which after fits and starts surpassed the half-century-old NAACP as the 1960s' leading civil rights organization, was one of the crucial ways that the Montgomery bus boycott prepared the ground for the nationwide black freedom movement that transformed American politics, culture, and values over the next decades. The bus boycott was "God's proving ground," manifesting the destiny of African Americans to achieve their own freedom and "redeem the soul of America." It forged and tested the strategies and methods, support networks and alliances, language and vision, and shared spiritual meaning that helped generate and came to fruition in the ensuing mass movement.

The Montgomery epic showed the power and potential of mass nonviolent action in the American grain. It set the standard for a profoundly democratic grassroots movement in which leadership multiplied. It proved that ordinary people could behold the beloved community by building it, day by day, in the storm of heartfelt struggle.

"FRANKLY, I'M WORRIED TO DEATH," Martin King confessed to his mentor J. Pius Barbour. "A man who hits the peak at twenty-seven has a tough job ahead. People will be expecting me to pull rabbits out of the hat for the rest of my life."[217]

Book Two

Middle Passage

1963–1966

Prologue:

New Birth of Freedom

Survivors called it a perfect hell on earth, the devil's slaughter pen. The ground that had grown swaying fields of corn and wheat was soaked with blood. Thousands of men's bodies lay putrefying in puddles of blood and mud. Some of the dead men embedded in this hell clutched their Bibles. The three-day Battle of Gettysburg in July 1863, the bloodiest battle ever in the Western Hemisphere, left nearly as many dead or debilitated as all the American soldiers felled in the decade-long Vietnam War. Although the Union forces had lost almost half of the casualties, "it was the most beautiful thing I ever saw," a victorious Union soldier exulted.[1] The battered Confederate remnants hobbled back home across the Potomac. From then on the rebels waged a defensive war whose days were numbered.

But the stench and pollution from the crashingly quiet battlefield, overrun by buzzards and black flies, alarmed the traumatized farming town of Gettysburg in southeastern Pennsylvania. "In many instances arms and legs and sometimes heads protrude," Gettysburg banker David Wills reported to the governor, "and my attention has been directed to several places where the hogs were actually rooting out the bodies and devouring them."[2] Wills cranked gears in motion to create a massive burial ground that became the Soldiers' National Cemetery. Like all cemeteries of the time, it had to be formally dedicated. When poets Henry Wadsworth Longfellow and John Greenleaf Whittier refused Wills's invitation, he turned to the greatest orator of the age,

Edward Everett, diplomat, ex-senator, and Harvard president. Belatedly Wills invited the president of the United States to make "a few appropriate remarks."

As in early July, thousands of Americans invaded the farm town just before Thanksgiving, but these people were older and well clothed, women and men, all on the same side. Everett spoke of the battle for two hours, enthralling the crowd. Abraham Lincoln followed him, for three minutes. He was disappointed by the tepid response.

Yet his melodic 272-word speech transmuted the grisly deaths on the battlefield—burying of the decayed bodies still not complete, Cemetery Ridge still pockmarked with rusted rifles, strips of blue and gray, skeletons of horses—into the vital value of the war. Out of these parched fields of death Americans would create new life, Lincoln proclaimed, a "new birth of freedom," national rebirth. His words rewrote the nation's founding document of 1776 as a commitment to equality more than to life or even liberty, and set the stage for postwar reform of the Constitution to follow suit. He accomplished a feat in a few phrases that history had belied and that the war had so far cruelly mocked: conjuring the meaning of America as a single people dedicated to a single proposition, their union defined by equality. Lincoln's incantation, which drew no distinction between North and South, forged the ideal of a new America that would complete the American Revolution, a second founding to fulfill what was promised in the first.[3]

But at what cost? Although the Union commander-in-chief may have confessed later that he became a Christian only after seeing the "graves of our dead heroes" at Gettysburg—"I then and there consecrated myself to Christ"—he was glorifying, even sacralizing, hideous, painful death, the mass destruction of the young men under his ultimate command who on this battlefield died senselessly.[4] Neither side had a compelling reason to fight at Gettysburg, no strategic necessity. And the suicidal "Pickett's charge" up Cemetery Hill was one of the craziest blunders in military history, for which Robert E. Lee asked his Confederate president to fire him.

Transubstantiating the flesh and blood of fifty thousand young Americans killed or wounded into an abstract promise of equality and union, himself as high priest of this Eucharist, Lincoln justified the mad horror of the war, no matter what the outcome. In four years over six hundred thousand Americans would die over Lincoln's lofty principles, seeding the national myth that it was a war of sacred justice. The war freed the slaves, and it launched a powerful industrial nation with railroads steaming from sea to shining sea. But equality of any sort would remain a mirage. Lincoln was speaking over the heads of his audience, beyond hearing of the buried heroes, to an America that did not exist. The heroes had died for Lincoln's dream.

Lincoln was neither the first nor the last to hallow the war as a holocaust, purifying fire, its primal power cleansing the nation of its sins to bring rebirth. Walt Whitman, who saw Lincoln often in Washington—"we exchange bows, and very cordial ones"—where he treated the war's wounded heroes in improvised hospitals, exalted the war's purgative violence that he witnessed firsthand.[5]

In an 1865 poem he wrote: "And ever the sound of the cannon far or near, (rousing even in dreams a devilish exultation and all the old mad joy in the depths of my soul,)."[6] After all the horror he had seen, touched, and smelled, he wrote:

Look down, fair moon, and bathe this scene;
Pour softly down night's nimbus floods, on faces ghastly, swollen, purple;
On the dead, on their backs, with their arms toss'd wide,
Pour down your unstinted nimbus, sacred moon.[7]

When the Civil War erupted, and especially after Lincoln's Emancipation Proclamation turned the conflict into a war against slavery, black and white abolitionists envisioned the bloodletting as a reenactment (on a vaster scale) of God's deliverance of the Israelites, or as the apocalyptic Judgment Day crashing down from the heavens. In a wartime sermon AME bishop Daniel Payne portrayed Confederate soldiers as Pharaoh's forces and Union armies as the chariots of the returning wrathful Messiah. Many northerners and southern slaves believed that the unearthly sacrifice of life, the unmerited suffering of millions of dead and wounded, would redeem the nation and its people and bring about reconciliation between North and South, slave and slaveholder.

This vision of redemption through blood was conveyed by the war's anthem, "Battle Hymn of the Republic," by Julia Ward Howe, the tune fittingly from "John Brown's Body." Dripping with Hebrew Scriptures and Revelation, it served as the favorite marching song of Union soldiers. Whether the "grapes of wrath" were those of God or of the slaves, or the two as one, the Messiah in the mold of marching feet, white and black, was "trampling out the vintage" from centuries of human suffering into blood flowing as wine that would resurrect the nation. Lincoln was said to have wept upon first hearing it.

When on March 4, 1865, the reelected president began his Second Inaugural Address under the Capitol's new gold dome, John Wilkes Booth watching within pistol range, the dark wintry clouds suddenly parted to let in a blast of sunshine. But the clouds closed up before he finished his short speech. People then as now chose to remember the consoling last lines of this great address, "With malice toward none; with charity for all . . ."

In his First Inaugural Address he had pleaded for such Christlike reconciliation, "devoted altogether to *saving* the Union without war." Despite seven states having seceded and the Confederacy in full revolt, Lincoln did not presume to know which side God was on.

"We must not be enemies," he proclaimed. "Though passion may have strained, it must not break our bonds of affection. The mystic chords of memory, stretching from every battle-field, and patriot grave, to every living heart and hearthstone, all over this broad land, will yet swell the chorus of the Union, when again touched, as surely they will be, by the better angels of our nature."

But his address four years later was "a fiery gospel, writ in burnished rows of steel," sanctifying a just and holy crusade to free the slaves.

"If we shall suppose," Lincoln said, "that American Slavery is one of those offences which, in the providence of God, must needs come, but which, having continued through His appointed time, He now wills to remove, and that He gives to both North and South, this terrible war, as the woe due to those by whom the offence came, shall we discern therein any departure from those divine attributes which the believers in a Living God always ascribe to Him?" By no means.

"Fondly do we hope—fervently do we pray—that this mighty scourge of war may speedily pass away. Yet, if God wills that it continue, until all the wealth piled by the bond-man's two hundred and fifty years of unrequited toil shall be sunk, and every drop of blood drawn with the lash, shall be paid by another drawn with the sword, as was said three thousand years ago, so still it must be said 'the judgments of the Lord, are true and righteous altogether.' " His black listeners called out, "bress de Lord."

When Lincoln asked him what he thought of the speech, ex-slave Frederick Douglass told him later that day at a White House reception—"no one of color" was allowed; he had been kicked out, then appealed to the President to let him in—"Mr. Lincoln, that was a sacred effort."[8]

God was punishing both sides for the sin of slavery, and would continue to punish the nation far into the future, well past Reconstruction—but Lincoln by now had no doubt that God was foursquare on the Union side. A month later the war was over, the rebels vanquished. More Americans had lost their lives than in all the nation's other wars put together, including two world wars of the next century.

When slaves were liberated from bondage by northern troops, many were certain that God had answered their prayers.

"Golly! de kingdom hab kim dis time for sure," a black man cried out in Richmond, Virginia, the second Confederate capital, when white and black soldiers captured the city, "dat ar what am promised in de generations to dem dat goes up tru great tribulations."[9] Richmond's black residents welcomed "Father Abraham" with ecstasy when he toured the city ten days before his death, surging around him, touching him, calling him their "Messiah."

When he was slain on Good Friday, blacks and northern whites believed it was no coincidence. If the war had not yet done it—Lincoln had not been sure—the captain of state had died to wash away his people's sins.

But the new birth of freedom did not arise out of the ashes of this war.

FOUR SCORE YEARS LATER, America reunited was caught up in a world war that was a crusade for freedom, this time on a global scale. Three months before the Normandy invasion turned the tide against the Nazis, a fifteen-year-old black boy in Atlanta won a high school debate contest sponsored by black Elks. His speech was titled "The Negro and the Constitution."

"Black America still wears chains," the high school junior asserted. "Even winners of our highest honors face the class color bar." He mentioned Marian Anderson being barred from singing at Constitution Hall five years before.

"But this tale had a different ending," he said. "The nation rose in protest and gave a stunning rebuke to the Daughters of the American Revolution and a tremendous ovation to the artist, who sang in Washington on Easter Sunday and fittingly, before the Lincoln Memorial." Still, he pointed out, the great contralto could not spend the night in a "good hotel." Even after being honored as the "most distinguished resident" of Philadelphia, "she cannot be served in many of the public restaurants of her home city.

"So, with their right hand they raise to high places the great who have dark skins, and with their left, they slap us down to keep us in 'our places.' Yes, America, you have stripped me of my garments, you have robbed me of my precious endowment.

"Today 13 million black sons and daughters of our forefathers continue the fight for the translation of the thirteenth, fourteenth, and fifteenth amendments from writing on the printed page to actuality. We may conquer southern armies by the sword, but it is another thing to conquer southern hate."

After delivering his oration to the state Elks' contest in Dublin, Martin King returned on a bus to Atlanta. Riding through the rural river valley in which King's slave great-grandfather had long before picked cotton and preached the Gospel, the bus driver ordered King and his teacher to give up their seats for white passengers boarding along the route.

"We didn't move quickly enough to suit him," King recalled, "so he began cursing us, calling us 'black sons of bitches.' I intended to stay right in that seat, but Mrs. Bradley finally urged me up, saying we had to obey the law. And so we stood up in the aisle for the ninety miles to Atlanta. That night will never leave my memory. It was the angriest I have ever been in my life."[10] He happened to be the same age and in the same grade as Claudette Colvin would be a decade later when she put up a fight.

Despite his teenage rage, King would not for long be steered away from the upbeat words that had closed his speech.

"The spirit of Lincoln still lives," he had said, "that spirit born of the teachings of the Nazarene, who promised mercy to the merciful, who lifted the lowly, strengthened the weak, ate with publicans, and made the captives free.

"America experiences a new birth of freedom in her sons and daughters," he concluded. "She incarnates the spirit of her martyred chief. Their loyalty is repledged; their devotion renewed to the work He left unfinished. My heart throbs anew in the hope that inspired by the example of Lincoln, imbued with the spirit of Christ, they will cast down the last barrier to perfect freedom."[11]

I

Good Friday, April 12, 1963

Things looked bleak for Martin Luther King Jr. and the stumbling Birmingham movement. Everything was going wrong. It was bad enough that the start of the Birmingham campaign had to be postponed twice—first until after the March city election, then until the April 2 runoff in which ex–lieutenant governor Albert Boutwell trounced Public Safety Commissioner Theophilius Eugene "Bull" Connor for mayor. But Connor, refusing to step down, was proving a cannier adversary than the movement had counted on.

Born in Selma, sixty-five-year-old Connor had started out as a railroad telegrapher and baseball radio announcer in the 1920s, earning his nickname for "shooting the bull," not his shape. After serving as a state legislator, in 1937 he was elected public safety commissioner, one of three (as in Montgomery) who ran the city. His baptism as a savior of Jim Crow came in November 1938, when the liberal Southern Conference for Human Welfare held its founding meeting in downtown Birmingham. Its focus was New Deal–style economic reform. But when Connor announced that "White and Negro are not to segregate together" and his men dragged a rope down the middle of Municipal Auditorium, he compelled the group to make an issue of segregated seating—all the more so when First Lady Eleanor Roosevelt pulled her folding chair out into the aisle as a protest but was not arrested. During the next quarter century Connor tacitly encouraged Ku Klux Klan bombings to block integrated housing and buses, letting the KKK do the dirty work. Now the Klan was backing off for a season to let Connor conquer a Negro invasion by official methods.

The early April sit-ins at downtown department stores got off to a lackluster start, partly because stores closed their lunch counters. The store boycott that had started several months before limped along. Notwithstanding SCLC executive director Wyatt Walker's meticulous planning of every last detail, including the number of seats in each lunchroom, within less than a week after the kickoff on April 3 SCLC leaders altered their strategy from sit-ins to protest marches (and even considered canning direct action in favor of voter registration). The city's black preachers and other African-American leaders were overwhelmingly resistant to SCLC's civic confrontation. They claimed lack of consultation, but in fact they hoped that Boutwell's new regime would make protests unnecessary. In his marathon meetings with black moderates King managed to turn some of them around.

The sit-ins and marches garnered a respectable three hundred arrests during the first week, but Connor got a midnight injunction from a cooperative state court judge banning further protests. He had overheard King on a police bug announce to a Wednesday mass meeting that he would be arrested on Friday.

"Everyone in the movement must live a sacrificial life," he had said at St. James AME Church. "I can't think of a better day than Good Friday for a move for freedom."[12] Next day at a press conference Rev. Ralph Abernathy raised the stakes: "Almost two thousand years ago Christ died on the cross for us. Tomorrow we will take it up for our people and die if necessary."[13] The specter of King's jailing finally put the Birmingham protests on the front page of the *New York Times,* a badly needed lift. But was he bluffing?

Things got worse on Maundy Thursday. SCLC's bail funds were hitting bottom when the bail bondsman reported that the city had put him out of business. Suddenly the cost of bailing prisoners jumped tenfold. Moreover, because contempt citations could be prosecuted in superior court, the potential bail would be much higher than simply for parading without a permit. King's advisers felt he had a higher responsibility to leave town and raise cold cash as only he could.

When he met with local leaders and SCLC staff on Good Friday morning to decide what to do, "a sense of doom" pervaded Room 30, King's small suite at the Gaston Motel. Owner Arthur G. Gaston, Birmingham's only black millionaire, and King's father were among those present. "I looked about me," King Jr. recalled, "and saw that, for the first time, our most dedicated and devoted leaders were overwhelmed by a feeling of hopelessness. No one knew what to say, for no one knew what to do." There was an atmosphere of utter gloom, Andrew Young recalled.

A staff member broke the somber silence. "Martin, this means you can't go to jail. We need money. We need a lot of money. We need it now. You are the only one who has the contacts to get it."

Did it occur to anyone in the stuffy room that King's "one-man team" approach to leadership, especially his one-man moneymaking show, had put them all in this untenable dilemma? He was still the six-year-old organization's only dependable fund-raiser. "If you go to jail," the staffer continued, "we are lost. The battle of Birmingham is lost." But if he did not go to jail, after making a public pledge, the nation's eyes upon him, the movement might die a less honorable death, and his leadership, already fragile, might be undone. Judges could then shut down any constitutional protest with the stroke of a pen.

Neither King nor SCLC could afford to lose in Birmingham. The future if not the survival of both were on the line. It was do or die in Birmingham, then the most segregated big city in America.

"I sat in the midst of the deepest quiet I have ever felt," King later wrote, "alone in that crowded room."[14] For the first time in his leadership career, the thirty-four-year-old preacher faced the prospect of going against the majority consensus of his team. Only Walker and Fred Shuttlesworth urged jail. All the other local leaders were adamantly opposed. Chain-smoking, King paid close attention to their objections. Compassionate listening was one of his ways of defusing stressful conflict.

Ever since in his Montgomery kitchen he was baptized in the power of prayer and had plumbed the depths of his faith, King sometimes sought to re-create that experience when crisis struck, but usually in private or with intimates. This time he made a show of his faith. Without a word he retreated to his bedroom and closed the door.

When he came out half an hour later to face the befuddled group, he was wearing a pressed blue-gray work shirt over his white dress shirt, and crisp blue jeans with cuffs rolled up. The denim outfit was meant both to show solidarity with poor blacks and to back the downtown store boycott by challenging the need to buy new Easter clothes.

"I don't know what will happen," King said grimly to his colleagues. "I don't know where the money will come from. But I have to make a faith act." He turned to his closest friend.

"I know you want to be in your pulpit on Easter Sunday, Ralph. But I am asking you to go with me."[15] As he had in Atlanta during the bus boycott, Daddy King pleaded with his son to avoid an arrest that might kill him. Like seven years before, Martin would not be swayed, neither by his father nor by other elders in the room.

"I have to go," he replied. "I am going to march if I have to march by myself. If we obey this injunction, we are out of business." Exasperated, his father rued, "Well, you didn't get this nonviolence from me. You must have got it from your mama."[16]

No one doubted he meant business. The group joined hands and sang "We Shall Overcome." Since the 1960 student sit-ins the slave spiritual rephrased by black South Carolina textile strikers, then polished by Pete Seeger and Guy Carawan, had become the movement's battle hymn. A few blocks away at Sixth Avenue Zion Hill Church fifty protesters were also singing freedom hymns as they patiently awaited their leader.

An hour later King, Abernathy, and Shuttlesworth led the trained protesters out of the church toward downtown white Birmingham. A growing crowd gathered around, joining in their chanting and singing, as they marched by black Kelly Ingram Park, boundary of the two Birminghams. Connor and his cops were waiting with paddy wagons. As if of one mind the column of twos suddenly turned, sidestepping the police blockade. Police caught up with them, motorcycle cops roaring to the front and ordering a halt. King and Abernathy fell to their knees in prayer. Burly cops grabbed each preacher by his shirt back and shoved them roughly into a paddy wagon. Police had trouble distinguishing protesters from onlookers, arresting a larger number than had marched out of the church. Shuttlesworth had not intended to go in this time, but he was swept up in the confusion. The crowd of several hundred cheered their heroes as they filled up the wagons.

At Birmingham city jail King and Abernathy were removed from the larger group that was stuffed into a drunk tank; each was locked in solitary confinement. King's cramped cell was completely dark. He had a cold metal cot without mattress, sheet, or blanket, and a filthy seatless toilet. Terror trumped his shock and disgust.

"Those were the longest, most frustrating and bewildering hours" of his life, he wrote later. "You will never know the meaning of utter darkness until you have lain in such a dungeon, knowing that sunlight is streaming overhead and still seeing only darkness below."[17] He feared that this might be his tomb, no bigger than Jesus' stone tomb in Jerusalem that he had once prayed within. Would this be his Golgotha? Would he never again hold his baby, Bernice, born a week before? The Montgomery movement had been born just after his first child, Yoki, had entered the world.

During his first two days of trembling darkness, when he was not praying or dozing fitfully, he could look back over seven years of daily facing death. The only time he had felt death embrace him was when in Harlem a deranged black woman stabbed him in the chest, September 1958—but God had let him survive the wound a hair from his heart. His fear of death had become a companion, a soul mate, which energized him while it also wore him down. Fear was intertwined with aching guilt for subjecting his wife and children, and parents, to the apparent inevitability of his death. Many times since December 1955 he had daydreamed about leaving the movement in others' hands. More than once he had resolved to do so. He had wanted out. But he always reminded himself of his covenant with the holy spirit, his midnight vow of January 1956 to fight on no matter what. Leaving the movement would mean betraying his faith, betraying his Lord, and leaving himself spiritually more alone than he was now physically in the "hole."

But what bruised fruit his leadership had netted since the bus boycott triumph. SCLC's voting rights campaign of the late 1950s, which had such potential, had fizzled, perhaps because he had not paid enough attention. During those early years he believed that his main job was to commit the uncommitted through oratory, to spread the political gospel like a black Billy Graham for justice, and always to raise money. It wasn't until the startling lunch-counter sit-ins of winter 1960 that he learned he must act with his body as well as his voice, and that black voting was not sufficient. And next year the freedom rides led by CORE and young SNCC (Student Nonviolent Coordinating Committee) members showed him that he was not alone in staring down death. SNCC activists who wrote wills before heading on a bus from Montgomery to Mississippi were upset when he refused to join them, after urging them onward. To derisive laugher "De Lawd" told them that he must choose the time and place of his Golgotha.[18] De Lawd was the nickname SNCC people had given him, only partly in jest.

Then came humiliating defeat in Albany, the southwest Georgia city that Bernice Johnson Reagan, born and raised there, called the "mother lode" of the movement, in which singing was as powerful as marching and sitting in.[19] SNCC's resentment toward King for his moral caution was deepened by his men's grabbing the helm of the Albany movement, then jumping ship when it ran into shoals. SCLC had earned a reputation for bringing a big media show that spotlighted King, then leaving town with the cameras, abandoning local people to fend for themselves against sheriffs and the Klan. Notwithstanding his sacred pledge, King might have already resigned from the movement for an ivoried college or seminary had the young militants not kept relighting his fire.

What King hated most about jail, and being alone, was the suffocating self-reproach he conjured up.

2

If the stench and darkness of Birmingham's hole represented the nadir of King's young life, the zenith had been a world away at the White House. In October 1961, a long-sought appointment was granted with the new president, who had been beleaguered by the failed Cuban invasion and a contest of wills with Khrushchev over Berlin. King found himself having an animated lunch with John and Jacqueline Kennedy upstairs in the family quarters, the first African American so honored. Afterward the Kennedys showed him around the rooms that the First Lady had famously redecorated. In the Lincoln bedroom, he and JFK saw their faces black and white reflected in a replica of the Emancipation Proclamation above Lincoln's fireplace.

"Mr. President," the preacher said softly, "I'd like to see you stand in this room and sign a Second Emancipation Proclamation outlawing segregation, one hundred years after Lincoln's. You could base it on the Fourteenth Amendment."[20] JFK warmed to the idea and asked King to prepare a draft.

King had always been wary of the wealthy, charismatic Irish Catholic whom much of the nation now admired like royalty. Before the 1960 election he had been cultivating a political friendship with Vice President Richard Nixon; the two had met in West Africa at the inauguration of Ghana's Kwame Nkrumah in March 1957. Candidate Kennedy's phone call to Coretta King days before the election had brought about her husband's release from state prison after an Atlanta lunch-counter sit-in—"they had me chained all the way down there." The call had clinched Kennedy's razor-thin victory with a windfall of black support; and it persuaded King that there might be more to Kennedy than his Irish Brahmin halo.[21]

Like many Americans, King was lifted by the new spirit of idealism and commitment that Kennedy's New Frontier was purveying to the nation. Was it just words and soaring metaphor, his own coin of the realm? He sought to harness this rejuvenated patriotism away from Kennedy's prime target, the Cold War, toward the unfinished revolution at home. Although JFK's magnetic inaugural address echoed Lincolnian tones, he did not draw upon Lincoln's call for equality as the essence of American union. He was leery of rekindling Civil War memories that might divide the nation when it sorely needed unity to face global communism—and that might alienate the white South that dominated Congress and could be crucial to his reelection. Play up Lincoln's image, play down what he stood for.

King on the contrary saw a one-time chance to wed New Frontier idealism to the "mystic chords of memory" of the Civil War, whose centennial was being commemorated, more vigorously South than North. Like A. Philip Randolph, Roy Wilkins, and other black leaders, King wanted the President to honor the centennial of the Emancipation Proclamation that had freed slaves by delivering a second Emancipation Proclamation to abolish slavery's afterlife of segregation; and in the same manner, an executive order that bypassed Congress. JFK could get cover from the commemoration to make such action more politically palatable. So far the commemoration had been exploited by white southerners who were using it to refight the Civil War and to defend the southern way of life. King and his colleagues wanted to exploit Civil War memories to bolster the civil rights crusade.

During his first hundred days Kennedy appeared to encourage this approach by making it clear to King and other black leaders that he saw no hope for congressional legislation against Jim Crow. In an Oval Office meeting he told them he would pursue a strategy of "executive action" to advance civil rights. But it did not take long to discover that executive action was a fig leaf for inaction. It did not translate into meaningful executive orders—made plain when JFK's promised order to ban housing discrimination was delayed for two years and watered down. Kennedy cautioned the leaders not to push him.

King did not heed this warning. Since Congress was deadlocked, he made it his mission to nudge the President to outlaw segregation by decree. Although he placed in Kennedy's hands a Lincolnesque proclamation for New Year's 1963, JFK ignored it. He had already avoided one opportunity to address the nation in late September 1962, the centennial of Lincoln's signing, while embroiled with Mississippi governor Ross Barnett over the admission of James Meredith to the University of Mississippi. He did not want to fan the flames of the true-life Gettysburg reenactment at Ole Miss. He sent in several thousand troops to quell the ferocious mobs. Many were injured and two people died, the only fatalities connected with military intervention in the South during this era.

By the time New Year's Day 1963 rolled around, the White House had decided to replace a commemoration of Emancipation with a gala presidential dinner on Lincoln's birthday to which black leaders and celebrities would be invited in droves. That February evening President Kennedy panicked upon discovering actor Sammy Davis Jr.—like his own brother-in-law Peter Lawford a member of Hollywood's fabled "Rat Pack"—wandering with his white wife into the Lincoln bedroom. He commanded his staff to use any ruse necessary to prevent the couple from being photographed. Like Lincoln before him, Kennedy believed that civil rights had limits; interracial marriage was still taboo. King, Randolph, and other leaders had boycotted the sham occasion.

BACK IN SPRING 1961, just a few weeks after the President had instructed black leaders not to push him—Khrushchev and Fidel Castro were pounding him hard enough—a squadron of youthful activists jolted him harder than King's entreaties ever could have. John and Robert Kennedy, fond of muscular activism by others, could not help but admire the daring of the freedom riders in Alabama, despite their being a royal pain.

Shortly after the Supreme Court declared segregated bus terminals unconstitutional, CORE resolved to enforce compliance with the ruling. In May 1961 a baker's dozen of activists, black and white, left Washington on two buses, headed for New Orleans. Outside of Anniston, Alabama, one bus was forced off the road and firebombed by the Klan. The choking riders barely escaped the inferno. In town eight men burst into the second bus and assaulted the passengers, nearly killing a retired white professor. Then a Klan mob ambushed the freedom riders on their arrival at the Birmingham bus station. Fred Shuttlesworth called an ambulance for white pacifist Jim Peck, who underwent hours of surgery for multiple head gashes.

CORE decided to declare victory and go home, but Diane Nash and other SNCC members were determined to complete the journey at all cost. Robert Kennedy, the greenhorn attorney general fresh from the Cuban Bay of Pigs morass, interceded with Alabama officials. The SNCC group rode safely from Birmingham a hundred miles south to Montgomery guarded by police cars and helicopters. But when the bus pulled into the Montgomery terminal the police disappeared. The riders were greeted by another vicious mob that beat them with pipes and baseball bats, almost killing two young men. President Kennedy's personal emissary, John Siegenthaler, was knocked out cold. The President publicly expressed his concern and called for peace.

A mass meeting was held the next night at Ralph Abernathy's church. King flew in to speak in support of the riders. He had already been on the phone with the attorney general. Before the meeting King conferred in the church basement with CORE's James Farmer and SNCC's Diane Nash about what to do. The phone rang. Robert Kennedy was calling again to ask King to stop the freedom ride to allow a cooling-off period. Keeping the attorney general on the line, he turned to his colleagues.

"Don't you think that maybe the freedom ride has already made its point and now should be called off, as the attorney general suggests?" Nash shook her head.

"The Nashville Student Movement wants to go on," she said sternly. Farmer instructed King, who was ambivalent, to "tell the attorney general that we have been cooling off for 350 years. If we cool off any more we will be in a deep freeze."

"I understand," King replied softly, and turned down Kennedy's request.[22]

Upstairs outside the mass meeting, several hundred rioters were besieging the church, firing rocks through stained-glass windows. Those inside, showered with glass, emboldened themselves for hours with tenacious singing. The mob was about to break down the doors when a battalion of U.S. marshals, sent by the attorney general, scattered them with tear gas.

Robert Kennedy recalled a late-night phone call from King, who feared for his life. "I said that our people were down there, and that as long as he was in church, he might say a prayer for us. He didn't think that was very humorous. He rather berated me for what was happening to him at the time. I said to him that I didn't think that he'd be alive if it wasn't for us, and that we were going to keep him alive, and that the marshals would keep the church from burning down."[23] The outnumbered marshals were reinforced later that night by national guard troops reluctantly activated by Governor John Patterson, a JFK political ally who reportedly had been evading the President's phone calls.

Three days later two busloads of freedom riders, national guard, and reporters left for Jackson, Mississippi, escorted by legions of police in cars and aircraft. Farmer remembered its being like a military maneuver. Jackson onlookers witnessed the spectacle of protesters being led into the interstate terminal by rifle-toting guardsmen, police opening doors for them, then being handcuffed and taken away. Robert Kennedy had made a secret deal with Mississippi politicians, permitting the bust if done with no violence. The riders served two months at tough Parchman penitentiary in the Delta, where prayer and defiant singing of freedom songs got them through. Over the summer of 1961 hundreds more flocked to Jackson and joined their peers in prison. Prodded by the attorney general, the Interstate Commerce Commission enforced the Supreme Court ruling banning segregation in terminals. The freedom rides gave SNCC its reputation for fearless militancy, steeling cadres for further combat.

While still not at his Golgotha, Martin King found himself in hand-to-hand combat in an unlikely setting, the SLC convention in Birmingham, September 1962. The sixth convention, in the wake of

SCLC's Albany defeat, convened in the steel city in part because Shuttlesworth had been lobbying to get SCLC to aggressively support the local movement—pleading to make Birmingham the next campaign. The irascible, tough-as-nails preacher had led boycotts and other protests for seven years since founding his Alabama Christian Movement for Human Rights (ACMHR) when the state NAACP was outlawed by Attorney General Patterson's court order in June 1956. A boycott of downtown stores begun by Miles College students in early 1962 was having surprising success. When SCLC descended upon the fractured city for its annual gathering, merchants agreed to pull the "colored" signs—cosmetic changes revoked when SCLC left town. King's own arrival was auspicious. At the airport he used the city's only desegregated men's room and found himself standing next to the city's staunchly segregationist mayor, Art Hanes. They did not pass words.

During King's keynote address on the final morning of the convention, a beefy white man sitting next to millionaire Gaston walked onto the stage and belted King several times in the face. Delegates and reporters were amazed to see the SCLC president, once a wrestler, take the blows without shielding his face. As Abernathy and Joe Lowery jumped up and readied their fists to strike back, King stared down his attacker and soothed him, protecting him from his colleagues' wrath. As if he were an honored guest King introduced the man, who lived in an American Nazi Party hostel. The young Nazi wept in King's arms.

When the police took the man away King said he would not press charges, but the police did so. The Nazi explained at his trial that he became enraged when King announced a benefit by Sammy Davis Jr., the comedian whose dark seed was polluting the womb of virtuous white womanhood.

After celebrating the Emancipation Day centennial at black-led rallies around the country, King gathered his inner circle for a two-day retreat in early January 1963 at Dorchester in southeastern Georgia. At the Congregational church missionary school, Wyatt Walker presented an elaborate plan for a four-stage campaign in Birmingham, "Project Confrontation": lunch-counter sit-ins, boycott of big stores, mass marches to support the boycott and jam the jails, and finally a call to outsiders to help immobilize the city.

The Albany movement had been too fresh a wound to dissect at the September conference, but here they probed it. Acting on its hard lessons might lead to redemption in the centennial year of the first emancipation. Unlike in the Albany struggle they would focus on a single target, rather than segregation in scattershot fashion, and a clear-cut goal: desegregating department stores. They would pursue a defined strategy, to split the business elite from city hall. Preempting competition by SNCC or other groups, the movement would remain unified under tight control by SCLC and its ACMHR affiliate. Above all, they planned to profit from the reckless abandon of a police czar who, unlike Albany's media savvy chief Laurie Pritchett, was presumably ready to use brutal tactics and expose the ugliness of white supremacy for the world to witness. They must provoke open violence by the opposition.

All of these lessons except the necessity of official violence were matters that King had done right in Montgomery. They were trying to re-create the glory of the bus boycott, adding civil disobedience and an escalating media drama that would pressure the federal government to intervene, preferably with a bill to abolish segregation. If cajoling in the Lincoln bedroom and King's bully pulpit could not force the President to act, mass jailings might do the trick.

But SCLC leaders had a deep concern about Birmingham that distinguished it from Albany and Montgomery—the conservative apathy of middle-class black leaders, especially preachers. Shuttlesworth's ACMHR spoke for a narrow evangelical spectrum of the black community of 150,000. Many local blacks considered him a wild man, seeker of martyrdom, too radical for the community's good no matter how courageous.

"Don't worry, Martin," he said. "I can handle the preachers." Could King trust his swaggering confidence?

"You better be right," he replied skeptically.[24]

Swallowing their doubts about the reliability of black allies, SCLC reached consensus for an all-out mobilization to crack segregation in Birmingham. They sought a morale-lifting victory—first in six years— that would set the pace for the South and force John Kennedy to grasp the mantle of Lincoln. Before SCLC could "redeem the soul of America," its stated mission, it had to redeem itself.

At the close King made sure that his dozen colleagues understood the personal risk they were taking together.

"I have to tell you that in my judgment," he said gravely, "some of the people sitting here today will not come back alive from this campaign. I want you to think about it." Andrew Young felt that once again their chief was being dragged into peril, this time by Shuttlesworth, against his will or even his best judgment. King knew better than anyone, Young recalled, "that every time he made a commitment to something like this he was committing his life. He thought in everything he did it meant his death."

"You better let me know what kind of eulogy you want," King said to his fellows.[25] Then, as was his habit, he parlayed the gravity into levity by delivering tongue-in-cheek eulogies for a few of his brothers in cloth, airing each one's dirty linen. He and his associates knew that it was his own funeral he was perseverating about. He had plenty of skeletons of his own.

His preoccupation with death and his own mortality was so familiar to those who knew him well that they sometimes tried to make light of it, as he sometimes would with his own gallows humor. When his college friend Mary McKinney Edmonds, a Spelman grad, lunched with him around this time in Cleveland, where he was preaching at her father's church, she sat with her back to the restaurant door and joked that this way an assassin must shoot her first.

"No, Mary," he said dryly, "when they get me, and they will, they will only get me." No gallows humor on this occasion. Edmonds blanched.[26]

3

King's dark night of the soul in his Birmingham dungeon was broken by a visit on Saturday by one of his lawyers, who brought a copy of that morning's Birmingham daily. While he was being held incommunicado, the local and national press lit into him. *Time*'s article was titled "Poorly Timed Protest." *Newsweek* and other media indicted King and Connor as equal extremists. Evangelist Billy Graham, whom King had once hoped to join forces with, publicly urged "my good personal friend" to "put the brakes on."[27] Birmingham's white and black moderates echoed this stand.

Although King was heartened by his lawyer's news on money being raised, his spirit sank upon reading a statement in the newspaper by eight prominent Alabama clergymen, leaders of the Protestant, Catholic, and Jewish faiths in the state, who denounced the protests as "unwise and untimely." By Deep South standards these were racially liberal churchmen. They had publicly opposed Governor George Wallace's inaugural pledge of "segregation forever." But they hadn't lifted a finger to help resolve the Montgomery bus boycott.

"Just as we formerly pointed out that 'hatred and violence have no sanction in our religious and political traditions,'" their words rang out on the front page, "we also point out that such actions as incite to hatred and violence, however technically peaceful actions may be, have not contributed to the resolution of our local problems. We do not believe that these days of new hope are days when extreme measures are justified in Birmingham." They urged the Negro community to withdraw support from the protests.[28]

For years King had felt an affinity with Saint Paul. He likened his own "kitchen conversion" in January 1956 to Paul's blinding vision on the road to Damascus in the first century C.E. The Greek Jew, like King, heard Jesus speaking to him. The heavenly light was so bright that Paul could not see in an earthly way for three days. King identified with the ex-persecutor's relentless persecution—"tried for heresy at Jerusalem, jailed at Philippi, beaten at Thessalonica, mobbed at Ephesus, depressed at Athens," and imprisoned and executed in Rome.

Not long after King's own vision he preached a sermon at Dexter in the persona of Paul, a letter to American Christians. Martin as Paul urged his audience to "be not conformed to this world," but to transform themselves into the divine image, a colony of heaven, to begin by refusing to conform to banal evil.[29] At least since his Albany jailing King had thought about writing a letter from jail as Paul had done. Now he transmuted the despair he felt reading the clergymen's letter into a furious burst of intellectual energy, to craft a Pauline epistle that sharpened themes he had previewed in his 1956 sermon.[30]

Like Paul of Tarsus, the Birmingham inmate penned an urgent letter for a particular place and time that took on universal meaning for all times and places. Scribbling on the margins of the newspaper in which the clergymen's letter appeared, then on scraps of paper slipped into his cell by a black jail trusty, he began with a warm greeting, "My dear fellow clergymen," and praised them as sincere men of "genuine good will."

He responded to criticism of him as an outsider by explaining that he and SCLC had been invited by their local affiliate; but that they were there "more basically" because "injustice is here." Just like the Hebrew prophets, and just as the Apostle Paul "left his village of Tarsus and carried the gospel of Jesus Christ to the far corners of the Greco-Roman world, so I am compelled to carry the gospel of freedom beyond my own home town. Like Paul, I must constantly respond to the Macedonian call for aid." He was likewise an apostle sent by God to correct false teachings of misguided Christians.[31]

Unlike the Hebrew prophets who chastised a chosen people, Paul was the unequaled prophet of human unity. He brooked no divisions in the body of Christ, no divisive spirit. So in his own epistle King stressed from the outset the interrelatedness of all people, partly as justification for his intervention, but more as source of segregation's sinfulness and that of his white clergy brethren.

"Injustice anywhere is a threat to justice everywhere," he asserted. "We are caught in an inescapable network of mutuality, tied in a single garment of destiny. Whatever affects one directly, affects all indirectly. Never again can we afford to live with the narrow, provincial 'outsider agitator' idea. Anyone who lives inside the United States can never be considered an outsider anywhere within its bounds." How far he had traveled since Montgomery, when he was troubled about the role of Bayard Rustin and other outsiders.

The heart of his message to his fellow clergy was that racial segregation had broken the interwoven body of humanity. This was the crisis—not the disorder in Birmingham streets that was aimed at mending the broken community. But the curveball he pitched to these clergy was to confess his disappointment that white (and black) moderates like themselves were not only not helping to repair the break, to reunify God's splintered creation. Notwithstanding their apparent sincerity and goodwill, they were more responsible for the crisis than white supremacists and the Klan. He was not the first to suggest that the worst sin was good people staying silent. But in the case of these religious leaders, and many other moderates, they were remaining silent *except* to criticize the protests and defend law and order. Even more damaging was that the moderates were not even aware of their complicity but in flagrant denial.

"Shallow understanding from people of good will," King wrote, was more the problem than "absolute misunderstanding from people of ill will," "lukewarm acceptance" worse than "outright rejection."

King was twisting the preachers' comfortable ethical world upside down, or right side up—and indirectly this included Birmingham's slacking black preachers. He argued that like antebellum ministers who tolerated slavery or gave lip service to abolition, the moderates, particularly moderate church people, were the primary linchpin bolstering

MLK speaking to crowd on his parsonage porch after Montgomery bombing, with mayor, police chief, and police commissioner, January 30, 1956 (© Bettman/Corbis)

Rev. Ralph Abernathy, MLK, and Bayard Rustin at Montgomery courthouse for boycott leaders' arraignment, February 24, 1956 (© AP/Wide World Photos)

Rev. Ralph Abernathy and MLK marching in Birmingham just before their arrest, April 12, 1963 (© Charles Moore/Black Star)

Fire hose attack on young protesters in Birmingham, May 1963

(© Charles Moore/Black Star)

Fannie Lou Hamer
picketing at SNCC
voter registration
protest, Hattiesburg,
Miss., fall 1963
(© Matt Herron /
Take Stock)

Three young women singing on Selma-to-Montgomery march,
March 1965 (© Charles Moore / Black Star)

MLK at Mississippi march against fear "summit meeting" debating Black Power, June 1966; Bernard Lee (with bottle), Andy Young (arm raised), Stokely Carmichael (lying on floor) (© Bob Fitch/Bob Fitch Photo)

MLK at Atlanta staff meeting with James Bevel (wearing cap), summer 1966 (© Bob Fitch/ Bob Fitch Photo)

MLK shooting pool in Chicago during SCLC housing rights campaign, 1966 (© Bob Fitch/ Bob Fitch Photo)

MLK resting during Mississippi
march against fear, June 1966
(© Bob Fitch / Black Star)

MLK escorting two girls to
desegregate public school,
Grenada, Miss., September 19, 1966
(© Bob Fitch / Black Star)

Women protesting Vietnam War, Central Park, New York, April 15, 1967,
first mass antiwar march; MLK condemned the war at the U.N. rally
(© Deborah Schneer)

Striking Memphis sanitation workers, March 1968 (© Bettmann/ Corbis)

MLK greeting children in Newark, N.J., while organizing the Poor People's Campaign, March 27, 1968 (© AP/ Wide World Photos)

MLK's family looking
at his body in casket,
Atlanta, April 1968
(© Bob Fitch / Black Star)

MLK's colleagues with
mule-drawn wagon
carrying his casket
in funeral procession
from Ebenezer Baptist
Church to Morehouse
College, Atlanta,
April 9, 1968
(© Lynn Pelham / Time Life
Pictures / Getty Images)

Coretta Scott King with daughter Bernice at MLK funeral, Ebenezer Baptist Church, Atlanta, April 9, 1968
(© Bob Fitch / Black Star)

the unconscionable status quo. He had borne a grudge since the Montgomery bus boycott, when he had naively hoped that white clergy in Alabama—the same ilk he was now addressing—could be persuaded to rally behind the boycott. This was the assignment he had given to Methodist minister Glenn Smiley. He believed then, as he did today about Birmingham, that such influence could have made a crucial difference in wearing down the resistance of the Montgomery city commissioners, so sensitive to white voters—in which case the boycott could have achieved its goals independently, without a Supreme Court decision. This rosy hope was one of the worst misjudgments of King's career. It had taught him to be wary of white ministers and moderates.

King's broadside against moderates echoed the words of white writer Lillian Smith, whom he singled out for praise, in her address to the MIA's Institute on Nonviolence and Social Change in December 1956, the bus boycott's first anniversary. Her speech, "The Right Way Is Not a Moderate Way," was delivered by a friend because she was at home in Georgia battling the cancer that eventually killed her.

Bemoaning moderation as "the slogan of our times," the controversial novelist had lauded the Montgomery movement for showing the world that moderation was a dangerous myth no longer affordable. Rather, there were simply extremes: the extreme of hate and the extreme of love, the extreme of the lie and the extreme of searching for truth.

"So, you have been extremists," she had said to the Montgomery black community, "good, creative, loving extremists, and I want to tell you I admire and respect you for it." Of many great things they had done, one of the most valuable was to dramatize "for all America to see that in times of ordeal, in times of crisis, only the extremist can meet the challenge. The question in crisis is not: Are you going to be an extremist? The question is: *What kind of extremist* are you going to be?" She drew an analogy with her own struggle with cancer. Moderation would not make the cancer go away. The time had come, she insisted, "when it is dangerous not to risk. We must take risks in order to save our integrity, our moral nature, our lives and our country."[32] It was perilous *not* to be an extremist when extremism was called for. One was guilty of harmful extremism by not engaging in the constructive version.

In his Birmingham letter six years later King embraced the arrow of extremism (after being wounded by it) and restated Lillian Smith's provocative question: not *whether*, but *what kind* of extremist shall they be? Jesus had been an extremist, for love, he suggested, as were the Hebrew prophets, for justice, and Paul, for the Christian gospel of unity; so was Lincoln for national union, and Jefferson for natural rights. And for sure God had been an extremist in flooding the world, nearly killing Isaac, slaughtering worshipers of the golden calf, and sending his only begotten son to an agonizing death.

King declared that he was being an extremist by standing "in the middle of two opposing forces in the Negro community," complacent apathy and bitter violence, the latter exemplified by the Nation of Islam and other black nationalist "hate" groups. "I have tried to stand between these two forces," like his extremist namesake, Martin Luther: "Here I stand; I cannot do otherwise, so help me God." Evoking Paul, he claimed that his middle-of-the-road extremism was to pursue "the more excellent way of love and nonviolent protest."

Like Lillian Smith but more subtly he was charting a tectonic shift in the moral landscape. In Montgomery and since, he had championed walking a middle road *between* extremes—for example, between capitalism and communism. In a new departure he now asserted that the good and true middle road replaced false moderation with a creative extreme that would navigate amid hazardous extremes on either side—in this case, of passivity and of vengeful retaliation. And just as there were different kinds of extremism, so there were different forms of militancy. Neither extremism nor militancy had to mean violence to body or spirit. So much for Aristotle's doctrine of the golden mean in which moderation was enshrined and extremes expunged. One ought not blame King's poor churchmen for their bewilderment: he was accusing them of worse evil than the Klan.

The creative extremist, the constructive militant, the compassionate radical—King was projecting a new center for the American political universe. Could this radical center take hold?

Part of King's radical moderation was, again like Paul's approach, to clothe his unflinching moral pounce in a tone of friendship and pastoral caring for fellow men of God. Despite his harsh criticisms of wayward Christians, Paul often expressed a longing to be with the recipients of his admonitions. In closing, King asked the clergymen to forgive him if he overstated the truth or showed "unreasonable impatience," while asking God to forgive him if he was not hard enough on them. He wished to meet each of the eight signers as a Judeo-Christian brother. He was not only acting out his commitment to rebuild broken community, but showing that the heart of community was face-to-face dialogue, fellowship, and forgiveness, breaking bread at the table of brotherhood.

Was King speaking only to the clergymen, to white ministers, and to moderates of all colors? In a semiconscious way he may have been addressing his own moderate, cautious, and passive side. He could identify with the middle-class white clergy; perhaps this was why he challenged them so artfully. He had always leaned toward caution and often appeared passive. He had not immediately backed the bus boycott in December 1955. He had resisted the robust voting rights campaign that acting director Ella Baker mapped out for SCLC. He had refused to join the freedom rides even after egging on the riders. He had wiggled and wavered in Albany, further infuriating his SNCC allies. He had reluctantly approved the Birmingham campaign only when Shuttlesworth's pleading could not be rebuffed. In his upbringing and temperament he was as much a moderate as the bishops and rabbi he was upbraiding. Putting aside his own comfortable moderate demeanor, he had to decide for himself, What kind of extremist shall I be?

He acted the part of extremist in smuggling drafts of his missive in and out of jail as Walker, one of few who could decipher his scrawls, frantically copyedited, his secretary typed them, and he returned typescripts by attorney courier for the prisoner to revise. He began the lengthy letter on Easter Sunday, while outside an SCLC crew sought to desegregate Birmingham's lily-white churches. The letter was released to the press on Thursday. It drew little comment and had small effect on the Birmingham movement. Rejected by the *New York Times Magazine,* it was published later that spring in three left-leaning journals and then in the *Atlantic.* Its rise to canon and classic did not come until it made waves as the core of King's second book, *Why We Can't Wait,* in the afterheat of 1963.

. . .

A PERSONAL EPISTLE ABOUT RACE relations that made a louder splash during spring 1963, and ripples into the next century, appeared as James Baldwin's *The Fire Next Time*. The best-selling book contained a short letter, "My Dungeon Shook: Letter to My Nephew on the One Hundredth Anniversary of the Emancipation," and a long essay, "Down at the Cross: Letter from a Region in My Mind." Like King the thirty-nine-year-old author was the son of a Baptist preacher and had become a preacher himself. Writing in the deceptively calm racial waters of mid-1962, Baldwin expressed an apocalyptic urgency that surpassed that of the SCLC leader in the Birmingham cauldron. If King wrote his soon-to-be-famous letter physically imprisoned, Baldwin wrote metaphorically as a prisoner in America, as a slave in all but name, psychologically shackled. He asserted that, whether born in Harlem like himself or in middle-class digs like King, the Negro was born into a mental ghetto from which he must break free.

To endure their psychic imprisonment African Americans had to toughen themselves, build up self-worth, and through religion find compassion to care for their own people and even for the oppressors, whose sin of racism, he optimistically believed, came more from ignorance and delusion than willfulness. White people must drastically change their ways, however, to forestall the racial Armageddon. In return for black forbearance, they must overturn their own identity in order to be able to relate to blacks as children of God. To see blacks differently, they must see themselves anew—as spiritually sick souls locked in their own psycho-spiritual prison, enslaved inside their debilitating myth of superiority (and terror of inferiority) that was ultimately as dehumanizing for themselves as for the oppressed.[33]

The white man, Baldwin wrote, is "in sore need of new standards, which will release him from his confusion and place him once again in fruitful communion with the depths of his own being." Why would blacks, or whites, want to be integrated into a burning house? White people could not be free themselves without helping to free the Other.

Despite Baldwin's tone of imminent doom, this work, as much as King's letter, was a veiled gift to the white world—if only it would be heard as such. But Baldwin's message was misunderstood by many white (and black) Americans. He was far from advocating the extreme of revolutionary violence if whites did not come to their senses. He like King was ardently trying to avoid black vengeance. With his passionate prose he too was calling for creative extremists to seize the center ground, spread it in all directions, and forestall the catastrophic extremism of either passivity or nihilism.

"Everything now, we must assume, is in our hands," he concluded. "If we—and now I mean the relatively conscious whites and the relatively conscious blacks, who must, like lovers, insist on, or create, the consciousness of the others—do not falter in our duty now, we may be able, handful that we are, to end the racial nightmare." If they did not dare, black and white together, Noah's prophecy would be fulfilled: in the words of a slave spiritual, "No more water, the fire next time!"[34]

4

While feverishly revising his prison letter, King was reading another black manifesto published sixty years before, *The Souls of Black Folk,* by W. E. B. Du Bois. The work foreshadowed Baldwin's apocalyptic black self-exploration and shared with both Baldwin and King's letter a tone of subdued outrage and reasoned passion. When King, Abernathy, and the other protesters were brought in for arraignment on Monday morning, the two leaders complained about their hard, bare beds and cold nights without covers. King, who had been fasting, was tired, weak, and grumpy. Later back in his cell King met with his attorney, Clarence Jones, who "lifted a thousand pounds from my heart" with word that King's close friend Harry Belafonte had raised fifty thousand dollars for protesters' bail money, which redeemed his decision to go to jail.[35]

Chained to three kids and a newborn, Coretta King in Atlanta was distressed that she had not heard from her husband, who always called from jail right away. Bull Connor had forbidden him a call to his wife or to anyone else. On Sunday—the first Easter she had not gone to church—she tried calling President Kennedy in Palm Beach, Florida. He owed her: his helpful phone call to her in October 1960 had probably won him the election. She couldn't reach the President, but the attorney general returned her call with reassurance. Robert Kennedy had been called by Belafonte, urging him to improve King's condition.

"Tell Reverend King we're doing all we can," he had told the singer, joking that "I'm not sure we can get into prison reform at this moment."[36]

When the President called Coretta back on Monday afternoon her two-year-old son, Dexter, picked up the phone. The leader of the free world had to break through a riff of baby talk to reach the movement's first lady. In his warm brogue JFK asked about her children and new baby and said that he had sent FBI agents to investigate her husband's plight; if he did so, no agents talked to the prisoner. He said that her husband would be phoning shortly. She got the call a few minutes later. Martin King was surprised when she excitedly told him of Kennedy's call. He urged her to get maximum media mileage from the White House intervention. Whatever Kennedy or his younger brother had done, King's and Abernathy's conditions had suddenly gotten better: mattresses, pillows, blankets, and now a phone call, with guards eavesdropping.

When King and Abernathy were released after eight days, they discovered that their jailing had not hot-wired the movement as they had hoped. It seemed to be running out of juice. After only three weeks people were weary. A young Mississippi native who had driven over from his home state on Good Friday almost single-handedly breathed new life into the withering crusade. King had urged him to come when he was about to get arrested.

"You can put me in jail," Rev. James Bevel roused Good Friday's mass meeting, "but you can't stop us. When the Holy Ghost gets to a man, nothing can stop him." He cajoled the teenagers to join in. "Some of these students say they have got to go to school, but they will get more education in five days in the city jail than they will get in five months in a segregated school."[37] A recent convert from SNCC to SCLC, now heading up the latter's limited Mississippi operations, Bevel arrived in Birmingham just as the Greenwood voter registration offensive had stalled. The Greenwood campaign in the Delta had been getting the kind of attention from the Kennedy brothers and the media that King had wished on Birmingham, after SNCC activist Jimmy Travis got shot, the SNCC office was burned out, and Bob Moses and several others were jailed for constitutionally protected activities. But the Justice Department pulled out at the pivotal moment, leaving SNCC in the lurch. Some SNCC people blamed King for diverting attention to Birmingham, where Project Confrontation was feeling its way.

Bevel, twenty-six, with shaved head topped by skullcap—his beloved father claimed Jewish blood (and changed his surname to a Hebrew word associated with God)—was already well tested in movement risk taking. Kidnapped from the Delta by his mother after she divorced his father, he spent his teenage years in Cleveland, then served a short stint in the navy until a black ship's cook with a Ph.D. gave him Tolstoy's *Kingdom of God Is Within You;* he could no longer serve in the military. Returning to Cleveland, he made good money as a steelworker, sang rhythm-and-blues at night, and was about to sign a recording contract when his godmother insisted he go to church with her. On that Sunday morning, hearing God's voice in the reading of Isaiah, he felt a divine call. Shortly he arrived at the black Baptist seminary in Nashville.

Although he was friends with John Lewis and other movement firebrands in Nashville, he spurned the workshops on nonviolent resistance taught by Rev. James Lawson, because the redemption he thirsted for was personal, not political. But Lawson reminded him of his father, who walked what Jesus taught, and he could not keep away. When the Nashville lunch-counter sit-ins erupted in early 1960 he was an eager recruit. Next spring when Nashville movement leader Diane Nash called for SNCC people to take over the freedom ride in Birmingham, Bevel joined up and found himself back in Mississippi, spending several weeks in Parchman pen. His glorious tenor kept his brothers' spirits up while infuriating the jailers. Although he and Nash, light-skinned, straitlaced Catholic beauty queen turned superwoman activist, were human opposites, she accepted his plea of marriage, despite his notoriety in the movement as a proud womanizer.

While King was in jail in Birmingham, Bevel was exhorting the faithful with his frenzied preaching at nightly mass meetings. He tangled with the authoritarian Walker, who had a penchant for antagonizing the young militants. Walker demanded that King fire him. "I can take orders from you," Bevel implored King, "but Wyatt is just an unprincipled motherfucker."[38] Both entranced and intimidated by him, King refused to let him go, especially since Bevel was his vital link with SNCC and younger activists. Although he had little of King's highfalutin religious training—he was the kind of hootin' and hollerin' country preacher that King had scorned—some considered the man they nicknamed the "Prophet" at least De Lawd's equal as a preacher. After getting out of jail King had to push to keep from getting upstaged.

"I would rather stay in jail the rest of my days," King enthralled a mass meeting, "than make a butchery of my conscience." This man who hated jail yelled out, "I will die there if necessary."[39] The preaching and the unearthly singing by the ACMHR gospel choir, making Birmingham's night music as thrilling as Albany's, conjured the illusion of a thriving mass movement.

But the gaggle of reporters and TV cameras were leaving town. Birmingham had fast become old news. If something was not done to dazzle them, the movement would fade as it had in Greenwood and Albany. Bevel was eager to deploy an unconventional weapon, but his superiors held him back. He wanted to unleash the power of teenagers and preteens whose explosive energy was bottled up in segregated schools. To this point most of those arrested had been adults, trained in the movement's nonviolent workshops led by Dorothy Cotton and others. King's marathon meetings in March had barely won the verbal backing of a majority of the city's black leaders. King knew that using children might undo that fragile support, as well as bring criticism from important white allies, especially in Washington. Racked with doubts, spending hours closeted in his motel suite, he was unable to make up his mind.

Assuming King's approval, Bevel and the kids' army did not wait for a final go-ahead from the Gaston Motel command center. D-Day had been set for Thursday, May 2. Bevel, Cotton, Andrew Young, and other SCLC organizers had spent the week proselytizing high school students by importuning athletic stars, prom queens, and student leaders to mobilize their own followers. On D-Day morning over a thousand youngsters, many in elementary school, high-fived over the school gates that their principals had locked to keep them inside and rushed into Sixteenth Street Baptist Church for quick schooling in nonviolent revolution.

After lunch, they streamed out of the church in orderly fashion, two by two, to march downtown to city hall. As they sang "We want our freedom!" Connor's police halted the rhythmic dancelike flow and escorted them into paddy wagons until filled up and then into commandeered school buses. Several hundred boys packed the city jail; several hundred girls were penned up at the state fairgrounds. There was something about the steely, purposeful dignity of those confident marching schoolchildren, an epiphany captured in film footage, that made them invincible. They had turned the corner. From this afternoon on, victory was palpable.

Betraying his reputation, for a trying month Connor had been copying the restraint of Albany's police chief, Pritchett, whom he had hired as a consultant. It had worked thus far. Minimal police violence had dammed the movement's flow. But D-Day got him stuck. The movement finally was filling the jails. The city was incapable of holding more prisoners; the courts were paralyzed. He could no longer afford to arrest protesters. He would have to stop them. Snarling dogs had made an appearance as a scare tactic. Something more punishing was imperative.

King and other SCLC doubters were relieved by the day's success. At that night's exultant mass meeting he christened the following day "Double D-Day." On Friday morning an even larger army of schoolkids vaulted from their school yards and packed the Baptist church for classes that ennobled them. With jittery excitement they playacted confrontations with police and angry bystanders that would soon be real life. Hormones popping, they readied for battle. When the kids in formation poured out of every orifice of the church heading toward the white downtown, Connor was ready: he had positioned a phalanx of firemen with high-powered fire hoses whose blasts of one hundred pounds per square inch could rip bark off trees. Fired from tripod-mounted nozzles that resembled Gatling guns, the ferocious water cannons hurled the kids against trees, walls, and pavement. Kids on the periphery were attacked by German shepherds lunging at their limbs. Girls wearing cotton skirts were most vulnerable.

The sight and sound of this water massacre—tiny girls screaming, shirts torn off boys, soaked children piled on each other—left an indelible memory on millions of television viewers, including this writer. I watched it on Dave Garroway's *Today* show on NBC before going to my western Massachusetts high school, where soon I formed a civil rights committee. This was as much a historic day for television as for the nation. During the freedom rides and Albany movement SCLC had awakened to the power of television. They had carefully planned to make Birmingham a media spectacle to dominate the networks' daily quarter hour of national news. Up to this day Connor's unexpected kid-gloves approach had sabotaged their hopes. Now Connor was revealing his true colors. Television that had first shown its pizzazz with Elvis Presley in 1956 and its ability to anoint presidents with the 1960 Kennedy-Nixon debates now showed its power to make history in the streets. May 3, 1963, was the birth of the television age. Not even President Kennedy would outdo Martin King's mastery of the medium, reaching its peak in Selma two years later.

Bruised and battered kids who could still walk, and legions of fresh troops—their sisters, brothers, pals—returned to the streets on Saturday. Over two hundred were arrested. Teenagers around the edges who had not been trained nor had pledged to obey the "ten commandments" nonviolent code fought back with rocks and bottles. Grabbing a police megaphone, Bevel on his own called off the protest and declared a weekend truce, to Walker's chagrin, for fear of rioting. Only nonviolent purists like Bevel and King minded the melee. Walker was thrilled that untrained youth were joining the protests. He noticed that press counts of protesters did not distinguish between the schooled and unschooled; thus numbers were inflated. He and other staff wondered if mass action would be more effective if strictly controlled—or allowed to be fluid in the margins.

Then came miracle Sunday. King and Abernathy were away, preaching at their home churches in Atlanta, where the former was praised as "Moses on earth." In the afternoon a thousand well-dressed adults gathered for a prayer service at New Pilgrim Baptist Church. A woman got up and testified that she and other mothers ought not to be afraid to let their kids go to jail. "Jail be the only thang leff t'do," she called out, "an ain't a disgrace lahk Ah always bin taught, no *suh. (Praise the Lord!)* It's a *honuh* t'go t'jail in the footsteps of ow-uh great leaduh, Dr. Mawtin Luthuh King!"[40] White troubadours Guy and Candie Carawan from Highlander Folk School were arrested at the church door for violating Jim Crow religion, while darker-skinned Joan Baez was seduced by soul music inside before being spirited away to perform at all-black Miles College. Preacher Bevel revved up the fellowship's anger at the Carawans' arrest.

"We're tired of this mess!" He broke the truce he had imposed. "Let's not march," he yelled, "let's walk."[41] They were determined to hold a prayer vigil at Southside jail, come what may.

Outside New Pilgrim the gathering doubled in size to two or three thousand, the largest march yet; mainly grown-ups in dark suits and bright dresses. In a few blocks, singing fervently "I Want Jesus to Walk with Me," they ran into a blockade of police and fire engines two blocks from the jail. For a minute Bevel thought the mounted fire hoses were machine guns. Since Walker could not stop the march, he had picked its leader, Rev. Charles Billups, an evangelist preacher and Shuttlesworth's longtime coworker. Up against the fire-engine barricade, water guns with bulging hoses poised to shoot, Billups knelt to pray, as did the serpentine procession behind him. He let loose his lungs.

"We're not turning back," he shouted. "All we want is our freedom. How do you feel doing these things?" Then in a mellifluous chant, tears flowing down his cheeks, he cried, "Turn on your water! Turn loose your dogs! We will stand here till we die." The huge chorus behind him echoed his words, all staring at the firemen and cops. Connor swiftly ordered his firefighters to open fire. They were still, as if in a spell.

"Dammit!" he bellowed. "Turn on the hoses!" A fireman was heard to say, "We're here to put out fires, not people."[42] A few firemen cried. They ignored Connor's frantic screams, their long hoses like sagging phalluses. They stepped aside as the marchers stood up and slowly walked by.

When Billups—a shipwreck survivor of World War II, shrapnel in his head from Korea—had joined Shuttlesworth's movement years before, he had confessed that he was "living on borrowed time," with "nothing to go for but life." In 1960 the Klan abducted him, tied him to a tree, beat him senseless with chains, and branded his belly with "KKK" while commanding, "Nigger, stop that praying." Billups felt more sorry for them than for himself. When one of his assailants later showed up at his home offering to turn himself in, the young preacher prayed with him instead.[43]

"You would have to say that the hand of God moved in that demonstration," New Pilgrim's pastor observed of miracle Sunday.[44] He believed that the protesters' spiritual delirium must have infected the firemen. King, who had missed this emotional and spiritual apex of the campaign, recalled nonetheless: "I saw there, I felt there, for the first time, the pride and the *power* of nonviolence."[45]

D-Day, Double D-Day, and the weekend marches had gotten Washington's attention. With the President keeping watch on the fast-breaking events, his brother sent assistant attorneys general Burke Marshall and Joe Dolan to push the stalled negotiations with business leaders. Communication was complicated by the businessmen's refusal to talk directly with black leaders, especially with outsider King, and by the downtown merchants' need to get approval for even cosmetic changes from the "Big Mules," the bankers and industrialists who really ran the city.

Moreover, SCLC had underestimated the intransigence of the business leaders. They might have had different priorities than Bull Connor, but they were less willing to jettison Jim Crow than was the Montgomery bus company in 1956. The store owners might have buckled sooner had it not been for the industrialists' dependence on segregation to keep the work force divided, and for fear of retribution by Connor and the Klan. Even black heavyweights like Gaston were slow to move—until Gaston looked out his office window and saw below a tiny girl get horsewhipped by water. With the help of the merchants' lawyer, David Vann, Marshall and Dolan shuttled between the Gaston Motel and the merchants and then made overtures to the Big Mules' Senior Citizens Committee.

Monday was the fourth day of massive young people's marches downtown as the protesters, many wearing raincoats, got acclimated to the water assaults; some found the spray refreshing in the ninety-degree heat. By that evening over twenty-five hundred people were incarcerated, most of them juveniles. The fairground 4-H dorms, which had always excluded black kids, now overflowed with boisterous black girl power.

Tuesday, May 7, was V-Day. Shuttlesworth, Bevel, and Cotton decided that this was the day for a midday show of force in the forbidden downtown. An hour earlier than police expected, squads of kids spun out of church doors and maneuvered cleverly into awed lunch-hour crowds, sitting down in restaurants and wandering through department stores. As only serendipity might permit, the merchants, making scant progress toward a settlement, broke for lunch at the height of the downtown hullabaloo. The Negroes had taken over their downtown. When a store owner found a black teenager sprawled out on the floor of his men's department chanting "Freedom!" he decided it was time to settle. When the shaken merchants regathered after their badly digested luncheon, they agreed on terms to put before the Big Mules, who had also been sobered by the downtown revolt.

The lunchtime foray was so successful that the leaders decided on a sequel in midafternoon. This time, however, the burgeoning crowds around the fringes let loose at the cops with rocks and bricks. It was one thing to have a little violence at the edges that could draw more TV cameras. It was a different matter when the newspaper of record, the *New York Times,* named it a riot. Though small and short by later standards, it was the first urban riot of a decade that would see hundreds more.

By late afternoon protest leaders managed to calm things down and pull their troops from the tempest. Remarkably, no one was killed. The five-week campaign had suffered lacerations and broken bones but no deaths. The day's heaviest casualty was Shuttlesworth. He was assaulted by a water gun outside Sixteenth Street Baptist Church, smashing him down a stairwell, breaking his ribs, nearly knocking him out. When Connor heard that he had been taken away in an ambulance he told reporters he wished he had been taken in a hearse.

Meanwhile SNCC leader Jim Forman, excited by the children's crusade but dismayed that little kids were deliberately put in harm's way, dropped in on King at the Gaston Motel. He was mortified to find this man of the people eating room-service steak in silk pajamas while children were doing battle in his name. Robert Kennedy and Malcolm X had found rare concord in likewise condemning the abuse of children. Kennedy said that "an injured, maimed or dead child is a price that none of us can afford to pay." The Nation of Islam minister was cutting: "Real men don't put their children on the firing line."[46]

The daily escalating street protests climaxing in the nonviolent takeover of downtown and the violent spasm of unaffiliated youth brought tentative agreement by the merchants and the Mules to desegregate the large stores' lunch counters, rest rooms, and clerk jobs with all deliberate speed, and to form a biracial committee to plan subsequent integration of schools, parks, and police. Key provisions remained to be worked out; it was not a done deal. With all of his rhetorical promises King was reluctant to settle for less than freedom *now,* but Burke Marshall's steady pressure made him cave in. Marshall had arranged a presidential press conference to announce the anticipated breakthrough—but they still faced a big hurdle.

In a low ebb for King's professed concern with pastoral care or simple compassion, neither he nor Abernathy had taken a moment to phone hospitalized Shuttlesworth, in great physical pain, much less pay a visit. This stung him. Well before the fire-hose blast that felled him Shuttlesworth, like SNCC activists in Albany, had felt rolled over by the SCLC juggernaut—even though he had beseeched them to come and admired King. Now, rather than come to his bedside with the sketchy agreement, which supposedly required his OK, they asked the heavily sedated patient to drive to a meeting across town at "Dynamite Hill," perhaps hoping he wouldn't show. At first King kept his back to him. No one would tell him what was up.

"Fred, we have decided to call off the demonstrations."

Shuttlesworth, woozy from painkillers, couldn't believe his ringing ears. "Say that again, Martin? Did I hear you right?" King repeated his words.

"Well, Martin, *who* decided?"

"We just decided that we can't have negotiations with all this going on."

"Well, Martin, it's hard for me to see how anybody could decide that without me. Hell no, we're not calling anything off."

"Well, uh—"

"Martin, you know what they said in Albany. You get things stirred up and then you pull out and leave the community with sickness and death and lost jobs. But I've been here. People have been hurt, and I've been here to help heal. That's why I'm respected in Birmingham. People trust me, and I have the responsibility after SCLC is gone, and I'm telling you it will not be called off. You and I promised that we would not stop demonstrating until we had the victory."

His rage rose. "You've been Mr. Big, Martin," he burst out, "but you'll be Mr. Shit if you pull out now! You'll be a nobody. If you want to call it off, you call it off, but I'm marching."

Marshall jumped in. "What about the press conference by the President? I made promises."

"Burke," he replied to the assistant attorney general for civil rights, "who gave you the authority to make promises to anybody?"

As Shuttlesworth hobbled to the door King said, "We got to have unity, Burke. We've just got to have unity. People have suffered. People will suffer."[47] His face was anguish. Shuttlesworth stormed out, his wife, Ruby, propping him up.

By next day he had calmed some but was still fuming that his friend Martin had double-crossed him. He could not abide ending the protests that he had staked his life on until a fair agreement was signed, sealed, and delivered. After all, the bus boycott was not called off even when the highest court of the land ratified its victory; they waited several weeks for the order to take effect. From Shuttlesworth's standpoint the proposed settlement was more P.R. than real: he had tasted the worth of white promises the past fall. Moreover, the young masses were eager to keep marching and cheered his reluctance, holding him to a higher standard than the usual compromise of half a loaf.

Shuttlesworth was heading out of the Gaston Motel to lead a march downtown when Andrew Young physically blocked him, ready to tackle him despite his injuries. "I was prepared to do whatever I had to do to keep him from going out that door and embarrassing Martin Luther King in front of the whole world." Dolan managed to get his boss, RFK, on the phone: "Reverend Shuttlesworth, the attorney general would like to speak with you." Kennedy reassured him that the settlement was sound.

The phone call, Young recalled, "saved me from punching him out."[48] Behind closed doors SCLC leaders' behavior did not always adhere to the nonviolent discipline imposed on their young followers in the streets. Shuttlesworth blamed suave Young, SCLC's lead negotiator, more than anyone for pulling wool over their eyes.

At separate but equal press conferences on Friday the two sides announced the agreement for phased desegregating of department stores and a biracial committee to oversee further desegregation. Despite its delayed timetable, the larger black community embraced the agreement with relief. Connor, whose incumbent city commission had refused to hand over power to the new mayor, giving the city rival regimes, publicly repudiated the pact. While white moderates backed it as the best they could get, supremacists were livid.

At a raucous Klan rally that night Grand Dragon Robert Shelton bitterly declared, "Martin Luther King's epitaph can be written here in Birmingham."[49] Later that night a powerful bomb with Klan signature obliterated Room 30 of the Gaston Hotel. King had checked out earlier that day, turning the room over to an aide, Joe Lowery, out celebrating. No one was hurt. Minutes before, a bomb had wrecked the home of King's younger brother, Rev. A. D. King, a protest leader. In response to the bombings blacks not part of the movement rose up in a true riot, torching several buildings downtown. The insurrection was worsened by the highway patrol battalion sent in by Governor Wallace, which made Connor's tactics seem timid: a preview of Selma's "Bloody Sunday" two years hence. Many blacks were injured, but incredibly, none were killed. The President deployed eighteen thousand troops, the first time in the postwar era that the military intervened to suppress disorder rather than enforce a court decree.

When Connor failed to hold the line against mongrelization, Bombingham had returned to business as usual. But change had come that could not be turned back. The city's despised black children had brought deliverance.

In retrospect, Young called King's bold decision to get arrested on Good Friday—popular only with Shuttlesworth and his own Christian soldiers—"the beginning of his true leadership."[50] He had done a remarkable job winning tepid support from moderate black leaders, even ones like the *Birmingham World*'s Emory Jackson, who had been so opposed as to editorialize that the protests were "wasteful and worthless."[51]

Although he handled Shuttlesworth poorly, he had kept feuding among subleaders, especially Walker and Bevel, from spilling into the public eye. He had performed masterfully as the symbolic focus of the campaign, until being overshadowed by the army of no-nonsense kids.

But time and again he had equivocated, delayed, refused to decide. If left to his discretion the children's crusade might never have materialized—and the Birmingham campaign, such a close thing, would almost surely have failed. In that case it was doubtful that King could have regained the prestige and moral authority he had lost after Albany. As Shuttlesworth had warned, Mr. Big would be Mr. Shit, or Mr. Nothing.

King had a lot to celebrate besides having left town hours before his motel room was blown up. His leadership of the Negro Revolution hung by a thread of his garment of destiny. Had his moment to shine come and gone? Would he forever be living in the long shadow cast by the Montgomery mass miracle?

During all the low days after Albany he had not often doubted that the Spirit still stood with him, that their covenant had not been broken, that he was called by God to lead his people to a second fuller emancipation. Although—despite his rational mind-set—he never looked hard for proof, he nonetheless appreciated signs and portents. These had been bountiful in Montgomery; they had helped to sustain his and the movement's ebullient energy.

Whatever his disappointments with Birmingham, with his own failures of leadership there, his temporizing, indecision, and paralysis of nerve, the epic spectacle—and the media's superlative spin on it—reaffirmed his faith in his personal mission, his worth to his God, his trust in having been anointed. It eased his mind to be facing certain death when he felt exalted, his feet firmly planted on a divine path. It was this spiritual release that energized him to write the prison epistle that would justify the civil rights struggle for posterity, as Lincoln's Gettysburg Address had etched the meaning of the first Civil War. But his sudden catapulting to "man of the year" (as *Time* would anoint him on its cover), with all of the hoopla of fame surrounding his elevated status, made him more conscious than ever of two Martin Kings at war, the exalted and the earthbound, sinful self.

If King did not expect his redemption in Birmingham and did not quite trust it, he and his colleagues had expected even less to discover in the steel city the holy grail, the elixir they had been seeking. In Montgomery King and the MIA had nearly perfected the boycott as a form of nonviolent mass action. But despite hundreds of exemplary group actions since, especially lunch-counter sit-ins and freedom rides, the American movement had not come close to approximating the large-scale direct action led by Gandhi in India.

Now, thanks to Bevel's zeal to unleash kid power, the desperation that allowed such an outlandish tactic, and most of all the brave beauty of the boys and girls, SCLC leaders had discovered the irresistible power of *mass* nonviolent action. It was not only its magnitude that stunned them. It was the complex catalytic role of violence. They had planned carefully for a violent response by Connor's cops, vexed when it took a month to bring it out. But they were taken aback by the dynamic supporting role played by uneducated, lower-class black youth with little to lose who joined the demonstrations spontaneously. The astounding impact of the disciplined children's marches, and of the telegenic fire spray and canine corps, was not devalued by their realization that the school dropouts and jobless youth who threw rocks and bottles, provoking even crueler police reprisal, proved indispensable to their victory.

Bevel, Cotton, and other street leaders mustered all their skill to stop the unplanned violence, believing it hurt their cause as well as their principles. SCLC repudiated it. Yet it was the disciplined mass marches combined with the parasitic fringe violence—the latter spilling into full-scale rioting—that brought the Big Mules to their knees. In the United States, the hidden power of Gandhian-style mass action would be the ever-present threat that police violence would beget people's violence into an escalating spiral of chaos. The ugliness of white supremacy forced into the light was not only the brutality of its perpetrators, but the pain of its hardest-pressed victims primed for release.

5

_____

Robert Kennedy saw in the Birmingham violence the specter of the urban underclass in revolt. He worried that it might spread to big cities in the North. He invited James Baldwin for a breakfast discussion at his Hickory Hill estate in Virginia, then asked the writer to assemble a small group of knowledgeable people to meet with him in New York. Among those who showed up at Kennedy's opulent Central Park West apartment in late May were singers Harry Belafonte and Lena Horne, playwright Lorraine Hansberry, and social psychologist Kenneth Clark, whose experiments with white and black dolls had undergirded the 1954 _Brown_ decision. To give the attorney general a taste of Jim Crow justice, Baldwin invited Louisiana CORE activist and freedom rider Jerome Smith, who had been jailed and beaten numerous times; he was getting medical treatment in New York for his battle wounds.

Smith set the tone for the evening by saying that meeting with Kennedy in his lap of luxury made him feel like throwing up. The attorney general had been upbraided by freedom riders the year before when SNCC's Charles Sherrod accused him of bribing the movement with voter registration funds (to move away from direct action), but Smith made Sherrod's barrage look tame. With volcanic black anger that Kennedy had never before witnessed—but that would unnerve many well-meaning whites in years to come—Smith recounted his experience in the Deep South. Kennedy turned to the more respectable

Negroes, but Horne replied, "You've got a great many very, very accomplished people in this room, Mr. Attorney General. But the only man who should be listened to is that man over there."

Smith confessed that he was questioning nonviolence. "When I pull the trigger," he said, "kiss it good-bye." Baldwin asked if he would fight for his country. "Never! Never! Never!" Kennedy, World War II vet and Cold War quarterback, was shocked.

"Bobby got redder and redder," Clark recalled, "and accused Jerome of treason. That made everybody move in to protect Jerome and to confirm his feelings. It became really an attack!"

"This boy," Horne said later, "just put it like it was. He communicated the plain, basic suffering of being a Negro. The primeval memory of everyone in that room went to work after that. He took us back to the common dirt of our existence and rubbed our noses in it." Tempers caught fire all around.

Hansberry, creator of the racial drama *A Raisin in the Sun*, admonished Kennedy: "Look, if *you* can't understand what this young man is saying, then we are without any hope at all because you and your brother are representatives of the best that white America can offer. If *you* are insensitive to this, then there's no alternative except our going into the streets, and chaos." Sounding like Baldwin in his new book, she said that whites were castrating blacks, and warned vaguely of Negroes in the street getting guns and killing white people.

The combat raged for three hours. Clark called it "one of the most violent, emotional verbal assaults that I had ever witnessed, the most intense, traumatic meeting in which I've ever taken part." Kennedy, hoping for constructive brainstorming, not destructive emotions, recalled that "they seemed possessed. They reacted as a unit. It was impossible to make contact with any of them. You can't talk to them the way you can talk to Martin Luther King or Roy Wilkins. It was all emotion, hysteria—they stood up and orated—they cursed—some of them wept and left the room."

His friend and biographer Arthur Schlesinger Jr. concluded that "he began, I believe, to grasp as from the inside the nature of black anguish. He resented the experience, but it pierced him all the same. His tormentors made no sense; but in a way they made all sense."[52] Kennedy brooded about the battle but let its meaning sink in. He began to understand why they could not wait.

Marshall and Dolan returned from the Birmingham battlefield with a new mission. The experience had convinced them that there would be many Birminghams in the months ahead, and that it would be impossible for the Justice Department to step in all over the South. Birmingham itself was a close call. On speaking tours King, Shuttlesworth, and others ratcheted up pressure on JFK to sign a second Emancipation Proclamation outlawing segregation. But the President had made it plain that executive action, such as the Birmingham intervention, would fall short of an executive *order*. Nor would the civil rights community have been satisfied with a milk-toast order like Kennedy's against housing discrimination. They felt that whatever Washington did had to be comprehensive, enforceable, irreversible. In the wake of Robert Kennedy's browbeating in Manhattan it did not take long for the attorney general and his deputies to decide that sweeping civil rights legislation was a must. RFK sensed too that the President's free-world leadership might depend on it.

On Memorial Day 1963 Vice President Lyndon Johnson, kept out of the loop on civil rights as on much else, delivered an uncharacteristically eloquent speech at Gettysburg.

"One hundred years ago, the slave was freed. One hundred years later, the Negro remains in bondage. The Negro today asks justice. We do not answer him—we do not answer those who lie beneath this soil—when we reply to the Negro by asking, 'Patience.' Our nation found its soul in honor on these fields of Gettysburg one hundred years ago. We must not lose that soul in dishonor now on the fields of hate."[53] LBJ was so charged up by his oration that he urged Kennedy to give a Gettysburg address of his own.

MADE FAMOUS AROUND THE GLOBE by TV, newspapers, and mass-market magazines, the electrifying Birmingham drama ignited a firestorm of largely nonviolent protest as spring turned to summer. Perhaps because there were so many protests so spread out, or because of the media's burnout after Birmingham, what King called the "Negro revolution of 1963" was poorly covered and thus underplayed. By the government's conservative data, during ten weeks through July, over 750 demonstrations occurred in 186 cities with 15,000 arrests. These were not only in southern hot spots like Jackson, Danville, Durham, and Orangeburg. Many protests, organized by CORE and allied groups, took place in northern and western cities. If the 1960 sit-ins launched the black student movement, CORE's civil disobedience in San Francisco, where hotels, restaurants, and car lots were forced to hire blacks, and in other cities and campus towns launched the white student movement, which focused on civil rights and liberties before turning to Vietnam in 1965.

Although Justice Department leaders had been born again to civil rights, White House political advisers—ever mindful of the 1960 squeaker—saw a Kennedy civil rights bill sinking his reelection. Then another media show in Alabama that absorbed the Justice Department finally pushed the President to rise above his traditional temporizing. Stung by the Birmingham sellout, cognizant that television was the culprit, Governor Wallace decided to stage a media spectacle of his own to block desegregation of the University of Alabama, still lily-white seven years after Autherine Lucy had been admitted, then kicked out after white rioting. As he had pledged, Wallace stood "in the schoolhouse door" on June 11 to symbolically bar Vivian Malone and James Hood from enrolling. But after JFK federalized the national guard he stepped aside to avoid arrest by U.S. marshals.

Just two days prior, another drama hidden from public view transpired in the hill country near the Mississippi Delta. Several rights workers, led by SCLC's Annell Ponder and ranging in age from forty-five-year-old Fannie Lou Hamer, from nearby Ruleville, to sixteen-year-old June Johnson from Greenwood, were returning by bus from an SCLC voter registration workshop in South Carolina. When the bus stopped in Winona on Sunday morning and they tried to have breakfast at the Jim Crow café, they were taken to jail. The bus driver, who had already harassed them, had called ahead. For hours they were tortured and sexually abused. The jailers stripped Johnson naked and beat her bloody. Hamer heard Ponder screaming, while praying God to have mercy on her captors. For refusing to call them "sir" they pulverized her face and she nearly lost an eye. They came for Hamer.

"You bitch, you," they yelled at her. "We gon' make you wish you was dead." The memory burned into her soul.

"The state highway patrolman came and carried me out of the cell into another cell where there were two Negro prisoners. The patrolman gave the first Negro a long blackjack that was heavy. It was loaded with something and they had me to lay down on the bunk with my face down, and I was beat. I was beat by the first Negro until he gave out. Then the patrolman ordered the other man to take the blackjack and he began to beat. That's when I started screaming." The patrolman lifted her dress and fondled her while she was being whipped. She could feel the cops' sadistic sexual gratification. After the beatings the jailer's wife and daughter, good Bible Belt Christians, surreptitiously brought them water. Hamer gave them Bible verses to contemplate.

The merciless beating blinded her in one eye, ruptured her kidneys, and crippled the polio survivor for life. Her battered face was unrecognizable for weeks. She overheard the jailers plotting to throw their bodies into the Big Black River. Quick action by SNCC and SCLC colleagues saved them—though SNCC's Lawrence Guyot was thrown in Winona jail himself, where the guards nearly burned off his penis. Several months later the torturers were brought to trial, but the white jury acquitted them.

Fired up by righteous anger, Hamer was out registering voters in the cotton fields as soon as she could walk, heedless of her limp. A year later she told her gruesome tale to a live national television audience.

In late May the White House refused King's request for a meeting with the President to talk about ending segregation. Kennedy stated to aides in a secretly recorded conversation that "King is so hot these days that it's like having Marx coming to the White House." He worried that if he proposed legislation, "it will look like he got me to do it."[54] On June 1 the attorney general convened an Oval Office meeting to decide whether to push the bill and what it would contain. He said he was dealing with thirty major protests that week. Backed by the vice president, who had never before been privy to civil rights policy, RFK persuaded his brother and doubting aides that the bill could not wait—regardless of his reelection or southern oligarchs on Capitol hill.

Ten days later, at the moment of Wallace's stand-down in Tuscaloosa, John Kennedy ordered his speechwriters to prepare an address to the American people that evening. Two days before, not knowing about the legislative breakthrough, King had criticized the President for his timidity. For once he might have wished he'd held his tongue.

JFK's hastily prepared speech—he fumbled with notes while facing the camera—was the most passionate presidential statement on race, from a man uncomfortable with both passion and race, since the Civil War president against whom he did not want to be measured.

We are confronted with a moral issue, he said, that "is as old as the Scriptures and is as clear as the American Constitution. We preach freedom around the world, and we mean it, and we cherish our freedom here at home, but are we to say to the world, and much more importantly, to each other that this is a land of the free except for the Negroes; that we have no second-class citizens except Negroes; that we have no class or caste system, no ghettos, no master race except with respect to Negroes?"

"Now the time has come for this nation to fulfill its promise. The events in Birmingham and elsewhere have so increased the cries for equality that no city or state or legislative body can prudently choose to ignore them." Who among us, he asked, would be "content with the counsels of patience and delay? One hundred years of delay have passed since President Lincoln freed the slaves, yet their heirs, their grandsons, are not fully free." Across the land, he said, "the fires of frustration and discord are busy in every city. Redress is sought in the street."[55]

With frank acknowledgment that he was responding to mass demands, he announced he was sending a measure to Congress that the White House had considered impossible just two months before: to banish segregation and discrimination in public accommodations. It would be the first meaningful civil rights legislation since Reconstruction.

Like most of the civil rights community King was happy with Kennedy's speech. Kennedy's chief adviser, Ted Sorensen, let it be known that his boss "was not averse to those who called his speech and bill 'the second Emancipation Proclamation.'"[56] King, who had been steering him in this direction ever since the unlikely pair had seen their reflections in Lincoln's proclamation two years before, would have concurred.

But black leaders' euphoria did not last the night. Minutes after the family of Medgar Evers in Jackson had cheered Kennedy's speech, the Mississippi NAACP leader, returning home after a long day shepherding the Jackson protests, was shot down in his driveway by a high-powered rifle. The President drew flak from southern whites when he ordered that the veteran of Europe's Normandy invasion be buried with full military honors at Arlington National Cemetery. It took four decades and three trials before Evers's assassin, Byron de la Beckwith, was finally convicted for murder. Beckwith had bragged to his Klan klavern that killing "the nigger" caused him no more grief than his wife felt in giving birth.

6

What the Kennedy administration was conspiring to forestall, King, his SCLC colleagues, and grassroots organizers were busily fomenting—a true nationwide mass movement not seen since the labor revolt of the 1930s. But the establishment civil rights leaders such as Roy Wilkins and Whitney Young and their white liberal allies worried that the civil rights revolution might get out of hand, as Birmingham and its sister protests warned. They felt it must be managed from above.

Shortly after Birmingham, multimillionaire philanthropist Stephen Currier funded the Council for United Civil Rights Leadership (CUCRL), a federation of the "Big Six" civil rights organizations (NAACP, Urban League, SCLC, CORE, SNCC, National Council of Negro Women). James Farmer of CORE discovered that "civil rights generalship was one-fourth leadership, one-fourth showmanship, one-fourth one-upsmanship, and one-fourth partnership." Though SNCC's Jim Forman disparaged it as mainly a fund-raising gimmick (with SNCC at the short end), CUCRL provided a forum to try to resolve intergroup gripes and to develop broader strategy. Division had surfaced about means and even ends. The elite council was often polarized between the bureaucratic inertia of Wilkins and Young, and Forman's and Farmer's impatient militancy. Caught in the middle, King's thoughtful, low-key presence served as a reconciling force between opposites.

To unify both the feuding leaders and the erupting masses, the next step seemed clear—to rev up the march on Washington that A. Philip Randolph and Bayard Rustin had been planning since March, at which time neither SCLC nor other civil rights groups showed interest. In late 1962 Randolph had proposed commemorating the centennial of emancipation with a mass protest in the capital drawing attention to black unemployment and poverty, issues virtually ignored by the mainstream movement. His threatened march on Washington by black workers in 1941 had forced President Roosevelt's executive order banning discrimination in war industry. When King got on board in May and dragged Wilkins and Young along, the price of their backing was to downplay economic issues and focus on passage of the civil rights bill that Birmingham had put on JFK's front burner. King wanted the protest "to unite in one luminous action all of the forces along the far-flung front," climaxing the "thundering events of the summer."

Randolph chose Bayard Rustin to direct the colossal organizing operation, overriding opposition from Wilkins and others concerned about Rustin's homosexuality and leftwing past. Trading on his vast Rolodex of contacts, Rustin rapidly pulled together a supercoalition of interracial civil rights, labor, and religious leaders, though he was unable to swing endorsement by George Meany's AFL-CIO. When civil rights leaders met with President Kennedy at the White House in late June, Randolph stood up to JFK's efforts to squelch the march because he feared disorder. A month later the President endorsed it.

On August 28, 1963, about three hundred thousand people arrived in Washington on twenty-two chartered trains, two thousand charter buses, thousands of car pools, and surged down the Mall. Moving from the Washington Monument toward the forty-year-old Lincoln Memorial, it was a symbolic march across history from the promises of the American Revolution to the unfinished business of the Civil War. The mass assembly was estimated to be about three-quarters black, one-quarter white and Latino. Many poor Negroes bused up from the Deep South. Large contingents represented religious faiths and labor unions. Haunting freedom songs by Odetta and Joan Baez and spirituals by Mahalia Jackson and Marian Anderson—back to the Memorial after a quarter century—blended with brief speeches by the civil rights generals. Although pressured by moderate leaders at the last minute to soften his words, SNCC's John Lewis pierced the optimistic mood with a candid speech that expressed reservations about Kennedy's legislation because it neglected police brutality and voting rights.

At the end of the long sun-baked afternoon King stood beneath the brooding stone face of Lincoln, a row of white-capped guards behind him. He waited for the cheers and chants to die down.

"I am happy to join with you today," he began, "in what will go down in history as the greatest demonstration for freedom in the history of our nation.

"Five score years ago, a great American, in whose symbolic shadow we stand today, signed the Emancipation Proclamation. This momentous decree came as a great beacon light of hope to millions of Negro slaves who had been seared in the flames of withering injustice. It came as a joyous daybreak to end the long night of their captivity.

"But one hundred years later, the Negro is still not free. One hundred years later, the life of the Negro is still sadly crippled by the manacles of segregation and the chains of discrimination. One hundred years later, the Negro lives on a lonely island of poverty in the midst of a vast ocean of material prosperity. One hundred years later, the Negro is still languishing in the corners of American society and finds himself in exile in his own land."

In this great sermon televised live, King did for the whole nation, indeed the globe, what the best of black preachers had long sought to do for their downcast flocks: to conjure the kingdom of God in their midst. But first he had to lead them out of slavery. He transported his listeners back to the now of 1863 and made them feel the hope of Lincoln's act of emancipation. Then he carried them a century into the future and made them feel the chains of slavery still suffocating its inheritors. He made slavery palpable in the eternal now. He painted in vivid strokes why "we can never be satisfied" with meager gains that perpetuated psychological enslavement. He showed how the "fierce urgency of now" required an end to gradualism.

Then just as surely as he pitched the present into the past and the past into the present, he flung the past-imbued present into the future—and pulled the future back into the present. He was shape-shifting time.

The sheer power of his entranced audience, and a nudge by Mahalia Jackson, inspired him to let go of his prepared text and grasp a phrase he had used before, recently in a big Detroit rally. The act of drawing his dream out of ether made it more tangible than words typed on paper. He was prophesying of the future, "one day," but the images spun by his spoken words made the invisible world visible, the Word flesh. If only for an instant, he was delivering Americans from the "warm threshold" on which they stood up into the "palace of justice," the eternal kingdom where all would break bread together at the table of brotherhood.

Although King made plain that only with faith would they be able to raise themselves into the kingdom of God, his words proclaimed that the kingdom was being lived on that very day by the people he was talking to. Below him along the reflecting pool, dipping their feet in water, and under the elms, seeking shade, were southerner and Yankee, black and white, Jew and gentile, Catholic and Protestant, women and men, old and young—sitting together, singing together, praying together, standing up for freedom together.

All that was left was for the prophet shaman to call the kingdom into being: "Let freedom ring." The future of racial justice had arrived, if fleetingly, on this hot August afternoon. "Thank God Almighty, we are free at last."[57]

None were more uplifted by the dream and the day's drama than the thousands of poor black people that SNCC had brought from the Deep South. "It helped them believe that they were not alone," a SNCC activist remarked, "that there really were people in the nation who cared what happened to them."[58] Yet some southern organizers had a hard time sharing De Lawd's dream. Sitting on the trampled grass, the young black activist Anne Moody of CORE told herself that back in Mississippi "we never had time to sleep, much less dream."[59] Abernathy wandered back to the Mall later that day and felt the holy spirit whistling through the leftover debris.

A WEEK LATER BIRMINGHAM fell into turmoil again. In fits and starts the new mayor, Albert Boutwell, and the biracial citizens committee had moved to implement the May agreement. Although the city council abrogated segregation laws, the merchants dragged their heels. Sitting together at lunch counters was bad enough, but the real threat of mongrelization was the commingling of black and white kids at school, where they could make friends. Spurred by the Klan, who bombed a black lawyer's home, whites rioted when a federal court ordered the admission of five black children to three white schools. Governor Wallace sent the Alabama National Guard to block desegregation. President Kennedy federalized the guard in order to pull them out. The kids enrolled in school.

On Saturday morning, September 14, "Dynamite Bob" Chambliss told his wife and niece that he had found the address of "the nigger girl that was going to integrate the school." His niece warned him to be careful. He boasted that he had enough "stuff put away to flatten half of Birmingham."

"What good do you think any of that would do?" his niece asked. He looked her straight in the eye.

"You just wait till after Sunday morning. They will beg us to let them segregate."[60]

Late that night Chambliss and three Klan colleagues stashed a powerful dynamite bomb in bushes outside Sixteenth Street Baptist Church, Birmingham's counterpart to middle-class Dexter in Montgomery. The church had been drawn reluctantly into the spring crusade by its new young pastor, John Cross. This bomb was unlike twenty others the Klan had set off in town, all unsolved crimes, since blowing up Shuttlesworth's home in December 1956. It had a delayed fuse and could be detonated remotely. At 10:22 A.M., with a roar heard all over the city, the bomb blasted a seven-foot-wide hole through the church basement's thick wall and decimated the women's lounge. The face of Jesus was blown out of a stained-glass window. Five girls had just finished their Sunday school class on "the love that forgives." They were in the lounge helping each other get dressed, all in white, to usher the youth day service. Addie Mae Collins, fourteen, was tying the sash of her friend Denise McNair, eleven. Carole Robertson and Cynthia Wesley, both fourteen, were fixing their hair.

After the explosion the smoke and rubble were so heavy that it took hard digging to reach the four blackened bodies buried on top of each other, one girl decapitated.

Their identities were revealed by shoes and rings. Addie Mae's younger sister Sarah barely survived the carnage.

With rioting breaking out, Rev. Cross stood on the church's front steps: "We should be forgiving as Christ was forgiving." He gave the megaphone to Rev. Billups: "Go home and pray for the men who did this evil deed," Billups told the angry crowd. "We must have love in our hearts for these men."[61]

One of the bombers, Bobby Cherry, surveyed the grisly scene and told a neighbor there would be more bombings. Apparently the Klan had not directly targeted the children, though black children were their worst enemy. By the hundreds they had streamed out of this devastated church in May to desegregate white Birmingham. Now in smaller numbers they were invading white schools.

The rest of Sunday, blacks seeking revenge fought street battles with police and Al Lingo's savage highway patrol. Cops killed a black man who was trying to get away. In another part of town a white teenager shot dead a thirteen-year-old black boy riding a bicycle. Black men patrolled their neighborhoods with shotguns. One of them, Rev. John Rice, was a high school guidance counselor who had urged students in the spring not to join the protests. But he had taken his eight-year-old daughter, Condoleezza, the future national security adviser, to witness them, and to accompany him as he aided his penned students at the fairgrounds. Four months later one of her schoolmates was killed in the church.

Martin King arrived Sunday night to a city about to implode.

"We feel that Birmingham is now in a state of civil disorder, an emergency situation," he told the press Monday morning. He called for the U.S. Army to take over the city. He wired the President that if he did not take drastic action, "we shall see the worst racial holocaust this nation has ever seen."[62] The White House demurred, disappointing King. As in many times past, black forbearance outpaced rage. Street violence diminished before it wrought civil war.

In his eulogy at the slain girls' funeral, King tried to do for their deaths what Lincoln had done a hundred years before in Gettysburg: transform gory suffering and dying into redemptive rebirth, a new birth of freedom. He had persuaded the parents of three girls to hold a combined funeral for the good of the movement.

The girls died nobly, he said. "They are the martyred heroines of a holy crusade for freedom and human dignity. So they have something to say to us in their death. They say to each of us, black and white alike"—here he was surely speaking to himself—"that we must substitute courage for caution.

"The innocent blood of these little girls may well serve as the redemptive force that will bring new light to this dark city. The spilt blood of these innocent girls may cause the whole citizenry of Birmingham to transform the negative extremes of a dark past into the positive extremes of a bright future."[63] His words soothed the girls' grief-stricken families and friends but, unlike on August 28, fell short of engendering new life in their midst, of delivering heaven to their hell.

SNCC's John Lewis shepherded car pools of Birmingham youngsters from the funeral to join a growing SNCC voting rights protest in Selma, an hour away, where three hundred were jailed that month.

7

His words over the girls' dead bodies did little to lift up King's own depressed spirit. The Birmingham triumph seemed more than ever like a media mirage. The glory of the August march seemed of a distant time and place, its meaning defiled by the slaughter of the four innocents.

As if to deny their paralysis the SCLC convention in Richmond spewed forth a babel of proposals for how to save the movement, and to save nonviolence, which some thought had been buried with the girls. Ideas ranged from protest campaigns in half a dozen cities, to a national economic boycott, to a massive return to Birmingham to hammer home the delayed desegregation. A renewed Birmingham thrust might include a march to Montgomery, part of a daring proposal by Diane Nash Bevel and her husband to shut down the Alabama capital with mass direct action and physically remove George Wallace from office. King had dismissed the Bevels' revolutionary script with a chuckle, but others thought it worth pursuing. After several days of heated talk leaders failed to agree on the next step, except for a boycott of Birmingham business and "selective buying" campaigns in other cities.

Rather than upbeat as before, King's presidential address as the convention closed was contrite, repentant, even despairing. "We knew, when we went into Birmingham," he said, "that this was the test, the acid test of whether the Negro Revolution would succeed. Today we are faced with the midnight of oppression which we had believed to be the dawn of redemption"—aggravated by the President's unwillingness to take action in the current Birmingham crisis. He admitted that his faith in the Kennedys had been naïve. "We are faced with an extreme situation, and therefore our remedies must be extreme." Yet he clung to his faith in nonviolence, telling the story of Lazarus and Dives, of Jesus loving his enemies, and of Lincoln explaining why he did not call the Confederates the enemy: "Do I not destroy my enemies when I make them my friends?"

Opening his heart to his coworkers, King avowed that his leadership was "standing still, doing nothing, going nowhere."[64] Never before had he made such a confession. It had been less than a month since he had delivered his effervescent dream on that warm afternoon. He had slid from the loftiest peak to the lowliest valley.

JUST AS KING was never able to savor the peaks in his life, at least not for long, so his rock-solid ego, self-esteem, and faith did not let his downtimes drown him. He brooded over his sins and those of the multitudes, he took refuge in partying and sexual excess (which the FBI began to record), but despite his depressed demeanor, during these years he never hit bottom and thus was always able to will himself back to impressive functionality.

Besides his faith, sense of calling, and emotional security, he found an additional tool to deal with adversity and crisis: his consciousness of inhabiting a divided world. Like many African Americans, but more self-consciously, he came to believe that the world, and each human soul, were divided into sacred and secular realms that flowed in and out of each other. For King, this fundamental duality of life infused every aspect of being.

When he had arrived at Boston University he discovered a name for this split but interwoven universe—dialectics—and a thinker who was its master: Hegel. But, reflecting Cartesian dualism, Hegel and his disciples, especially Karl Marx, grandly oversimplified the divided world and did not grasp how it was one, two, and many simultaneously, how in order to be united it had to be divided. While Hegel's own thinking was more complex than that of his interpreters, the basic Hegelian formula of thesis, antithesis, and synthesis was the gist of his legacy. Although King had applied this formula frequently in his preaching, writing, and leading, he understood there was more to it than met the eye.

So King synthesized everywhere—justice and love, militancy and moderation, persuasion and coercion, legal and extralegal, communism and democracy, individual and community; on Sunday mornings, heaven and hell, sin and salvation, good and evil, life and death. Whether or not he had read about it for the first time in Birmingham jail, he experienced acutely the divided self of black people that Du Bois rendered so tenderly in *The Souls of Black Folk*.

"It is a peculiar sensation," Du Bois wrote at the turn of the century, "this double-consciousness, this sense of always looking at one's self through the eyes of others. . . . One ever feels his twoness,—an American, a Negro; two souls, two thoughts, two unreconciled strivings; two warring ideals in one dark body, whose dogged strength alone keeps it from being torn asunder.

"The history of the American Negro is the history of this strife,— this longing to attain self-conscious manhood, to merge his double self into a better and truer self. In this merging he wishes neither of the other selves to be lost."

Many times in many idioms King had preached Du Bois's plea "to make it possible for a man to be both a Negro and an American, without being cursed and spit upon by his fellows, without having the doors of Opportunity closed roughly in his face."[65] After a long life of often bitter struggle, Du Bois had finally concluded that this was an impossibility in America. He renounced his citizenship and left his country for good. The great scholar activist died at ninety-five in Ghana, on the eve of the March on Washington.

King never gave up faith in America and its promise, although he came perilously close later on. He endured every day his anguished twoness but made it a tool of emancipation.

Whether African Americans' attunement to double consciousness resulted from resistance to white oppression or was rooted in African worldviews or both, King's basic philosophy of life was to deny dichotomies and to affirm the unity of opposites in every facet of experience. For him almost every dichotomy was a false dichotomy. As a Hegelian he believed that unity could be experienced *only* through conjoining opposites. But his perspective treated opposites not as nullifying but fulfilling each other, as ambiguously coexisting. It was most often a matter not of either/or, but of both/and, the simultaneous embracing of unresolvable opposites.[66] Synthesis was the lived experience of continuous creative tension in the relationship between opposites, a relationship whose conflict brought clarity and change.

ABRAHAM LINCOLN STOOD out as an oddity in American history in part because he shared the homespun dialectical thinking that was common to African Americans. This had much to do with his greatness. His genius was to master the ambiguity of holding two opposing "truths" in creative tension and charting a middle path to reconcile and transcend the two poles.

From October 1854 well into his presidency he asserted that slavery was an "unqualified," "monstrous" moral wrong, yet it could not simply be abolished. His middle path was rhetorically to condemn the evil—and to mean it—while practically tolerating it (even the draconian Fugitive Slave Law of 1850), opposing only its expansion. When war broke out, he presided over the most horrible warfare the world had yet seen, the most destructive war ever in the Americas. But unlike virtually all other Union voices including preachers', he did not solely blame the South and held all Americans responsible for slavery and its fruit of carnage. He declared, notably in his Second Inaugural Address, that God probably sided with the North, but that no one could be sure. Although God could be on only one side, the Lord was punishing both sides for their sins. Unlike Hebrew prophets to whom he was later compared, Lincoln did not aspire to speak for God, to pronounce God's will, but sought to clarify divine meaning.

He condemned slavery but did not condemn the white South, hating the sin but not the sinner. Yet while not hating or even blaming the Confederates, he was responsible for their mass destruction. At the same time as killing them by the hundreds of thousands he pardoned prisoners of war by the handful. He invoked moral absolutes, particularly in justifying his near dictatorial war powers, but he usually expressed his absolutes nonjudgmentally; and supremely in the Second Inaugural, with ambivalence and uncertainty. He somehow got away with being righteous ("the judgments of the Lord, are true and righteous altogether") without being self-righteous. While he called for "malice toward none, charity for all" and sincerely desired reconciliation, his soldiers were still slaughtering the bloom of southern youth.

As King's prison letter had done in proposing a moral equivalent of war, Lincoln shifted the moral landscape to pursue the middle path of nonjudgmental but total war, transforming what had been an extreme solution—pushed by hardly an abolitionist—into the moral center of American life. How many Americans today, outside the Deep South, would judge Lincoln's methods (even his authoritarian rule) extreme or radical? In full command of the battlefield of ambiguity, of incertitude, he redefined the drastic extreme of war as the moderate, the even-handed, the reasonable, the balancing of macro justice with micro compassion.

No better epitaph for Lincoln was composed than by Frederick Douglass:

"Viewed from the genuine abolition ground," he declared, "Mr. Lincoln seemed tardy, cold, dull, indifferent. But, measuring him by the sentiment of his country, the sentiment he was bound as a statesman to consult, he was swift, zealous, radical, and determined. Taking him all in all, measuring the tremendous magnitude of the work before him, considering the necessary means to ends, infinite wisdom has seldom sent any man into the world better fitted for his mission than Abraham Lincoln."[67]

How successful was Lincoln's stance of radical moderation? In the short run the nation was devastated by unprecedented casualties of war—not only lives and limbs lost, but homes and farms wrecked, psychological death on a colossal scale. Yet the Union was preserved, and slavery abolished. But slavery in another form—some felt more virulent—continued for another century. Despite Lincoln's prophetic words and deeds, his supremely bloody war against southern white supremacy had not attained justice for black people, and certainly not racial equality. Rather, it led to a century of white revenge and a tightened noose around black lives. Even if racial justice had been achieved—the way it looked for a few short years in early Reconstruction—King was convinced that justice without reconciliation was nearly worthless, sowing seeds of future hatred and hostility.

His storied humility not withstanding, King saw his own messianic mission, and that of his movement, as being to succeed where Lincoln failed, to fulfill the first and second American revolutions with a third one a century hence.

KING HAD FIRST PRACTICED radical moderation during the bus boycott. It was startlingly successful. Beginning with his address on December 5, 1955, he had heralded a means of struggle that combined the militant and the moderate, persuasion and coercion, passion and compassion. But, rhetoric to the contrary, moderation had had the upper hand. Initial demands were moderate, as was the tactic: refraining from riding a bus. Participants did not engage in civil disobedience, but rather civil obedience when they reported for arrest en masse. Even when the state court shut down the car pool in November 1956—an ideal opportunity to disobey the ruling and obey a higher law, that of the Supreme Court and the Constitution—they walked for the last five weeks. Through it all King was more concerned in practice with tempering militancy than firing it up. His greatest feat of leadership was keeping the protest nonviolent.

He witnessed true militancy for the first time in the freedom rides and then in the Albany movement. He wasn't sure he liked what he saw, especially lack of structure, control, order. He was awed—but how does one *lead* something so volatile and unpredictable? What should his role be? Out in front or pulling strings? As we have seen, Birmingham was intended to be a manageable alternative—as orderly as the bus boycott. Meticulous planning with unified control was expected to ensure a positive result. The initial lunch-counter sit-ins by Miles students would have won attention three years before, but in April 1963 they were old hat. There was no fire in the belly. Project Confrontation almost died stillborn.

King's true leadership might indeed have emerged when he gambled on going to jail on Good Friday. His prison epistle conveyed his Easter epiphany, thanks to the moderate clergy who attacked him, that he and his coworkers were extremists. They had no choice but to fulfill their God-given mission. His creative extremism of mass nonviolent action would be the middle path between the intolerable extremes of silence, from white and black, and nihilism. Who could have been more extreme than the shortsighted black preachers and businessmen on one side, or Bull Connor's forces of public safety on the other—in equal measure guardians of the unconscionable status quo?

The power of King's epistle came from the rawness of his conversion, in the bleak blackness of his dungeon, to nonviolent extremism. Yet it was one thing to articulate the word, his unique talent, another to make it flesh. Released from jail, he seemed to lose the flame of his captivity. One might suppose that the children's crusade would have been just the type of creative extremism he had called for from his dark cell. But in the comfort of his motel room he wavered and wobbled until the spirited youngsters were led by their feet, and perhaps a nudge from God.

In spite of himself and his old god caution, creative extremism won the day. Within months, in sharp relief to the riots that broke out in Birmingham and dozens of other cities, the once controversial children's marches appeared to many as a necessary and even restrained maneuver. Of course nothing makes radical look moderate like success and the passage of time—true of Lincoln in the Civil War and of the American Revolution. Without endorsing its tactics, the President himself lent his moral support to the Birmingham movement.

King's wielding of radical moderation underwent a metamorphosis between Montgomery and Birmingham. Still for him it was more radical in words, more moderate in deeds. Like Lincoln, he was moderate by temperament, a reluctant radical by the pull of his times and his conscience. Like Lincoln, he believed that real change would come only when public attitudes changed. He knew well, as he said many times, that a law would not get a white racist to like him, but it might keep the man from lynching him. Although laws were vital, moral suasion and education were ultimately more so, especially in the long run that King always kept an eye on (another dichotomy he tried to transcend). The radical edge of confrontation would trouble the conscience of the uncommitted or indifferent majority. But reassurance and lack of blaming and vengefulness, conveyed by rhetoric and behavior, would give the majority the safety it needed to accept a change in the rules, especially in the white South.

The March on Washington put forth this double message: The movement in its widening dimensions had the power to disrupt the nation's business as usual, and to give it a black eye in the rest of the world. But the national, mass-based movement was guided by wisdom, restraint, and goodwill. The march succeeded, Rustin commented, "because it was the product of sound political philosophy and intelligent, responsible strategy."[68] The march and what led up to it made it easier for the American people to accept the principles, if not the practice, espoused by the civil rights movement.

Then came the church bombing, and all bets were off from the movement's point of view. Within SCLC Diane Nash and Jim Bevel, backed by others, pushed King to launch a last-resort, all-out campaign to shut down Alabama government as long as blacks were locked out. Stung by defeat in the Delta, Bob Moses and SNCC were concocting a less confrontational but more dangerous plan to overthrow the Mississippi Democratic Party democratically.

Now that movement voices all around him were goading him to walk the talk of creative extremism, to practice what he had been preaching, King once again was immobilized. Although moving forward with Operation Breadbasket, its selective buying campaign (or boycott) to compel black hiring, SCLC found itself once more in the doldrums. The leaders discovered that nothing failed like success. Were the late fifties repeating themselves, when a glorious triumph stemmed by white terrorism brought the movement to a standstill? But autumn 1963 was a very different time. A people's army had been unleashed upon the land.

SOMETHING ELSE HAD CHANGED since the 1950s that hinted at a different political strategy to actualize the Negro revolution. Throughout American history, citizens had turned to direct action when governmental channels seemed closed. With the Civil War, government itself turned to direct action of the most horrific sort when its own checks and balances failed to halt the irrepressible conflict. Now by mid-1963 a dynamic liberal presidency seemed to have found its soul, black and other progressive voters were finding their voice, and meaningful legislation to remedy racial and economic injustice appeared within reach.

Rustin and Randolph believed that the March on Washington meant more than that the civil rights movement had come of age, had become the spunky center of American politics. The diverse, interracial, multi-class composition of the marchers signaled to them that blacks and whites, middle-class and working-class, could be brought together around a common program of economic reform. The march's little-noticed "ten demands" that Rustin announced to the assemblage included "a massive federal program to train and place all unemployed workers—Negro and white—in meaningful and dignified jobs at decent wages" and a ban on discrimination in employment and housing.[69]

These two men, democratic socialists for decades, considered racism inextricable from class oppression and had long called for black alliances with organized labor and other liberal forces. Could this be the moment for the first successful progressive interracial electoral coalition in American history? During the Populist movement of the 1890s and the New Deal "popular front" of the 1930s, blacks had played third fiddle. Now they might be equal partners. Since June 1963 progressives looked to a president who might carry the torch to make his reelection a mandate for social justice.

King was no stranger to democratic socialism. He was known to have had a "socialist orientation" as early as 1960. But he had higher priorities and more urgent claims on his attention, it didn't speak his prophetic language, and it was too sectarian for a leader who clung to unity. Rustin and Stanley Levison, his closest advisers, were pressing him to focus more on economic issues and the impoverishment of both blacks and whites that socialist Michael Harrington had recently exposed in his book *The Other America*, which awakened JFK to the problem.

Shortly after the Birmingham crusade, King was pushed in this direction by an unlikely player, Whitney Young of the mainstream National Urban League. Even before he assumed leadership of the Urban League in fall 1961, he had been framing a proposal for "compensatory" or "preferential treatment" for disadvantaged African Americans. After he won over his board of trustees, the league called in June 1963 for "an immediate, dramatic, and tangible domestic Marshall Plan," a "special effort"—which Young distinguished from special privileges—of massive compensatory action, over ten years, by government, business, and foundations, to improve employment, education, housing, and health for urban blacks.[70]

Speaking on NBC television three weeks later, King for the first time advocated a "concrete, practical preferential program" for African Americans. In St. Louis, right after he had eulogized the four Birmingham martyrs, he asserted: "It is now only normal and moral to atone for past injustices to Negroes with a crash program of special treatment."[71]

Was King's glimmer of hope that JFK's second term might be as progressive as FDR's first a victim of the Kennedy flash and polish that was so often belied by Kennedy realpolitik—an ethical contradiction King himself was guilty of? Was he being seduced by the specter of a new Kennedy emerging after Birmingham who was leaving behind the cautious Kennedy of the first two years? He later spoke of "two Kennedys," the second reborn during the Negro revolution of 1963.[72]

He had been more upset than he let on about the President's passivity in the wake of the Birmingham church bombing and the rioting that followed. His idealistic side hoped that Kennedy would seize Lincoln's mantle and finish the unfinished emancipation. His practical side, the side that identified with Kennedy's hesitancy, feared that he and the movement had pushed him to his limit. JFK's unwillingness to take further risks frustrated him.

It was worse than he realized. He had long suspected that the FBI was spying on him and blamed it on J. Edgar Hoover's racism. But the wiretapping of his home and office did not start till September 1963; the Kennedy brothers wanted it as much as the FBI boss. Shortly after the March on Washington, RFK approved Hoover's request for electronic surveillance. FBI informants had disclosed that two of King's most trusted aides, Jack O'Dell, a black SCLC organizer, and Stanley Levison (already being wiretapped), had been Communist Party activists. While it was not clear that Levison had ever been an actual CP member (he denied it), he had been a party fund-raiser and had managed CP business ventures. But he had fully cut his ties from the CP when he decided in early 1957 that King, not communism, was the answer to his social conscience. O'Dell had been a party operative more recently but had also cut his ties.[73]

Although the Kennedys did not believe that King himself was or ever had been a communist or sympathizer, the FBI had gathered more than enough secret evidence to make a strong case for one or the other. Hundreds of progressive activists, writers, artists, filmmakers, and scholars had been ruined by far weaker dossiers compiled by the FBI for McCarthyite congressional hearings. During a June 1963 meeting Kennedy had walked King out to the White House rose garden and leaned on him to fire O'Dell and break off all contact with Levison. King did dismiss O'Dell, but the Kennedys were chagrined to discover through subsequent spying that he had continued to confer with Levison, directly or indirectly. As a matter of principle as well as friendship, he refused to end his six-year relationship with his close confidant.

"I have to weigh other factors," he told another white friend, "before I can shun anybody like that. You see, I have a pastoral responsibility."[74] His commitment to nonviolent soul force required that he not break off a connection with anyone, certainly not with a devoted friend. This man who always feared being ostracized himself would not stoop so low as to ostracize somebody else. If he could keep lines of communication open with segregationists who hated him, he could do so with Levison, who loved him. On top of this he felt himself in a pastoral relationship with Levison (though the latter was Jewish), as he did with all of his close disciples.

But King, as he would freely admit to his friends, was no saint. The initial wiretap logs revealed that his overnight stays in various cities were not all business. Hoover was more agitated and obsessed by this charismatic black man's sexual adventurism than by his leftwing associations, though the two were blurred in the FBI czar's paranoid mind.

By late fall 1963, unbeknownst to the civil rights leader, the Kennedys were not feeling sanguine about a future partnership with him. The tenuous mutual trust built up by the March on Washington and King's deft containment of black rage was being washed away.

Whatever John Kennedy was thinking about King, and whatever JFK's promise for 1964 and beyond, mattered no longer after a high-powered bullet destroyed his brain on November 22. King was watching television at home in Atlanta when he heard the horrid news. He called to Coretta downstairs.

"Corrie, I just heard that President Kennedy has been shot—maybe killed." After learning that he was dead, they sat together in silent shock. Despite his disappointments, King had not only liked and admired Kennedy—who had called Coretta twice in crises—he felt linked to him as a flawed leader. He felt a peculiar bond of understanding and empathy with JFK's trials and tribulations. He felt that starting with the Ole Miss battle and the Cuban missile crisis of a year before, Kennedy "went through what Lincoln went through."[75] Now he realized that all three of them shared the same fate.

"This is what is going to happen to me," he said to Coretta. "I keep telling you, this is a sick society."[76]

He grieved not only about Kennedy's death but about its message that hate and violence were on the loose in America. Hurt that the bereaved family did not invite him to the funeral mass at National Cathedral, he flew to Washington nonetheless and stood alone unknown in the crowd, praying, as the black-shrouded, horse-drawn wagon clip-clopped past him.

On Thanksgiving eve the new president spoke to a joint session of Congress seeking to reassure the nation, especially African Americans, that he would stay the course.

"So let us here highly resolve," LBJ evoked Lincoln at Gettysburg, "that John Fitzgerald Kennedy did not live—or die—in vain."

8

On the Sunday after Thanksgiving, nine days after Kennedy's killing, the Nation of Islam's newly promoted "national minister" spoke at a Nation rally in New York City, where he headed the big Harlem mosque. The title of Malcolm's address, "God's Judgment of White America," foreshadowed its unanticipated bombshell. It was about "divine justice" and "how the hypocritical American white man was reaping what he had sowed."

Although he criticized the "late President" a number of times, including his alleged manipulation of the March on Washington—Malcolm had called it "the Farce on Washington"—he did not mention the assassination. The Nation's supreme leader, Elijah Muhammad, revered as semidivine by Malcolm and all the faithful, had specifically ordered him and all ministers not to comment on the national trauma. But in the question period someone asked him about it. Probably expecting the question, Malcolm deliberately disobeyed the man who had saved him from a hellish life on earth.

"Being an old farm boy myself," he replied with his infamous grin, "chickens coming home to roost never did make me sad; they've always made me glad." The audience howled with delighted surprise. He was referring to America's legacy of slavery and white supremacy, and across the seas, to what he considered an imperial foreign policy that targeted popular Third World leaders like Fidel Castro and the Congo's

Patrice Lumumba. More generally he meant "America's climate of hate," which also worried King—but which Malcolm had been complicit in perpetuating.

"The seeds that America had sown—in enslavement, in many things that followed since then—all these seeds were coming up today; it was harvest time."[77] The media, leading off with the *New York Times,* excoriated him for the seemingly offhand comment. The Nation of Islam, which under Muhammad's leadership had striven to remain rigorously nonpolitical, was suddenly thrust into the dead center of American politics. The supreme leader shocked Malcolm, whom he had always treated like a favored son, by commanding his silence for three months and suspending his ministry.

Both Malcolm and his father surrogate may have been waiting for such an incident to bring their growing tensions to a head. During the past year Malcolm had been so tortured by rumors of Muhammad's sexual immorality—impregnating his secretaries, then silencing them—that he had confronted him about it. Muhammad explained to him that he was merely fulfilling biblical prophecies—that as King David and other prophets were philanderers so he must be. Malcolm, on the contrary, had strictly obeyed the Nation's ascetic moral code of sexual abstinence outside of marriage. Wanting to turn the rage of the urban underclass that he was so attuned to in a fruitful direction, he had also been frustrated by the Nation's ban on political activity. By the time of Muhammad's edict of silence, which he later made indefinite, Malcolm was aware that his rivals in the chain of command were conspiring to oust him, or worse. Most Muslims still considered him the heir apparent.

Ever since his jailhouse conversion in 1948—the same year that nineteen-year-old Martin King was ordained a Baptist minister—and ever more strongly in his twelve years as a street preacher, Malcolm held faith in his divinely appointed mission to rescue and redeem the lives of black people who were laying waste their souls as he had during his reckless youth. The covenant was clear: black people poisoned by white sin must wage an internal holy war to purify themselves; in return Allah, the avenging God of justice, would destroy the devilish master race and its decadent civilization. If they freed themselves on the inside, Allah would free them from external chains. So Malcolm preached moral purity while at the same time that "white America is doomed!" No one shall escape except those who accepted Allah as God, Islam as the only true religion, and Elijah Muhammad as God's Messenger "to the 22 million ex-slaves here in America.

"If America will repent," Malcolm cried out like Jeremiah, "God will overlook some of its wicked deeds, but if America refuses, then like the biblical houses of Egypt and Babylon, God will erase the American government and the entire white race from this planet." White America, he warned, "wake up and take heed, before it is too late!" America's "racial powder keg" was ready to set off the "Great Doomsday," a "day of slaughter for this sinful white world."[78] No more water, the fire next time.

Although Malcolm was spouting familiar Black Muslim diatribe, his and the Nation's rhetoric rejuvenated a black tradition of prophetic invective as old as the slaves' baptism to Christianity. Black abolitionists had condemned slavery in similar terms, calling upon whites to repent in the face of a just, wrathful God.

"Beware Americans!" wrote Othello, a free Maryland black, in 1788. "Consider the difference between the mild effulgence of approving Providence," enjoyed in the American Revolution, "and the angry countenance of incensed divinity." Forty years later, Boston abolitionist David Walker printed a fiery pamphlet banned both South and North:

"Americans, unless you speedily alter your course, you and your Country are gone!!!!!! Your DESTRUCTION is at hand, and will be speedily consummated unless you REPENT." Many abolitionists, invigorated by the fervent evangelism of the Second Great Awakening, argued that collective atonement was the surest path to both emancipation and the kingdom of God on earth. But atonement did not come calmly. The irrepressible conflict over slavery led to the ghastly Armageddon of the Civil War. What new Armageddon lay in store for white America in the 1960s?

After three months of painful silence, Malcolm decided to break away from his spiritual and personal home of a quarter century. In early March 1964 he announced that he was leaving the Nation because of "internal differences," not "of my own free will." But now that he had "more independence of action," he intended "to use a more flexible approach toward working with others." He was "prepared to cooperate in local civil-rights actions in the South and elsewhere and shall do so because every campaign for specific objectives can only heighten the political consciousness of the Negroes and intensify their identification against white society." He created the Muslim Mosque, Inc., as a vehicle for unifying black people both Muslim and non-Muslim.

Although still calling himself a black nationalist, he downplayed racial separation. "We cannot think of uniting with others, until after we have first united among ourselves." He held fast to the right of armed self-defense and of retaliation.[79] He envisioned his new movement as not competing with but complementing both the Nation of Islam and the civil rights movement. He saw his prophetic role as doing for Black Muslims and the urban poor what King had done for southern black Christians. But the nature of his constituency might require him to play by different rules.

Malcolm sought to reinterpret the civil rights movement and to strengthen it with new allies from the urban ghettos, and from overseas. His strategy for doing so was to "expand the civil-rights struggle to a higher level—to the level of human rights," and to put American racism on trial before the United Nations. Malcolm argued that as long as black activists confined the movement to "the jurisdiction of Uncle Sam," they were lost. They must globalize the struggle—fighting in the world arena in which people of color were the majority—and get support from newly freed African nations as well as Asians and Latin Americans. Still he went out of his way to threaten organized violence if the government, or white extremists, responded to the multiclass black movement with violent suppression. It would be "ballots or bullets."[80]

To escape bullets from Muslim rivals—death threats were climbing by the week—and to forge personal alliances with African and Arab leaders, Malcolm left his country for the first time on a five-week journey to Egypt, Lebanon, Nigeria, Ghana, Morocco, Algeria, and Saudi Arabia, meeting with students, journalists, politicians, diplomats, and heads of state. He made the pilgrimage to Mecca, a cardinal duty of all Muslims, which allowed him to adopt the Sunni Muslim name El Hajj Malik El Shabazz. He had thought that his main mission was to link up with fellow dark-skinned leaders, but the hajj brought about what he called his "spiritual rebirth." It was no less a political rebirth.

"Never have I witnessed such sincere hospitality and the overwhelming spirit of true brotherhood," he wrote from Jedda, "as is practiced by people *of all colors and races* here in this ancient holy land, the home of Abraham, Muhammad and all the other prophets of the Holy Scriptures." It made him "utterly speechless and spellbound." He saw tens of thousands of pilgrims from all over the globe, "*of all colors,* from blue-eyed blonds to black-skinned Africans," all embodying a spirit of unity "that my experiences in America had led me to believe could never exist between the white and the non-white." He added, "I was not conscious of color for the first time in my life.

"America needs to understand Islam," he insisted, "because this is the one religion that erases the race problem. Before America allows herself to be destroyed by the 'cancer of racism' she should become better acquainted with the religious philosophy of Islam, a religion that has already molded people of all colors into one vast family." In sum, "Islam removes racism."

Upon returning to robustious welcomes in New York and Chicago he declared that "I no longer subscribe to sweeping indictments of one race. My pilgrimage to Mecca served to convince me that perhaps American whites can be cured of the rampant racism which is consuming them and about to destroy this country. I am not a racist and do not subscribe to any of the tenets of racism."[81] Before he left on his journey he had downplayed the spiritual spur of the broadened freedom movement he pressed for. Now he saw orthodox Islam as a force of liberation in its own right that could not only mobilize poor blacks but help bridge the divide between black and white America. In July 1964, after founding the Organization of Afro-American Unity, modeled on a federation of African nations, he took off on a longer journey seeking a global alliance to fight American racism.

MALCOLM TALKED ABOUT it hardly more than King and mainstream black leaders, but his true enemy was hard-core deadening poverty. He blamed it on white racism more than capitalism, which he saw through the prism of race, not class. Malcolm barely recognized the white victims of poverty, who constituted the majority of American poor.

Unlike his superrich predecessor, the new president of the United States had tasted poverty, growing up amid poor whites and Mexicans in south Texas. In his twenties he had joined the New Deal with activist zeal to fight the Depression, heading the New Deal's youth-assistance program in Texas. After assuming the presidency he resolved not only to continue Kennedy's social programs but to go further—to carry out his hero FDR's unfulfilled legacy. So in his first State of the Union address, in early January 1964, he declared a "war against poverty." The Kennedy White House had set the stage for it but was not ready to promote it in the reelection year, and not before the civil rights bill. LBJ had expedient priorities as well as noble ones: he could steal thunder from the civil rights crusade, win support from voters of color, and appease southern whites who stood to benefit. Enough of a populist legacy had survived in the white South to support ambitious economic remedies, especially if they headed off touchier rights laws.

President Johnson threw a curveball when he called the civil rights generals to meet with him in mid-January. King, Wilkins, Whitney Young, and James Farmer expected LBJ to bend their ears if not their arms to accept a weakening of the civil rights bill then being considered by the House Rules Committee, a civil rights graveyard. Rather, he reassured them that he would secure the bill without any changes. Not stopping there, he urged them to mobilize support for his war on poverty.

Through midwinter 1964 King and SCLC colleagues debated how serious Johnson was about ending poverty, and whether it should affect their own wobbly strategy. They understood that LBJ's initiative, unlike the civil rights measure, was not a direct response to movement pressure. But the movement had had a decisive indirect influence by producing a favorable moral and political environment and by raising poor people's expectations. While the civil rights community fully endorsed the antipoverty program, it did not want to deflect momentum from the full-court press behind the civil rights bill, whose passage was touch and go, especially with a dreaded Senate filibuster. Although a majority of African Americans hovered around poverty, most black leaders held that obtaining constitutional rights must be the foundation for economic advances—the same position pushed by American leaders on the world stage about nations of color. Johnson and congressional liberals launched the war on poverty largely on their own.

The antipoverty effort would likely have been more effective had rights leaders been more involved. The long-term aim of preventing poverty was more ambitious than the New Deal's goal of stabilizing it, but Johnson's means were paltry in comparison. The strategy behind the "war" was the old American ideal of expanding opportunity while rehabilitating the poor. The various programs, delivering services and not cash to the inner-city and rural poor, aimed at helping them to help themselves rise out of poverty. It was criticized by activists and social workers for not giving poor people what they most needed: jobs or income.

The poverty war's chief weapon was the decentralized Community Action Program (CAP), which marshaled legal, educational, social work, and health resources to give poor people more control of their lives. A controversial feature mandated "maximum feasible participation of residents." But just as the phrase "all deliberate speed" had marred the *Brown* desegregation decision, so the qualifier "feasible" encouraged noncompliance. Nowhere was "involvement of the poor" converted into real power. In his later study of the poverty war, social psychologist Kenneth Clark branded it a "charade," not resulting "in any observable changes in the predicament of the poor."[82]

Regardless of its strategy, weaponry, or prospect of victory, the Johnson administration's will to combat poverty delighted the two men who had wanted their great Washington march to focus on poverty and unemployment. Rustin and Randolph had long insisted that black people could not move forward without pulling up the economic roots of racism. They were astonished to see the Texan not known for racial enlightenment leading the way toward economic justice. For Rustin, this turn of events was nearly as revelatory as Malcolm's discovery of white Muslims in Mecca. Had Johnson dealt them in?

.   .   .

President Johnson's unexpected boldness in putting poverty on the nation's agenda—though his program would barely dent it—complicated King's difficulties in crafting his second and most important book, *Why We Can't Wait*. Was racism or poverty the driving issue of the day? How were they connected? A group effort, largely ghostwritten, the slender volume appeared in early June 1964, published by Harper & Row (as was his Montgomery memoir). Its composition was challenged not only by churning political tides, but by the delicacy of collaborating with a coauthor, Levison, whom President Kennedy had ordered King to excommunicate. But the book, with "Letter from Birmingham Jail" as its centerpiece, proved a masterstroke of passionate reasonableness, practical idealism, and radical moderation.

Although as with *Stride Toward Freedom* he put himself front and center in his narrative, he testified that the masses in revolt were the prime actors: "it was the people who moved their leaders, not the leaders who moved the people." In summer 1963, "the Negroes of America wrote an emancipation proclamation to themselves. They shook off three hundred years of psychological slavery and said: 'We can make ourselves free.'" The Revolution of 1963 all but finished off "slaveries other than the physical" that had endured since 1863, especially the guts of slavery, the psychic and spiritual servitude that had hardly diminished since the Civil War. "Is not freedom the negation of servitude? Does not one have to end totally for the other to begin?"

Reprising his jail letter, he rejected the opposite extremes of incrementalism and unplanned or "directionless spontaneity." In words that contradicted his own deeds/misdeeds, he declared that in "the bursting mood that has overtaken the Negro," compromise was "profane and pernicious," that the current black leadership was "innately opposed to compromise." Clearly he referred to unprincipled compromise, like the corrupt Compromise of 1877 that summarily ended Reconstruction, but he sounded absolute.

As if to meet any doubt about his newfound extremism, he submitted that "when you are right you cannot be too radical." Then he countered his own extremist tone by asserting that the Negro wanted only to secure his rightful place within the economic system, not overturn it; that direct action must be complemented by electoral gains; and that black people needed nothing more radical than the benefits given to veterans after World War II. But the book made an airtight case for freedom now.

His most far-reaching proposal for reform was the "Bill of Rights for the Disadvantaged." King had conceived of it as the "Negro Bill of Rights," but he and his coauthors decided that such a narrow scope was neither expedient nor right. "The moral justification for special measures for Negroes," he wrote, "is rooted in the robberies inherent in the institution of slavery," not least the billions in unpaid wages. He rationalized extending these entitlements to disadvantaged whites on the grounds of what he called "derivative bondage"—the impact of slavery on the control and exploitation of the white labor force. "As long as labor was cheapened by the involuntary servitude of the black man, the freedom of white labor, especially in the South, was little more than a myth." White labor was cheapened further when formal slavery was replaced by systematic racial discrimination, which made black workers a reserve army to keep wages low and to break strikes. This was the most damaging linkage of race and class, the most malignant economic root of racism. Still, the concept of derivative bondage was something of a stretch. Compensatory justice appropriate for a chosen people liberated from slavery did not have the same moral charge when applied to a larger group not sharing this heritage.

No doubt other peoples of color would have been included in King's proposal, but in the mid-1960s, when the combined population of Latinos, American Indians, and Asians did not equal that of African Americans, smaller racial minorities appeared as invisible to King as to the public at large. America was white and black.

The economic and social rights he envisioned, similar to the GI Bill of Rights, would give "veterans of the long siege of denial" full educational support with living expenses, loan subsidies for home and business, preferential employment (especially in civil service jobs), medical care, and other compensation. Intended for a ten-year period, the entitlements would aim at the "basic psychological and motivational transformation" of recipients, affecting "social evils" like family breakups, school dropout, crime, unmarried births, and "swollen relief rolls."

Although "change in human psychology is normally a slow process," King was convinced that the catalyst of black revolt would hasten transformation from within.

To undergird the economic bill of rights King called for a massive federal effort to foster full employment in the teeth of automation, and the "full resources of the society" to attack tenacious poverty. Admirable as they were, King's vague reform proposals did not match the power of his moral indictment of racism and prophetic call for change. Irresistible in the realm of civil rights, King's rhetorical magic had not found its footing in the intractable realm of human rights—or in the slippery sphere of public-policy reform.

To activists on the street, many of whom could not even vote, King's contemplation of macroeconomic reform must have seemed as remote from their hand-to-mouth lives as was Plato's ethereal realm of ideas from the shadowy cave. King would have liked nothing better than hiding out on a tropical island with Plato's *Republic,* his second favorite book, but the murky real life of movement politics dogged his waking hours. SCLC's strategic confusion of late fall had not been straightened out six months later. Drift drove. The "revolutionary" plan Nash and Bevel had concocted in the afternoon of the church bombing—a saner alternative to their grieving impulse to track down and kill the bombers—had picked up support from SCLC staff. They toned it down from a militant nonviolent shutdown of the state capital (including lie-ins on highways, runways, and railroad tracks), which upset President Kennedy when he got wind of it, to a "nonviolent army" marching on Montgomery and mobilizing for voting rights throughout Alabama.

By late winter 1964 the Alabama campaign, including a renewed push in Birmingham, where the mayor and merchants had reneged on the year-old settlement, was poised for takeoff. Throughout the spring King heralded the "Alabama freedom army" as SCLC's next big push, hitting the road by June or July. But an unexpected turn on Florida's Atlantic coast, and the mounting drama of SNCC's Mississippi Freedom Summer, forced SCLC to postpone its Alabama rendezvous with destiny. King and SCLC needed a timely victory to stay afloat, and to keep from getting drowned out by the revolution in Mississippi.

Settled by the Spanish in 1564, St. Augustine, Florida, was the oldest nonnative city in North America; its flourishing slave trade predated the arrival of slaves in Virginia by half a century. Preparing to celebrate its quadricentennial, the tourist city with Deep South racial mores got swept up in the Negro Revolution of 1963. Apart from usual demands, the black community was protesting use of federal funds for a racially exclusive historical commemoration.

Both whites and blacks lived in fear of a thousand-strong armed Klan militia, calling itself Ancient City Hunting Club, whose chieftain, "Hoss" Manucy, a pig farmer and bootlegger, told a journalist that "my only bad habit is fightin' nigguhs."[83] Manucy shared law-enforcement duties with the sheriff, his former football coach, who had deputized him and his gang. Skirmishes between black activists, newly affiliated with SCLC, and Manucy's posse escalated to pitched battles after the Klan torched a cottage where King had stayed and local leader Robert Hayling, a dentist, armed his followers. "We were not totally nonviolent," Hayling later admitted.[84] Although King was unhappy about this ethical lapse, he did not reject having armed bodyguards in St. Augustine, protection he had eventually vetoed in the bus boycott. Six months after the President's murder, his own assassination seemed more likely than ever.

"This is the most lawless city I've ever been in," he told a reporter. "I've never seen this kind of wide-open violence." At mass meetings he announced his readiness to die: "If physical death is the price I must pay to free my white brother and all my brothers and sisters from a permanent death of the spirit, then nothing can be more redemptive."[85]

King and entourage flew in and out of St. Augustine during May and June 1964 while he was trying to manage SCLC's disarray and money woes, promote his new book, and fight for Senate passage of the civil rights bill, in danger of death by filibuster. The House had passed it by a wide margin in February. On June 10, after mighty political arm-twisting by LBJ, the Senate shut off (71–29) the two-month southern filibuster, longest ever, the last big hurdle toward passage.

Next morning King, Abernathy, and eight others were arrested seeking to desegregate the Monson Motor Lodge restaurant. Taken to the Jacksonville jail, King told a black woman employee who greeted him: "Hello, sister. I've been in fifteen jails, but this is the first time that I have been treated like a hog." As in Birmingham he was put in solitary, "a very lonely, dark and desolate cell by myself, cut off from everybody."[86]

A few days later black and white protesters plunged into the first movement "swim-in" in the Monson motel pool, King watching across the street. The owner poured a noxious chemical into the water to scare them out. Protesters sought as well to integrate the Atlantic Ocean, which had swallowed black bodies as human cargo for centuries. They were attacked on the hot beach by crazed mobs of white toughs, male and female. Despite the governor's ban on night marches, night after night protesters marched in the old city at dusk toward the historic slave market, the prime tourist attraction. Street battles with Manucy's Klan posse, who sometimes outnumbered them, grew increasingly violent until all hell broke loose after dark on Thursday, June 24.

The Klan had gathered a large rally at the Old Slave Market, where, under a full moon, supremacists J. B. Stoner and Connie Lynch whipped the crowd into a frenzy of hatred. The civil rights forces, mainly teenagers in boy-girl pairs, had marched as usual from their church headquarters toward the slave market that was now taken over by the slaveholders' scions.

"There they are!" Lynch shrieked. "Here come the niggers now!" Armed with bats, tire tools, logging chains, and cue sticks, heaving trash cans and other makeshift missiles, the enraged white crowd overran state troopers sent by the governor and attacked the protesters in a real-life reenactment of Civil War combat. The bloodied protesters, a score lying on the ground, many having to be hospitalized, found an escape route with whites in hot pursuit. A woman yelled: "Don't let 'em git away, boys, go git 'em!"[87] The New York Times reported that "a number of Negro women had their clothes torn off while they were being clawed and beaten by screaming terrorists."[88]

Standing alone on a dark porch, King watched his followers "stumbling past him in the dim shine of the streetlights like the tattered remnant of a brigade filtering back from a battlefield disaster, girls in shredded clothes, sobs now lifting up from them, a few scattered screams like a long-pent breath at last released—he watching them with that stricken expression of amazement, horror, but also captivation."[89] He did what he could to shepherd his wounded flock back to the church. Abernathy performed oratorical wonders to calm the troops in the sanctuary, transmuting that night's "sweltering fevers for vengeance" back into the "higher, finally mysterious will to love despite everything."[90]

King found a telephone to call Washington for help to stave off a racial nightmare. Waiting to get through to the Justice Department, he sat in a supporter's parlor, shirt soaking in sweat, wearily whispering: "When things happen like this tonight, you question sometimes, what are we doing to these people?" Sipping ice water, he said to Abernathy, Young, and Shuttlesworth: "It can't go on like this. It just can't go on like this."[91]

As in Birmingham the specter of all-out racial violence finally forced the white establishment to give way. The governor announced he had formed the biracial committee that black leaders had long demanded, but promptly told the intransigent mayor, "There is no committee"; it was make believe.[92] Despite fears of Klan reprisal, eighty white businessmen quietly voted to comply with the imminent Civil Rights Act. With no actual settlement like they got in Birmingham and only the fig leaf of a fragile détente (similar to the Albany outcome), King left St. Augustine in palpable relief. It was not the victory he had gambled on, but the impasse might be moot with the new civil rights law.

A few days later, July 2, he joined other black leaders (including Rosa Parks) in the White House to witness President Johnson sign the civil rights bill into law, using six dozen pens that he dispensed to his guests. LBJ corralled the civil rights generals into the Cabinet Room and asked them to halt demonstrations until after the election, calling them unnecessary and self-defeating. While Wilkins and Whitney Young (no fans of street protest) readily agreed, King and more-radical leaders were noncommittal. How could the new law be enforced without doses of direct action?

The 1964 Civil Rights Act set a national policy prohibiting legally sanctioned segregation. It outlawed racial discrimination in public accommodations and schools, authorizing the attorney general to sue offenders; it banned discrimination in employment by race or gender. The law was not as strong as activists wanted—it soft-pedaled voting rights—but it was better than Kennedy's original proposal of June 1963. In historian C. Vann Woodward's words, Jim Crow as a legal entity was dead.[93]

The test would be its effect on racism and altering race relations, South and North. The major difficulty, as always, was implementation, which depended on a committed attorney general with political will. The law provided only judicial remedies inaccessible to ordinary citizens lacking legal resources. Nevertheless, fear of prosecution compelled desegregation of public accommodations more rapidly than expected, though not much changed with segregated housing and jobs. School integration did not advance until the federal bureaucracy swung into action in the late 1960s, and then only by fits and starts. The long-term trend, especially in northern cities, was for de facto school segregation to worsen.

While most black leaders applauded the law, some were troubled by its shortcomings, particularly its irrelevance to the African-American majority living outside the South. A CORE analysis pointed out that "the ghetto minorities in the urban North are ignored."[94] Malcolm X lambasted it as "only a valve, a vent, that was designed to enable us to let off our frustrations"—not "to solve our problems" but to "lessen the explosion."[95]

9

When Ella Baker, SCLC executive director, heard about the February 1960 lunch-counter sit-ins that were spreading like a fever, she called her long list of contacts at southern colleges. "It is time to move," she told them in her deep, resonant voice. Defiance of racial oppression had been a tradition in her family. When she was a child her grandmother told her tales of slave revolts and of how she had been whipped for refusing to marry the man chosen by her owner. She wed instead a rebellious slave who became a Baptist preacher and was an important role model for his granddaughter. Baker, fifty-six, had been organizing for thirty years, setting up black consumer cooperatives during the Depression, recruiting NAACP members throughout the South, serving as NAACP director of branches, then heading its New York office before helping to found SCLC. She had an extraordinary ability to inspire people of all ages, especially young people, and to give them a deeper perspective on social change. Rising to the challenge of directing SCLC's Atlanta headquarters, she was never accepted as an equal by King and fellow ministers, despite her organizing genius. She felt that SCLC's centralized charismatic leadership had undermined the voting rights campaign she created.

Baker realized that the momentous sit-in movement would not endure without a structure to coordinate the local groups. On Easter weekend 1960 she convened a conference of sit-in leaders from over fifty black southern colleges at Shaw University in Raleigh, North Carolina, where she had been class valedictorian. King spoke to the two hundred fervent students, but Baker fought SCLC's effort to capture the student groups as its youth wing. She believed that the students needed an autonomous organization "with the right to direct their own affairs and even make their own mistakes."[96] She hoped they would be bolder than SCLC. The young activists set up a loosely structured Student Nonviolent Coordinating Committee (SNCC) and adopted a statement of purpose that affirmed its Christian-based nonviolent philosophy. As the sit-in movement slowed, SNCC shifted from a coordinating body to a cadre of ex-students committed to long-term organizing in rural southern communities.

Inspired by Baker, who had grown so critical of SCLC's preacher hierarchy that she resigned in summer 1960, SNCC embodied an alternative style of participatory "group-centered leadership" that would clash with SCLC. She believed that what movements needed was "the development of people who are interested not in being leaders as much as in developing leadership among other people."[97] SNCC activists lived out the idea that real change came through empowerment of people at the grass roots. They understood that to overcome subjugation, especially in the rural South, black people had to rely on themselves, not on media stars who came and went. Because SNCC activists believed that they had to exemplify their values, prefiguring the redemptive society they sought to create—and because they shared a common risk of death—they were reluctant to recognize leaders among themselves. "We are all leaders," they proclaimed. Their slogan: "Let the people decide."

In late August 1962, a tired, strong-willed woman with a great smile and shining eyes strode into a meeting at her Baptist church in Ruleville, a Mississippi Delta town not far from where Emmett Till had been bludgeoned to death. "Until then I'd never heard of no mass meeting and I didn't know that a Negro could register and vote," Fannie Lou Hamer remembered. SNCC organizers Bob Moses, James Forman, and Jim Bevel led the meeting at the rural church. Bevel preached to the poor sharecroppers (from Matthew's Gospel) that they must "discern the signs of the times." God's time was upon them, and they must act for their freedom.[98]

"When they asked for those to raise their hands who'd go down to the courthouse the next day," Hamer recalled, "I raised mine. Had it up high as I could get it. I guess if I'd had any sense I'd a-been a little scared, but what was the point of being scared? The only thing they could do to me was kill me, and it seemed like they'd been trying to do that a little bit at a time ever since I could remember."

Forty-four years old, she was the youngest of twenty children of sharecropper parents. She had picked cotton since she was seven, for the previous eighteen years with her husband, Pap, on a nearby plantation. She had always known poverty and injustice. When she was a young girl, a white farmer had poisoned their mules just when her family was getting ahead. For a long time she had wanted to help her kind. "Just listenin' at 'em, I could just see myself votin' people outa office that I know was wrong and didn't do nothin' to help the poor. I said, you know, that's sumpin' I really wanna be involved in."[99] Chief among those who did not care about poor people, in her opinion, was powerful Senator James Eastland, owner of a huge cotton plantation in Hamer's county. He ruled the county like a feudal baron.

Hamer rode with seventeen others on a SNCC-chartered bus to the county seat of Indianola, birthplace of the White Citizens Councils in 1954. The registrar "brought a big old book out there, and he gave me the sixteenth section of the Constitution of Mississippi, and that was dealing with de facto laws, and I didn't know nothin' about no de facto laws." She "flunked out" along with the others. Driving home, they were all arrested because the bus was "too yellow." She sang spirituals to strengthen them. When she got home the plantation owner kicked her off her land. "I didn't have no other choice because for one time I wanted things to be different." The house where she stayed in town was shot up by vigilantes. It was one hell of a winter.

"Pap couldn't get a job nowhere 'cause everybody knew he was my husband. We made it on through, though, and since then I just been trying to work and get our people organized."[100] Bob Moses recruited the "lady who sings the hymns" to join SNCC, its oldest field organizer. Why was she drawn to this brash young outfit?

This country has "divided us into classes," she explained, "and if you hadn't arrived at a certain level, you wasn't treated no better by the blacks than you was by the whites. It was these kids what broke a lot of this down. They treated us like we were special and we loved 'em. We didn't feel uneasy about our language might not be right or something. We just felt like we could talk to 'em. We trusted 'em, and I can tell the world those kids done their share in Mississippi."

SNCC had been struggling for a year to register black voters in the "closed society" of Mississippi, the kingpin of white supremacy, where rural blacks were still treated much like slaves. The state's terrorism had kept it off-limits to SCLC. Blacks were almost half the population, but only 5 percent were registered, in some counties none at all, owing to intimidation and reprisals in general, the literacy test and poll tax in particular. Registering black people was incendiary.

Bob Moses, driving force behind the voting campaign, had moved to McComb, in southern Mississippi, where he set up the first of a string of registration "schools." In his mid-twenties, the contemplative young man with fiery eyes had grown up in Harlem and had been a Harvard graduate student in philosophy, drawn to Camus and existentialism. While teaching high school in New York he had organized with Bayard Rustin. Inspired by the lunch-counter sit-ins, he volunteered for duty at SNCC's makeshift Atlanta office. On a visit to Mississippi he was persuaded by Amzie Moore, a local NAACP leader, that enfranchising black people should be SNCC's main mission. Moses would become a legend in SNCC not only for courage but for his ability to motivate leadership in others. With his guidance SNCC activists learned "how to find potential leadership, how to groom it," Lawrence Guyot recalled, "and the most painful lesson for some of us was how to let it go once you've set it into motion."[101]

McComb tested the mettle of Moses and his small cadre. They were routinely beaten and arrested when they accompanied local blacks to the county courthouse. Herbert Lee, a brave farmer who supported them, a father of nine, was gunned down by a state legislator who was never prosecuted. After a march to protest the cold-blooded murder, Moses and associates were jailed for two months. They left McComb in December 1961 and fanned out into several counties around the Delta.

Risk and repression became a way of life. SNCC workers were shot at in their cars, and mobs invaded their offices. When county supervisors cut off federal food aid to poor blacks as punishment, SNCC went all out to mobilize food caravans from the North, helped by comedian Dick Gregory. This boosted the registration campaign as activists drew the connection between children going hungry and lack of political power. In several county seats SNCC organized Freedom Days with courthouse marches seeking registration.

Success in turning out disfranchised voters to vote in the November 1963 election—though their votes were not counted—convinced SNCC and its partners in the Council of Federated Organizations (COFO) that black citizens could build an electoral vehicle independent of the segregated state Democratic Party. As its immediate goal the Mississippi Freedom Democratic Party (MFDP), founded in early 1964, prepared to challenge the all-white regulars for seating at the August Democratic national convention. When as expected MFDP members were excluded from the party's precinct and county meetings, they set up their own, meticulously adhering to proper procedures. Four MFDP activists qualified for the June primary, including Hamer as candidate for Congress. Unsuccessful, they ran as independents in the fall.

Meanwhile, SNCC launched the Mississippi Summer Project, which brought a thousand northern college students, mainly white, to join a climactic registration crusade entwined with the MFDP effort. SNCC activists were risking their lives, and the lives of local people, for little gain in black voters. Their desperate gambit was to create a national crisis. Moses and other SNCC leaders calculated that if white students were beaten or killed, it would grab the nation's attention and might lead to federal protection of voting rights. Black victims of Mississippi's reign of terror had been ignored. Many in SNCC were concerned, however, that the white students would overshadow the indigenous organizers, take over leadership roles, and worsen the powerlessness of poor blacks.

In mid-June, while volunteers learned the ropes in a marathon training workshop at an Ohio college—Hamer lifting them to the heavens with her singing, Moses preparing them for possible death—three Freedom Summer activists disappeared in Neshoba County after a traffic arrest. Two were white, CORE's Michael Schwerner and Andrew Goodman, fresh from the first Ohio training session. One was black, eighteen-year-old James Chaney, from Meridian, Mississippi. Despite sensational media coverage, Robert Kennedy—champion of voter registration—claimed he had no authority to intervene. Six weeks later searchers found the three mutilated bodies buried in an earthen dam. The deputy sheriff who arrested them had turned them over to the Klan. The triple lynching fastened the eyes of the nation on Mississippi Freedom Summer.

By late June 1964 the white student army was settling into communities all over the state. The young women and men stayed with black families or in ramshackle "freedom houses." In hundred-degree heat they trudged along dusty dirt roads in their straw hats and blue denim and nervously talked with people on cabin porches about their right to vote. The students escorted the few who dared register to the courthouse, where most failed the rigged exam. Rejected for the ninth time, one old man looked down as he walked out and said wistfully, "I want my freedom all right. I do mighty bad."[102]

Over the summer more black people were assaulted for aspiring to be citizens, and dozens of church headquarters were burned or bombed. Volunteers helped organize marches to protest brutality by police and the Klan, and many were jailed. At times even SNCC had trouble keeping up with the feisty militancy of local teenagers bent on integrating their towns. "The kids were moving, with or without us."[103]

Unable to make much progress, voter registration gave way to the building of the MFDP. "Have you freedom-registered?" organizers asked, in churches, on backwoods roads, and riding plantation buses with cotton pickers long before sunup. MFDP conventions in each county chose delegates to five congressional district conventions, which in turn sent delegates to the state convention in Jackson. "People straight out of tarpaper shacks, many illiterate, some wearing a (borrowed) suit for the first time, disenfranchised for three generations, without a living memory of political power, yet caught on with some extraordinary inner sense to how the process worked, down to its smallest nuance and finagle."[104]

Ella Baker gave a passionate address to the song- and prayer-filled Jackson convention. Most of the eight hundred delegates were black and poor; many were women. Sixty-eight men and women were chosen to fight for the party's recognition at the national convention in Atlantic City, New Jersey. The MFDP had sprouted into a serious threat to the Democratic power structure of the Magnolia State, and of the nation.

ON AUGUST 4, 1964, the day that FBI and navy searchers found the bodies of Chaney, Goodman, and Schwerner, President Johnson sent sixty-four jet fighters to cripple an oil depot and naval port in North Vietnam. He announced on TV that the bombing, the first by his country since the Korean War, was a justified retaliation for a torpedo assault on an American destroyer in the Gulf of Tonkin. That incident never happened. But two days earlier, the destroyer had been attacked a few miles offshore by North Vietnamese patrol boats that suspected its involvement in a raid on two nearby islands, part of intensifying covert warfare against the North led by the CIA. In response the destroyer had blasted three patrol boats, sinking one.

Johnson and his national security advisers had wanted to leave it at that, but when the media got wind of it, LBJ feared that Arizona senator Barry Goldwater, the Republican presidential nominee, would have a field day haranguing the President for being soft. Goldwater sounded as hawkish on the Vietnam problem, turning it into a hot-button issue, as he was in condemning the Civil Rights Act he had just voted against. Referring to both fronts, he had declared in his acceptance speech that "extremism in the defense of liberty is no vice! Moderation in the pursuit of justice is no virtue!" It was as if he had taken a leaf from King's Birmingham letter (his speechwriter had probably read it). But Goldwater's liberty and justice were the opposite of King's, as were his means of pursuing them.

For half a year, LBJ's inner circle had been looking for a dramatic provocation to secure congressional backing for deeper military involvement in Southeast Asia. Once it hit the airwaves and became a campaign issue, this shadow skirmish in waters claimed by North Vietnam did the trick. After meetings between the President and leaders of Congress, especially J. William Fulbright, head of the Senate Foreign Relations Committee, the Gulf of Tonkin Resolution sailed through the House

unanimously, the Senate with only two dissents. It gave Johnson authority "to take all the necessary measures to repel any armed attack against
the forces of the United States to prevent further aggression."[105] Even
Fulbright did not know that the administration deemed it a blank check,
equivalent to a declaration of war. And the war came.

THE BALLOONS, BRIGHT LIGHTS, and glitter of Atlantic City—
its ocean air smelling of seaweed and popcorn—felt like another world
to the MFDP delegates arriving by bus from faraway Mississippi. Not
that they had left the Magnolia State behind. Hundreds of their constituents followed them to the fading resort town, all wearing their Sunday best. They intended to buttonhole every delegate they could find to
back the MFDP challenge, while their people kept a round-the-clock
vigil on the famous boardwalk in front of the convention hall. SNCC
organizers were dressed up in Ivy League suits and pressed the flesh
like their lives depended on it.

With nine state delegations lined up and an unimpeachable legal
case submitted by prominent Democratic broker Joseph Rauh, United
Auto Workers counsel, the MFDP strategy was to garner enough votes
in the credentials committee to force a floor vote to decide on recognition. Their trump card was that their state's all-white delegation, like
the Wallace-controlled delegates from neighboring Alabama, refused
to declare loyalty to the national party and its nominees. They were
defiantly in the Goldwater camp.

King, Wilkins, James Farmer, and other notables testified on the
MFDP's behalf at a nationally televised hearing, but more telling oratory came from black Mississippians who explained what happened
when they tried to vote. Limping to the table, Fannie Lou Hamer, the
MFDP vice chair, stole the show and won her country's heart with her
gripping tale of being beaten in Winona jail till her body "was as navy
blue as anything you ever seen." Her melodic voice rose to a shout. "All
of this is on account we want to register," she sang out, "to become
first-class citizens. And if the Freedom Democratic Party is not seated
now, I question America. Is this America," she asked, "the land of the
free and the home of the brave?"[106]

The millions watching did not catch the end of Hamer's live testimony (though it was replayed that night) because President Johnson deliberately cut it off with an abrupt press conference about trivia. The big man from Texas was more frightened by the little people from Mississippi than by the North Vietnamese peasant army he had just rained bombs upon.

If not the whole loaf, MFDP delegates realistically hoped to get half the seats—how such a dispute had been settled in the past. But LBJ feared that giving the MFDP *any* seats would deliver the message that Negroes had taken over the Democratic Party. Feeling vulnerable because of the Civil Rights Act, which had more bark than bite, the supreme vote counter had calculated that fifteen southern and border states could be lost to Goldwater if Mississippi and other Deep South regulars stormed out of the convention. To keep a lid on the black insurgency that obsessed him, he had badgered Hoover into approving an elephantine FBI spy operation in Atlantic City, thirty agents plus informants aimed at King, SNCC, and the MFDP.

Watching telegenic Hamer in all of her righteous glory, he was determined, as Senator Hubert Humphrey put it privately to black leaders, to "not allow that illiterate woman to speak from the floor of the convention."[107] This was an unlettered crippled sharecropper whose words could shake the nation to its roots, and possibly drive the President from office. "I felt just like I was telling it from the mountain," she tearfully told a reporter.[108] After her high-voltage performance the Democrats were flooded with telegrams and phone calls backing the MFDP. Hamer had to be kept off the convention floor at all cost.

As the convention opened, the prospect of a successful floor vote for the MFDP challenge brought Johnson teetering toward an emotional breakdown. If the Negroes' victory did not open the floodgate to Robert Kennedy's stealing the nomination, his terror, it might lead to repudiation by the voters in November. LBJ could not imagine winning the election without a healthy chunk of the South, his home. Now he might even lose the Lone Star State. In any event, a narrow win without a strong mandate would doom his dreams of greatness.

On Monday evening, August 24, Johnson spoke on the phone to his close ally Walter Reuther, the auto workers' chief. "I think the Negroes are going back to the Reconstruction period," he said. "They set themselves back a hundred years." The next morning his depression had deepened. He read to his press secretary, George Reedy, a handwritten statement withdrawing himself from the race: he was "absolutely unavailable."

"This will throw the nation into quite an uproar, sir," Reedy scrambled to reply.

Minutes later he bared himself to special assistant Walter Jenkins: "I don't see any reason why I ought to seek the right to endure anguish," he said. People "think I want great power. What I want is great solace—and a little love. That's all *I* want."

"You have a lot more of that," his confidant struggled to reassure him. The President was listening only to himself.

"Goldwater's had a couple of nervous breakdowns," he said. "I don't want to be in this place like Wilson," paralyzed by a stroke during his last seventeen months in the White House. Johnson had suffered a major heart attack in 1955, his father had died at his age, and he had had nightmares of paralysis since childhood. "I do not believe I can physically and mentally carry the responsibilities of the Bomb and the world and the nigras and the South. I know my own limitations."[109] He did not want to die in office like his father figure, FDR.

After vigorous debate on Sunday, the MFDP delegates had voted to accept a compromise proposed by Oregon congresswoman Edith Green: to seat members of both delegations who would swear loyalty to the party. The Johnson forces countermanded with their own offer: a loyalty oath, two at-large nonvoting seats for the delegation cochairs, guest passes for the rest, plus a nondiscrimination pledge for future conventions. Unlike Green's "honorable" compromise, Johnson's felt like a slap in the face—two token seats, not even representing Mississippi, handpicked by the white party bosses. The nondiscrimination pledge meant little without guaranteeing black voting rights. The bottom line of Johnson's compromise was simple: Hamer was to be silenced.

At a Monday meeting Hamer and Humphrey shed tears together after she shamed him: "I been praying about you," she said, "and you're a good man. The trouble is, you're afraid to do what you know is right."

LBJ had put it to him that the price of the vice presidential nod was for him to squelch the Mississippi uprising.

"God will take care of you," she told the senator, "even if you lose this job. But Mr. Humphrey, if you take this job, you won't be worth anything. Mr. Humphrey, I'm going to pray for you again."[110]

MFDP leaders felt betrayed by Humphrey's kowtowing because he had long been a courageous fighter for civil rights, recently in shepherding Senate passage of the Civil Rights Act. At the Democrats' convention back in 1948, the Minneapolis mayor's electric oratory supporting the strong civil rights plank caused southern delegates led by South Carolina governor Strom Thurmond to walk out and form the Dixiecrat Party. "The time has arrived for the Democratic Party to get out of the shadow of states' rights," young Mayor Humphrey had exclaimed, "and walk forthrightly into the bright sunshine of human rights."[111] Sixteen years later it was Humphrey's strange mission to stem another southern walkout over civil rights. Now with so much at stake he seemed to be sliding backward from sunshine to shadow. Hamer and her MFDP colleagues told him they would accept nothing less than the Green compromise.

On Tuesday, after an MFDP mass meeting ratified the Green compromise, Senator Humphrey convened in his hotel bedroom a summit meeting of movement leaders and LBJ loyalists from which he barred Hamer. He played hardball LBJ-style to hit home the Johnson compromise. With King, Moses, Rustin, MFDP chair Aaron Henry, white Tougaloo chaplain Edwin King (cochair), and others huddled around queen-size beds, UAW's Reuther warned King: "Your funding is on the line. The kind of money you got from us in Birmingham is there again for Mississippi, but you've got to help us and we've got to help Johnson."[112] Reuther had threatened to fire Rauh as UAW counsel. King, used to the final say in such decisions, turned to the MFDP leaders. They tried to find wiggle room, but Humphrey indicated that it was take it or leave it, above all on the question of Hamer's participation.

The struggle for a tolerable compromise was cut short by a shock from the convention hall. TV anchors announced that the credentials committee had voted, unanimously, to adopt Johnson's compromise. Rauh, who in fact voted against it along with others, tried to stave off a vote until he conferred with MFDP leaders, but the Johnson juggernaut, not even permitting a roll-call vote, bulldozed it through. Because of fearsome White House pressure, the MFDP no longer had the votes to bring their minority report to the floor.

Back in the hotel suite Moses, known for his calm manner, yelled to Humphrey, "You cheated!" and slammed the door in fury. "I have never seen such just really blatant use of power," Congresswoman Green recalled, to block her proposal from floor debate.[113]

In the next twenty-four hours the embattled MFDP held two meetings on the Johnson compromise and rejected it unanimously both times. King, Rauh, Rustin, Farmer, and other leaders tried to sway them. As if repudiating his own quarter century of direct-action devotion, Rustin urged them to make a courageous but painful shift from protest politics to electoral coalition building.

"There is a difference between protest and politics," he explained. "The former is based on morality and the latter is based on reality and compromise. If you are going to engage in politics then you must give up protest."

SNCC's Mendy Samstein stood up. "You're a traitor, Bayard!"[114] If Rustin had spent the summer in Mississippi, he would have witnessed politics and protest in fruitful collaboration, each indispensable to the other. Instead he was trapped in a false dichotomy. What he didn't seem to realize was that in order for electoral politics to achieve large goals of socioeconomic reform, to move toward democratic socialism, the electoral process and party politics would have to be transformed by the moral force of the civil rights movement. This was the importance of refusing the Johnson compromise that meant politics as usual.

If ever there were two Martin Kings cohabiting one body, two minds in one, it was in these meetings. In the face of suffocating pressure by Reuther, Humphrey, and others, he held fast to his rock of ambivalence, seeing things both ways.

"I am not going to counsel you to accept or reject. That is your decision." He said that he could see good reasons for either. He affirmed Rustin's view that the movement was moving from protest to politics and that in the electoral arena odious compromises were unavoidable. He knew of course that this was hardly less true of protest politics. He had succumbed to as many dubious compromises as he had seen jail cells. But the MFDP and its delegates were, even by the movement's high standards, of exceptional integrity. Time and again MFDP delegates argued that they were beholden to the folks back home who had chosen them. But they had been willing to accept a respectful compromise like Green's.

Despite his ambivalence and deference to the delegates, King offered his view that accepting the two seats was the wiser course. "He did not pressure us strongly to take it," Rev. Ed King remembered. "His position, as he told me, was that he wanted to see us take this compromise because this would mean strength for him, help for him in Negro voter registration throughout the South and in the North. He said, 'So being a Negro leader, I want you to take this, but if I were a Mississippi Negro, I would vote against it.'" Accepting the compromise might help to build a progressive electoral coalition. But what would be lost?

After listening to the luminaries the delegates argued back and forth. Moses pleaded that it was not a choice between morality and politics. Their duty was to bring morality into the political arena. Hamer, who herself had wavered, captured the consensus in a memorable utterance: "We didn't come all this way for no two seats!"

On the brink of torpedoing his political life, President Johnson had been relieved to hear from Humphrey and Reuther that the credentials committee had crumbled. But later Tuesday afternoon he was alerted that it was too late. In a last hurrah, half of the MFDP delegates staged a televised sit-in in the abandoned seats of the Mississippi delegation. Hamer got to speak from the floor after all. Merely floating a compromise with the Negroes had propelled most of the Mississippi regulars to walk out. They could stomach no MFDP delegates, even at-large, and sneered at a loyalty oath. A handful of holdouts turned tail when the black contingent claimed the vacant seats amid a media frenzy.

Johnson's fears returned with a vengeance when he talked by phone with two southern allies, governors John Connally (Texas) and Carl Sanders (Georgia). "It looks like we're turning the Democratic party over to the nigras," Sanders chided him. As both Montgomery and Birmingham proved, *any* concession to black demand was seen as a slippery slope toward Reconstruction-style black rule. "It's gonna cut our throats from ear to ear."

LBJ replied that the MFDP deserved recognition: "Pistols kept 'em out." He pleaded with his cronies to keep the rest of the Deep South from walking out. They were not encouraging. The South seemed to be seceding this time from the Democratic Party itself—his worst nightmare. At midnight, less than twenty-four hours before his own coronation, the crown he had always coveted, he was ready to throw in the towel.

"By God, I'm gonna go up there and quit," he told his distressed press secretary, who was ready to resign himself. "Fuck 'em all."[115]

By the time Johnson arrived in Atlantic City next afternoon with Humphrey in tow, his operatives had managed to hold off any further walkouts; Alabama was cocked to go. All on the surface was harmonious uniformity as LBJ was nominated by acclamation on Wednesday night, then Humphrey the next. *Defeated* would be too noble a word for what had happened to the true democrats of Mississippi. Moses was right: they had been cheated in a rigged game.

The boardwalk vigil grew monumental on the last night. A thousand spirited voices chanted "Freedom now!" With Hamer leading, they sang the movement's anthem, tightly linking arms. The grassroots troops who had tried valiantly to inject moral passion and principle into cautious and unprincipled electoral politics returned to the southern battlefield dejected, disillusioned, angry, but far from giving up. Many had learned that, whether or not they could ever hope to build alliances with white liberals, they had to first have power of their own.

Hamer of course was disappointed with the Democrats, but willing to forgive, able to see that "regardless of what they act like, there's some good there." Despite their punishing trials she looked back on Freedom Summer as "the result of all our faith. Our prayers and all we had lived for started to be translated into action." It was "the beginning of a New Kingdom right here on earth," grounded in the Mississippi movement's ethos of trust, integrity, moral courage, and spiritual connectedness.[116] SNCC and MFDP activists could not see it at the time, but Mississippi Freedom Summer was no less crucial than the Selma movement in achieving the Voting Rights Act a year later. It was also the catalyst of Black Power.

IO

Nothing exposed the chasm between civil rights elite and foot soldiers like the lessons each brought home from the Atlantic City debacle. The latter saw it as the cup half empty, the former as the cup half full. King, perhaps alone, saw both what was lost and what was gained. The MFDP delegation and their retinue returned to Mississippi with the bitter but defiant realization that they must go it alone. They could depend on no one in high places, not even in their own movement. They had been abandoned by the national party for which they had risked their lives and livelihoods.

The civil rights generals, to the contrary, had an unbeatable presidential candidate who had just rammed through Congress the most significant civil rights legislation since Reconstruction and had also declared an "unconditional war on poverty." They had a vice presidential nominee, whatever his backsliding in Atlantic City, who had fought hard for the civil rights bill and had been the Senate's conscience on civil rights for fifteen years. They had a commitment from the national party to ban discrimination in delegate selection to future conventions (though no promise on voting rights). Not least, they had forced a walkout of the Mississippi segregationists, possibly the first step toward wholesale party realignment benefiting the civil rights forces, at least in the long run. The sharpest difference was that while grassroots leaders felt deserted by Machiavellian liberal allies, the elite felt upbeat that they could work profitably with the Democratic power structure. It was not surprising that Andrew Young assessed the Atlantic City outcome as comparable to Birmingham.

Evidence of the civil rights generals' new hubris was their willingness to honor LBJ's request to halt demonstrations for the duration of the presidential campaign. Wilkins and Whitney Young insisted on an outright ban. Leaders of CORE (which had virtually invented civil rights direct action in the 1940s) and of SNCC were against the idea of a breather. Neither group wanted to brake the momentum of Freedom Summer. CORE believed there was no better time for militant protest, which they had been spearheading all over the country, especially around employment and housing issues.

As usual when the movement's left and right flanks clashed, King assumed the position of mediator—the self-styled unifier of opposites, seeking to clarify and merge the strengths of each side. James Farmer and John Lewis hoped that King would back them up, but he recoiled from tangling with the combative Wilkins. "Martin was not an arguer at all or a debater," Farmer recalled.[117] "He never was able to infight," Rustin observed. "He always took a neutralist position, and let the decision be made."[118]

While it was true that he was no infighter and assumed an outwardly passive pose in such confrontations, he was not a neutralist, one who took no position. Having faith in a larger unity, King held both positions at once, in creative if chaotic tension—his interest in each cloaked by compassionate listening—as he sought to blend them into a principled compromise agreeable to both sides. At this late summer summit, the generals hammered out a statement calling for a "broad curtailment, if not total moratorium of all mass marches, picketing and demonstrations"—not quite what the President had in mind, but SNCC and CORE would accept nothing more binding.[119]

King's October 1 address to the SCLC convention in Savannah, Georgia, showed that Rustin's influence on him was as strong as ever. If SCLC was to move beyond its southern base, lead a national movement, and focus on economic justice, he said, it must place greater priority on electoral coalition building, and not just in the pressure cooker of a presidential campaign. "We are now facing basic social and economic problems that require political reform."[120] To fight a full war on poverty, the movement would have to exercise control over Congress and the bureaucracy, necessitating new allies and new methods.

Both the movement elite and the foot soldiers agreed that they must shape power nonviolently through the electoral process. But the former believed in political breadth, the latter in moral depth—an expanding universe versus a solid moral core.

While King called for a shift in priorities, unlike Rustin he did not propose replacing protest with politics. Although the unexpectedly high degree of compliance with the Civil Rights Act's public-accommodations provisions meant that the movement would not need to engage in direct-action enforcement like the freedom rides, on a large scale, King had no illusions that voting rights could be achieved without nonviolent combat. Rather than the false dichotomy of direct action versus electoral politics, he wanted to combine the two—the best of each tradition—into a creative if ambiguous synthesis, working simultaneously outside and inside the political system. He was vague on the details, in which the devil would no doubt be found. His experiences in Montgomery and Birmingham had taught him that on a local level, direct action was never divorced from municipal politics; for disfranchised black citizens, direct action was usually an expression of politics by other means.

His personal effort to combine the two approaches—shepherding a direct-action organization while barnstorming city after city against Goldwater, sometimes with parades honoring King, and to get out the vote—landed him in an Atlanta hospital with a virus and high blood pressure, "completely exhausted, tired and empty," according to his wife.[121] As he was sleeping in his hospital bed, Coretta King called him with news that he had won the Nobel Peace Prize.

Although hesitant to disrupt his rest, she "realized that this was exactly the sort of lift Martin desperately needed."[122] He had not felt exalted when chosen as *Time*'s "Man of the Year" back in January, but this was the highest earthly honor that leadership could attain, his own and the grassroots leadership of the movement. At his bedside he gathered Coretta and three assistants in solemn prayer that they would bear the heavier cross that the prize bestowed.

"History has thrust me into this position," he told the crush of reporters who invaded the hospital.[123]

Now it would be harder than ever for him to reclaim the old Martin King who had been swallowed up by this gargantuan persona. It would be harder than ever for him to distinguish between the two realities, to determine which self was more real—the Whitmanesque cosmic Self containing multitudes, with a mission to save them, or the bantering Baptist minister whose favorite pastime was devouring barbecued pig's ears and trading "nigger jokes" with his preacher pals, listening to the blues.

In early November Lyndon Johnson trounced Barry Goldwater by the largest popular-vote margin in U.S. history (61 percent to 39 percent). The Arizona senator carried only his own state and the Deep South. LBJ's strategy of campaigning as president of all the people and showing restrained forcefulness abroad and at home had paid off. Coattails of Camelot gave the Democrats an increased majority in the Senate and even more in the House; they now controlled two-thirds of each chamber. Johnson's "Great Society" seemed more than a mirage. Although Goldwater, the jet-piloting senator from Phoenix, and his right-banking party had hit the ground, a longer-winged phoenix would before long take flight from the Republican ashes.

SHORTLY AFTER THE HISTORIC election SNCC held a retreat in Waveland, Mississippi. In a turbulent atmosphere belied by the Gulf of Mexico's calm waters, weary activists grappled with pressing internal conflicts, particularly between blacks and whites (also between men and women), and charted new directions. Anger festering over summer and fall now burst its seams. Many black organizers, especially from poorer families, were steamed that the army of white college students, despite noble intentions, had sometimes disrespected and pushed aside native blacks, dampening their budding somebodiness. Betrayal in Atlantic City combined with the white students' insensitivity had led SNCC's black majority to deeply question its interracial basis. The brave white students had served their purpose as cannon fodder, but the price might have been too steep. To survive and grow, many came to feel, the movement had to get blacker.

· · ·

THROUGH DOGGED WILLPOWER King kept his fractured self intact during the final climactic weeks of 1964. The Nobel glory—he was feted by global leaders—lifted his public persona into the stratosphere while depression plagued his soul.

The FBI was in hot pursuit. Meeting with women journalists in mid-November, J. Edgar Hoover attacked King as "the most notorious liar in the country" for his criticisms of southern FBI agents, particularly in Albany, Georgia. King and his aides were blindsided. What was Hoover up to? Should they fight or try to make up? King issued a conciliatory statement and arranged an appointment with Hoover to clear the air, which turned out to be pure show, a "completely nonfunctional meeting," in Young's words.[124]

A week later King met with Farmer at Kennedy airport and flatly denied charges of Communist ties or financial misdealings that the FBI was gearing up to hit him with. Playing down the sexual rumors, he nonetheless confided in Farmer that "when a man travels like you and I do, there are bound to be women."[125] In fact he was terrified that his compulsive sexual romping would catch up with him—and his divine anointment might crumble into dust.

In early December, as King was flying to Oslo with a princely entourage of thirty friends and family, his inner self was as despondent as his public one was triumphant. Pressing royal flesh and hobnobbing with European bigwigs, he showed no sign of the black mood within. But he could not hide it from Coretta and those who knew him best. Besides sexual guilt eating at him, he was distressed by Abernathy's juvenile jealousy in petulantly claiming his share of the Oslo limelight and of the fifty-four thousand dollars prize money. King had decided to give it all to the movement that had won it with him, vetoing Coretta's plea that half be saved for their children's college education.

"Only Martin's family and close staff members knew how depressed he was during the entire Nobel trip," Coretta King revealed later. "He was worried that the rumors might hurt the movement and he was concerned about what black people would think. He always worried about that. We had to work with him and help him out of his depression. Somehow he managed all the official functions, the speeches, the whole trip and the public never knew what he was going through."[126]

After receiving the gold medallion on a grand stage in Oslo frosted with carnations, he declared that he was accepting the award as trustee on behalf of the entire civil rights movement. In his public lecture at Oslo University he extolled the power of nonviolent methods and urged they be used to bring about world peace and disarmament, the highest aim of humanity.

"Those who pioneer in the struggle for peace and freedom will still face uncomfortable jail terms, painful threats of death. They will still be battered by the storms of persecution, leading them to nagging feelings that they can no longer bear such a heavy burden." Nonviolent warriors would always face "the temptation of wanting to retreat to a more quiet and serene life," as he surely did in his inward soul, but they must not succumb. They must carry their cross to the bitter end.

Returning to New York, he was given a tumultuous welcome as though he were the pope or had won the World Series. He was now world famous. The American president hosted him, his wife, and parents at a warm White House reception.

II

Following the White House welcome, King met alone with the President, who sang the praises of his war on poverty. King applauded the new program but insisted that the movement's higher priority was strong voting rights legislation.

"Martin, you're right about that," Johnson replied. "I'm going to do it eventually, but I can't get a voting rights bill through in this session of Congress."[127] He wanted to wait until the dust had settled from the Civil Rights Act, just five months old. Like the cautious JFK he could not forfeit the support of southern barons in Congress for his Great Society programs. As shown by his response to the MFDP insurgency, black voting rights were not as important to him as substantive reforms like medical care for the aged and aid to education and to cities.

The Nash and Bevel master plan to enfranchise black Alabamians, conceived as a permanent memorial, and the moral equivalent of revenge, for the four slain girls, was finally coming to fruition fifteen months after the church bombing. King called a staff retreat in Birmingham shortly after the election, where he stressed the need to export nonviolent methods to the urban North, but they decided that an Alabama voting rights campaign was the next order of business. Should it be statewide, they debated, which would scatter their forces; should it focus on the state capital; or should it apply concentrated force on one city or county that was notably resistant to black registration?

Longtime Selma activist Amelia Boynton, a Tuskegee graduate, gave the answer when she reported on the awful situation in Dallas County, where 2 percent of eligible black voters were registered, registration was restricted to two days a month, and local judge James Hare had flouted the First Amendment by banning all demonstrations. Local leaders were convinced that only by electing their own city and county officials could they overcome the racist repression that plagued the black community. For two years a small band of SNCC activists had been organizing ward meetings and registration marches in the central Alabama city fifty miles west of Montgomery. The marchers had braved fierce attacks by Sheriff Jim Clark and his Klan-ridden posse similar to St. Augustine's. But the 1964 Mississippi campaign had depleted SNCC's efforts and small progress had been made. Moderate black leaders were hopeful, as they had been in Birmingham, that the election of a new mayor, Joe Smitherman, replacing a staunch segregationist, would alleviate racial conflict.

Boynton and the Dallas County Voters League invited SCLC to help them boost registration locally. The new strategy was for SCLC to go first to Selma (population thirty thousand, about half black), then fan out into several neighboring counties in Alabama's Black Belt, culminating in Montgomery. They made plans to challenge the seating of the all-white legislature and discussed creating a Freedom Democratic Party in Alabama. Boynton and her colleagues worried, though, that SCLC would leave town before the local battle was won. Nor did they want SCLC to run the show, weakening indigenous leadership. But they were willing to take the risk. The two groups planned a kickoff rally in Selma for the day after Emancipation Day.

Before heading to Selma, King had his own local concern to deal with—helping to resolve a strike by black workers at Atlanta's Scripto pen company, a few blocks from "Sweet Auburn" Avenue. Some strikers worshiped at his church. One night he disappeared from home and stood alone at the plant gate in the midnight chill, talking with workers at the shift change. They won a decent settlement by Christmas. Ahead of many of his movement peers, King was attentive to economic deprivation and workers' rights. But he was at a loss for how to translate his concern into a strategy.

The Selma rally on Saturday, January 2, filled the red-brick, twin-steepled Brown Chapel AME Church across from a black housing project. Defying Judge Hare's prohibition, it was the first black political gathering in six months. But Selma's director of public safety, Wilson Baker, part of the new city leadership, had no intention of halting the peaceful if rambunctious rally. Although Christmas radiance and the Nobel afterglow had not relieved his depression, King's spirited pep talk betrayed no hint of his inner roiling.

"At the rate they are letting us register now," he asserted, "it will take a hundred and three years to register all of the fifteen thousand Negroes in Dallas County who are qualified to vote."

"That's right!"

"But we don't *have* that *long* to wait!" The audience roared.

"Today marks the beginning of a determined, organized, mobilized campaign to get the right to vote everywhere in Alabama. If we are refused, we will appeal to Governor George Wallace. If he refuses to listen, we will appeal to the legislature. If they don't listen, we will appeal to the conscience of the Congress in another dramatic march on Washington.

"Give us the ballot!" he belted out again and again as the assembly's rising shouts shook the walls and stained-glass windows.[128]

Three days later 75 million Americans, a record TV audience, watched President Johnson deliver his second State of the Union address to Congress. Plugging voting rights in passing, he spotlighted his Great Society reforms that constituted the most ambitious progressive legislation since America's halfhearted welfare state was born in 1935. The measures passed in 1964 and 1965 would bring the nation a quantum leap closer to the social democracies of western Europe and Canada, while still falling short without fundamentals like national health insurance and economic planning. No wonder conservatives condemned the Great Society agenda as a communist five-year plan.

Unlike Kennedy, Johnson reveled in Civil War echoes and analogies. In his address he called for a "new quest for union" as the nation began its second century after the Civil War's "terrible test of blood and fire." Somewhere in his soul he may have sensed that a new civil war of blood and fire was about to break loose. If he was to be another Great Emancipator he would, like Lincoln, have to pay a price in national blood.

The FBI was surely after King's blood. Just before his meeting with Hoover at Thanksgiving an anonymous package landed in his Atlanta mailbox, secretly delivered by FBI agents—a bombshell as politically deadly as the dynamite tossed on his porch in Montgomery. The package contained an audiotape of King and friends having an apparent sexual party in a hotel room, along with a letter purportedly from a black man (composed by the FBI) urging King to commit suicide. Damning him as "a great liability for all of us Negroes," the hand-scrawled letter stated that "Satan could not do more. What incredible evilness. Your end is approaching. You are done. There is but one way out for you. You better take it before your filthy, abnormal fraudulent self is bared to the nation."[129]

The letter showed that, whatever its failures at capturing hooded killers in the Deep South, the agency's yearlong surveillance of King had hooked into his psychological Achilles' heel. How did the FBI know that he felt himself to be a fraud, an impostor? What if the world found out that he was not really a man of God underneath his robes? Because mail piled up at the King home, the suicide package was not opened—by Coretta King—until after New Year's. She read the letter and listened to her husband's earthly exaltations. Shaken, she called him to come home. He played the tape over and over.

THROUGHOUT JANUARY 1965 SCLC and the Voters League organized marches to the courthouse to seek registration, and tested desegregation of restaurants. Run-ins with Sheriff Clark resulted in clusters of arrests. King led a Monday-morning march of four hundred, many of them teenagers, to the courthouse, where they were blocked by Clark and harassed by George Lincoln Rockwell and his Nazi thugs. King invited the American Nazi führer to speak at that night's mass meeting, a ploy to tantalize the media. He and his aides then checked in to the grand antebellum Hotel Albert, a replica of the Doges' Palace in Venice, to test desegregation. When King and Dorothy Cotton encountered a white supremacist in the lobby, he asked the man, "You're still going to be with us tonight?"

"I'm afraid not," he replied, then hit King in the face and, as he fell to the floor, kicked him in the groin. He was more startled than injured. Baker quickly arrested the attacker. That evening at the mass meeting the public safety director seized Rockwell and his Nazi band when they rose to King's bait. Despite this adrenaline release, the movement, with few new voters, appeared to be stalling.

As the unleashing of children turned the corner in Birmingham, teachers broke the impasse in Selma. On January 22, with King back in Atlanta, Voters League president Frederick Reese, a high school teacher and pastor, led an after-school march of over a hundred teachers— nearly all the black schoolteachers—to the courthouse. Although female teachers such as Jo Ann Robinson in Montgomery had spear-headed the bus boycott, in other Deep South towns teachers scared for their jobs had been among the last to join in; even in Montgomery they never protested openly. Often as in Birmingham teachers conspired with principals to keep students captive. Reese had labored hard to get the teachers out, shaming them when need be.

The miracle of these marching teachers, some already registered, risking their livelihoods and the administrators' wrath, gave black Selma a feeling that they might win the battle. Their students felt proud of them. Now the principals had to keep both teachers and pupils penned up. Teachers were the first middle-class citizens to march; they were followed by beauticians and undertakers. Activists started saying to one another, "Brother, we got a *move*-ment goin' on in Selma!"

Physical encounters with Sheriff Clark revved up as well. He decked campaign director Bevel and Rev. C. T. Vivian when, eyeball to eyeball, each tried to speak truth to power on the courthouse steps.

When King led another courthouse march in late January, the sheriff roughly shoved Annie Lee Cooper, who had been fired from a white-owned nursing home for organizing employees to vote. "With a curse under her breath," an eyewitness recounted, "she slugged Clark near the left eye with her fist. She was a tall, powerfully built woman, and Clark staggered to his knees under the blow; as he did, she hit him again."[130] When deputies grabbed her, she pummeled and kicked them, then ran over to punch the fallen sheriff once more for good measure. Three deputies wrestled her to the ground. The sheriff got to his feet and bashed her with his club. She wrenched it away and knocked Clark's helmet off as they fought over the stick. With trembling hands he finally pulled it free and smashed her again on the skull as deputies dragged her away in double handcuffs.

"Don't bother with it!" King yelled out, to keep the marchers from striking back.[131]

After a month of marching and jail-going they had a movement in Selma, but it was not having national impact. Bevel and other leaders decided that, as in Birmingham, King needed to be arrested in order to stir up the media. On Monday, February 1, King led a march of three hundred adults out of Brown Chapel, all in one body rather than in clumps in order to force arrest by Baker, the Laurie Pritchett of Selma. If they made it to the courthouse Sheriff Clark would be waiting for them, which would put King at risk of bodily harm if not death. He and Abernathy were the last to be arrested. Baker did not want them jailed, but they gave him no choice.

At first they were placed with a hundred other protesters in a steaming, ninety-foot holding tank, where King was able to greet and talk with ordinary inmates through the bars. He was appalled to hear from some who had been in for months or even years without knowing the charges. In no mood to make a speech, he proposed a Quaker-type meeting where any of the protesters could speak, sing, or pray as the spirit said do. Abernathy read Psalm 27: "The Lord is my light and my salvation; whom shall I fear?"[132] Fervent testimony, prayer, and freedom songs brought bodies and emotions to a fever in this Quaker meeting like none other.

Transferred to a small cell with Abernathy and white SCLC staffer Charles Fager (the jail had just been desegregated), King fasted as usual for the first two days and conducted his jail routine of prayer, meditation, hymn singing, and workouts. He chatted with Fager about the obstacles that lay ahead to fundamental change. "If we are going to achieve real equality," he said, "the United States will have to adopt a modified form of socialism."[133] He liked what he had tasted in Norway and Sweden.

As leaders hoped, the tempo of protest stepped up during the first week of February. In the afternoon after King was jailed, five hundred schoolchildren, inspired by teachers and parents, joined the grown-ups behind bars. In Marion, Coretta King's hometown, thirty miles north in Perry County, several hundred adults and young people were jailed in their first Freedom Day. Hundreds more got arrested in both counties by the end of the week, the total of three thousand prisoners surpassing Birmingham's peak.

Before the chain reaction of arrests that week, SCLC leaders had anticipated a breakthrough in Selma, then moving on to adjoining counties like Perry and Lowndes, where virtually no blacks voted and repression was heavier.

A federal judge's decision easing registration rules seemed to offer a way for SCLC to leave Selma gracefully. Bevel and Young ordered a moratorium on marching. King might have gone along with such an exit strategy a year or two before, as he had accepted the Birmingham compromise that Shuttlesworth had opposed. He learned from that experience that Shuttlesworth had been right about the city's backsliding, just as he himself had been right that the truce was adequate to gain national legislation. Now in February 1965 he was not willing to settle for a half-a-loaf victory that would not appreciably expand Selma's black electorate. Tensions had been rising already between the Voters League and SNCC's concern with local empowerment on one hand and SCLC's larger goal of a voting rights law on the other.

From his jail cell King criticized Young for the pause, ordered a new round of protests, and wrote out a detailed game plan for upping the ante, with presidential and congressional intervention and a media offensive. He was not ready to leave town.

In the first month of Selma protests the small SNCC team found itself as an awkward third wheel squeezed between SCLC and the Voters League, not sure of its rightful role. What could they do to further mobilize Selma's youth? While King was in jail two SNCC organizers drove an hour east to Tuskegee to hear Malcolm X address a packed hall at famed Tuskegee Institute, built by Booker T. Washington. When they met with him afterward, Malcolm encouraged their work and they invited him to visit Selma.

Next morning, to Bevel's and Young's shocked chagrin, he showed up at Brown Chapel in time for a morning youth rally. In a hurried parley in the pastor's study the SCLC staff sought to fence in what he might say, to which he retorted, "Nobody puts words in my mouth."[134] The SNCC workers insisted that he speak, freely. Bevel and Young gave in.

Malcolm's message to the youth rally was restrained and constructive. Calling himself a field slave, with a different perspective than "house Negroes," he declared that the white folk "should thank Dr. King for holding people in check, for there are others who do not believe in these measures. But I'm not going to try to stir you up and make you do something you wouldn't have done anyway." He urged them to take their grievance to the United Nations and put the racists on trial before the world. The young people clapped and cheered.

"I pray that God will bless you in everything that you do," he concluded. "I pray that you will grow intellectually"—as he had shown the way, especially in the past year—"and I pray that all the fear that has ever been in your heart will be taken out."[135] When he returned to the church study Diane Nash apologized for the ministers who had tried to censor him. She confessed that some of them did not understand nonviolence themselves. During the rally he talked with Coretta King, in Selma to visit her jailed husband. She had spoken to the young people to reaffirm the urgency of nonviolent principles.

"Mrs. King," he said to her, "will you tell Dr. King that I had planned to visit with him in jail." He couldn't now because he was late for an African students' conference in London. It was doubtful he would have gotten in to see him. The two men had met once briefly, the past March, a chance encounter at the Capitol during debate over the civil rights bill.

"I want Dr. King to know that I didn't come to Selma to make his job difficult. I really did come thinking that I could make it easier. If the white people realize what the alternative is, perhaps they will be more willing to hear Dr. King."

She was moved by his sincerity and goodwill and told her husband about their conversation when she visited him later that day. "He didn't react too much one way or the other," she recalled.[136]

Two weeks later, the chickens came home to roost for Malcolm X. On February 21, he appeared at Harlem's Audobon Ballroom to unveil the new political program of his Organization of Afro-American Unity, which he wanted to ally with the civil rights movement. He was convinced that he could work with SNCC and even with King. He had been highly impressed by the Selma movement on his brief visit. As he began his address, his wife and children in front of him, Nation of Islam assassins shot him down in a burst of gunfire. They were presumably acting on orders of Malcolm's rivals in the Nation, who had openly called for the apostate's death.

THE DAY AFTER Malcolm's Selma visit, King walked out of jail in time to meet with fifteen mostly liberal congressmen on a fact-finding trip. In a breach of protocol that showed his clout, he announced that he would be meeting with the President, though uninvited. LBJ and his aides were put off by King's chutzpah, but they acquiesced to a meeting at which Johnson for the first time publicly supported a voting rights bill that his Justice Department was drawing up. Guided by the federal court's new rules, white and black Selma leaders met and worked with the obstinate county registrar to make black registration swifter and easier. While the Voters League was pleased with incremental progress, SCLC wanted to step up protests in Selma to build pressure for national reform.

The morning after his release from jail, King attended a meeting to decide whether to send two SNCC activists as scouts to forbidding Lowndes County to investigate the climate for voting rights work. The plan was for them to leave early the next morning, Sunday, and get out before dark. Sometimes during meetings King would excuse himself, go into another room, and pray on the decision at hand. When he returned Abernathy would announce with biblical pomp that the word of God was about to be spoken, and King would reveal to them what God had told him. No one was willing to gainsay or second-guess the Lord.

At this meeting, according to a participant, King abruptly started reciting by heart the passage from Hebrew Scriptures about Moses sending twelve scouts into Canaan to scope out the Promised Land.

When they came back after forty days, two of the scouts encouraged the Israelites to fight for the Promised Land of milk and honey; the other ten terrified them with reports of giants who would slaughter them. Defying the command of God and of Moses, the people refused to go forward. Moses beseeched God not to kill them all, so instead the Lord banished the Hebrews to the wilderness for forty years. The ten cowardly spies died from a plague. The brave ones, Joshua and Caleb, were the only two of that generation allowed to enter the Promised Land. After reciting his Torah portion, King was followed without pause by other preachers in the circle: Abernathy, then C. T. Vivian, then Hosea Williams, all speaking from memory. The land of milk and honey, one said, would be a land flowing with black people exercising the vote. Telling the biblical tale in this round-robin prayer gave the group courage while revealing the answer. King insisted that the two SNCC spies take the fastest car to Canaan.[137]

Next week King returned to Selma from Washington, ill with a virus, as marches built momentum. Jails full, the sheriff's frustration led him to loose his posse on young marchers, chasing them with whips and electric cattle prods on a long-distance run into outlying woods. Soon after, Clark was hospitalized with heart pains; in their next court-house foray marchers prayed for his recovery. At a mass meeting King called for night marches, the explosive element in St. Augustine, to escalate the struggle.

The movement was spreading out through the Black Belt with protests in Perry and Wilcox counties, in Montgomery, and a planned move north to Birmingham. Just out of jail, Rev. Vivian reluctantly answered a call by activists in Marion, the Perry County seat, to speak at a mass meeting that would spill out into the night. After his pep talk at Zion's Chapel Methodist Church, driving back toward Selma, he was alarmed to pass a twenty-car convoy of siren-blaring state police racing toward Marion. Protesters left the church intending a short march to the courthouse. They were met by a phalanx of state troopers who gave them no chance to turn around. Streetlights went out as the troopers clobbered them with heavy clubs. White toughs attacked newsmen, giving NBC's Richard Valeriani a near-fatal head wound, beating up UPI photographers, smashing their cameras.

Protesters retreated back to the church but were blocked by people still coming out. A few dozen found refuge in Mack's Café, but troopers burst inside, shot out the lights, and brutalized people indiscriminately. Cager Lee, eighty-two, beaten bloody on the street, had run into the café after his daughter Viola Jackson. Lee's grandson Jimmie Lee Jackson, twenty-six, was trying to lead the old man to medical help, but troopers forced them back inside. When they attacked Jackson's mother, who was aiding her father and son, Jimmie shielded her with his body. Troopers slammed him against a cigarette machine and shot him twice in the stomach. Crawling through a gauntlet of beatings, Jackson managed to escape from the café, then collapsed on the street, bleeding heavily. A friend took him to the small Marion hospital; he was ambulanced to Selma, where they could give him blood.

During the rampage someone ran into Sheriff Clark, off duty in civilian clothes, and asked why he had left his own turf. Things were too quiet in Selma, he replied with a smirk.

Thousands prayed for the devout Jimmie Lee Jackson, a well-loved pulpwood-mill worker and youngest deacon of Marion's St. James Baptist Church. He had attempted five times to register in Perry County courthouse. Rather than the voting card he risked his life for, Col. Al Lingo, head of the state police, served him at his hospital bed with a warrant for assault and battery with intent to murder a state trooper. Eight days after the shooting he died.

Bevel and Bernard Lafayette mourned with Jackson's bandaged family in their small house by a creek. The family told Bevel they should keep moving. Cager Lee said he was ready to march again. Weeping as he left their house, Bevel asked Lafayette if he would trek with him to Montgomery. The idea for a march to the state capital, starting from Marion, had come to him in the dark hours before Jackson died, as he walked his own garden of Gethsemane outside the Torch Motel.

"I tell you," Bevel said to the mass meeting at Brown Chapel the next night, "the death of that man is pushing me kind of hard." People wailed. He spoke two Bible passages, one about King Herod killing James, the other from Hebrew Scriptures in which Esther was called to go to the king to save the Jews from destruction. The king in this kairos time was George Wallace, their chief oppressor.

Personifying Esther, he yelled out, "I must go see the king!" The assembly pledged that like Esther they would all go on foot. "Be prepared to walk to Montgomery," he cried. "Be prepared to sleep on the highway!"[138]

Bevel was not the only one driven by a vision of marching to confront the king, but the most vocal. Marion activists felt the same boiling urge; they wanted to carry Jackson's coffin to Wallace's office. SCLC staff had been contemplating a march to the capital for months. Ever since Bevel and Diane Nash had dreamed up their Alabama battle plan in the hours after the four girls were blown apart, they knew that the climax would be in Montgomery, where the movement had started out a decade before. But the impulsive Bevel did not seek approval from King or the Voters League before trumpeting the march. A preacher's fighting call to reenact a biblical journey could not be turned back easily.

"I had to get the people out of a state of grief," Bevel recalled of his motivation. "If you don't deal with negative violence and grief, it turns into bitterness. So what I recommended was that people walk to Montgomery, which would give them time to work through their hostility and resentments. If you went back to some of the classical strategies of Gandhi, when you have a great violation of the people and there's a great sense of injury, you have to give people an honorable means and context in which to express and eliminate that grief and speak decisively back to the issue. Otherwise the movement will break down in violence and chaos."[139]

SCLC staff and Selma leaders went along with Bevel and grassroots rage and set the date: the journey would begin the next Sunday, March 7, from Selma. King reluctantly OK'd the decision. Bevel persuaded him to stay in Atlanta for his safety. The air was thick with death threats against him. He also felt obligated to lead the communion service at his church after being absent for weeks. They did not expect to get past the bridge over the Alabama River, named for Edmund Pettus, Selma's own Confederate general, who ruled the county after the Civil War.

On Tuesday, March 2, King spoke at Howard University in Washington, appending his first public criticism of the Vietnam intervention, as "accomplishing nothing."[140] Three weeks before, National Liberation Front guerrillas, aka Vietcong, assaulted a U.S. base at Pleiku in the

Central Highlands of South Vietnam, killing several soldiers. Just as the Gulf of Tonkin incident provided the pretext for August's air attacks and a congressional blank check for more, so the Pleiku incident was the awaited provocation to unleash the "sustained reprisal" bombardment of North Vietnam code-named "Rolling Thunder." Little could King imagine that these air attacks would mushroom into an air war whose bomb tonnage surpassed the Allied bombing of Europe, Japan, and Korea combined. Six days after King's Howard speech the first combat marines arrived to defend the sprawling air base at Da Nang. A few weeks later President Johnson secretly changed the marines' assignment to "search and destroy" the Vietcong.

"THERE WAS THAT PILE of rolled-up blankets," marcher Maria Varela scribbled on a scrap of paper, "taken off beds and wrapped up with belts, or old ties, or string. There they were in the corner by the altar—a patchwork mountain of rolled-up trust. 'We are going,' 'WE ARE GOING' spoke that patchwork mountain in its unvalued dignity."

After workshops in Brown Chapel that included lessons by medics on coping with tear gas, Hosea Williams of SCLC and SNCC's John Lewis led six hundred people carrying rolled-up blankets past the housing project toward the Alabama River, walking two by two. They were defying an order by Governor Wallace prohibiting the march.

Crossing the Edmund Pettus Bridge, the large-framed Williams whispered to slender Lewis, "John, can you swim?" Lewis shook his head. "I can't either, and I'm sure we're gonna end up in that river." On the downward end of the arching bridge the long thin column, keeping to the sidewalk, was halted by a solid body of gas-masked state troopers. With little warning they lunged at the marchers, smashing heads and lobbing tear-gas grenades, the first thrown by Sheriff Clark as he shrieked, "Get those god-damned niggers! Get those god-damned white niggers!"[141] Felled Amelia Boynton, knocked unconscious, barely avoided suffocation by a gas-spewing grenade a trooper had placed by her face.

Troopers and Clark's mounted posse, the riders with bone-chilling rebel yells, chased and trampled the marchers all the way back to the church headquarters, madly flailing whips, clubs wrapped in barbed wire, and electric cattle prods. Scores were injured, some severely, the lucky ones rescued by movement ambulances. At a Baptist church cops hurled a youth through a stained-glass window of Jesus. Despite a fractured skull, blood flowing, Lewis found strength to direct his fallen comrades out of danger. Back at Brown Chapel Bevel, Williams, and Lewis conferred by phone with King at home in Atlanta. He was upset about the unexpected rampage, regretful that he wasn't there.

"HE DIDN'T COME, and they went without him," Varela's poem, found crumpled in a raincoat, exclaimed. "Picked up their bedrolls, umbrellas (we had laughed about what 'de lawd' would do if it rained) and brown paper sacks with toothbrushes.

"I wonder would it have been different had he been there? But no matter.

"A man is allowed his weak moments, and other christs always seem to rise up to take their place. Many hundreds did that day."[142]

As happened in Birmingham, the graphic televised brutality—sharply contrasting with the protesters' nonviolent discipline—won over much of the American public. In a rare act of media morality ABC interrupted its national broadcast of the film *Judgment at Nuremberg*, starring Spencer Tracy as the war-crimes judge, to show the Selma racial pogrom in living color.

Protests against "Bloody Sunday," demanding federal action, erupted in cities all over the country, including a SNCC sit-in at the attorney general's office—protesters dragged out late at night—and a ballooning White House vigil and picket line. Congress members called Bloody Sunday "an exercise in terror."[143]

At King's direction SCLC flashed telegrams to hundreds of northern clergy urging them to join him two days later to carry on the march. Federal judge Frank Johnson, the swing vote in desegregating Montgomery's buses, enjoined the Tuesday march pending a hearing. King agonized under opposite pulls from the feds and the locals. At one point he decided to call it off, but finally resolved to proceed. He was not sure he could stop the march without being spurned. But he had never before violated a federal court order. If he could disobey a federal court, why couldn't white supremacists?

The two thousand singing and chanting marchers, ranks swelled by a Who's Who of religious notables and a large Unitarian contingent, recrossed the river. A forbidding line of troopers stopped them at the same point as on Sunday. King led the gathering in prayer, then ordered the long column to turn back. They retreated to Brown Chapel singing "Ain't Gonna Let Nobody Turn Me 'Round," the Selma theme song— an irony not lost on many. Back at the church he promised his followers that they would still get to Montgomery.

King's unilateral move, apparently a secret last-minute deal with federal officials, angered more-militant protesters and deepened SNCC's distrust of De Lawd. In King's view, marching across the bridge to the police barricade and turning back was a reasonable, even honorable compromise, a middle way between unacceptable extremes. He violated the injunction, but to a limited extent. SNCC's Forman called King's compromise "a classic example of trickery against the people."[144] King denied that he had made an agreement with the feds to turn around, claiming that he had decided to halt when they faced an impassable helmeted blockade.

COURTHOUSE MARCHES CONTINUED in Selma. A quiet procession led by youthful Jimmy Webb was halted by deputy sheriff L. C. Crocker, who told them the courthouse was closed.

> Webb: All we want to do is go to the lawn of the courthouse, kneel in prayer, and we'll gladly return—
> Crocker: You take your prayers back to your church. That's the proper place to pray. I'm sure that God'll hear your prayer just as well down there as he will up here, but you're not going on this courthouse lawn.
> Webb: Sir, whenever there are men in a sinful condition, prayer should be uttered wherever they are.
> Crocker: Then why don't you pray where you are? Go back down there and pray. You think you're lily white? You think you're not sinful?
> Webb: No.
> Crocker: Well then, go back to your church and pray.
> Webb: Sir, can we pray together, you and I?

> Crocker: *You do your prayin' and I do mine, big boy. You don't pray for me. I don't want you to pray for me! Because I don't think your prayers get above your head.*
>
> Webb: *Will you pray for us?*
>
> Crocker: *No, I'm not going to pray for you. I tend to my business, you tend to yours.*

"What about love?" a young woman asked him

Crocker: I don't have to love anybody I don't want to love. You do your own lovin'. You love your little niggers. I'll love who I please.

THE RAPID-FIRE EVENTS in Selma, especially the vigilante slaying of Rev. James Reeb, a Boston Unitarian minister—arousing national concern and presidential attention that Jackson's killing had not—worked magic on Washington politicians, not least the supreme politician in the Oval Office. A sit-in disrupted his own home, a first in the White House. As demonstrations mounted around the country Johnson resolved to make a bill ensuring universal suffrage, with federal registrars and a ban on literacy tests, his most urgent domestic priority. He and Attorney General Nicholas Katzenbach quickly crafted a coalition to enact the bill.

George Wallace wired LBJ for a meeting about the crisis. On Saturday morning, March 13, the President gave Wallace the "Johnson treatment" in the Oval Office. Sitting practically on top of him, his steely eyes locked on Wallace's for three hours, LBJ cajoled and scolded the much smaller man about black people's right to vote in Alabama, and why the governor should do all in his power to help rather than hinder them. This would stop all the protests. "Why don't you let the niggers vote?" When Wallace nervously insisted there was nothing he could do, LBJ shot back, "Don't you shit me, George Wallace!"[145] He goaded Wallace to live a hundred years in the future, instead of a hundred years in the past.

Taking the governor in tow for a Rose Garden press conference, a thousand chanting protesters outside the gate, the President declared that Bloody Sunday and the Reverend Reeb's killing were "an American tragedy." Embracing the Selma protests, he called for immediate passage of a strict voting rights bill. He said he had urged Wallace, standing mute by the big guy's side, to support universal suffrage and the right of peaceful assembly.

The cowed governor admitted to the press that "I have much more respect for him than I thought I'd ever have. If I hadn't left when I did," he quipped, "he'd have had me coming out for civil rights."[146] But Wallace in Johnson's maw was a different animal than the fox in his Alabama lair.

Selma protesters huddled around worn black-and-white TV sets on Monday evening, March 15, to watch the President plead for the bill, with uncharacteristic passion, before a joint session of Congress and 70 million viewers. No president had made such an address on a domestic matter for two decades, never before on television.

"At times history and fate meet in a single time in a single place," he began, his big frame hunched over the lectern, "to shape a turning point in man's unending search for freedom. So it was at Lexington and Concord. So it was a century ago at Appomattox. So it was last week in Selma, Alabama." He recalled his own encounters with discrimination against Mexicans as a young Texas schoolteacher and declared: "I do not want to be the president who built empires, or sought grandeur, or extended domain. I want to be the president who helped to feed the hungry."[147] No doubt LBJ's finest hour.

SCLC leaders were watching the speech at a Selma participant's home. When Johnson promised the nation that "we shall overcome," a subdued Martin King blinked tears while his colleagues cheered. They had never seen him cry before.

After a Montgomery hearing Judge Frank Johnson ruled that the extreme nature of wrongs black citizens were facing justified redress to the outer limit of the First Amendment's right of peaceful assembly. He permitted protesters to march on the highway to Montgomery, even if disrupting traffic; the state of Alabama was responsible for protecting them; and if the state failed to, the federal government would step in. The protest would be limited to three hundred where Highway 80 was two lanes, but unlimited for the first and last legs, especially entering the capital.

Under fierce presidential pressure Wallace agreed to provide protection, then reneged, wiring LBJ that he did not have adequate forces. Infuriated at this double cross, Johnson urged him to call up the Alabama National Guard. When Wallace balked, playing into his hand, the President federalized the Alabama guard and sent in two thousand army troops, including two field hospitals, one of the largest military deployments in the South since Union forces pulled out in 1877.

Before the trek could commence, SCLC staff had to pull together a monumental logistics operation: inviting a multitude of outsiders, setting up encampments along the route, requisitioning food, blankets, and sleeping bags for thousands, recruiting medical teams—and the delicate task of choosing three hundred privileged souls to carry the torch all fifty miles. At a mass meeting logistics czar Hosea Williams pleaded "dire need of personnel with formal training and experience in the following categories: portable latrines, water tanks, bath trucks, garbage trucks, medical service, camp housing, parade marshals, campsite security guards, food, office administration, finance, transportation, communications, press, public relations, electricity and the screening of marchers."[148] A team of white theologians signed up to cook garbage cans full of hot meals and drive them to the nightly encampments at black farms along the way.

King ventured to Montgomery in advance of his troops to make sure that its black community would welcome them. Partly because he (and then Abernathy) had left town, little of the spirit of '56 had endured. Ministers and other local leaders were displeased when SNCC activists organized courthouse marches in support of Selma sisters and brothers. The day after the President's historic speech to Congress, peaceful Montgomery protesters were brutally attacked by sheriff's men in a less noticed reprise of Bloody Sunday. King led another march to the courthouse, negotiated a public apology from old nemesis Sheriff Mac Butler, and mediated among angry SNCC activists, arrogant SCLC staff like Bevel, and put-upon preachers resting on dried-up laurels.

On the first day of spring, Sunday, March 21, several thousand pilgrims flowed over the Pettus Bridge. Wearing flower leis brought by a Hawaiian delegation, King and other leaders in the front row marched arm in arm with white clergy, including a guest of honor,

Jewish theologian and Hasidic rabbi Abraham Joshua Heschel. King and Heschel, a Polish émigré, had first met at a conference on religion and race in Chicago two years before. They saw eye to eye on the imperative of the prophetic voice calling passionately for social justice in the modern world, a voice each of them exemplified. The white-bearded Heschel had just led a march in New York to FBI headquarters protesting brutality against Selma protesters. Now in Selma, he wrote in his diary that "I felt a sense of the Holy in what I was doing." He felt "as though my legs were praying."[149]

The marchers paused at the site of the bloody assault. This time there was no turning back. Flanked on either side by rows of bayonet-wielding soldiers, marchers passed crowds of whites who yelled out ugly words but couldn't get close. For five days the mud-caked assembly snaked through the humid heat and drenching rain, through the spooky swamps of Lowndes County, past rickety Baptist churches, half-collapsed shacks whose inhabitants waved warmly, and a dilapidated black school in Trickem with no roof.

King marched along Jefferson Davis Highway for the first three days, appearing "terribly tired" and aloof. "He seemed to have his mind on something else all the time," a marcher recalled. "He wasn't anything like a leader in the sense of communicating with people" openly, a theologian rued.[150] To the extent that he was detached and uncommunicative, this was a different King than the one who loved to talk and listen to ordinary people, especially black folk with whom he felt more comfortable. The depression that had spiked in Oslo had not eased its grip. He had withdrawn into inner recesses, seeking sanctuary in the privacy of his own soul.

And the long march was strenuous. King's feet like all the others' got painfully blistered. The foot soldiers' feet were treated every night by volunteer docs. But unlike all the others, who slept on cots or the ground, King camped out in a mobile home that accompanied him. In midweek he flew off to a fund-raising gig in Cleveland and returned for the climax.

The marchers multiplied as they approached Montgomery. On the last night they were regaled by Belafonte, Joan Baez, and other entertainers. Next morning, Thursday, March 25, at least twenty-five thousand people strode confidently into downtown Montgomery and up Dexter Avenue, filling the wide street toward the white statehouse flying the Confederate flag. Wallace peered sheepishly at the surging masses below his window who were petitioning him for freedom—impressed in spite of himself. King stood near the bronze star marking the 1861 inaugural site of Confederate president Jefferson Davis, covered with plywood to protect it from the black rabble. A few feet away stood a Confederate cannon and Davis's statue.

King must have felt wistful as he looked down to the left of the vast assemblage at the red brick church he had pastored. There it had all begun for him. In ten years the movement had traversed the South and grown into the nation's preeminent political force. On this day many thousands of participants had come back to its birthplace for the largest-ever freedom gathering in the South. King's address was a breathtaking synthesis of realism and hope, forbearance and faith, courage and love.

"My people, my people, listen! The battle is in our hands. I must admit to you there are still some difficulties ahead. We are still in for a season of suffering. I must admit to you there are still jail cells waiting for us, dark and difficult moments.

"We will be able to change all of these conditions.

"How long?" he asked the faithful below. "Not long," he answered, offering the litany over and over as a multitude of voices joined in the rhythmic crescendo.

"How long?" he concluded. "Not long, 'cause mine eyes have seen the glory of the coming of the Lord, trampling out the vintage where the grapes of wrath are stored. He has loosed the fateful lightning of his terrible swift sword. His truth is marching on.

"He has sounded forth the trumpets that shall never call retreat. He is lifting up the hearts of man before His judgment seat. Oh, be swift, my soul, to answer Him. Be jubilant, my feet. Our God is marching on."[151]

One of his rapt listeners was Viola Gregg Liuzzo, a white Unitarian activist from Detroit who had labored with boundless energy to make the march triumph. That morning she had felt a strong premonition that someone would be killed. As she drove her conspicuous green Oldsmobile back to Montgomery that night with a black teenage boy to ferry another carload home to Selma, she was shot to death by four Klansmen, one of them FBI informant Gary Thomas Rowe, on a desolate stretch of Lowndes County.

12

SCLC left a skeletal crew in Selma as it prepared to create more Selmas across Alabama's Black Belt, and as the voting rights measure moved forward through Congress more quickly than the 1964 bill. Frederick Reese, Amelia Boynton, and other local leaders—their stature raised by the protest campaign—resented SCLC's expected departure. SCLC's fourth bug-out in as many years—it seemed almost an annual rite of passage—aggravated SNCC's mistrust of King and his staff. They felt that De Lawd had let them down once again.

But SCLC had left Selma in better shape than St. Augustine, Birmingham, Albany, or even Montgomery. Those black communities had sometimes felt worse off after King's departure—and more vulnerable to retaliation—even while the regional and national movement gained ground. In Selma voter registration did rise, with expectation of full enfranchisement by the new voting rights law. Tested by protesters, Selma had desegregated public accommodations and was taking steps to integrate schools. The climate of intimidation and fear had cooled, as the new moderate city government negotiated with Reese, Boynton, and other black leaders to improve race relations. These talks upset the White Citizens Council types. Even if officials were only going through the motions, waiting for the burnout of black assertion, a Reconstruction to be replaced by Redemption, they were compelled to take black demands seriously. Unlike the other battlegrounds, black voters could potentially win control of Selma and Dallas County, as they later did. Local black leadership had been strengthened not diminished by SCLC's political tornado, which was SNCC's benchmark for a successful campaign.

SNCC was not content to criticize its big brother. As always, it walked the talk. They would show the movement and the world what local empowerment could mean, in an Alabama Black Belt county where the Confederacy still held sway.

The day after Viola Liuzzo's murder, seasoned SNCC organizer Stokely Carmichael arrived in Lowndes County with a sleeping bag and the name of someone to stay with. He had pressed the flesh with Lowndes residents along the march, winning their trust. He was joined by a handful of others, including Scott B. Smith Jr., just recovered from a gang shooting in Chicago; in the hospital his mother had told him it was time for him to do something right for his people.[152]

Carmichael hailed from a much different world. Born in Trinidad, he had grown up in New York ghettos and graduated from elite Bronx High School of Science, where he hung with Old Left children, white and black. He had attended Howard University in Washington, D.C., and had thrown himself into the sit-ins and freedom rides, one whose baptism by fire was Mississippi's Parchman penitentiary. He had recently won praise as a district director of Mississippi Freedom Summer.

SNCC leaders decided that if they could get impoverished blacks to vote in this "totalitarian" county—where they were four-fifths of the population and not one voted—it could be a prototype for the Deep South. Having learned from the MFDP crusade that blacks could not rely on white allies and must create their own base of power independent of the Democrats, Carmichael's cadre carefully organized local folk, notably ministers and older women, to form the Lowndes County Freedom Organization (LCFO). An obscure law made it feasible to qualify an alternative county party. LCFO's symbol was a black panther. When pressured the panther "moves back until it is cornered," explained LCFO chair John Hulett, longtime local activist, father of seven, "then it comes out fighting for life or death. We felt we had been pushed back long enough."[153]

The plan was simple, wrote SNCC program secretary Cleveland Sellers: "We intended to register as many blacks as we could, and take over the county." After achieving success in Lowndes "we intended to widen our base by branching out and doing the same thing in surrounding counties. We were convinced that we had found The Lever we had been searching for."[154]

Black enfranchisement steadily took hold in Lowndes, boosted by federal registrars who came with the Voting Rights Act. White retaliation spiked. In the county seat of Hayneville Jonathan Daniels, a white Episcopal seminarian involved in voting work, was murdered in broad daylight by a deputy sheriff as he shielded a black girl from getting shot.

A grassroots LCFO convention chose candidates for county offices and conducted a remarkable grassroots campaign during summer and fall 1966. At a spirited church rally on election eve, the candidate for tax assessor, Alice Moore, gave a short speech. "My platform is tax the rich and feed the poor," she announced to roaring applause. Hulett pledged that they would govern the county "as a model for democracy."[155] Although they lost every seat, the party of the black panther made a worthy start toward building a network of indigenous black political organizations. Some years later the black majority took power in Lowndes County. Hulett was elected sheriff and county supervisor.

ON THE SUNDAY AFTER the marvelous march on Montgomery, King appeared on NBC's *Meet the Press* from San Francisco. He let it be known that the Alabama campaign, far from finished, was about to intensify. Liuzzo's death had distressed him. It sharpened his animus toward Alabama politicians, whom he blamed as much as the Klan. The next step, he announced, would be a national boycott of Alabama products. Unions would refuse to ship goods to or from the state. SCLC would lean on the feds to suspend contracts with Alabama firms. The boycott would aim at getting Alabama's white moderates to pressure the statehouse to enfranchise black citizens and end the reign of terror. His words recalled the intemperance of SNCC's John Lewis at the great march in August 1963, so controversial at the time. It was a measure of how far King had traveled in eighteen turbulent months.

The response of media commentators and liberal allies was uniformly negative. Perhaps they had hoped King and his legions would ride off into history after he had told his people in Montgomery that victory would not be long. Movement heavyweights scored the boycott plan. Rustin called it stupid. It was the first time a King initiative had been publicly rebuked by liberals, a turning point in his relationship with them. But he would not back off, yet.

The bittersweet Selma aftermath marked the beginning of a two-year interval in which Bevel would shape King's course as much as Rustin and Levison had earlier. While most Selma activists and SCLC were burned out, King beyond exhaustion, Bevel had gotten warmed up. He saw the Selma-to-Montgomery march as the dam break in his grand plan to free Alabama from tyranny. His strategic vision sometimes crossing the line of rationality, he nonetheless won King's backing for a scenario that climaxed with mass arrests in Montgomery for disrupting state operations. Bevel imagined shutting down the legislature and even removing Governor Wallace by nonviolent abduction. This was roughly the script by Bevel and Nash that King had scoffed at a year earlier.

The SCLC board met in Baltimore in late March 1965 to hear proposals for new directions. The circumspect Young called for a "new militancy." Less than wholeheartedly the board approved the boycott of Alabama, watered down, but King failed to link it with the mass civil disobedience in Montgomery that Bevel had designed the boycott to support; one without the other would not reach the goal. King and his board also approved a competing plan by Hosea Williams for a summer campaign, SCOPE, that would take Mississippi Freedom Summer to the rest of the South, combining voter registration with citizenship education, conducted by hundreds of northern students. With some reservation the board backed King's resolution to focus more on poverty and to move into northern cities.

In typical fashion King juggled the dueling projects of SCLC's two field marshals, giving both Bevel and Williams a nod. But the strapped organization could not handle both enterprises. When SCLC committed half a million dollars to SCOPE and gave Williams control over all southern field staff (including Bevel), it was evident that King had made a choice. He had not been up-front about it. He suffered a severe hit of depression during April 1965 (caused, his doctors thought, by extreme fatigue) and was not fully in charge. By the time he returned from a week's rest in Miami and Nassau, SCOPE was revving up and the Alabama Project sputtering. Withering criticism of the Alabama boycott combined with the exhaustion of grassroots forces and Bevel's alienation from Montgomery's local leadership would have made the Alabama revolt dubious at best. But SCOPE, rife with mismanagement and lax supervision of its young organizers, proved an embarrassment, a shadow of Freedom Summer 1964. SCLC was drifting once again.

By summer the dispirited Bevel had moved to Chicago to plant new seeds. In the northern battleground, where Mississippi-born Bevel had grown up, King would follow his lead.

During spring 1965, as marines landed both in Vietnam and in the Dominican Republic, King worried more about relations with the SNCC community than his own staff's infighting. The conflict was all about the use and abuse of leadership. SNCC organizers accused SCLC of exploiting local people for the sake of King's aggrandizement and SCLC's reach for national power. They did not believe in leadership trickling down but rather in its welling up. They had long felt that the cult of personality around De Lawd undermined the emergence of grassroots leaders who, facing retaliatory violence, had to keep the local movement going after the media show left town.

King felt guilty about his royal status and was stressed by its demands; it contributed mightily to his depression. But he was convinced of its necessity and addicted to its comforts. It was like a drug, with fearsome highs and lows. Although he suffered from serious depression, he did not show signs of bipolar disorder (manic depression) as did an unsettling number of 1960s' radical organizers, black and white. His highs were not so high (and always modulated); his lows not quite so low, until later. He did not exhibit the kind of manic excitement that, for example, Bevel was known for.

While SNCC people bristled at SCLC's haughtiness, the latter group felt that despite their principled dedication, SNCC cadres were undisciplined, anarchistic, and heading toward separatism. King shared these criticisms, though he was fond of the SNCC people and had friendly relations with them as individuals. Although they felt hostility toward his staff, SNCC's umbrage toward King was more about disappointment than disrespect.

On April 30, Harry Belafonte mediated a respectful gripe session between the two groups to grapple with their differences. Putting aside the most divisive issues that might have been unresolvable, they reached consensus on all major points except SCLC's insistence on excluding Communists from the movement. To reporters after, King downplayed feuding between the groups that the media had been sensationalizing since Selma. They hammered out a unity statement that finessed the split over radicalism. The movement "is by its very nature a radical movement which seeks to eliminate an established order of racism and segregation."[156]

Tutored by Levison, Clarence Jones, and other New York advisers, King grew alarmed about President Johnson's belligerent foreign policy in Southeast Asia and the Caribbean. He opposed LBJ's intervention in the Dominican Republic, which upheld the military junta that had overthrown democratically elected Juan Bosch. The furtive escalation in Vietnam, which Johnson refused to explain or even own up to, impelled him to speak out against it firmly.

At a rally in Petersburg, Virginia, in early July he declared that the war in Vietnam "must be stopped," with a negotiated settlement that included the Vietcong. "I'm not going to sit by and see war escalated without saying anything about it." He urged citizens to conduct "peace rallies just like we have freedom rallies," but later denied calling for antiwar protest.[157] In mid-April 1965 Students for a Democratic Society had mounted the first large Vietnam peace march, bringing twenty-five thousand protesters to Washington. When a journalist asked him why he was sounding off about Vietnam, King replied, "I'm much more than a civil rights leader."[158]

Five days after the Petersburg rally he spoke on the phone with LBJ to strategize about a snag in the voting rights bill nearing passage. He claimed that his recent statement on Vietnam "in no way is an attempt to engage in a criticism of your policies," but that the press "lifted it out of context." Johnson countered that it had "distressed" him.

"I'd welcome a chance to review with you my problems and our alternatives there." He tried to justify his current policy and why the bombing of North Vietnam was necessary.

"I don't want to pull down the flag and come home running with my tail between my legs." But "I don't want to get us in a war with China and Russia. So I've got a pretty tough problem. And I'm not all wise." Aware of whom he was talking to, "I pray every night to get direction and judgment and leadership that permit me to do what's right."

Biting his tongue, King complimented him for his "true leadership and true greatness," especially in civil rights.[159]

In fact, the commander-in-chief's stealth in escalating the war bespoke his grave doubts about it. He did not think he could win in Vietnam—only stave off defeat. After three months of wrangling, including a long but spineless Senate filibuster, an exceptionally strong voting rights bill passed Congress. LBJ signed it amid the usual pomp on August 6, 1965, a bust of Lincoln peering over his shoulder in the Capitol Rotunda. Here Lincoln had signed the Emancipation Proclamation. The Selma crusade, culmination of the entire southern movement, especially voting rights campaigns, not only turned the White House around but sped up the legislative process, toughened the bill, and won over the wavering. New York Democrat Emanuel Celler, head of the House judiciary subcommittee that shaped it, acknowledged that the "climate of public opinion throughout the nation has so changed because of the Alabama outrages, as to make assured passage of this solid bill—a bill that would have been inconceivable a year ago."[160] Activists had walked a long, tortuous road since black suffrage agitation had begun in the North a century and a quarter past.

Implementation of the Voting Rights Act in the eleven covered southern states, particularly the ban on literacy tests and use of federal registrars, brought a big jump in black registration. From 1967 on, a growing majority of those eligible were registered. The number of southern black officeholders rose substantially, though not proportionately with black voters. Nearly all were local positions. Another generation passed before black politicians won statewide office. Although fear of reprisal diminished with blacks now serving on juries, white elites still conspired to subvert black voting with intimidation, evasions of the law, registration obstacles, purging voting rolls, gerrymandering districts, and other practices that lasted into the twenty-first century.

Five days after Johnson signed the Voting Rights Act, the arrest and beating of a young black man for drunk driving in the Watts ghetto of Los Angeles set off rioting by several thousand blacks. Violence escalated over the week in a sweltering heat wave, as black men and women looted stores and firebombed businesses. The California National Guard, aided by the army, belatedly restored order with excessive firepower. Thirty-four people died, mostly black, hundreds were injured, about four thousand jailed.

Black ministers in Los Angeles beseeched King to help calm the fever. He arrived in the burned-out ghetto as the uprising subsided and spoke to gatherings of stunned residents. Next day he met with the rightwing mayor and police chief about police brutality and urged a civilian review board. Both officials denounced him.

King was shaken by the warlike destruction he witnessed, block after block in smoky ruin, his first swallowing of the strange fruit of ghetto rage. "He was absolutely undone," Rustin recalled. For over two years Rustin had been trying to convince him that the inner cities were time bombs of mad misery, that black oppression was economic as much as racial. "I think it was the first time he really understood."

King called the rioting "a class revolt of underprivileged against privileged."[161] But he was disheartened to hear from the young rebels that despite loss of black life and gutting of black business, they believed they had won. They had drawn the nation's attention to their desperation.

After the Watts revolt of August 1965, which wrenched his soul, Martin King began his journey from moderate radical to revolutionary. He was leaping beyond Lincoln into an unknown land.

IN EARLY JUNE 1966 quixotic James Meredith, thirty-three, set off on a solitary march through his native Mississippi to make the point that black people could live like human beings. After serving for nine years in the U.S. Air Force, Meredith, born to a poor farm family, had integrated "Ole Miss" in 1962 with the strong arm of federal troops—two people were killed in the white rioting—and became its first black graduate a year later. Just after commencing his "march against fear," a white racist ambushed him by shotgun, seriously injuring him, which precipitated a dramatic conflict among the movement's leaders that had historic repercussions.

The civil rights generals converged at Meredith's hospital bedside in Memphis. They resolved to jointly continue his march against fear, to reunify the movement and to push voter registration in places where the feds were delinquent in enforcing the new voting law. King had just started an SCLC campaign in Chicago, ultimately unsuccessful, to force Mayor Richard Daley to end racism in housing and hiring and to prove that nonviolent action could work in explosive northern ghettos. Stokely Carmichael had been elected chair of SNCC in May. Dynamic ex–freedom rider Ruby Doris Robinson replaced Jim Forman as executive secretary, the first woman in a SNCC leadership position. At this pivotal meeting the organization decided that white SNCC members should organize only in white communities. SNCC had crossed the Rubicon toward becoming a separatist, black nationalist organization that no longer adhered to nonviolent principles. CORE was pursuing a parallel path of black militancy, with a particular focus on black economic development.

In Memphis Roy Wilkins and Whitney Young angrily packed their bags when Carmichael, backed by CORE's Floyd McKissick, won King's reluctant assent for the march to minimize white participation, to have protection from the armed Deacons for Defense, and to promote independent black organization.

As the marchers trod through familiar SNCC territory in the Delta, they roused the local folk and expanded voting rolls but were met by ferocious police assaults. After being jailed for setting up sleeping tents, Carmichael was warmly welcomed by a huge night rally in Greenwood.

"This is the twenty-seventh time I have been arrested—and I ain't going to jail no more!" The crowd cheered him on. "The only way we gonna stop them white men from whuppin' us is to take over. We been saying freedom for six years and we ain't got nothin'. What we gonna start saying now is Black Power!" SNCC's Willie Ricks led the assembly in passionate cries of "Black Power!" repeated over and over. The expression, which starkly encapsulated SNCC's new political vision, had been used before by Richard Wright, Paul Robeson, Adam Clayton Powell Jr., and others, but now caught on and electrified black youth all over the country as it ignited a storm of criticism from older leaders and white allies. On the march the nightly rallies turned into contests over which chant, "Black Power" or "Freedom now," could drown out the other.

In Yazoo City, where to his chagrin he had been booed by some marchers, King held a long summit meeting with Carmichael, McKissick, and other leaders to try to resolve the antagonism. He said he understood the new slogan's magnetic draw to young blacks, whose expectations had been lifted by himself and others, but who felt bitter and betrayed because their elders were unable to deliver on their promises. Yet he argued that the slogan would be self-defeating for the movement. Leaders must be concerned with how their rhetoric was interpreted, he counseled. No one doubted his genius for shaping his own words to be understood as he meant them. Words must both fire up and cool down.

While the concept of black power was sound, he said, the slogan had the "wrong connotations." He worried about the violent images it conjured up and the media's alarmism. Carmichael replied that the issue of violence or nonviolence was irrelevant, a remark bruising to King.

"Power is the only thing respected in this world," he asserted, "and we must get it at any cost." He looked King straight in the eyes. "Martin, you know as well as I do that practically every other ethnic group in America has done just this," creating its own political and economic power base to advance itself. "The Jews, the Irish and the Italians did it. Why can't we?"

"That is just the point," King answered. "No one has ever heard the Jews publicly chant a slogan of Jewish power, but they have power. The same thing is true of the Irish and Italians. Neither group has used a slogan of Irish or Italian power, but they have worked hard to achieve it. This is exactly what we must do. We must use every constructive means to amass economic and political power. This is the kind of legitimate power we need. We must work to build racial pride and refute the notion that black is evil and ugly. But this must come through a program, not merely through a slogan."

Carmichael and McKissick insisted that slogans were crucial, as they had been all along. "What we need is a new slogan with 'black' in it." King, master sloganeer, did not gainsay the need for one.

"Why not use the slogan 'black consciousness' or 'black equality'?" he asked. "The words 'black' and 'power' together give the impression that we are talking about black domination rather than black equality." He didn't have to be reminded how white hysteria about "black domination," "black rule," had damaged black-led Reconstruction after the Civil War. Carmichael countered that neither slogan would have the appeal and rhetorical force of 'black power.'

"Martin," Carmichael confessed, "I deliberately decided to raise this issue on the march in order to give it a national forum, and force you to take a stand for Black Power." King let out his full-throated baritone laugh.

"I have been used before. One more time won't hurt."[162] He and his younger adversaries were unbending, neither side swaying the other. Out of respect for De Lawd the SNCC and CORE chiefs agreed to cease using either slogan until the expedition was over. Later King disavowed the Black Power slogan, but he never repudiated Carmichael or SNCC. He still hoped for a united black movement.

Despite the acrimony, some SNCC activists were impressed with King when they made friends with him hiking along the hot highway, "discussing strategy, tactics and our dreams." SNCC leader Cleveland Sellers found that King had an engaging sense of humor and an open mind, and that he was "much less conservative than we initially believed. I will never forget his magnificent speeches at the nightly rallies. Nor the humble smile that spread across his face when throngs of admirers rushed forward to touch him." He was "a staunch ally and a true brother."[163]

Book Three

Crossing to Jerusalem

1967–1968

I

New York
April 4, 1967

Christian churches were shaped like crosses to symbolize the church as the body of Christ. Their steeples scraped the sky to connect earth with heaven. The tallest point on Manhattan Island, high over the Hudson River, was Morningside Heights, home of Columbia University and Union Theological Seminary. Upon this promontory the Rockefeller family, staunch Southern Baptists, built nondenominational Riverside Church in the depth of the Great Depression. Its twin steeples soared higher than those of the twelfth-century French cathedral at Chartres, its model.

Like a medieval castle towering over a valley of serfs, the Rockefellers' grand cathedral stood heavenly guard over the valley of Harlem down below. Once the crown jewel of African-American cultural revival and economic hope, this black community that had been the promised land for many southern immigrants had sunk since the Depression into an impoverished ghetto. Like poor blacks in other cities, thousands of its citizens rose up in revolt during a hot summer the year before Watts.

"I come to this magnificent house of worship tonight," Martin Luther King Jr. declared to the audience overflowing the long nave, "because my conscience leaves me no other choice." He affirmed the sponsoring group, Clergy and Laymen Concerned About Vietnam, and its statement that "a time comes when silence is betrayal, and that time has come for us in relation to Vietnam."

He had preached at Riverside Church before; this would be his last time there. He was on familiar intellectual ground. Riverside's ministers, founder Harry Emerson Fosdick and successor Robert McCracken, had influenced his preaching. The luminaries of Union Seminary next door, Reinhold Niebuhr and Paul Tillich, had shaped his thinking, especially about justice and love. Although he supported the war, Niebuhr bore witness in the audience that night.

"Some of us who have already begun to break the silence of the night," King continued, "have found that the calling to speak is often a vocation of agony. But we must speak." He spoke not only to break the betrayal of his own silence, but to break the ghastly silence of the war's victims. In a larger sense he sought to give voice to voiceless humanity, forever the prophet's duty.

He felt compelled to condemn the war for multiple reasons that bled into each other. First was the war's destruction of the war on poverty at home that had appeared as a beacon of hope for America's poor. "I watched this program broken and eviscerated as if it were some idle political plaything of a society gone mad on war. I knew that America would never invest the necessary funds or energies in rehabilitation of its poor, so long as adventures like Vietnam continued to draw men and skills and money like some demonic destructive suction tube, so I was increasingly compelled to see the war as an enemy of the poor."

Grievously, this demonic suction tube was ripping poor youth from their families to "fight and die in extraordinarily high proportions relative to the rest of the population. We were taking the black young men who had been crippled by our society and sending them eight thousand miles away to guarantee liberties in Southeast Asia which they had not found in Southwest Georgia and East Harlem. We have been repeatedly faced with the cruel irony of watching Negro and white boys on TV screens as they kill and die together for a nation that has been unable to seat them together in the same schools. We watch them in brutal solidarity burning the huts of a poor village, but we realize that they would hardly live on the same block in Chicago. I could not be silent in the face of such cruel manipulation of the poor."

How could he ask the angry and desperate young men of the inner cities to trade their Molotov cocktails for picket signs when they would ask him: What about Vietnam? "I knew that I could never again raise my voice against the violence of the oppressed in the ghettos without having first spoken clearly to the greatest purveyor of violence in the world today, my own government."

Giving voice to the muted murmurs of the world's faiths that all people were One, he imagined how the war, and the American government, were experienced by Vietnamese peasants and the "enemy," not easily distinguished from the peasant sea. He encapsulated the history that few Americans knew: how the United States had refused to back Vietnamese independence after World War II, had paid for the French war to reconquer its former colony, had tricked Vietnamese nationalists in 1954 to accept temporary partition, had supported the corrupt Saigon regime in defying mandated elections to reunify the country, and had protected the regime with military advisers, covert action, air power, and finally ground troops, when repression, especially against Buddhists, provoked indigenous revolt led by communists.

"Surely we must understand their feelings," King spoke of South Vietnam's National Liberation Front (NLF), "even if we do not condone their actions. Surely we must see that the men we supported pressed them to their violence. Here is the true meaning and value of compassion and nonviolence when it helps us to see the enemy's point of view, to hear his questions, to know his assessment of ourselves." Americans must have the wisdom to learn from the adversary's story. Only then could a middle way of truth be found.

After calling for cessation of bombing and a cease-fire, he urged Americans to protest. He encouraged draft-age men to apply for conscientious objector status. He told his audience that they must understand the war as "but a symptom of a far deeper malady within the American spirit. When machines and computers, profit motives and property rights are considered more important than people," the triple evils of racism, materialism, and militarism "are incapable of being conquered." He warned of future Vietnams in other Third World countries where U.S. foreign policy served the needs of corporate investment, rather than support the striving of the world's poor for freedom from economic bondage.

"I am convinced that if we are to get on the right side of the world revolution, we as a nation must undergo a radical revolution of values. We must rapidly begin the shift from a thing oriented society to a person oriented society. A nation that continues year after year to spend more on military defense than on programs of social uplift is approaching spiritual death.

"These are revolutionary times. Our only hope today lies in our ability to recapture the revolutionary spirit and go out into a sometimes hostile world declaring eternal hostility to poverty, racism, and militarism."

He did not stop there. "Every nation must now develop an overriding loyalty to mankind as a whole in order to preserve the best in their individual societies. This call for a worldwide fellowship that lifts neighborly concern beyond one's tribe, race, class, and nation is in reality a call for an all-embracing and unconditional love for mankind. I am speaking of that force which all of the great religions have seen as the supreme unifying principle of life."[1]

In his softly incendiary address, he gave air to "the burnings of my own heart." He not only put forth, in the most public way, in the world's media capital, a wrenching critique of U.S. policy in Vietnam; not only called for the obligation of protest and refusing to fight the war; not only condemned what leftists called imperialism. Sounding for all their differences like Malcolm X in his climactic year, he urged Americans to stop resisting the revolutionary tide in the world, rather to *lead* a world revolution against poverty, injustice, and exploitation. At the moment when "revolution" was starting to be fashionable, even faddish, among young radicals and the media, he exhorted Americans to make a true revolution driven by the power of love. He faced an uphill battle to make revolution, once again, a patriotic call, resonating with the American creed.

Unlike many Americans who came to oppose the war by 1967 or 1968, King never had any illusions about its moral soundness, never doubted whether it was right or wrong. Other influential Americans had been held back by ignorance, denial, partisanship, or uncertainty. What held King back from condemning the war unequivocally was a mix of fear, exhaustion, and concern about his effectiveness. He dreaded an ugly, all-out battle with the president who had done more for African Americans and civil rights than any president except Lincoln, more for poor people than any except FDR. King admired Johnson for his domestic reform (despite its shortcomings) as much as he loathed his bellicosity overseas. They had had an amicable personal relationship that it was important to King to preserve.

His own moral cowardice and hypocrisy had anguished him for two long years. To be sure, he had spoken out against the war from time to time, especially during the first six months of major escalation. But he had pulled his punches and spoken where he thought the media would not pay much attention. He was taken aback when his criticisms at a July 1965 civil rights rally in rural Virginia made news and upset President Johnson. King verged on apologetic in a phone conversation with him a few days later. He realized that he could not attack the war without directly attacking his nation's commander-in-chief.

King's early antiwar stand was bolstered by a letter he received in June 1965 from a South Vietnamese Buddhist monk, Thich Nhat Hanh, who pleaded with him to oppose the war loudly. The letter tried to explain why his brother monks had immolated themselves in protest, which had spurred MLK's initial opposition:

> The Vietnamese monk, by burning himself, says with all his strength and determination that he can endure the greatest sufferings to protect his people. The importance is not to take one's life, but to burn. What he really aims at is the expression of his will and determination, not death. To express will by burning oneself, therefore, is not to commit an act of destruction but to perform an act of construction, i.e., to suffer and die for the sake of one's people.
>
> I am sure that since you have been engaged in one of the hardest struggles for equality and human rights, you are among those who understand fully, and who share with all their hearts, the indescribable suffering of the Vietnamese people. The world's greatest humanists would not remain silent.

You yourself cannot remain silent. You cannot be silent since you have already been in action and you are in action because, in you, God is in action, too.[2]

King must have been struck by the consanguinity of the burning monks' passion to that of Jesus dying on the cross, their faith like his that their unearned suffering would prove redemptive. Like Christian stalwarts the Buddhist monks strove to forge the fire of suffering into an instrument of social rebirth. The difference was also striking. The Buddhists chose this path of self-destruction, lit their own fire. Although King like Christ was suffering deeply for his commitments, and knew he would sacrifice his life, he did not feel it was his choice to die and he did not want to die before his appointed time. He would live a long life, if it were in his hands. The Buddhists had no God to make this decision; they had to decide for themselves. King's own actions, like those of Jesus, were nonetheless sealing his fate. Like Jesus, he could have turned back at any time. But instead of turning back, he would keep doing God's will until forces beyond his control hammered him to the cross.

King took his antiwar candle to the SCLC convention in August 1965. Four days after President Johnson signed the Voting Rights Act, handing the first pen to King, the SCLC chief announced to the Birmingham convention that he was launching his own peacemaking mission. The recent Nobel Peace Prize laureate wrote to leaders of all nations involved in the war, particularly LBJ and North Vietnam's Ho Chi Minh, urging serious negotiations. He called on Johnson to stop the bombing and to talk with the NLF. A resolution supporting King's initiative cautioned that SCLC should not be distracted from the civil rights cause.

The White House blindsided him. Johnson had him briefed by U.N. ambassador Arthur Goldberg about apparent peace feelers that his effort might harm. Then the White House got Senator Thomas Dodd and other Congress members to rip his ineptness and disloyalty. He expressed his distress in a conference call with Stanley Levison, Andrew Young, and other advisers, in mid-September 1965, recorded by the FBI.

"The press is being stacked against me," he complained. They would accuse him of being "power drunk and that I feel that I can do anything because I got the Nobel Prize and it went to my head. I really don't have the strength to fight this issue *and* keep my civil rights fight going. They have all the news media and TV and I just don't have the strength to fight all these things. The deeper you get involved the deeper you have to go, and I'm already overloaded and almost emotionally fatigued. I think we have to admit that I am going too far." Without objection from his advisers he decided to drop his peace mission.

"I have to find out how I can gracefully pull out," he told them, "so that I can get on with the civil rights issue, because I have come to the conclusion that I can't battle these forces who are out to defeat my influence," that "are going to try to cut me down." A year and a half later he confided to his staff that "my name then wouldn't have been written in any book called *Profiles in Courage,*" the Pulitzer Prize–winning bestseller by John F. Kennedy.[3]

He might have been emboldened to carry on had he been supported by the civil rights community, but his initiative—not wholly backed by his own organization—was criticized by mainstream groups such as the NAACP. Nor did SNCC or CORE embrace his actions.

Like King, SNCC activists had nursed anger about the war since early 1965, especially when field staff were called for induction. A handful refused to go and were handed maximum five-year terms by southern federal judges. But except for Robert Moses, whom American Nazis had pelted with red paint in an August protest, they had remained fairly quiet. By January 1966 SNCC leaders could no longer contain their outrage. They put out a strong statement opposing the war, reviling the government for hypocrisy in pretending to defend freedom and democracy in Southeast Asia when it refused to do so in southeast America. The statement supported those who resisted the draft in order to build democracy at home. It asked plaintively, "Where is the draft for the freedom fight in the United States?"[4] Protesting at the Atlanta induction center, SNCC coined the slogan "Hell no, we won't go!" SNCC was attacked by the media, politicians, and black moderates. The Georgia legislature refused to seat newly elected state representative Julian Bond, a SNCC activist, for opposing the war. King lambasted the legislature for violating the Constitution and suppressing dissent.

Although SNCC had not joined King earlier against the war, now they were pushing him to speak out more strongly, partly to give their own antiwar stand legitimacy, to shield themselves from recrimination. Stokely Carmichael, who replaced John Lewis as SNCC's chairman in May 1966, made it his mission to move King forward on the war. As the Black Power movement emerged out of Lowndes County, Alabama, it condemned the war as fiercely as it did racism, seeing them as sides of the same coin.

Throughout 1966 King spoke occasionally against the war and the massive bombing and once appeared with Thich Nhat Hanh at a Chicago press conference. Although SCLC officially scorned the war, he turned down invitations to speak at peace rallies, rallies he had earlier encouraged. A few times he asked Coretta King, longtime pacifist and member of Women Strike for Peace, to speak in his place. King and advisers rationalized his rationing of antiwar rhetoric as more effective than continuous salvos. But he was lying low, praying for peace but not acting, risking. The slamming of his 1965 peace mission taught him that Vietnam was a political minefield. Unlike Vietnamese monks, he was not ready to burn. And he did not want the lash of Lyndon Johnson's wrath. If nonviolence was about turning enemies into friends, he was unhappy about turning his tall Texan friend into a foe.

But the war kept hemorrhaging. By end of 1966, nearly four hundred thousand U.S. troops were deployed in South Vietnam, twice as many as a year earlier. Several thousand had come home in coffins. Tens of thousands of Vietnamese civilians had been killed; hundreds of thousands were forced to flee their villages. The negotiation route was going nowhere. King's outward passivity belied his growing disquiet, the rumbling of his conscience. Friends joining him for the 1966 Thanksgiving holiday recalled his obsession with the war and nonstop arguments. He was groping his way out of his prison cell of silence.

The point of no return came in mid-January 1967. He was waiting for a plane at Atlanta airport, flying to Jamaica for a month of rest and reflection and to write his fourth and final book, *Where Do We Go from*

Here. He bought a copy of *Ramparts,* the glossy New Left magazine, at a newsstand. Over lunch his eyes seized on an article, "The Children of Vietnam," graphic photos of kids fiendishly burned by American napalm bombs. His aide Bernard Lee recalled that "he froze as he looked at the pictures from Vietnam. He saw a picture of a Vietnamese mother holding her dead baby, a baby killed by our military." He pushed his plate away from him.

"Doesn't it taste any good?" Lee knew how his boss loved to eat.

"Nothing will ever taste any good for me," he replied testily, "until I do everything I can to end that war."[5] This was the moment that he committed himself to stop it, regardless of the political or personal cost.

SMALL PROTESTS AGAINST the Vietnam intervention, organized mainly by radical pacifists, had occurred sporadically ever since an August 1963 demonstration against the Saigon regime's harsh persecution of Buddhists, some of whom had set themselves on fire. The groundswell had become a "movement," though small compared to its civil rights sister, when in April 1965 Students for a Democratic Society pulled off an unexpectedly impressive march of about twenty-five thousand who picketed the White House, rallied at the Washington Monument, and marched on the Capitol. A month earlier University of Michigan students and faculty organized an all-night "teach-in" that drew thousands. The idea was quickly copied at a hundred other campuses. Antiwar scholars debated State Department "truth teams" before large audiences.

That summer, during the twentieth anniversary of the Hiroshima and Nagasaki nuclear bombings, the "Assembly of Unrepresented People" gathered in Washington for workshops and direct action. It was designed to connect Vietnam with voting rights and other issues, to create a peace *and* freedom movement. On the final day a few hundred were arrested as they tried nonviolently to invade the Capitol with a "Declaration of Peace." On the West Coast, protesters in Oakland sat down in front of army trains carrying soldiers bound for Vietnam. The Assembly of Unrepresented People gave birth to the first antiwar coalition, composed of thirty-three organizations. In mid-October 1965 a worldwide protest filled the streets of a hundred cities from New York to Tokyo. Another big Washington march took place over Thanksgiving.

As the war expanded, opponents felt an increasing urgency to end it, testified by the hundreds who engaged in civil disobedience. A handful chose to sacrifice everything. In early November Norman Morrison, a thirty-two-year-old Quaker from Baltimore, sat down below Defense Secretary Robert McNamara's office window at the Pentagon, poured kerosene over his body, and died in a small inferno.

"I reacted to the horror of his action," McNamara recalled, "by bottling up my emotions and avoided talking about them with anyone—even my family. I knew Marg and our three children shared many of Morrison's feelings about the war, as did the wives and children of several of my cabinet colleagues. I believed I understood and shared some of his thoughts. The episode created tension at home that only deepened as dissent and criticism of the war continued to grow."[6]

A week later Roger LaPorte, a young Catholic worker who had just witnessed a draft-card burning—hecklers had yelled, "Burn yourselves, not your cards!"—immolated himself in front of the United Nations. Alice Herz, an eighty-two-year-old refugee from Nazi Germany, had set herself aflame on a Detroit street. She wrote a note to her daughter: "I choose the illuminating death of a Buddhist to protest against a great country trying to wipe out a small country for no reason."[7]

The movement that grew so quickly in 1965 appeared to drag its feet the next year. Little noticed by the media, much was stirring at the grass roots, especially on campuses. Activists were building for the long haul. Key events took place that enlarged the opposition, including Senator J. William Fulbright's televised Vietnam hearings, peace campaigns for Congress, and more marching. Antiwar pop songs climbed to the top of the charts, notably Barry McGuire's "Eve of Destruction."

Though belied by his official rhetoric, the commander-in-chief seemed to be getting the message. With the failure of air attacks on oil-storage depots in North Vietnam, the Joint Chiefs of Staff pushed Johnson to order unrestrained bombing of Hanoi and Haiphong in late 1966. At his request they brought a team of Pentagon "whiz kids" to the Oval Office to prove their case.

"I have one more problem for your computer," said LBJ. "Will you feed into it how long it will take five hundred thousand angry Americans to climb that White House wall out there and lynch their president if he does something like that?"[8] Although some populated targets remained off-limits, the air war steadily expanded. American troops kept pouring into South Vietnam, to reach half a million by end of 1967. The war seemed as relentless and intractable as it was indeterminate. It was truly a "stalemate machine," as Pentagon analyst Daniel Ellsberg called it.[9]

2

Despite his mystical aura and prophetic bearing, James Bevel was not as demonstrative about talking to God as was King, who did not hesitate to inform meetings large or small that God was speaking through him. He would habitually interrupt staff meetings to divine God's answers to their strategic or tactical questions. But it was Bevel's hearing of God's voice in a reading of Isaiah, which landed him in a Baptist seminary in Nashville, that led him to the freedom movement. Now nearly a decade later he was living in Chicago's west side. The hero of Birmingham and Selma was heading up SCLC's first and most extensive northern campaign, to transform slum conditions in the nation's largest black ghetto. King's decisive encounter with divinity occurred in his kitchen. Bevel's took place in the basement laundry room of his Chicago tenement, while he was washing his baby son's diapers.

He heard a voice firmly instructing him to stop the war. "James Bevel, my children are dying in Vietnam. My children are suffering. They are your brothers and sisters too. You must help them." He was certain it was the voice of Jesus. It admonished him for urging nonviolence in the American South but not toward the Vietnamese. It was hypocritical for him to denounce protesters for throwing rocks in Birmingham or Chicago and not to denounce the President for raining bombs on women and children. Bevel tried to defend himself, but the voice would have none of his rationalizations. "I can't answer your prayers here in this country," it insisted, "if you are killing people in Vietnam."

Bevel told his story to a skeptical Andrew Young, who urged him to talk to King when he returned from Jamaica. He could not wait. Impulsive as ever, he borrowed money to fly to Jamaica in January 1967 and found a cab driver who knew where King was hiding out. King and Bernard Lee were astonished to see him getting out of a cab at their beach house. After sharing his conversation with Jesus, Bevel pressed his boss to take the risk of all-out opposition to Johnson's war. King may well have already decided to act. These secondhand words from Jesus no doubt fortified his resolve. He spent a good deal of his time in Jamaica praying and meditating about the war, what God wanted him to do.

Bevel had taken leave from his labors in Chicago to accept an offer from A. J. Muste and Dave Dellinger to take charge of the Spring Mobilization Committee's mass protests against the war on April 15. They chose him partly in hopes that he would bring King on board, as well as a large black constituency. The national antiwar coalition had trouble staying intact during 1966 due to factional conflicts of Communists, Trotskyists, and pacifists. A fragile unity was maintained by the war's urgency and by Muste's skillful piloting. King's involvement would not only put more bodies in the street but provide a veneer of solidarity. Bevel was determined that King would lead the peace march from Central Park to the United Nations.

Two weeks after returning from Jamaica, King delivered his first full speech on Vietnam at a Los Angeles symposium. The featured speaker on a panel with four antiwar senators, he spelled out the human, moral, political, and diplomatic casualties of the war—in Vietnam, the United States, and around the world.

"We must combine the fervor of the civil rights movement with the peace movement," he concluded. "We must demonstrate, teach, and preach, until the very foundations of our nation are shaken." On March 25 in Chicago, where like Bevel he had been living in a slum while campaigning for housing rights, he delivered the same fighting words at his first peace march, organized by Veterans for Peace. He led the march with famed baby doctor Benjamin Spock, who had also been nudging him to act.[10]

DESPITE THEIR PERSONAL HOSTILITY to the war, hardly any SCLC staff, advisers, or board members backed King's walking out on a limb, or down the gangplank. Many were concerned about losing financial support at a precarious time when SCLC was laying off staff. Andy Young wanted King and SCLC to oppose the war but on SCLC's terms. As in Birmingham and Selma, he wanted SCLC to be in control. Worried that King's message would be distorted or misunderstood in the cacophony of April 15, Young arranged his address at Riverside Church. Young was also King's liaison with the Spring Mobilization Committee, headed by Dellinger following Muste's death in February at age eighty-one. Muste had just returned from a peace journey to North Vietnam, where he talked with Ho Chi Minh.

As before, the Mobilization Committee comprised a coalition of contentious leftists: radical pacifists, progressive clergy, SNCC, student activists, Trotskyites, and Communists. King and Young were alarmed about the presence of Communist Party members, the result of a nonexclusion policy meant to be a final repudiation of McCarthyism, as well as to broaden support. But CP involvement had kept Norman Thomas, other democratic socialists, and influential liberals from joining up. Young pressured the committee to remove a Communist from its list of sponsors, to no avail. King was also troubled by the prospect of sharing the platform with his friend Stokely Carmichael, who had abandoned nonviolence in pushing for greater black militancy.

In a mid-March letter to Bevel and Dellinger, Young pointed to the underlying conflict between radical and liberal peace leaders. Rustin and Levison had been steering King through the thickets of liberal/radical animosity for several years. Although the radical peace leaders had bitter differences among themselves, especially Stalinists and Trotskyites who had battled for decades, their common goal was to build a broad American left. Over time they foresaw the left growing into a majority force for progressive, even revolutionary change. Liberals and democratic socialists, on the contrary, strove to build a majority coalition to win political power. Some like Rustin believed they were unlikely to get a better deal than the Johnson administration and its Democratic Congress. Others, like Allard Lowenstein, favored replacing Johnson with a president as strong on peace as LBJ had been on civil rights and poverty, possibly Senator Robert Kennedy.

The Spring Mobilization Committee was pleased with the breadth of their coalition in unifying the left. But for liberals and democratic socialists, this leftwing solidarity meant the exclusion of the vast majority of Americans. In their eyes the strategy of deferred transformation was not only pie in the sky but jeopardizing the short-term prospects for a majority movement to stop the war.

Young conveyed King's concern that their base of support was not wide enough to win over the uncommitted. Would they be preaching to the choir? King wanted more diverse speakers, including liberal academics and labor leaders, and a plan for withdrawal that ordinary Americans could rally around. Hoping to draw in peace activists who were feeling uncomfortable, he proposed a meeting to fashion a principled compromise to expand participation from liberals and moderates. That meeting apparently never happened. Prominent liberals like Norman Thomas and Norman Cousins sat out the march.

"Never has there been so much opposition to a war," Young's letter concluded, "or so pregnant a climate to witness for Peace. This sentiment must not be allowed to become splintered into a thousand institutional factions and rendered ineffective and irrelevant. There is a real opportunity to organize the prevailing mood and lead the newly awakened consciences into a meaningful political program for the ending of the War."[11]

Despite threats of funding cutoffs by big SCLC donors, reservations about militant speakers like Carmichael whose words might overshadow his, and an assassination plot, King resolved to speak his mind on April 15.

"At times you do things to satisfy your conscience," he told Levison in an FBI-recorded phone call, "and they may be altogether unrealistic or wrong tactically, but you feel better. I will get a lot of criticism and I know it can hurt SCLC." But, he insisted, "I can no longer be cautious about this matter. I feel so deep in my heart that we are so wrong in this country. The time has come for a real prophecy and I'm willing to go that road."[12]

Withstanding rain, light then heavy, a quarter to half a million people gathered at sprawling Sheep Meadow in New York's Central Park on Saturday, April 15, 1967—a diverse assemblage of all ages and races, predominantly young, white, and middle-class. Myriads of hippies flowed through the crowd with painted faces and flowered hair. The nonviolent tenor of the day was expressed by such posters as "They Are Our Brothers Whom We Kill." Some carried Vietcong flags. A front line of notables—King, Spock, Carmichael, Bevel, and a towering photograph of Muste—led the peace army along 59th Street and down Madison Avenue to the U.N. It was so vast that tens of thousands never got out of Central Park. The organizers were dizzied by the size of the march, and the one in San Francisco to which Coretta King spoke.

King turned to Dellinger on the speakers' platform at the U.N. and told him that more people had turned out than for the 1963 March on Washington. It was the largest demonstration in American history. Dellinger believed that at last they had a real peace movement. "I somehow felt like 'we're in.'"[13] Carmichael's angry speech evoked chants of "Black Power!" King's talk was toned down from his Riverside jeremiad.

"The promises of the Great Society," he said, "have been shot down on the battlefield of Vietnam. The bombs in Vietnam explode at home. They destroy the hopes and possibilities for a decent America."

Responding to critics of his Riverside address, he explained: "I have not urged a mechanical fusion of the civil rights and peace movements. There are people who have come to see the moral imperative of equality but who cannot yet see the moral imperative of world brotherhood. I would like to see the fervor of the civil rights movement imbued into the peace movement to instill it with greater strength, but I am not urging a single organizational form.

"I believe everyone has a duty to be in both the civil rights and peace movements, but for those who presently choose but one, I would hope they will finally come to see the moral roots common to both. I hope they will understand that brotherhood is indivisible, that equality of races is connected with the equality of nations in a single harmonious coexistence of all human beings."[14]

Earlier in the day at Sheep Meadow, in an action not approved by the march officialdom, about seventy young men, many of them Cornell students, stood on a rocky cliff facing TV cameras and burned their draft cards in a coffee can filled with paraffin. A few were lit by supportive wives and women friends. As they finished their task, the contagious spirit of shared defiance moved a hundred more to come up from the edges and put their cards to flame.

DRAFT RESISTANCE IN AMERICA had been around for a century, ever since conscription was first instituted during the Civil War, two months after the Emancipation Proclamation. In July 1863 poor whites in New York City, largely Irish immigrants, rioted against the draft, incensed that rich people could buy their way out. Mobs attacked those supporting the Union cause. They targeted African Americans with venomous rage, since they were being forced to fight and die to free the slaves, when they themselves were hardly free. Over a hundred New Yorkers, mainly blacks, were killed in five days of burning, looting, and carnage.

In the twentieth century resistance to conscription took peaceful and nonracist forms. Five hundred were imprisoned for draft refusal during World War I. During the Second World War those who were granted conscientious objector status for religious reasons were sent to civilian public-service camps. About six thousand pacifists refused this option out of principle and served time in federal prison—among them King's advisers Bayard Rustin and Glenn Smiley.

Draft resistance during the Vietnam era involved only the isolated burning of draft cards until the draft system itself provoked widespread dissent. In February 1966 the crusty czar of selective service, General Lewis Hershey, declared that draft boards could induct male college students with lower academic standing. With draft calls approaching forty thousand per month, middle-class students were no longer insulated from the war. Only a small proportion of students were inducted while in college; most of these were black, brown, or working-class. But the draft, seen as inseparable from the war that it fueled, had emerged as the most critical issue facing students. It became the driving force of mass antiwar opposition among the younger generation.

As an organized movement, draft resistance grew up both in and outside of SDS. Thousands of college students signed "We Won't Go" pledges. The influence of SNCC was pervasive—its early support of draft defiance, draft refusal by several SNCC activists, and the controversial decision that whites should leave SNCC and organize their own people.

The day after the great peace march, King was interviewed on CBS's *Face the Nation*. He was asked how he felt about protesters burning draft cards and carrying Vietcong flags. He averred that the Mobilization Committee had nothing to do with either and did not condone them.

"I do feel, however, that this war has gone so far and has done such damage to the nation and to many of the values that we hold very dear that something must be done on a much more massive scale to oppose it. I do not at this point advocate civil disobedience. I think we have to do a lot of groundwork in massive education before that," reflecting his Gandhian approach. He reiterated his encouragement of young men to apply for conscientious objector status. He probably did not know how discriminatory the CO process was. A person of color, especially from a poor family, had little chance of being granted CO status by his local draft board. Even articulate white middle-class men not associated with a peace church like the Quakers had a tough time getting through the hoop. Draft boards frowned upon CO applicants, considering them unmanly if not un-American. It would be all the harder for a young black man to face inquisition by an all-white board.

Reporter Martin Agronsky asked King if he advocated draft resistance.

"Well, I have certainly advocated this," he replied, now speaking to an audience of millions, "because I myself would be a conscientious objector if I had to face it." But a CO was not a resister. With his usual ambiguity he seemed to be calling for noncooperation within the law. One might have seen a parallel with the Montgomery bus boycott's initial demand for more reasonable segregation within the law.

"In the true spirit of nonviolence," he explained, "I have only advocated doing what we do to resist it openly, cheerfully, and with a desire to reconcile rather than to estrange."[15] He opposed burning draft cards (a federal crime) not only because it was inflammatory but because, by destroying the evidence, it might be seen as evading prosecution. No one asked him where he stood on publicly breaking the draft law with willingness to accept the consequences, the kind of "extreme" action he had promoted with such passion in his letter from Birmingham jail.

Such an approach had been set forth at the huge rally in San Francisco's Golden Gate Park the day before. In the winter David Harris, Dennis Sweeney, and other members of the Peace and Liberation Commune in East Palo Alto, California, had joined with Berkeley activists to create "the Resistance." They named it after the French struggle against the Nazis. At the San Francisco rally Harris announced the newborn group's call for a nationwide "turn-in" of draft cards in October. A former high school football star from the farm town of Fresno, where he had been Boy of the Year, bearded, scruffy-haired Harris had recently resigned as Stanford student-body president to pour his energy into antidraft organizing. He and his commune brothers had already sent their draft cards back to the government and were preparing to go to prison.

Harris and Sweeney had worked with SNCC in Mississippi and envisioned the Resistance as a "white SNCC." It came to life as a blend of the risk-taking, openness, and direct democracy of SNCC, principles of Gandhian nonviolence, and an "exploration of selfhood" that arose from the flourishing California counterculture with its libertarian values.[16] They saw defying the draft as an existential act of self-liberation—from the manipulation of life choices that the government called "channeling," from the "white skin privilege" of deferments, and above all, from immoral complicity in the war machine. It was a "personal, deep communication type of politics," as SDS activist Tom Bell put it, a fusion of the personal and the political that would build, they dreamed, toward a nonviolent revolution.[17]

As an immediate strategy, draft resisters believed noncooperation could provide crucial leverage to stop the war. Organizer Paul Rupert commented that the Resistance "had a very material grasp that we were potential cannon fodder and could have a real part in making it impossible for the war to be waged."[18] Success hinged on getting enough men to take the first big step of renouncing their deferments and facing induction.

KING ANTICIPATED CRITICISM for his antiwar stand from both allies and adversaries; he had been through this before. He did not expect the deluge of recrimination. Nor did he expect the biting condescension that he felt as veiled racism: denying his *right* to speak out. The liberal media led the charge, right after his Riverside crossing of the Rubicon. Lambasting his "sheer inventions of unsupported fantasy," the *Washington Post* accused him of "grave injury to those who are his natural allies. Many who have listened to him with respect will never again accord him the same confidence. He has diminished his usefulness to his cause, to his country and to his people. And that is a great tragedy."[19] He was stung by these words.

Critics zeroed in on his alleged effort to "fuse" the civil rights and antiwar movements. His ambiguity did not help him. "In linking the civil rights movement with total opposition to our position in Vietnam," *Life* editorialized, he "comes close to betraying the cause for which he has worked so long. He goes beyond his personal right to dissent when he connects progress in civil rights here with a proposal that amounts to abject surrender in Vietnam," negotiating with the NLF, and urged youth to become COs rather than serve. "Much of his speech was a demagogic slander that sounded like a script for Radio Hanoi."[20]

He was criticized though less vehemently by the black press, a campaign orchestrated by the President's black assistant Louis Martin, who brought African-American publishers to the White House to hear LBJ's rebuttal.[21] Some newspapers and commentators praised King's stand, but they were drowned out by the media's big guns.

Out of necessity King had grown a thick skin to absorb white criticism, but he was wounded by black attacks, brought to tears. Baseball legend Jackie Robinson, a friend, questioned his judgment. The NAACP officially rebuked him, warning that merging the peace and freedom movements would be a serious mistake. Whitney Young of the Urban League attacked him harshly. A month earlier he and Young had nearly come to blows at a fund-raising dinner on Long Island. Young had scolded him for his recent antiwar talk in Los Angeles because it might have angered LBJ. King told his colleague that he didn't have to agree with his position, but "I do expect you to defend my right to say it." The movement generals lit into each other.

"Whitney," King let loose, "what you're saying may get you a foundation grant, but it won't get you into the kingdom of truth." Young, whose daughter was hunger-fasting against the war at Bryn Mawr, pointed at King's paunch: "You're eating well." An aide pulled King away. As his anger died down, he felt disgusted by his behavior and called Young later to apologize. Before long Young backed away from his unequivocal support of the war and confessed in later years that King was right.[22]

When the attacks rained down on him in April, King vigorously defended himself. He argued that he had the obligation to speak about the war not only as a citizen, but as a minister and a Nobel Peace Prize winner. He was offended by the *New York Times* and others who belittled him for ignorance of world affairs. He had closely followed his country's involvement in Southeast Asia and was well briefed by European journalists he had befriended over the years.

On fusing the two movements he tried to explain that they were linked by their content but not form, raising more questions than he answered. Was he being disingenuous? Surely Bevel and other antiwar colleagues he respected were seeking to merge civil rights, economic justice, and peace into One Big Movement. This had been the aim of SNCC and the New Left for a while. Although it opposed the war, he had no desire for SCLC to become an antiwar organization. But he expected that it would join in peace coalitions if they reached further into the mainstream than the April 15 alliance and involved more people of color.

President Johnson "flushed with anger" when he got wind of King's Riverside speech. Aides fed his hostility and paranoia. Cold War liberal John Roche, a political scientist and ex–democratic socialist, was his assistant in charge of wringing support from intellectuals. He reported to his boss that King, "inordinately ambitious and quite stupid," had "thrown in with the commies," jettisoning his black leadership. The "Communist-oriented 'peace' types have played him (and his driving wife) like trout." FBI's Hoover echoed this line to LBJ: "Based on King's recent activities and public utterances, it is clear that he is an instrument in the hands of subversive forces seeking to undermine our nation."[23] King and his staff right away felt stepped-up surveillance by Hoover's men: more frequent phone clicks, unmarked cars tailing them.

No one could doubt that King's spring peace offensive, with all its fateful ramifications, marked a major turning in his life, politically, emotionally, and spiritually. It also brought an irreparable rupture of his relationship with the President. Ever since he began the Vietnam escalation two years before, LBJ had felt more and more besieged by the media and opponents left and right. He knew better than anyone that Vietnam was a lost cause. If King was hurt most by black people attacking him, Johnson was unhinged by disloyalty and betrayal. King, for whom he had done so much, for whom he had risked his presidency, had turned against him, had made him the enemy. Armed with the full power of his office, he would now turn on King, make him the scapegoat. He blamed "that goddamned nigger preacher" for all his troubles.[24]

On Sunday, April 9, King preached at a Chicago church. "I don't know how long I'll live," he exclaimed, "but I hope I can live so well that the preacher can get up and say he was faithful. That's all, that's enough.

"That's where I want to go from this point on, the rest of my days. 'He who is greatest among you shall be your servant.' I want to be a servant. I want to be a witness for my Lord, do something for others."[25]

3

The stormy spring of 1967 marked a turning point not only for Martin King, the antiwar movement, and Lyndon Johnson, but for the nation and the world. Vietnam was the axis around which the whole planet seemed to be seeking new directions, new ways out of darkness. The coming twelve months would draw a dividing line in world history as critical as any in the twentieth century.

Amid the vertigo of events King may not have known whether he wanted one movement or two, or what their relationship ought to be. His double consciousness allowed him to see the peace and justice movements as both separate and combined; it depended partly on the audience he was speaking to. For several weeks in April and May he felt called to lead both movements. The dramatic entrance of the most prominent American to oppose the war had energized the movement like nothing else. Many thousands marched in New York because King was there.

Yet though he was used to the quarrelsome civil rights movement, he was not prepared for the chaotic new movement whose divisions made the civil rights community look harmonious. Unlike the latter, antiwar leaders desired King's symbolic might as much as they spurned his calling the shots. The peace train did not hanker for a new Gandhi.

But during the weeks that he stood front and center he focused on charting a viable strategy to end the war. Bevel and key white activists had threatened mass civil disobedience in Washington as the next step. King insisted that he was not ready to support civil disobedience. Nor at the other extreme would he heed pressure to run for president in 1968 as a peace candidate. He considered meeting with North Vietnamese leaders in Paris, but decided it would not be prudent. He gave guarded support to the "Dump Johnson" effort while promoting grassroots pressure for "negotiations now." He proposed a march on Washington like the one in 1963, that would link the war with poverty-program cuts. That sounded too tame for most antiwar leaders, who wanted to escalate their tactics—but were not sure how.

He joined with Spock in launching Vietnam Summer, an effort to mobilize thousands of students to go door-to-door and educate their communities about the war, to build the mainstream opposition that he felt essential to stopping the war. And he took a further step toward advocating outright resistance to the draft.

In February 1964, when young Cassius Clay won the world heavyweight boxing title, he announced that he had joined the Nation of Islam (he had secretly joined in 1961) and changed his name to Muhammad Ali. Three years later, now a Black Muslim minister and a captain of Elijah Muhammad's elite guard, he professed to be a conscientious objector to the Vietnam War. His white draft board denied his CO claim and ordered him into the army. After his lawyers exhausted all appeals up to the Supreme Court, he refused induction on April 28, 1967, in Houston.

"I'll never wear the uniform of the United States military forces," he told the press in Chicago. "I am not going ten thousand miles from here to help murder and kill and burn another poor people simply to help continue the domination of white slave masters over the darker people the world over." At the induction center "I will meet them head-on," the champion asserted, "and I'll be looking right into their pale blue eyes."[26] The government swiftly indicted him for induction refusal. He was convicted and sentenced to five years in prison. The boxing associations stripped him of his title. Whatever their opinion of Black Muslims, African Americans felt the assault on their hero as an assault on them all.

In a major sermon at Ebenezer spelling out his Vietnam stand—

Carmichael tapping his feet in the front pew—King congratulated Ali for his moral courage. "Here is a young man willing to give up fame, if necessary, willing to give up millions of dollars in order to stand up for what conscience tells him is right. It seems that I can hear the voice crying out through all the eternities saying to him this morning, 'Blessed are ye when men shall persecute you and shall call you all manner of evil for righteousness' sake.'"

As for himself, he declared, "I answered a call, and when God speaks, who can but prophesy?" He called for Americans to repent. "The kingdom of God is at hand." He heard God saying to America, you are too arrogant. "If you don't change your ways, I will rise up and break the backbone of your power." Ali was showing the way. Americans must take up the cross. "Before the crown we wear there is the cross that we must bear."[27] He was speaking, of course, to a Christian congregation. Other faiths had their own strong metaphors for sacrifice and redemption.

Ten days later, at an open-housing protest in Louisville, Kentucky, King was hit in the head by a rock after trying to reason with white teenagers menacing his car. "We've got to learn to live together as brothers," he had told them.[28] That night he gripped the rock in his hand as he spoke at a rally. Soon after, he and Coretta picketed the White House with other activists in their first joint antiwar action. She had been protesting the war for years, quietly urging her husband along. Finally he was following her example. The Nobel Peace Prize laureate who was used to talking with presidents face-to-face was now joining ordinary citizens who had to shout their peace chants through the wrought-iron White House gates.

AT THE END OF MAY SCLC held a staff retreat at a Quaker center on St. Helena Island off the coast of South Carolina. The center was originally one of the first schools for freed slaves. For three centuries black people slaving in the rice plantations had held tight to African customs on the sea islands, a cultural way station between West Africa and mainland America. The balmy seaside setting hardly distracted participants from the crisis they faced.

SCLC staff, mostly men with large egos, had always fought each other for King's favor. He encouraged among his subordinates the verbal sparring he was unable to engage in himself. Much of the internal conflict was healthy and productive. But since the stymied Chicago campaign, infighting had swung out of control.

King was a harried chief wearing three heavy hats—Ebenezer pastor, prophetic voice, and SCLC executive. Yet he had been unable to bring in a strong manager to handle the chaos, unwilling to give up the illusion of control. Morale had plummeted with confusion over SCLC's mission and funding cuts that resulted partly from King's Vietnam stand. The staff had to downsize. Except in Grenada, Mississippi, SCLC's fieldwork in the South had virtually dissolved. Was the civil rights movement over? Did SCLC have a future?

He answered yes to both questions at the retreat in a lengthy talk, "To Chart Our Course for the Future." King had often turned to oratory as an arbiter of or an escape from conflict, as if the power of his words could transcend the sticky wickets of human impasse, lifting himself and others to their higher selves, if only long enough to change the subject.

"It is necessary for us to realize," he explained, "that we have moved from the era of civil rights to the era of human rights. When you deal with human rights you are not dealing with something clearly defined in the Constitution. They are rights that are clearly defined by the mandates of a humanitarian concern."

During the previous two years, when it became evident that the historic civil rights laws would not sweep away racism or poverty, he had come to see the inadequacy of individual rights. He grasped that "civil rights" carried too much baggage of the dominant tradition of American individualism and not enough counterweight from a tradition of communitarian impulses, collective striving, and common good. This subterranean tradition had been kept alive by peoples of color, especially blacks and American Indians. The polar strains of individualism and collectivism needed to be reconciled, as he strove to reconcile other opposites. His conception of rights shifted to a richer, comprehensive meaning that reflected his underlying biblical values.

By 1967 King seemed to be following the example of Malcolm X, who near the end of his life stressed the need to "expand the civil-rights struggle to a higher level—to the level of human rights." If the two leaders had been able to compare notes during Malcolm's last year, they would have discovered that each was drawing similar conclusions about the necessity to go beyond constitutional rights.

Both Martin and Malcolm were reconstructing the legacy of their forebears, such as Gabriel Prosser, Frederick Douglass, John Mercer Langston, Ida B. Wells, and Du Bois. From the end of the eighteenth century, African-American leaders had grounded their interpretation of rights in black spirituality and in what they saw as the divinely authorized Declaration of Independence, with its "amazing universalism," in King's words. Many African Americans had perceived their human rights, no matter how poorly fulfilled, as a covenant with their personal God intervening in history on the side of justice. "Blacks always believed in rights in some larger, mythologic sense—as a pantheon of possibility," legal scholar Patricia Williams noted.[29]

According to this deeper view that King took on, rights were more than private possessions. They were a moral imperative that transcended individual needs. He was rehabilitating the old preindustrial meaning of *right*: something that was right or just (righteous), that one therefore had a "right" to. Rights rightly understood were not whatever a person claimed as his or her due, with no boundaries; but what was required for all people, and thus for each, by the higher laws of justice and love. They were those entitlements that constituted the moral foundation of the beloved community.

Proper rights were limited by the same moral laws. Rights and responsibility were not a dichotomy but interwoven. Individuals had a moral responsibility to secure just rights for themselves and others. That was why, rooted in biblical faith, many African Americans experienced rights as shared resources. And why many have felt a duty to realize them not just on an individual basis, but for their people as a community or nation. This perspective diverged sharply from the classic liberal ideology of unbounded rights, owned by isolated, unencumbered selves devoid of community ties. King came to have hardly more affinity for such individualistic rights than he had for unbounded freedom or democracy, coins of the same realm.

"The great glory of American democracy," he said many times, "is the right to protest for right." The right to protest was authorized by the rightness or justice of the moral aim, not simply as a constitutional right justified in and of itself. "It is morally right," he wrote in his last book, "to insist that every person have a decent house, an adequate education, and enough money to provide basic necessities for one's family."[30] Rights could no longer be traded off or compartmentalized. They were a body, indivisible, as illustrated by the U.N. Declaration of Human Rights, which Malcolm had tied his kite to.

King had moved beyond the principle of compensatory justice—that disadvantaged African Americans, and whites as well, deserved an economic bill of rights justified by slavery. This was a linchpin of his 1964 book, *Why We Can't Wait*. All people had human rights, he now believed, because they were children of God. No further justification was needed. On the sunny sea island he was calling for a full-blown human rights movement, a "human rights revolution" that would place economic justice at the center.

The aim of the human rights movement would be to achieve genuine integration—meaning shared power—and genuine equality, requiring a "radical redistribution of economic and political power."

"For the last twelve years we have been in a reform movement." But "after Selma and the voting rights bill, we moved into a new era, which must be an era of revolution. We must see the great distinction between a reform movement and a revolutionary movement. We are called upon to raise certain basic questions about the whole society." The rules must be changed. There must be a revolution of values. Only by reallocating and *redefining* power would it be possible to wipe out the triple interlocking evils of racism, exploitation, and militarism.

"You really can't get rid of one without getting rid of the others," he said. "Jesus confronted this problem of the interrelatedness of evil one day." In the Gospel of John a rich man named Nicodemus came to Jesus and asked, What must I do to be saved?

"Jesus didn't get bogged down in a specific evil. He didn't say, now Nicodemus you must not drink liquor. He didn't say, Nicodemus you must not commit adultery. He didn't say, Nicodemus you must not lie. He didn't say, Nicodemus you must not steal. He said, Nicodemus you must be born again. Nicodemus, the whole structure of your life must be changed.

"What America must be told today is that she must be born again. The whole structure of American life must be changed."[31]

When he finished his talk the gathering sang a rousing "Ain't Gonna Study War No More," his lovely baritone clear as a bell.

WHETHER SINGING ISAIAH'S CALL for peace or invoking the Israelites' defeat of Pharaoh's forces to escape from Egyptian slavery, African Americans lived the Hebrew Scriptures in the present tense. It was a shock to the world, no less to the fighters themselves, when modern Israelites trounced Egypt and its neighbors in a six-day blitzkrieg and reconquered Jerusalem after two millennia of exile. The Bible was born again in June 1967.

During the spring, while much of the world was watching Vietnam and the American peace movement, hostile moves by Israel and surrounding Arab states rose to a level not seen since the Suez crisis of 1956. After Israel shot down Syrian jet fighters, Egyptian president Nasser mobilized his army menacingly on Israel's southern border. Suddenly on the morning of June 5, hundreds of Israeli jets swooped down on Egyptian air bases and in minutes pulverized Egypt's air force on the ground. Then Israeli jets decimated the Syrian and Jordanian air forces. With mastery of the air, Israel defeated Egyptian, Jordanian, and finally Syrian troops on their own turf. After a fierce battle between the Israeli and Jordanian sectors of Jerusalem, Israeli soldiers marched deliriously through the Lion's Gate into the Old City. They prayed in awe at the Western Wall, where the Jewish temple had been destroyed by Romans forty years after Jesus died.

No one at the time foresaw that Israel would hold on to the occupied Palestinian territories into the twenty-first century. The Arab states were humiliated by their defeat, but Palestinians were the real losers. Under Yasser Arafat's leadership they launched a guerrilla war that adopted terrorist tactics, emulating the pre-1948 Jewish resistance, out of desperation. For Israelis, the victory soured, as peace remained a mirage.

King was shaken by the Israeli blitzkrieg, which he heard about while returning from the second Peace on Earth conference in Geneva. Besides thousands of deaths, overwhelmingly the darker skinned, he realized that Israel's victory, and the triumphalism of most American Jews, would set back his peace work. The Six-Day War stole headlines from the Vietnam drama, providing cover for Johnson to pour in more troops. More serious was the long-term damage of dividing the peace forces, already fractious enough. "Half of the peace movement is Jewish," Stanley Levison observed, "and the Jews have all become hawks."[32] Many leftist Jews devoutly backed what they saw as Israel's war of self-preservation. But many other activists supported Palestinian self-determination.

Despite his warnings about Dante's inner circle of hell, King tried to remain noncommittal about Israel's war, while steadfastly defending its right to exist. For years he had condemned anti-Semitism, considering it racism. He even supported a moderate Zionism. But he believed that "the great powers have the obligation to recognize that the Arab world is in a state of imposed poverty and backwardness that must threaten peace and harmony." Lust for oil was "the heart of the problem." He called for a Marshall Plan for the Middle East.[33]

As he feared, besides militarizing the Mideast and ramping up the Cold War, the Six-Day War dealt a blow to the American left, making the prospect of unity more elusive. This became evident when SNCC leaders embraced Palestinian resistance to Israeli occupation. The heretical stand, which marginalized SNCC more than had its Vietnam opposition, complicated efforts to forge a broader antiwar coalition.

4

Rather than talk about war in the Mideast or in Vietnam, King spent most of June 1967 promoting his new book, published by Harper & Row, *Where Do We Go from Here: Chaos or Community?* He had taken up Levison's suggestion to write his fourth book during fall 1966 when, at a low ebb, he felt that his message wasn't getting across. This was in part because he wasn't clear what it was. The fading of the southern movement, the upheaval in northern cities, the impetuous rise of Black Power, the stalemate of SCLC's Chicago drive, and the mad horror of the war—all of these, sewn together in his mind, signified that the strategies and goals of the decade after Montgomery had to be refigured before they were made irrelevant by the crush of global revolt.

Fitting for a revolutionary time, he would write a book about power. Starting with an overview of the movement at this crossroads, it explained and challenged the Black Power phenomenon and, in an end run, offered an alternative picture of power serving an alternative vision of revolution—to create a "socially conscious democracy" that reconciled the opposing truths of individualism and collectivism.

The book was also an exposition of the lessons King thought he had learned from the movement's successes and failures, most recently in the Chicago campaign. While the Black Power movement in the South began in spring 1965 when SNCC joined forces with the Lowndes County Freedom Organization to run candidates for county office, organized Black Power in the North originated in SCLC's August 1965 decision, just after the Watts revolt, to launch a major campaign in Chicago, the nation's most segregated metropolis. They were invited in by the Coordinating Council of Community Organizations (CCCO), a grassroots federation that had made headway in fighting school segregation. Bevel took a leave as SCLC's director of direct action to work with an interracial group on the west side that had been applying militant nonviolent action to ghetto problems. When King appointed him director of the Chicago campaign, he got SCLC to embrace a strategy to create a federation of neighborhood tenant unions to empower residents to eliminate slum conditions. Bevel and his coworkers sought to combine CCCO's well-tested community organizing with SCLC's mass direct action. They aimed at mobilizing a nonviolent army to confront Chicago's power structure much as SCLC had done in Birmingham.

To dramatize slum conditions and his own commitment, King moved with his family into a dingy, urine-stenched tenement in one of the Windy City's worst slums. But the vision of "Unions to End Slums" proved to be only that. The Chicago Freedom Movement shifted from transforming the ghetto from within to fighting the financial and real-estate interests that intentionally segregated the city for their own profit. By summer 1966 the thrust of the campaign was to march against housing discrimination in ethnic white neighborhoods. The marches brought hostility from working-class mobs that King, who was felled by a rock in the head, felt was worse than anything he had encountered in the Deep South. He found Mayor Richard Daley's political machine, which had co-opted many black leaders, to be impregnable. He had ignored Rustin's warning to stay away from Chicago.

A summit meeting with Daley in August 1966 achieved a "half a loaf" compromise agreement with hollow promises for housing integration. A subsequent voter registration campaign led by Hosea Williams, aimed at challenging the Daley machine, proved a failure. King's turn toward the war in spring 1967 was, besides its moral impulse, a way of saving face after the Chicago disgrace.

WHILE IN *Where Do We Go from Here* King criticized Black Power as a slogan without program, as flash without back, he praised its essential meaning. He suggested that Black Power and the urban riots did not cause the growing white backlash—"massive resistance" of the 1950s gone national—but were the consequence. Black militancy slouching toward violence was the bitter fruit of promises unfulfilled, rights not implemented, lack of economic justice. The call for Black Power was a "psychological reaction to the psychological indoctrination that led to the creation of the perfect slave," he wrote. It was a healthy response to slavery's emasculation of black manhood, black humanity, its demonization of blackness.

"Psychological freedom, a firm sense of self-esteem, is the most powerful weapon against the long night of physical slavery." Certainly he valued this trait in himself and knew its potency. His gift of self-esteem set him apart from most other leaders, black or white, whose elephantine egos tried to fill their void of self-regard. He embraced Black Power's celebration of black pride and racial identity, a staple of his own rhetoric since he had first exalted the "new Negro in the South." Sounding like Du Bois, he interpreted Black Power as the latest manifestation of a centuries-old struggle by black people to reconcile their African past with their American present and future.

"The Negro's greatest dilemma is that in order to be healthy he must accept his ambivalence. The problem is that in the search for wholeness all too many Negroes seek to embrace only one side of their natures. The old Hegelian synthesis still offers the best answer to many of life's dilemmas. The American Negro is neither totally African nor totally Western. He is Afro-American, a true hybrid, a combination of two cultures."

While King was preparing his manuscript, *black* was replacing *Negro* among many segments of the black community, especially in the urban North. If his book had come out just a year later, many readers would have found his use of *Negro* outdated, for some offensive. The book appeared in a moment of transition between *Negro* and *black* that corresponded to the end of the civil rights movement and the takeoff of black liberation.

King endorsed Black Power in principle but objected to how most militants practiced it: rejection of integration for separatism, swaggering nationalism, inflammatory rhetoric, support, even glorification, of violent resistance, dehumanization of white people. He criticized its prioritizing of race over class (Black Panthers did the reverse), self-determination over economic justice, instead of exploring their inter-dependence, the task he took on in this book. He was troubled by its lack of effectiveness. They might celebrate black pride and beauty till kingdom come, but it might not make a dent in chronic black jobless-ness, or transforming the ghetto into a livable community. Dignity was no longer enough.

A treatise on power must be anchored in first principles. King wrote that power was the ability to achieve purpose, especially moral pur-pose. Philosophers culminating in Nietzsche had mistakenly divorced power from love, making them polar opposites. King professed that the "collision of immoral power with powerless morality" constituted the major crisis of our times, echoing his mentors Tillich and Niebuhr. Power without love was "reckless and abusive." Love without power was "sentimental and anemic." The rightful exercise of power was "love implementing the demands of justice," which was "power cor-recting everything that stands against love." If these principles were left in such airy abstraction, a contemporary Nietzsche might have dis-missed them as more idealistic Christian weakness that sapped the will to power. But King got down to earth.

He confessed that his own attempt to exercise moral power, and that of the civil rights movement, had fallen short. He confirmed much of the growing criticism by the left, especially from SNCC.

"In candor and self-criticism it is necessary to acknowledge that the tortuous job of organizing solidly and simultaneously in thousands of places was not a feature of our work." SCLC and other civil rights groups often defeated themselves by lackluster organization, by dis-unity and "petty competition." He did not object to healthy debate about contending strategies. Nor did he mind SNCC's refusal to "can-onize me." In an unpublished draft he wrote: "I have never been sensi-tive to being called 'De Lawd' by many younger activists," which he saw as fending off a damaging cult of personality. The nickname was also a sign of backhanded reverence.

The disunity that was destructive, he continued in the early draft, was "that which embodies misrepresentation and distortion." When, to make organizational hay, "false rumors are circulated that some leaders have 'sold out' to the power structure"—himself?—"or are opportunistically making alliances with one or another major political party to gain individual advantage, the whole movement suffers."[34] Such was immoral power born of powerless morality.

In the book he criticized SCLC for overstressing media drama and explosive events that did not "assemble and unify the support for new stages of struggle. Recognizing that no army can mobilize and demobilize and remain a fighting unit, we will have to build far-flung, workmanlike and experienced organizations in the future. We shall have to have people tied together in a long-term relationship instead of evanescent enthusiasts who lose their experience, spirit and unity because they have no mechanism that directs them to new tasks."

He called for a creative array of new organizations to be vehicles for expressions of democratic power. In addition to reinvigorated and democratized labor unions, they would include unions of tenants and of welfare recipients, their rights protected by a new Wagner Act relevant to a mature welfare state. Such grassroots unions of the poor and disadvantaged would coalesce with other groups into a bottom-up coalition, a "true alliance."

A true alliance, he explained, was "based upon some self-interest of each component group and a common interest into which they merge. For an alliance to have permanence and loyal commitment from its various elements, each of them must have a goal from which it benefits and none must have an outlook in basic conflict with the others." One would not ally with a group that disagreed on fundamental values or principles, like antiracism, even if sharing the same goals. The idea was to create alliances broader and deeper than the April peace mobilization, for example, but not so loose as to be "least common denominator" coalitions that agreed only on the narrowest single-issue objective. Rather than top-down coalitions jealously guarded by movement generals, true alliances would have mechanisms of participatory decision making built in. Those who knew King's decision-making style might have found his plea for internal democracy unconvincing.

Hierarchy and authoritarian control told only part of the story of King's leadership, however. They contrasted with, yet made room for, his keen ability to listen, pay attention, learn. People who knew him were struck by his gift for patient listening. Top-down control reverberated with democratic intimacy to produce a mode of leadership whose authority, whose claim to obedience and loyalty, was rooted in his engaged relationship with subleaders and followers. Until the last season of his life, his leadership offered a trusted setting for volatile, free-wheeling deliberation and dissent, encouraging conflict but keeping it in bounds. His charisma and personal power, like those of Lincoln, another grand master of the authority and democracy dialectic, proved compelling because they were embedded in a personal connection, felt as mystical by some. He sought to create with participants the "I and Thou" relationship that he held as a personalist ideal.

Over the years he had striven to exercise authority with compassionate understanding, even if the former often trumped the latter. Although he knew that he had made mistakes, had been undemocratic and manipulative, he was drawn to the "personal, deep communication" politics that animated younger activists. Despite his authoritarian manner, he had exemplified reciprocal leadership through fostering relationship. A decade of democracy in the streets, which he had helped midwife, could not have helped but wean him from his black Baptist orientation of preacher as boss. He was searching for better ways to express loving power and powerful love.

Only a true alliance, or alliance of true alliances, he believed, could eliminate the triple evils of racism, exploitation, and militarism—and as an eventual electoral coalition, move toward a democratic socialist society that would institutionalize power guided by compassion. The Johnson administration had shown in 1964 and 1965 that an American-style social democracy was not impossible. But LBJ sabotaged his Great Society and his own greatness by immoral power carried to the extreme: his Ahab-like obsession with the Moby Dick of Vietnam.

5

Even if it better fit his temperament and training, King was finding himself less able to lead the top-down coalition that he was familiar with. Gone were the days when he played the mediator between generals on the left and right of the civil rights movement. Terrain had shifted. As he had prophesied in his letter from Birmingham jail, the center that he commanded had moved to the left, moderate had become radical, perhaps even revolutionary. SNCC and CORE had abandoned the grand coalition, leaving King holding down its left end, an untenable position.

A sign of how much had changed for him, politically and emotionally, was how hard it had become to keep his anger wrapped up, especially in face-to-face meetings that he had usually handled with agility. He always had a deep well of anger, inherited from his father and the cruelty inflicted on his race. We saw his fury at fifteen when he was forced to move to the back of a bus in rural Georgia. But one of his supreme gifts, tied to the strong self-esteem that his parents had drummed into him, was his capacity to cap his anger and transform its energy into disarming humor and oratorical passion. Reeling now from the onslaught of invective for his Vietnam stand, he lost his temper more and more frequently. His ease with banter left him.

In a summit meeting with Wilkins, Whitney Young, and other leaders in late May 1967, he blew up at Wilkins when the combative NAACP chief did not let up on King's Vietnam apostasy. His longtime friend Kenneth Clark, the social psychologist, who had gathered the leaders at his home near New York, said it was "the first time I'd ever seen Martin angry."[35] The bitter exchange was escalating when Young, who had also skirmished with King on the war, jumped in to cool the fire. Getting nowhere, the leaders agreed to meet again soon.

SCLC colleagues were more concerned than ever about their boss's emotional state. Septima Clark had worked with him longer than anyone except Abernathy. "I have never seen you in the kind of mood that I witnessed" in early June, she wrote in a note. "Dr. King, if we are to keep a world renowned leader healthy, wholesome and efficient, some of the burdens must be shared." In Atlanta and in field offices she had encountered "many smoldering grievances." As a friend, she worried about his survival. "You are certainly more valuable healthy than sick, and God help us all if you become exhausted to the point of a non-active person. May God help you to help yourself."[36]

His physical and emotional exhaustion along with a lull in the peace campaign pushed him to brake his antiwar drive. At May's sea island retreat SCLC had committed to a summer program in Cleveland that would, they hoped, get better results than Chicago. The Ohio city had suffered rioting over the previous summer; its racially primitive white mayor only made things worse. The black ministers' association, with the blessing of the local NAACP, invited King to help alleviate the city's racial crisis. In June SCLC staff launched a community-organizing campaign that focused on tenant organizing, voter registration, and an Operation Breadbasket project to get jobs for poor blacks from local companies. The Chicago Breadbasket campaign, led by movement prodigy Jesse Jackson, a divinity student from South Carolina, had forced deals with two giant supermarket chains, garnering over a thousand jobs and sales of black products. Breadbasket, SCLC's most dependable success, was about to go national.

When King met again with fellow civil rights generals in mid-June, tension over Vietnam had calmed because he and SCLC were jetting up their northern campaign after the Chicago slump. King insisted that his priority was poverty but that the media ran amok with his comments on Vietnam. Wilkins, Young, and other leaders threw their support to the Cleveland project, the focal point of their unity statement. The alliance of black forces in Cleveland boded well for the summer.

SEEMINGLY IN SYNC with the war in Southeast Asia, the war in America's "domestic colonies" had escalated every summer since the Harlem riot of 1964, then Watts the next year, both of which King had tasted firsthand. In Harlem, acting at the mayor's behest, he had alienated militants by appearing to be on the side of the Man. In Watts he played an after-the-fact role but found the rebels and the rulers in utterly different worlds.

Racist police practices, lack of jobs, subhuman housing, and related ills had produced an "explosive mixture which had been accumulating in our cities since the end of World War II," the National Advisory Commission on Civil Disorders concluded in early 1968.[37] The unfulfilled promises of the freedom movement, and its lip service to cities outside the South, persuaded many young ghetto dwellers that they would have to act on their own, without plan, organization, or allies. A black reporter arrested in the Detroit riot noted that the majority of his jailmates "were hustlers and two-bit gangsters. They boasted about how much loot they got. Listening to them I became convinced there was no outside conspiracy or special organization that welded them together." They were bonded by hatred for the cops.[38]

In July 1967, as SCLC was signing up voters and organizing slum tenants in Cleveland, the ghettos' spontaneous combustion verged on civil war in Newark and Detroit and scores of other cities. Pent-up powerlessness in Newark resulting from an unresponsive city hall fueled a rampage of looting and wreckage. It was triggered by the police beating of a black cab driver. Poorly led police and national guard units stifled the revolt with indiscriminate gunfire, often against imaginary snipers. Half of the two dozen blacks they killed were not involved, including a seventy-three-year-old man, six women, and two young children.

The most catastrophic urban rebellion in U.S. history erupted a week later in Detroit. The Motor City had seen a bloody race riot in 1943, mainly whites attacking black newcomers. By the mid-1960s, after further migration from the South, the once integrated area around 12th Street was one of the nation's most densely populated districts, with overcrowded, dilapidated tenement buildings and rampant unemployment. Black residents and white cops were at war.

A late-night raid of a black club drew a furious crowd that started a chain reaction of looting and burning. Young blacks seemed to be "dancing amidst the flames." Dodging high-powered bullets, they howled and shrieked as they ran off with TVs and stereos and enough shoes to open a store.

How did it all start? a looter was asked.

"It takes too long to tell you."

"Yeah, it start two hundred years ago," his buddy replied.

"Why did it start now?"

"It didn't start now. You know a rash? You know how it spread. That's what this is. This is a rash and it spreadin' and spreadin'."[39]

Most of several hundred gutted buildings were hit by spreading, windswept fires. Firefighters reportedly withdrew three hundred times when police failed to protect them. Governor George Romney, then the GOP presidential front-runner, flew over the battleground at dusk on the second day. "It looked like the city had been bombed on the west side," he testified later. "There was an area two-and-a-half miles by three-and-a-half miles with major fires, with entire blocks in flames."[40] Five thousand Michigan national guardsmen were reinforced by four thousand army paratroopers dispatched reluctantly by President Johnson; he didn't want to help his likely opponent. He insisted to the commanding general that the troops not have bullets in their guns. "I don't want it said that one of my soldiers shot a pregnant nigger."[41]

As in Newark and Watts the devastation was compounded by chaos within the armies of the law. Guardsmen and state police often did not know who, where, or why they were shooting. Most of the forty-three reported deaths from the weeklong carnage, thirty-three of them blacks, were "accidental." Detroit's congressman and others believed the true death toll to be over a hundred.

During the Newark and Detroit riots King was shuttling between Atlanta, Chicago, and Cleveland. "There were dark days before," he told Levison over the phone, "but this is the darkest." In a conference call he and his advisers debated how to respond to the urban violence and decided he would send a public telegram to LBJ, who had denounced the rioting without offering a remedy.

King confided to his advisers that Chicago contacts "gave me the plan" for a Chicago revolt. "They don't plan to just burn down the west side, they are planning to get the Loop in Chicago."[42] FBI wiretappers sent this instantly to Hoover, who alerted Johnson within the hour that King knew about a conspiracy to torch Chicago's downtown. Since April the President had been hungry for juicy evidence to tar King with subversive militancy. Chicago did not burn this time.

He was far less interested in King's telegram, announced at an Ebenezer press conference on July 24.

There was no question that the violence and destruction must be halted, King wired his erstwhile ally, "but Congress has consistently refused to vote a halt to the destruction of the lives of Negroes in the ghetto." He lambasted defeat of a rent-supplement bill and even a rat-control program that lawmakers laughed at. They had never seen a black infant chewed up by a voracious rodent. "The suicidal and irrational acts which plagued our streets daily are being sowed and watered by the irrational, irrelevant and equally suicidal debate and delay in Congress," which he called "moral degradation" and hypocrisy.

White society bore ultimate responsibility for the rioting. "The turmoil of the ghetto is the externalization of the Negro's inner torment and rage. It has turned outward the frustration that formerly was suppressed in agony." He identified with this rage and the need to release it.

Because this was a state of emergency and "the life of our nation is at stake," he urged the President to deal with the root problem of unemployment by creating a new federal agency, modeled on the New Deal's Works Progress Administration (WPA), dear to LBJ's heart. The proposed agency would provide jobs for the jobless.[43] But the President was in no mood to be lectured by his Judas.

After reading the telegram King fielded reporters' questions. This time, he explained, he was not going to Detroit or Newark to help calm the flames. His job was not to stop riots but to prevent them from starting, to wipe out the conditions that stoked them. Thus he would continue his local empowerment efforts in Cleveland and Chicago. He had gone to Harlem and to Watts as a fireman, fool's errands. He no longer had time to put out fires, rather to build a larger fire of the Spirit to extinguish fires of the flesh.

"These are evil times," he preached to his Ebenezer faithful in early August. Their nation was still the "greatest purveyor of violence," in the ghetto jungles as well as in Asian ones.

He recounted that the other day a young man had told him that he needed to take a trip. No, he replied, he was on the road far too much already. "I'm tired of all this traveling I have to do," he complained to his flock. "I'm killing myself. Always away from my children and my family." He didn't need another trip. That wasn't what he meant, the fellow had rejoined. To relieve his troubles, to be born again, he wanted King to take LSD.[44]

IT WAS THE SUMMER of bitter despair. It was the Summer of Love. While desultory black youth threw Molotov cocktails in the inner cities, other young people, mainly of lighter skin, were calmly seeking liberation through marijuana and psychedelic drugs. Although both camps used illicit drugs, reveled in rock or soul, and considered themselves social outcasts, they were worlds apart, rent by class as much as race. Yet the bearded or bra-less hippie proselytizing LSD was very much the scion of the black hipster of the nation's dark ghettos.

The semimythical Summer of Love was launched in January 1967 with the Gathering of the Tribes festival in San Francisco's Golden Gate Park. Amid acid rock and surreal pageantry, an anarchist cadre called the Diggers handed out LSD to thousands. The organizers of the "Human Be-In" aimed at joining together youth turned on by drugs with those turned on by radical politics (many were both). The name itself reflected the mission. If sit-ins had conjured one kind of beloved community, be-ins conjured another. Each was a conjuring of the kingdom of God, a new Jerusalem. It did not take prophesy to imagine the power of merging the political and cultural rebels, making the youth movement one.

The mass media ran wild with the Human Be-In and lured a multitude of young people to San Francisco wearing flowers in their hair.

They settled in a rundown neighborhood called Haight-Ashbury. While playing with psychedelics and free sex, they also set up an instant cooperative commonwealth of communes, "free stores," free clinics, and other free spaces. Little Haight-Ashburys sprang up in other cities. Here was a revolution of values, but very different from the one King had in mind. Or was it?

Ten years before, writing about the Beat Generation, Norman Mailer had explored the confluence of cultural and political nonconformity in America. "If the fate of twentieth century man is to live with death," the threat of annihilation, "then the only life-giving answer is to accept the terms of death, to divorce oneself from society, to exist without roots, to set out on that uncharted journey into the rebellious imperatives of the self. One is Hip or one is Square, one is a rebel or one conforms. So it is no accident that the source of Hip is the Negro for he has been living on the margin between totalitarianism and democracy for two centuries."

The common ethos of hip blacks and whites, said Mailer, was their "burning consciousness of the present," to be engaged "in one primal battle: to open the limits of the possible for oneself. Yet in widening the arena of the possible, one widens it reciprocally for others as well," such that each person's fulfillment contains "its antithesis of human cooperation."

Writing after the triumph of the Montgomery bus boycott, Mailer foresaw that if black people continued to break free of their chains, it might unleash the hipster's "psychically armed rebellion" upon the broad expanses of American life; to "bring into the air such animosities, antipathies, that the mean empty hypocrisies of mass conformity will no longer work. A time of violence, new hysteria, confusion and rebellion will then be likely to replace the time of conformity."[45] The armies of the night were stirring.

Black and white activists, and eventually the hippie hordes, dressed themselves in the cool, existential style of the rebel, the "psychic outlaw." Grandchildren of Walt Whitman and the transcendentalists, hippies took participatory democracy to deeper regions of the psyche. The counterculture offered a world of spontaneous pleasure to mold cooperatively. While SNCC and the New Left arose partly as an answer to conformist alienation, the counterculture made this their Goliath. They took King's call to be creatively maladjusted to an extreme that would appall him.

The counterculture's motley mobilization assaulted the mores of the technocratic "death culture," including the scientific worldview and the capitalist work ethic. In a twist on Orwell, hippies were showing how Work was to be Play. They were subverting technique, efficiency, and joyless labor with the power of imagination, challenging not merely authority but its ethical grounding. A new culture appeared to be gestating in which spiritual capacities that "take fire from visionary splendor and the experience of human communion" were storming the barricades of a psychologically dying world.[46]

KING WAS NOT COMPLETELY ALIEN to the philosophy of the counterculture. Indeed he had inadvertently helped father it. For a long time he had preached that the worst evil was "psychological death"— worse than physical death, than physical suffering. Psychological death took many forms, from the sacred to the profane. It was the death of human personality, of the soul, of the Spirit within. Psychological death was depersonalization, the bitter fruit of racism, exploitation, and militarism, and of the soulless society that bred them.

Depersonalization meant that one's personality dis-integrated, one's divine essence severed from the rest of one's self, from other persons, from society. King saw this most frighteningly in the ghetto. "The depersonalized manipulation of persons as though they were things," he testified to a Senate hearing, "is as much responsible for the perpetuation of grief and misery in our cities as is the absence of wealth and natural resources."[47] When people were depersonalized they were turned into things—objects, numbers, commodities, caseloads. The "I-it" relationship replaced the possibility of "I and Thou," I itself reduced to "it." Objectification by the society, and worse, by one's own self. As the hippies and the ghetto dwellers acted out in their arenas, as writers like Ralph Ellison had spelled out in prose, as singers like Otis Redding and Simon and Garfunkel cried out in song, alienation was the plague of modern humanity. In Tillich's simple words, "Sin is separation."

While racism and segregation were the most blatant forms of alienation, and served as metaphors for the larger evil, King also spoke out against more subtle and insidious manifestations. He had come of age in the early Cold War era, when social critics like David Riesman, William H. Whyte Jr., and Erich Fromm were warning Americans of the dangers of mass conformity. He was familiar with Riesman's 1950 best-seller, *The Lonely Crowd*, its thesis that postwar America's mass-consumption society had replaced an "inner-directed" personality type who "acquire early in life an internalized set of goals" with an "other-directed" personality in tow to others' expectations, ruled by peer pressure, loyal to prevailing norms.[48]

As far back as May 1956, McCarthyism just past its peak, King questioned the concept of "maladjustment," which he called "the ringing cry of the new child psychology." Speaking to an NAACP gathering, he declared "there are some things in our social system to which I am proud to be maladjusted, and to which I suggest that you too ought to be maladjusted"—including segregation, discrimination, exploitation, and the "madness of militarism."[49] He was drawn to the new field of humanistic psychology, relevant both to his philosophy of personalism and to his pastoral counseling. Besides encouraging "creative maladjustment" to harmful norms and conformism, he spoke about internalized oppression and about subconscious destructive forces in society, a Jungian collective unconscious that needed to be healed through public witness. His political strategy of exposing the brutal underside of segregation in places like Birmingham, St. Augustine, and Selma was a means of healing the repressed id of subconscious racism that he believed all Americans shared.

He understood that science and technology had become a new religion threatening to extinguish traditional religious faiths. He also saw the technological revolution as the material force behind the emergent "new age" with its seemingly unlimited possibilities. He extolled technology's capacity to make the world a neighborhood, even while organized religion had failed to make it a "brotherhood." With all of its promise, however, he saw technology as more a curse than a blessing. Nowhere was he more prophetic than in his condemnation of automation and cybernetics, metaphors as well as touchstones of depersonalization.

Critiques of automation and cybernetics set off alarm bells in the mid–twentieth century that stopped tolling by century's end. Once portrayed as dehumanizing, these wonders of "progress" were later, by force of the Information Revolution, treated as liberating. Influenced by Bayard Rustin, King worried not only about the millions whose jobs would be replaced by machines—black workers the most vulnerable—but about the psychological deadening inflicted on the remaining workers controlled by technology rather than controlling it. Robotization would not only replace workers with robots robbing their jobs. It would turn them into robots.

He could already see how computers were regimenting the workplace—regimenting minds—in ways that Frederick Taylor's time and motion engineers could barely have dreamed of. The educated world was adopting a new faith that computer technology would emancipate humans from ignorance and drudgery. King saw the potential for psychological freedom, but he feared a greater danger of enslavement—just at the time when African Americans were throwing off the yoke of mental slavery that had endured for a century after the Civil War.

By 1967, biographer Marshall Frady suggested, "King had come to feel an unease of soul that he was trapped in some accelerating contest between the last hopes for a true, interconnected human community in America and the progressive deadening of its heart by the advance of a new sort of technotronic, corporate totalitarianism—a national order of power, composed of the megaconglomerates and the huge machineries of government acting in their interests, that was working a systematic impoverishment of modern man's very humanity, conducting the country ever further into a computerized, materialistic void. His forebodings about this brought him to a radicalization of perspective ranged against, as it were, the very nature and shape of his times."[50]

He did not have to look far to see how modern technologies were depersonalizing people. He took aim at the technology of bureaucracy. Since the 1964 Berkeley revolt students in the "multiversity" were protesting not only suppression of free speech and complicity with the war machine, but how they were bent, spindled, and mutilated like IBM cards—not educated for life, but trained for the work of death. Young men defied the draft not only because they despised the war, but also because they hated being channeled by the "pressurized guidance" of the Selective Service System, its "club of induction" terrifying registrants into conformity. Most degrading was the welfare bureaucracy, which helped poor families survive physically at the price of psychic servitude, druglike dependency.

In his December 1966 Senate testimony King tore into the welfare bureaucracy for its manipulation of the poor (others called it regimentation) and backed recipients' demands for dignity as well as decent benefits. "With the expansion of government and private bureaucracy," he told senators investigating the urban crisis, "and the growing complexity of society as a whole, the question of what are the rights of citizens becomes increasingly crucial." Poor people "are forging new forms of rights in relation to the welfare state which are important for all Americans, not only the poor and Negro.

"What is the citizen's right of participation," he asked, "in the decisions which so directly affect his community? Are these decisions to be made by professional elites?" Government by the people was needed, especially in public bureaucracies, that "involves the citizen in new and significant ways." He was implicitly criticizing the charade of poor people's participation in antipoverty programs. The "enhanced role of the citizen," he suggested, "may be as vital as additional money to the reemergence of the city as the springboard of hope for its populace."[51] Democratizing bureaucracies might be the only way to humanize them, forcing them to treat their clients as persons. More than ever he was embracing, in words at least, the ethos of participatory democracy that was the zeitgeist of the 1960s.

Fighting depersonalization, moreover, must begin at home. He believed that his movement, and any that he associated with, should set an example and refuse to be complicit in society's depersonalizing of citizens. Progressive movements had a moral responsibility, he felt, to offer an alternative stance that affirmed people's humanness while standing up to behavior that depersonalized others, inside or outside the movement. If activists did not strike a balance between asserting their responsibilities and respecting the rights of others, an equilibrium between justice and love, they would depersonalize not only their adversaries but themselves and their allies. They would lose their own humanity, and ultimate effectiveness, in the name of moral correctness.

6

_____

If Martin King had had more time to reflect, if he had been able to take the sabbatical from the movement that he lusted for, he might have expanded his critique of depersonalization into a full-fledged philosophy. He started pursuing these ideas during the bus boycott and its aftermath as a way to flesh out his understanding of how to integrate personal and social reformation. The American sickness was simultaneously institutional and personal. He witnessed how in myriad ways the boycott and the ensuing civil rights crusade had engaged this duality. He was alarmed now that the two poles of liberation, personal and structural, were shooting off in opposite directions. "Do your own thing," "anything goes," whether smoking grass or looting stores, was not his idea of freedom but a mockery. Neither hippies nor hipsters were looking beyond their own pleasure to the "principalities and powers" that created the gaping chasm between white middle-class kids who were free to drop out and turn on and the black ghetto youth who were forced to. For the latter, freedom meant "nothing left to lose," the refrain of a Janis Joplin hit song.

Yet the young Marxists and black nationalists had become so obsessed with "structure" that they lost sight of the actual people inhabiting the structures. King understood that the religions of structurelessness and of soulless structuralism—quests for meaning, for truth, for certitude—each led to dead ends, to a nihilism of the Spirit.

As he surveyed the shattered landscape of summer 1967, the summer of love and hate, he agonized not only about broken promises, his and others, but about all the centrifugal forces pulling the society apart. Chaos was drowning community. After all the movement's trials and triumphs over the past decade, how could so many alienated youth of all colors hold such shallow understandings of freedom? How had he contributed to this tragic misunderstanding? "Freedom now" did not mean freedom from responsibility. Black Power should not mean freedom to shoot cops, to "burn, baby, burn." As Plato had warned in his slamming of democracy, as Tocqueville had feared, freedom—which so many black people had died for—had become license, whether in the Haight-Ashbury hippie ghetto or on Detroit's flaming streets. And, on a far grander scale, in the corporate boardroom, the congressional cloakroom, the White House situation room.

In an Ebenezer sermon at the beginning of July 1967, King seemed to foresee the conflagration that would engulf over a hundred cities by the end of the month.

"America is a great nation," he shouted out, but if America doesn't deal with its racism, "I'm convinced that God will bring down the curtains on this nation, the curtains of doom.

"You know," he said, "there are times that you reap what you sow in history." He pounded his big King James Bible on the pulpit. "I believe it! Be not deceived. God is not mocked. Whatsoever a man soweth, that shall he also reap. America must resolve this race problem, or this race problem will doom America."[52]

Like the prophets Isaiah and Jeremiah whom he personified, he believed he was speaking God's own words in calling Americans to repent in order to ward off Armageddon. But he was pained as much by his emptiness of answers as by the overarching dilemma. He knew not what to do, where to go, to forestall civil war, to save the Union, to heal the national trauma. "We've got to learn to live together" was all he was sure of.

WITH THE FORTITUDE of a black woman reared in the rural South, Coretta King had lived with the ebbs and flows of her husband's worsening depression for several years. She and his close aides could no longer deny his condition when it nearly incapacitated him on his Nobel Prize journey in December 1964. We will never know how much his chronic depression was caused by current stresses, genetic predisposition, early childhood pressures, or growing up black. He was never treated by psychotherapy or drugs, neither of which he would have considered.

Instead he self-medicated. On the road at least three weeks out of four, he was usually able to control his mood by willpower, frenetic activity, and partying. At home in Atlanta the depression was harder to keep hidden. Coretta bore the brunt of it. But through all the storm and stress she remained his most loyal and steadfast supporter. More than once she kept him from falling apart. Her faith in him and in "God with us" was unshakable.

Although she had seen him through many black moods, she was more worried than ever at the time of the July riots. He fell into a state of depression "greater than I had ever seen it before."

"People expect me to have answers," he confided to her. "I don't have any answers. I don't feel like speaking to people." This was the man who thrived on human interaction. "I don't have anything to tell them."

She remembered a plaintive phone call from him at the Atlanta airport, on the edge of tears, telling her he had missed his flight to Louisville for a voter registration rally.

"I know why I missed my flight," he said. "I really don't want to go. I get tired of going and not having any answers."

He had "begun to take this very personally," she recalled, not knowing where the movement should head. "He would take on all these problems" as personal failures—the ghetto revolts, the unending brutal war—as if it were his God-given obligation to solve single-handedly the nation's ills, to prevent the nation's imminent doom. This was his voluminous public self speaking, his Whitmanesque cosmic self. It was all or nothing, opposite extremes. Was there no solid middle ground he could rest upon?

"People feel that nonviolence is failing," he told her.

"This is not so," she countered. "You mustn't believe that people are losing faith in you. There are millions of people who have faith in you and believe in you and feel that you are our best hope. I believe in you, if that means anything."

"Yes, that means a great deal."

"Somehow," she said, "you've just got to pull yourself out of this and go on. Too many people believe in you, and you're going to have to believe that you're right."

Once again he groused that he didn't have any answers.

"Somehow the answers will come," she consoled him. "I'm sure they will."[53] Several hours past his usual lateness, he finally landed in Louisville and rallied the troops, despite his own despondency. He could count on his public self to go on automatic pilot when his inner self ran out of fuel.

He would not allow America to rest, he told the people in Louisville.

HE HAD HABITUALLY USED rich metaphors of darkness as a rhetorical device, sometimes sounding melodramatic. But now when he said it was "midnight in our world today," he meant it. "We are experiencing a darkness so deep," he told a Los Angeles congregation, "that we can hardly see which way to turn."[54] In his soul's relentless tug-of-war between hope and despair, he usually managed to give hope the edge, in his public words anyway. But now the dark chambers of pessimism were closing in on him like claustrophobic jail cells.

He clung to his faith, however, that the divine force was buried in the deepest darkness. That if he carried his candle of faith deeper and still deeper into the heart of darkness, the darkness at the heart of life, he would discover the blinding light at the center of God's creation, the fire at the core of his own soul. Like ebony skin, the darkest dark emitted the brightest glow. The dark, absorbing all light, was not the absence but the fullness of light. But the light in deepest darkness was invisible to the mortal eye.

FEELING GUILTY AND UNWORTHY for not having answers, he nevertheless knew, like Augustine and all true Christians, that his faith had integrity only if it was permeated by doubt. His faith would be weak if it did not wrestle ceaselessly with doubt. Faith had no meaning, certainly no might, unless it was called into question, raked over the coals of inquisition. In a paradox of the Spirit, doubt fortified his faith. Faith tested by doubt, doubt enlightened by faith, lay at the core of his double consciousness. He lived in both worlds at once.

Notwithstanding his perpetual questioning, he had always felt so certain of what was right and wrong, to the point of preacherly arrogance, but his moral certainties were not helping him to find the right way forward. While generally praising, reviewers of his new book found a "weariness and bewilderment" in his prognosis, "confusion and doubt" in his ideas, a book "groping for something which it never finds."[55] He did not intend the work to be programmatic, but neither did he want it read as a confession of paralysis. *Why We Can't Wait* had answered its question. *Where Do We Go from Here* did not.

Where to go was a much tougher question, perhaps unanswerable in 1967. In calling for new expressions of grassroots democratic power, King was following Bob Moses's precept that good leaders ask certain questions and ordinary people answer them. Asking the right questions, in the right ways, might be the best servanthood he could offer.

SCLC PULLED OUT all the stops for its tenth-anniversary convention at Ebenezer in mid-August 1967. Even a special award for and speech by actor Sidney Poitier, first black winner of a best-actor Oscar, did not upstage King's centrality. Firmly in command, he betrayed little hint, except on his weary face, of his ravaging doubts, his beleaguered faith. That was reserved for his inner circle. In his presidential address, probably the most militant he ever gave, he dwelt on the overriding theme of revolution in the streets. He did not mince words.

He commenced by quoting Victor Hugo, whose *Les Misérables* was a favorite novel: "If the soul is left in darkness, sins will be committed. The guilty one is not he who commits the sin, but he who causes the darkness."

The leaders of white society caused the darkness. "They created discrimination. They created slums. They perpetuate unemployment, ignorance, and poverty." The crimes of the rioters were "derivative crimes. They are born of the greater crimes of the white society.

"Let us say it boldly, that if the total slum violations of law by the white man over the years were calculated and were compared with the lawbreaking of a few days of riots, the hardened criminal would be the white man." Congress, which dutifully spent billions on the war but had refused paltry millions to free children from rats, "is now running amuck with racism."

He quoted the warning of the conservative McCone commission after Watts that "the existing breech, if allowed to persist, could in time split our society irretrievably."

He was far from condoning violent revolt. He denied that the riots were insurrections, because they were leaderless, unorganized, and lacked goals, thus flaming out quickly. He deplored the recklessness of "self-styled revolutionists" like Carmichael and Rap Brown who called for insurrection without foot soldiers, without chance of victory. Their rhetoric was not even helpful to raise consciousness because lack of broad support for revolt doomed it to defeat, bringing "deeper despair and helplessness." If armed struggle could not win victories, it could never win a mass following. But it was equally self-defeating for moderate leaders, as they had done from Birmingham to Detroit, to urge enraged black people not to ruffle white feathers.

King's prophecy from his Birmingham jail cell, which he himself had left fallow, was now bursting from him like overripe fruit. He was advocating a dynamic middle course between pseudo-insurrection and complacent gradualism that pursued the creative extremism of militant civil disobedience. He called it the "militant middle." He explained that mass marches had been powerful tools in the South because they were outlawed. It was rebellion. But in northern cities mass marches were familiar, respectable, and generally nonthreatening. Something more audacious was needed to turn the ghettos around.

"To raise protest to an appropriate level for cities," he announced, "to invest it with aggressive but nonviolent qualities," it was now necessary to apply mass civil disobedience as an alternative to rioting. "To dislocate the functioning of a city without destroying it can be more effective than a riot because it can be longer lasting, costly to the society but not wantonly destructive. Moreover, it is more difficult for government to quell it by superior force. Mass civil disobedience can use rage as a constructive and creative force. It is purposeless to tell Negroes they should not be enraged when they should be. Indeed"—here he sounded like anticolonial revolutionary Frantz Fanon in *The Wretched of the Earth*, the bible of black nationalism—"they will be mentally healthier if they do not suppress rage but vent it constructively and use its energy peacefully but forcefully to cripple the operations of an oppressive society." He believed that nonviolent insurrection could finally free poor blacks from the psychological death of ghetto slavery.

He pointed out that civil disobedience had never been tried on a mass scale in the North. Even in the South it had "rarely been seriously organized and resolutely pursued." Too often "it was employed incorrectly" and "resorted to only when there was an absence of mass support and its purpose was headline-hunting." Was he pointing the finger at himself? He recommended to this full house of organizers that mass civil disobedience in northern cities be conducted weekly along with sit-ins for jobs at plant gates, and thousands of jobless youth camping out in Washington like the Bonus Marchers during the Great Depression. Disrupting business as usual in such ways would have an impact of "earthquake proportions," he predicted.

All of this was urgent, but it was not enough. Mass direct action must be combined with the continuing quest to build an effective coalition to win electoral power. They must replace Johnson with a candidate committed to both peace and economic justice (King had made it clear he himself was not running) and elect a new congressional majority to stem its rightward spin. Were these strategies at loggerheads? Although he no doubt worried about it, he did not publicly question whether mass urban disruption, while sublimating riots, would sharpen the white backlash and hinder efforts to win a progressive majority. He may have hoped that disciplined and principled disruption would shake loose the conscience-stricken elements of the growing backlash bloc from the hard-core racists and mindless patriots.

To see coalition politics as the "exclusive method," which Rustin had long been urging, "is as futile as it is disastrous. Negroes are not in a mood to wait for change by the slower, tedious, often frustrating road of political action." This dilemma recalled the early 1960s' contention between desegregation and voting rights campaigns, but now with higher stakes. King said that while urban blacks were learning to value electoral insurgency for long-term progress, they needed "the social adrenaline of quick changes" offered by direct action. It would be difficult to mix electoral action with nonviolent disruption, and each might fray the other, but he saw no sense in giving up one for the other.

He concluded his dramatic address to the convention by imploring Americans to heed Jefferson's warning: "I tremble for my country when I reflect that God is just."[56] America was living on borrowed time. Judgment Day was coming closer.

7

Martin King was able to let down his veil preaching at black Baptist churches. He was able to reveal slivers of his hidden self, as he rarely did to racially mixed congregations or in public speeches. So he did on the last Sunday of August 1967 at Mount Pisgah Missionary Baptist Church, in the heart of the Chicago slums that he had made his home the year before. Near the end of a long sermon decrying the abandonment of spiritual ends for material pleasure, he advised that people needed to value not only their interdependence with each other, all over the globe, but their dependence on God. For the first time in a decade, he publicly relived his kitchen conversion of January 1956.

"You can have some strange experiences at midnight," he said. This time, he made clear to rapt listeners that the inner voice he heard commanding him to hang on for righteousness was the voice of Jesus. He was preaching to black Baptists, of course. But it also reflected something deeper: his feeling dependent not only on God, but more than ever on his personal relationship with Jesus, to help him get through these midnight days. Jesus had become his personal God.

"And so I'm not worried about tomorrow. I get weary every now and then. The future looks difficult and dim, but I'm not worried about it ultimately because I have faith in God.

"I don't mind telling you this morning that sometimes I feel discouraged. (*All right*) I felt discouraged in Chicago. As I move through Mississippi and Georgia and Alabama, I feel discouraged. (*Yes, sir*) Living every day under the threat of death, I feel discouraged sometimes. Living every day under extensive criticisms, even from Negroes, I feel discouraged sometimes. (*Applause*) Yes, sometimes I feel discouraged and feel my work's in vain. But then the Holy Spirit (*Yes*) revives my soul again.

"There is a balm in Gilead to make the wounded whole. There is a balm in Gilead to heal the sin-sick soul."[57]

WHEN YOUNG NAACP LAWYER Marian Wright was a senior at Spelman College in 1960, she heard King give the Founders' Day address. More than the elegant power of his oratory, she was impressed with his openness about his doubts and uncertainties. "He talked about taking that one step even if you can't see the whole way, and how you just have to keep moving." As she was growing up in rural South Carolina, her parents instilled in her a mission to serve society. At Spelman she was jailed in an Atlanta lunch-counter sit-in, graduated as valedictorian, then went on to Yale Law School. In 1963 she worked on voter registration in Mississippi. After NAACP leader Medgar Evers was gunned down she moved in with the movement. The first black woman to pass the Mississippi bar, she devoted herself to legal help for poor blacks.

It felt like ages since Freedom Summer had shed some light on the misery of the Mississippi poor. Since then Wright had been searching for ways to keep Mississippi in the public eye, to show that the black poor were only getting poorer. Even the progress in voting rights was a mixed blessing. In many cases people who dared register, like Fannie Lou Hamer, were thrown out of work, kicked out of their homes, driven from poverty to penury. In March 1967 Wright testified before the Senate subcommittee on poverty about starvation in the Magnolia State, tenant-farm families going hungry while Senator Eastland and his ilk were raking in millions for not growing crops. The affluent senators were skeptical of her claims. She took them on a tour of the Delta.

She walked into a hot, filthy shack with New York senator Robert Kennedy, who had won a Senate seat in 1964 after resigning as attorney general. She could hardly believe her eyes when the well-dressed senator, who had barred cameras at the door, got down on his knees on the grimy floor with a child who looked dead. Nearly in tears, the father of ten said soothing words and touched the ragged child. The emaciated mom was scrubbing dishes in a tin tub.

When in July President Johnson reacted to the riots with one-sided hostility toward the rioters, RFK became convinced that the President would do nothing more to fight poverty. In late summer the senator was lounging by his pool at his Virginia estate with Wright and his aide Peter Edelman (whom Wright later married).

"The only way there's going to be change," he said to his guests, "is if it's more uncomfortable for the Congress not to act than it is for them to act. You've got to get a whole lot of poor people who just come to Washington and stay here until Congress gets really embarrassed and they have to act."[58] When Wright said good-bye she mentioned that she would stop to see King in Atlanta on her way home to Mississippi.

"Tell him to bring the poor people to Washington." The man who six years before had tried to persuade activists to halt their freedom ride and then, behind their backs, permitted Mississippi officials to jail them in Jackson was now calling, in effect, for a freedom ride in reverse.

Wright was shaken by how depressed King was. "He was real down that day when I walked in," she recalled, distressed about what to do. His dark mood lifted abruptly when she passed on Kennedy's offhand suggestion. He "instinctively felt that that was right and treated me as if I was an emissary of grace, something that brought him some light. Out of that, the Poor People's Campaign was born."[59]

That evening Coretta King was surprised to see her husband in a good mood. He was excited about the new idea.

KING'S CALL at the August SCLC gathering for nonviolent "dislocation" in cities to overcome poverty had drawn headlines all over the country. How committed was he to this path of creative extremism? The address had been drafted mainly by Levison. Was he doing more than mouthing his leftwing adviser's script? Was there a gap, as there had often been in the past, between his fighting words and his more temperate actions? Was he crying wolf?

Moreover, he would need prodigious energy to lead this gutsy campaign but was more depleted than ever. "I'm tired now," he said to an Atlanta mass meeting. "I've been in this thing thirteen years now and I'm really tired." Folksinger Joan Baez recalled his despondency at a September staff retreat. As people were relaxing after a long day of talk, King drinking whiskey, "I heard him saying that he wanted to just be a preacher, and he was sick of it all. That the Lord called him to be a preacher, and not to do all this stuff, and he wanted to leave it."[60]

At this mid-September retreat in rural Virginia, SCLC staff debated strategies and tactics for the new urban campaign. While Bevel pushed for a primary focus on the war, including supporting draft resistance, and Hosea Williams pleaded for them not to abandon the South, their chief pulled rank and insisted that a poor people's presence in Washington be the driving priority.

THE COLLISION WOULD LIKELY have happened sooner or later. The summer's conflagration in the cities carried its fury from the burned-out streets to a more civilized venue in which to "get whitey," Chicago's swank Palmer House. The drive for Black Power was now at flood tide, overpowering hesitation on the left with its arsenal of guilt. Many whites seemed to enjoy the role of victim rather than executioner, blind to the path of moral equality. The ghost of Atlantic City resurrected in Chicago. SNCC and allies were getting Pyrrhic revenge for their clobbering by the Johnson forces in August 1964. But on Labor Day weekend 1967, what the insurgents wrecked was not the crowning of Johnson but an effort to dethrone him.

The National Conference for New Politics was founded in fall 1965 to run peace candidates for Congress. It had little success in that arena, but pinned its hopes on challenging LBJ's reelection. Even though he disavowed interest, King felt flattered that, after April 15, many left liberals who had not given up on electoral politics were enthralled by the prospect of a King peace candidacy, with Spock as running mate. The pediatrician was as gung-ho about a third-party campaign as the preacher was reticent. Despite reservations King had accepted an invitation to give the keynote address at the NCNP convention in Chicago, called to craft an electoral strategy for 1968. It would have been hard to turn it down when the husband of SCLC's biggest donor was a main organizer.

Focusing on the three great evils of racism, exploitation, and the Vietnam War, his speech hit all of the notes he had been blowing for months. He stood before an assembly of over three thousand activists from two hundred organizations, a historic coming together of the American left.

"Seldom, if ever," he began, "has such a diverse and truly ecumenical gathering convened under the aegis of politics in our nation." They had come from dusty plantations and depressing ghettos, from universities and flourishing suburbs, "from Appalachian poverty and from conscience stricken wealth." They had come to Chicago because they had all seen "the coming of Judgment."[61]

He had been warned that young militants might heckle him. They did. What disturbed him more was that some ignored him, talked among themselves, walked out. They would not listen to a message that he believed spoke to their rage, filled in the gaps of revolutionary appeals that were otherwise sound and fury signifying nothing. Dispirited, he left town right after, followed by Andy Young, an NCNP board member, and Julian Bond, its cochair.

King's rude reception by the black and white New Left was only the prelude to a weekend of guilt supreme. The gathering surfaced divisions never to be healed—a day of judgment for the movement, if not for the nation.

The black caucus led by SNCC and the Black Panthers, comprising about one-tenth of the assembly, emotionally strong-armed the majority into giving them half the votes and committee seats; these were "tests of sincerity." They then bulldozed passage of a thirteen-point manifesto that included "white civilizing committees" to humanize the savage whites, and a condemnation of the "imperialist Zionist war" fought by Israel in June. "We are just a little tail," one white delegate reportedly gushed, "on the end of a very powerful black panther. And I want to be on that tail—if they'll let me."

The near majority who opposed the radical takeover were embittered. NCNP founder Arthur Waskow railed that "one thousand liberals are trying to become good radicals and they think they can do it by castrating themselves." When the black caucus took control, a woman set fire to her delegate card and walked out. "This is the old politics," she said, "not the new politics."[62]

The women's caucus was incensed. These radical women were already fed up with treatment as second-class activists by "male chauvinists" in SDS and other New Left groups. (The term *sexist* had not been invented quite yet.) When in a condescending manner those in charge blocked Shulamith Firestone from reading the caucus's resolution on male privilege—on the ground that women's oppression was trivial next to racism—the women boiled over. It wasn't like Rosa Parks in Montgomery, but this was the spark they needed to launch their own movement. Firestone and her sisters stormed out and formed the first women's liberation groups.

NCNP and its dream of a new populist party for peace and justice came crashing down. Now the antiwar movement, growing fast, was polarized between the "Dump Johnson" forces who chose to work within the Democratic Party and the radical legions who felt contempt for "establishment politics." They were determined to build democracy in the streets. On more of a tightrope walk than ever, King was still trying to straddle insurgency inside and outside the electoral system. He was finding it more and more difficult to talk out of both sides of his mouth. He might have to make a choice.

Presidential politics might be a chimera for the left, but black voters in big northern cities were poised to elect African-American mayors for the first time. This would be a breakthrough for black empowerment. King showed his commitment both to the electoral route and to black self-determination in Cleveland, eighth-largest U.S. city, where SCLC was conducting voter registration and rent strikes. Ohio state legislator Carl Stokes, who had grown up poor in a Cleveland project, had nearly defeated the Democratic mayor in 1965 and was trying again. He felt ambivalent about SCLC's presence. They proved indispensable in mobilizing the black vote, but he worried they would alienate liberal whites he depended on. King and SCLC felt they deserved credit for

Stokes's primary victory over the incumbent, one of the first times that a registration campaign actually delivered the goods. But Stokes never acknowledged SCLC's assistance. He asked King not to help out in the general election, which he narrowly won, making history.

King discovered in Cleveland, where he had invested considerable resources, that if militant black nationalists considered him an Uncle Tom, moderate purveyors of Black Power saw him as incendiary, a threat to gradual racial progress. Rather than expanding, the turf of radical moderation he had been cultivating seemed to be shrinking, especially now that he himself had adopted the language of revolution. His balancing act was facing a free fall.

8

When King had looked out over the sea of antiwar protesters on April 15 at the U.N., a greater sea than that of 1963, he must have wondered whether a similar march on Washington might turn the tide of war. In the following weeks, while pursuing other peace strategies like Vietnam Summer and the long-shot effort to replace Johnson, he moved forward with a notion to re-create the magic of "I Have a Dream." Could he unify the far-flung forces of peace as, in his glory days, he had done for the civil rights crusade? He called a meeting of peace leaders in early July across the street from Riverside Church, where he pushed his idea for a mass march in Washington that would couple opposition to the war and to dismantling the poverty program, linking the triple evils. A few days later the Newark riots exploded across the Hudson River. Everything changed.

As July turned to August the idea of a peaceful march on Washington, which might have caught the movement's imagination three months before, now seemed to many like a relic of the past. No matter how much activists disdained the ghetto violence, and the incendiary rhetoric of SNCC and the Black Panthers, all were caught up in the rush to escalate tactics to stop the war. In late May the Spring Mobilization Committee gathered several hundred activists in Washington to plan a different kind of spectacle in the capital. They would march on the Pentagon in October to "confront the warmakers." Even though a rally at the Lincoln Memorial was part of the plan, King chose to steer clear. He couldn't help but feel resentful that peace leaders weren't listening to him, when he had gone so far out on a limb for peace.

Liberal critics continued to pillory him. Black columnist Carl Rowan, who had alerted King to the false boycott settlement in January 1956, had criticized his antiwar stand back in April. In a September *Reader's Digest* article that reached millions, the ex-director of the U.S. Information Agency condemned King's "tragic decision" to oppose the war, blaming his hubris and his Communist ties.[63] King countered in an ABC News interview that Rowan was accusing dissenters of disloyalty, that he was engaging in McCarthy's tactics in alleging Communist influence on him.[64] As he weathered public blows and invasive espionage, he saw that the price of the mad war was not only blood in the streets at home, but the specter of a new McCarthyism eroding the Bill of Rights and laying waste fundamental freedoms.

A NEW ERA of McCarthyite repression seemed to be falling hardest on those young men refusing to cooperate with conscription. Antidraft activists had had a field day likening the Selective Service to totalitarian rule, not only induction but the channeling process that denied free choice of a job or career. Now in an ironic twist it was those publicly saying no to this arguably un-American institution who were being red-baited as Communist pawns. Congress had moved with alacrity to criminalize destruction or nonpossession of draft cards after a handful of pacifists had burned theirs. Caught without your draft card, go to prison for up to five years. This sounded like the Soviet Union, or South Africa. Murderers and rapists often got off with less.

So it was not surprising, in the face of such high risks, that the movement to renounce deferments, return draft cards, and openly refuse induction had taken hold by fall 1967 as the moral cutting edge of the antiwar cause. Through the summer of love and hate, David Harris and his cohorts roamed the West Coast from San Diego to Seattle, searching out prospective noncooperators, telling their story to small groups or one-to-one, explaining why they had chosen the role of criminal. Sometimes they played music and smoked marijuana together. "Part of the process was creating a sense of intimacy between us," Harris recalled, "which we felt was the basis of our organization."[65] The organizers planted a seedbed of local Resistance groups, mainly around campuses, that sprouted in all parts of the country, coalescing into a loose federation linked by common action and political style. Rejecting formal leadership, stressing consensus decision making, Resistance chapters did not have officers, because resisters faced the shared risk of prison, and thus, like early SNCC, everyone was a leader.

As Harris had promised at April's big San Francisco rally, on October 16 about fifteen hundred men turned in their draft cards at churches and federal buildings on the first National Day of Noncooperation, beating expectations. Thousands more sent back draft cards in later turn-ins. Spock, Yale chaplain William Sloane Coffin, and other members of Resist, a support group, delivered a briefcase packed with forsaken cards to the Justice Department. Spock, Coffin, and two others were later convicted in a celebrated trial of conspiring to aid and abet draft refusal.

In the San Francisco Bay Area the Resistance had joined in coalition with SDS and pacifist groups to mount Stop the Draft Week, aimed at shutting or slowing down the Oakland induction center. The tense coalition broke apart over tactics: traditional symbolic civil disobedience versus something more assertive that might actually close the facility serving the heart of the West Coast. The latter camp, desiring to march in step with Black Power, sought to demonstrate the "seriousness" of white radicals. The factions compromised by dividing the week. The Resistance and War Resisters League conducted a peaceful sit-in the same day cards were collected at the San Francisco federal building. Next day troops led by Berkeley SDS aggressively blocked the induction center and nearby streets in a taste of guerrilla warfare. Police routed them.

In a return engagement on Friday they outwitted the cops and kept them at bay, for a while surrounded, using cars, benches, and potted trees as barricades. This spontaneous action prevented inductee-laden buses from getting in for three hours. In the heat of battle protesters had invented a controversial new weapon, "mobile tactics," that lay in a gray area between militant nonviolence and armed struggle.

That fall SDS and the New Left were growing faster than ever. SDS chapters in every state except Alaska numbered more than three hundred. Although they supported draft resistance and joined Stop the Draft Week, their main target was university complicity, particularly war-related recruiting. Campus confrontations proliferated. Some were aimed at Dow Chemical, whose flesh-frying jellied gasoline, napalm, served as the most heinous symbol of the Vietnam carnage. Its child victims splayed in living color across *Ramparts* magazine had propelled King on his irreversible antiwar path.

The autumn's most explosive campus action occurred at the University of Wisconsin in Madison. A determined nonviolent obstruction of Dow recruiting by several hundred students brought a ferocious assault by riot-clad police who bloodied students in the manner of Selma and Birmingham. A shocked crowd did what they could to aid the injured and stymie the cops. A daring cadre let air out of a paddy wagon's tires and immobilized it with their bodies. Police responded with more beatings, tear gas, and Mace, a paralyzing nerve gas. The furious crowd counterattacked with rocks and bricks until the battle died down. Never before had an American campus witnessed such flagrant police brutality, not even in the South. It sparked a short-lived strike by students and sympathetic faculty.

The battles of Oakland and Madison built up to the frontal assault that weekend on the global headquarters of the American military colossus. Organized by the National Mobilization Committee, successor to the Spring Mobilization and the widest left coalition yet—despite SCLC's absence—the spectacle drew a potpourri of participants by offering a peaceful rally for newcomers, a kaleidoscopic "be-in" for hippies, and militant civil disobedience for those choosing to put their bodies on the line. They intended the confrontation at the Pentagon to be a "creative synthesis of Gandhi and guerrilla," as chief organizer Dave Dellinger depicted it, nonviolent but forceful. SDS had reluctantly endorsed the April mobilization; like SNCC's criticism of King, they felt that big media-centered marches stifled long-term grassroots organizing. SDS chapters decided to take part in this one when it appeared a real confrontation was brewing. The feds delayed granting permits and deployed thousands of combat-ready troops, fresh from

Vietnam, Santo Domingo, and Detroit, to defend the Pentagon from its own citizens.

The steering committee stayed up most of the night before, arguing tactics. Should they treat the troops as the enemy, or as fellow victims and potential allies? Unlike in Oakland, the views of the radical pacifists prevailed. They would conduct a teach-in to the troops, who were the same age as most protesters, but darker skinned. Had he known about it, King might have been pleasantly surprised. Here was a constructive middle course between pacifist moral witness and tactical adventurism that might spiral into chaos.

The next morning tens of thousands rallied at the Lincoln Memorial, listening to speeches and to singing by Phil Ochs and Peter, Paul, and Mary. To stunned silence a speaker announced the execution of Latin American revolutionary Che Guevara, who personified the spirit of revolt. Half the crowd crossed the Potomac River and congregated in a vast Pentagon parking lot. They witnessed an odd spectacle. A congeries of "witches, warlocks, holymen, seers, prophets, mystics, saints, sorcerers, shamans, troubadours, minstrels, bards, roadmen, and madmen" led by the anarchist Diggers and the Fugs rock band invoked all the magic they could muster to levitate the Pentagon and exorcise its evil spirits.[66] Chants of "Out, demon, out!" filled the crisp autumn air. Eyewitnesses reported the mighty fortress rising ten feet off the ground.

An SDS cadre and a "Revolutionary Contingent" broke through a cordon of MPs and paratroopers and seized high ground on a plaza at the Pentagon's north entrance. Some made it inside but were beaten and busted by troops lying in wait. A group of notables—including Spock, poet Robert Lowell, writer Dwight MacDonald, and linguist Noam Chomsky—maneuvered to another side of the complex to do quiet civil disobedience. MPs swooped down on them but arrested only the less famous. By late afternoon several thousand had mounted the steps to the plaza. Their front lines pressed up against solid rows of rigid young soldiers clutching bayoneted M-14s.

Following the eleventh-hour scenario, protesters communicated directly to the troops, through bullhorns and face-to-face, to try to win their hearts and minds. Over and over they urged the soldiers to "join us!" They talked gently—"You are our brothers"—and sang to them, stuck flowers in their rifle barrels. Three or four put down their rifles and seemed about to switch sides when MPs swiftly stole them away. Other soldiers reportedly abandoned the front line and were locked up in the Pentagon stockade. According to GIs' testimony a lot of them opposed the war and were touched by the teach-in.[67]

Defense secretary Robert McNamara and a top general oversaw the massing of forces from the Pentagon's roof. When he had met with the President to prepare for the protest, he recalled, "I told him we faced a difficult problem, because the Pentagon has no natural defenses." As he looked down upon the siege, "I was scared," McNamara confessed to a reporter. "An uncontrolled mob is a frightening thing. At the same time, I could not help but think that had the protesters been more disciplined—Gandhi-like—they could have achieved their objective of shutting us down. All they had to do was lie on the pavement around the building. We would have found it impossible to remove enough of them fast enough to keep the Pentagon open."[68]

As night fell and cold set in, protesters built campfires out of posters and debris. Marijuana joints floated around. Someone yelled, "Burn a draft card! Keep warm!" Hundreds of tiny flames flickered in the darkness. In an intense moment of solidarity and awe, people sang "Silent Night." But the military high command would not let all be calm. MPs and U.S. marshals sporadically beat and arrested people all evening. Late at night, TV cameras gone to bed, troops formed a flying wedge and attacked their unarmed foes, thrashing them with clubs and rifle butts. Young women were hurt the most. Blood stained the steps.

Peace returned by Sunday dawn. Many of the weary protesters departed. But a hard core of a few hundred stayed put until midnight, when they were ordered to disperse. Singing Woody Guthrie's "This Land Is Your Land," "America the Beautiful," and, over and over, "We Shall Overcome," they calmly offered themselves for jail. Packed into army trucks, they were driven underground into the bowels of the Pentagon, kept in utter darkness. They had made their destination at last, though in custody of Uncle Sam. At dawn, like a few hundred arrested earlier, the prisoners found themselves in a federal workhouse in Occoquan, Virginia. It was the same prison where suffragists, arrested for vigiling at the White House gate, had held hunger strikes during World War I, force-fed through tubes.

Fifty years later protesters (women and men separated) sat on bunks in the large barracks and made plans for furthering the revolution. Jesuit priest Daniel Berrigan and a few others fasted. March leaders Jerry Rubin and Abbie Hoffman concocted a new guerrilla group called the Yippies to lead the hippie masses. Hoffman wrapped himself in a white sheet and danced around like a madman.

The nonviolent siege of the Pentagon and Stop the Draft Week turned the corner for the antiwar movement. It now became broader, bolder, and more divided. Movement liberals and radicals parted company, committed to divergent strategies. The former aimed at winning over the majority to oppose the war, to be consummated, they hoped, in the 1968 elections. Radicals, lacking faith in electoral politics, aimed at raising the social cost of the war to a level that would make it unmanageable. Or if Johnson stayed his course, to make the nation ungovernable until the war ended. A big debate ensued about whether this critical mass of disruption could be achieved nonviolently.

SDS leader Greg Calvert had been one of those pushing hardest on the Pentagon protest's steering committee for the tactic of compassionate militancy. "I left the Pentagon absolutely convinced radical nonviolence had worked, that it was possible to confront the state nonviolently and effectively without falling into adventuristic tactics."[69] Other Pentagon veterans, including Calvert's SDS comrades, were just as convinced that the protesters were not aggressive enough, that the lesson of the Pentagon was that the military establishment was more vulnerable than they had thought. They should have fought harder to break through the lines.

Two images of revolution vied for the movement's future, Calvert suggested in retrospect. "One was a vision of long-range organizing born of the New Left's traditions of decentralist democracy and the spiritual and moral values embodied in nonviolence, but coupled now with a new sense of the power of *active* nonviolence focused on communication to new constituencies rather than simply on moral protest through civil disobedience. The other image projected direct confrontations and street disruptions, and increasingly abandoned the nonviolent tradition of the Movement in favor of a new brand of macho militancy."[70] As we will see, King was groping toward a way of reconciling these clashing images.

Never distinct, these two images cast dividing lines within the movement. The adventurists, whose tactics played well with their black nationalist allies, captured the imagination of the youth revolt and "seized the time." The alternative of militant compassion, especially of appealing to soldiers, and potential soldiers, not to fight—that strategy persevered against mounting odds but eventually was overrun.

The Pentagon siege was a turning point too for the Johnson administration. Despite LBJ's smug pronouncements, the administration was thrown awry by its magnitude and militancy. McNamara, who kept to himself his grave doubts about the war, was on his way out as defense czar. He didn't know whether he resigned or was fired. The White House berated the military chiefs for lousy intelligence. Johnson ordered the FBI, CIA, and other agencies drastically to step up surveillance and infiltration of antiwar groups. Soon the FBI had over a thousand agents spying on the New Left, plus several thousand informants. The CIA unleashed its illegal "Operation Chaos" to disrupt radical activism. But as quickening events would tell, it was too late for the Johnson administration to stem the tide.

KING WAS MUTE about Stop the Draft Week and the Pentagon. By October, with Bevel prodding him to support draft resistance, he had all but explicitly endorsed refusal to cooperate with conscription. For months he had been calling for conscientious objection. Did he mean official CO status with alternate service (even a noncombatant role in the military), which few could attain, or did he mean illegal noncooperation? He probably meant legal if possible, illegal if no other recourse. No doubt in private he supported the national draft-card turn-in and the disciplined sit-in in Oakland, where his friend Joan Baez was arrested. The activist folksinger, along with Harry Belafonte, had been performing benefit concerts for SCLC during the fall.

Apparently he had felt the proposed Pentagon protest to be unwise, misguided, even foolhardy. But wasn't it the kind of militant nonviolent disruption he had called for in August? Did he have a double standard when it came to the peace movement?

Besides feeling snubbed, he had good reason not to hook up with the Pentagon operation. The decentralized civil disobedience must have looked like a minefield. Unlike SCLC direct actions, it would be neither organized nor disciplined—McNamara was correct—nor would there be nonviolent training. The protesters did not have a broad base of national support, nor had they prepared the ground with educational work, which Gandhi deemed essential. King's call for militant disruption in the cities, by contrast, culminated a dozen years of steady movement building, successive stages of protest.

Yet despite its chaotic moments and lack of discipline, the Pentagon protest proved to be an invigorating step forward for the peace movement. With surprising success it had offered a palette of civil disobedience, small and large—draft-card burning, dialogue with soldiers, sit-ins, sit-downs, stand-ups, and the final refusal to leave. If King had swallowed his doubts, he might have been able to shape it into a disciplined nonviolent confrontation of a size and impact not seen since Gandhi's salt *satyagraha* in 1930. In any event, it was clear that by fall 1967 he did not oppose mass civil disobedience against the war. He simply held high standards for any direct action he might support, especially if he risked jail.

He publicly stated that he wished he was of draft age so he could resist the draft like Muhammad Ali.[71] But age did not have to hold him back. If he had unequivocally supported draft resistance, actively "aided and abetted" young men to renounce deferments and to refuse induction, he might have helped make resistance to conscription a more effective strategy. A critical mass of draft resisters in 1967 and 1968 would have made it harder to prosecute the ground war in South Vietnam, both by withdrawing conscripts and by hurting combat morale. King might have been accused of sedition if not treason and faced a long prison term. It would have been the trial of the century.

Draft resistance did keep growing during the next two years, but it proved more successful in ending the draft than in stopping the war.

9

One reason that King didn't join Spock, Coffin, Norman Mailer, and other notables sitting in at the Pentagon was purely practical. He had been ordered to go to jail in Birmingham. The Supreme Court in June had narrowly affirmed King's conviction, along with the convictions of Abernathy, Fred Shuttlesworth, Wyatt Walker, and a few others, for contempt of court when they marched in violation of the injunction on Good Friday 1963. King felt frustrated that he was to be penalized a second time for a peaceful assembly that had led to a noble end, the historic Civil Rights Act. Just when he was striving to make nonviolence the weapon of the strong, it was being shown as not worth the price.

Dressed in his denim going-to-jail garb, he looked depressed to well-wishers who gave him and three companions a jubilant send-off at Atlanta airport just before Halloween. He had plenty to read for five days behind bars. Besides the Bible, he brought William Styron's just published *Confessions of Nat Turner* and John Kenneth Galbraith's *New Industrial State*. His choice of reading hinted at his mind's wanderlust. In the historical novel Styron idealized Turner's bloody 1831 slave revolt as a prophetic mission and probed whether violence against racial oppression was justified. Economist Galbraith's new book examined how large corporations dominated the government.

Hardly had the steel doors closed than he got sick with a bad cold. He had little voice when he and his jailmates were cheered at a Birmingham mass meeting upon their release. But he found enough strength to assert that their 1963 Birmingham movement would be the model for his militant campaign for economic justice. Their troubled city had showed the world how powerful nonviolent disruption could be. Still adept at turning a bad deal to his advantage, he was getting mileage from his jail sojourn after all.

"Now we started out here in Birmingham," he said. "We struggled. And you know we got this city to the place it couldn't function. Birmingham could not function until it dealt with our problem. You remember that?

"We've got to take this same Birmingham experience and apply it to the economic situation that we face." Through his hoarse voice he vented his anger:

"We've got to make it known that until our problem is solved, America may have many, many days, but they will be full of trouble. There will be no rest, there will be no tranquility in this country, until the nation comes to terms with our problem."[72]

AFTER THANKSGIVING, at another staff retreat on St. Helena Island, King offered a full analysis of "the state of the movement." Again he played down the immorality of rioting in the "domestic colony"—stressing its damage to property, not people—and played up the sins of white society.

"The Negro who runs wild in a riot has been given the example of his own government running wild in the world." Reaffirming his faith in nonviolence, despite its battering by the year's events, he explained that it "must be adapted to urban conditions and urban moods." It must "mature to a new level, to correspond to heightened black impatience and stiffened white resistance." The disruption it inflicted must not be clandestine or surreptitious, but open. "It is not necessary to infest it with guerrilla romanticism"—a swipe at the Black Panthers and SNCC as well as the white New Left. Just five days earlier, Black Panther minister of defense Huey Newton, patrolling the police with a pistol and a law book, was pulled over by two Oakland cops. In the ensuing gunfight he was shot in the stomach, killed one cop, and wounded the other. The shots were heard round the world and made Newton, charged with murder, a guerrilla superstar on the scale of freshly dead Che Guevara.

King was determined to seek a better way. Mass civil disobedience "as a new stage of struggle," he claimed, "can transmute the deep anger of the ghetto into a creative force."

Like any revolutionary strategist worth his salt, he spelled out the agents of revolutionary change—disaffected American youth. They comprised three overlapping groups. First, the majority of young people (white and black) who were alienated to some degree, but not willing to take risks that might jeopardize their futures. Second, a large minority who had become hippies. Third, a smaller minority, the radicals, who hungered for action, "direct, self-transforming, and structure-transforming action." The hippies were not seeking social change but flight from society. When occasionally they protested, it was not "to better the political world, but to give expression to their own world." But escapism was no solution. The nonconformity and creative maladjustment of all three groups, he claimed, were spawned by committed black youth, who had transformed themselves and their values to build a culture of resistance.

He believed that SCLC's new strategy of "massive active nonviolent resistance to the evils of the modern system" could bring about an "action synthesis" that might unify the disaffected youth in a shared journey toward meaningful change, getting tangible results while healing divisions of race, class, and politics. Radicals would offer the burning urgency of action, the hippie sector the need for inner peace, and the silent majority of youth would bring to the table realism, respect for traditional values, and openness to honorable compromise.

Then he took a leaf from the book that had fanned the fire of young militants as his own new book had not—Fanon's *Wretched of the Earth*. He invoked the French-trained psychiatrist's call to advance humanity to a higher level by refusing to emulate values of the old order; the revolutionary must "set afoot a new man." Unlike Fanon, he insisted that the people reborn must reject the old order's addiction to violence.

He always liked to surprise his staff. Just as abruptly as he would go off to pray, he suddenly performed a wedding ceremony, to marry himself. Was he being funny or dead serious?

"I have taken a vow," he said. "I, Martin Luther King, take thee, non-violence, to be my wedded wife, for better or for worse, for richer or for poorer, in sickness and in health, till death do us part."[73] It was not a jest.

"I am going on in that faith and with that determination." He said that if they could escalate nonviolent action, "we will be able to go to Washington, we will be able to move through the cities of our country. Many will wonder where we are coming from. Our only answer will be that we are coming up out of great trials and tribulations. We will be seeking a city whose Builder and Maker is God, and if we will do this we will be able to turn this nation upside down and right side up."[74]

ALTHOUGH WHITE RADICALS could never match the drama of Huey Newton's shoot-out with Oakland police, they sought to apply "mobile tactics" wherever they could. Running around midtown Manhattan after dark, throwing eggs and blood at limousines, scattered by police on horseback, a few thousand protesters failed to prevent Secretary of State Dean Rusk from speaking at the New York Hilton, where he was protected by a thousand cops manning barricades. During the first week of December protesters replayed Oakland's Stop the Draft Week at the New York induction center, with hundreds of arrests. Like the Oakland antidraft protests, the New York actions were mostly not nonviolent—though ubiquitous Dr. Spock led symbolic civil disobedience at the induction center. But the sporadic violence by protesters was mainly verbal, in self-defense, or aimed at property.

Despite his new rhetoric of disruption and dislocation, King never condoned destruction of property. For this reason, and because it was done by men of cloth using religious imagery, he did not approve of a daring new tactic of militant nonviolence. A few days after the Pentagon siege Philip Berrigan, a Josephite priest, and three other Catholics poured their blood on draft files at a Baltimore draft board—a further experiment in combining Gandhian and guerrilla tactics, taking nonviolent action to its limit. The most notorious of a dozen draft-board raids was carried out the following spring outside of Baltimore. The "Catonsville Nine"—Berrigan, his brother Daniel (who had fasted at Occoquan prison), and seven other radical Catholics—made a bonfire of draft files with homemade napalm, declaring that "we believe some property has no right to exist."[75] Participants in these actions avoided harming anybody, stayed around to be arrested, and accepted the consequences. After the Catonsville trial, however, the Berrigans went underground until the FBI caught up with them.

Like King's own escalation of tactics, the "ultra resistance" draft raids were a creative effort to halt the relentless spiral toward armed struggle by modeling a militant nonviolent alternative. But by this midnight hour many white and black activists were losing patience with even the boldest expression of nonviolence.

Violent posturing was one form of militancy. Another was separatism, which had manifested itself during the long history of black struggle whenever interracial avenues appeared blocked. By late 1967 separatism had become more than ever the basis of black liberation.

White women who felt oppressed in the peace and justice movements identified with the subordinate position of African Americans. When a few nonconforming women began speaking out for their own freedom in the mid-1960s, they hoped to be able to change SNCC and SDS from within. It didn't work. After black activists demanded a black-only movement, dissident women adopted that course for themselves.

Shulamith Firestone, still smarting from her Labor Day humiliation, founded New York Radical Women in the fall. They helped to organize an antiwar march in Washington by the Jeannette Rankin Brigade, led by the eighty-seven-year-old feminist, the first woman in Congress and the only lawmaker to vote against World War II. They handed out leaflets along the march announcing "Sisterhood is powerful." The event included a torchlight procession at Arlington National Cemetery symbolizing "the burial of traditional womanhood." Participants went home to form more feminist collectives.

Charlotte Bunch started a group in Washington, D.C. Raised in New Mexico, graduate of Duke, a youth leader in the Southern Methodist Church, she had been a civil rights activist who had marched from Selma to Montgomery and then a community organizer in a D.C. ghetto. She had identified both with the New Left and with Christianity's radical wing, inspired by the black church, that "sought to put the gospel into action for social justice." She remembered that in her first women's group, "we spent months convincing ourselves that it was politically okay to meet separately as women and to focus on women's concerns. We felt somewhat more secure because we saw a parallel to the arguments of blacks who had been establishing their right and need to have their own space."[76]

Radical feminist groups sprouted rapidly as word spread through female networks. "I had never known anything as easy as organizing women's groups," Heather Booth recalled, "as easy and as exciting and as dramatic."[77] New Left ranks were depleted as legions of radical women declared their independence and fashioned a movement of their own.

Because they perceived it as the key to their liberation, they pursued self-discovery through consciousness-raising groups. Partly modeled on SNCC's testimonies about racism, the CR group was a recruitment tool, a process for unlearning sexism (a word they coined), and a microcosm of an egalitarian community that prefigured a feminist society. Through intimate dialogue they learned that their personal problems were "political" and required collective solutions. Radical feminists dug down to the root, as they saw it: the subjugation of women in relationships with men and in the family division of labor (especially childbearing). They demanded not equality of sex roles, which they likened to Jim Crow's separate but equal, but their elimination. This new creed struck chords in a multitude of young, mainly white, middle-class women who convinced themselves that, like black people, they had the right to define themselves and to shape their own destinies.

LIKE MOST AMERICANS King was little aware of radical feminist rumblings. CR groups were proliferating underground, and hardly at all in the South. The movement did not announce itself to the world until September 1968, when activists protested the Miss America Pageant in Atlantic City for allegedly celebrating women as sex objects. King knew about the National Organization for Women, founded by Betty Friedan and colleagues in 1966, but he was not on record as having endorsed NOW's campaign against sex discrimination. Like Frederick Douglass in the mid–nineteenth century and many black and white reform leaders in the 1960s—the NCNP convention an apotheosis—he placed racial discrimination well above gender bias on his scale of evils. If he was not noticeably concerned about women's plight in education and the work world, how much less would he have been sensitive to the major grievance of radical feminists—female subjugation in home and family. Given his background and his own patriarchal assumptions, he simply would not have understood where they were coming from.

In his own life he did not question his wife's primary obligation to raise their four children. She struggled with his neglect of parenting responsibilities, easily justified by his public mission but still painful. Just as the preacher was the center of the black church, the father was the center of the family, even if absent. Just as he firmly believed that leadership in the church never ascended from the pew to the pulpit, so he did not see any major role for movement women, with rare exceptions such as Jo Ann Robinson, beyond being "helpmates" for male leaders.

Ella Baker bristled at her treatment by King and other ministers when she was director of SCLC. They did not listen to her (King's listening gift notwithstanding) even though she had better ideas and far more experience. Dorothy Cotton had a less troubled relationship with him, in part because they were emotionally close. Although she didn't protest when he asked her, the director of citizenship education, to get coffee at staff meetings, she like Baker was well aware of his chauvinist attitudes and behavior.

King may have been more unabashed in his sexism, but he was hardly worse than many younger movement men, both black and white, who might have been slyer in mistreating their sisters, but still expected them to be the movement secretaries and "shit workers" as well as to service their sexual needs. In Robin Morgan's words, radical feminists were saying "good-bye to all that."

IN A CHRISTMAS EVE SERMON at Ebenezer, King confessed that over the past four years he had witnessed his dream "turn into a nightmare." But now he was striving, with whatever time he had left, to transfigure the nightmare into a bolder dream, a dream not of reform but of revolution, that this time would not be deferred.

Half a million American soldiers were fighting for their lives in the defoliated forests and jungles of Vietnam. Troops had invaded America's own cities to put down native insurgencies. Draft induction centers, military bases, the Pentagon fortress were under siege by protesters in time of war. Thousands were openly flouting the draft. Stoned soldiers were refusing to fight, deserting the battlefield, blowing up their commanders. At home, black and white, young and old, poor and rich inhabited different nations, unable to communicate across the social chasms. The white backlash, a new name for aggressive white privilege, had fired up the revolt by blacks and youth; they in turn fueled the backlash. It was a civil war, not of geography but of mind. A civil war for America's soul.

IO

In Matthew's Gospel, Jesus laid down principles by which, on the Day of Judgment, he would decide who will be saved and who will be damned. Those he will save will have fed and clothed the hungry, welcomed the stranger, cared for the sick, and visited the imprisoned. Perhaps because he hated jails, or because he had been jailed himself nineteen times, Martin King had never visited fellow protesters behind bars.

Joan Baez had first heard King speak, in Monterey, California, during the Montgomery bus boycott, when she was a fifteen-year-old high school girl. She cried when he talked about the bus boycott. Seven years later she sang "We Shall Overcome" to the March on Washington. In fall 1966 she and her mentor Ira Sandperl helped King desegregate schools in Grenada, Mississippi, walking black kids through rocks to a white school. After she was jailed a second time for sitting in at the Oakland induction center, sentenced to forty-five days, King decided to visit her. Baez, her mother, and sixty other war protesters had been at Santa Rita jail, east of San Francisco Bay, since before Christmas.

The "regular" inmates, black and brown women, were bouncing off the walls when rumors flew that the great man was coming to see the dark-skinned mestiza who lulled them to sleep with angelic lullabies. In the visiting cell on January 14, 1968, King and Andy Young gave Baez and her mother bear hugs. The daughter wiped her tears. The two men looked weary.

"We sat at the small table under a bare lightbulb," Joan Baez Sr. recalled, "and they went round and round with stories of old times, jokes, and ringing laughter such as the holding cell and its guards had never heard before. A warm and comfortable glow settled around me as if God were in his heaven, even if we were behind bars." Joan and her mom noticed a few familiar "wishful black faces peeking through the mesh screen." Joan asked King if he would say hello to her friends.

"Why shor', babies," he said in his southern drawl, "you jus' come right on in," as though it were his parlor. He looked at the guard, who opened the door. The teenagers darted in. Smiling warmly, King hugged each girl, saying "God bless you, babies." They danced back out of the cell, beaming to their bones and whooping. The girls lost their "privileges" as punishment; they couldn't have cared less. "I shook his han' and touched him and talked t'him," one girl exulted later to Baez. "Nuthin' kin ever take that away from me!"[78]

Before leaving the cramped visiting cell, King bowed his head over the small table and said a prayer full of hope.

King looked anything but hopeful when next they visited Ira Sandperl, Joan's partner in crime, on the men's side. The depression King had cloaked visiting his "very dear friend" Baez flared up full force. Sandperl, Jewish, was a peace activist and Gandhian scholar in his mid-forties who always wore Brooks Brothers suits to protests. He felt embarrassed, "reeking to high heaven" in his smelly jail clothes, sitting with his famous friends in their polished outfits. But King's spiffy exterior belied inner bedlam. Sandperl had never before seen his friend less than fully composed. Something was wrong.

"You guys, what's the matter?" he asked with his trademark chuckle. "I'm the one who should be feeling lousy. What are you upset about?" King peered around the visiting cell as if afraid he would be locked in. In fact it was his last time behind bars.

King said he "really felt awful," Sandperl remembered. He was mad at himself and guilt stricken. He said that "recently there were black hate groups that were both phoning him and writing him, threatening his life."

"I shouldn't feel any different," he confessed, than he did about white groups who had been plotting to kill him for eleven years. "I do feel differently," he said plaintively to his friend. "I am really annoyed at myself. I can't believe that these black groups are people who really want my death." After all of his years of battling white racism, it had come to this: black people mattered to him more than white.[79] But this man who walked every extra mile to preserve black unity, who had fought so hard against hate, can be forgiven for being mortified by the thought that some blacks hated his guts. And for being afraid that, like Malcolm, like Gandhi, he might be slain by one of his own. A black woman had come close in 1958, slipping in a knife a hair from his heart.

Struggling to maintain his equilibrium in these dark days, he could have been spared this unnecessary heartache. These threats did not come from black liberation groups. They were all fabricated by the FBI. Hoover's men were hell-bent on torturing his soul.

As King left the cell he mused, "Ira, if you're not in jail in the poor people's march, visit me in jail, because I will certainly be there." Sandperl replied that certainly he would.[80] On his way out of the sprawling county jail complex, hundreds of black and brown inmates ran to their windows and shouted their complaints to him—poor heating, lousy food, many other things.

"I just stood there listening to their complaints," he recounted to his staff three days later. "Finally, as I was getting ready to walk off, almost with tears in my eyes, one young man said, 'Doctor, you all be sure to fix it up now, so I can get me a job when I get out of here.'"[81]

King spoke to a support vigil for the protesters outside the Santa Rita gate. He had visited his friends, he said, to show his appreciation for their work for peace and justice, and because "I see these two struggles as one struggle. There can be no justice without peace, and there can be no peace without justice." Justice was indivisible. This was his clearest statement yet that he wanted to build One Big Movement to transform the nation.

"I'm going to continue with all of my might, with all of my energy, and with all of my action, to oppose that abominable, evil, unjust war in Vietnam." He expressed alarm about the growing repression of antiwar protest, which was bedeviling him personally. He saw a definite move by the government "to go all out now to silence dissenters," now zooming in on draft resistance.

"We cannot allow this to happen. We've got to make it clear that to indict Dr. Spock and Bill Coffin and the other courageous souls will mean indicting all of us, if they think that this draft resistance movement is going to be stopped."[82] King was not only, for the first time, publicly backing draft noncooperation as honorable and necessary in the tradition of Thoreau and Gandhi. He was identifying himself with it. Radical pacifists he respected who, like himself, were not subject to conscription were challenging the draft system in creative ways—sitting in at induction centers, aiding and abetting resisters, burning draft files. He had put the government on notice that he might have to share their jeopardy.

WAS THIS RHETORIC of the moment, or was he challenging the government to prosecute him? Standing outside Santa Rita jail in the California winter, he sounded as if he were ready to go to prison for his opposition to the war. But he had made other commitments. He expected that he might be spending time in prison for shutting down the nation's capital in the spring.

He had given marching orders to his staff at the sea island retreat in late November. The Poor People's Campaign would be a "last, desperate demand for the nation to respond to nonviolence. We've got to go for broke this time." The most extreme tactical proposals came not from Bevel or the usual firebrands but from one whom King counted on to hold up the cautious, conservative end of staff debate. His newly anointed executive vice president, Andy Young, suggested lying down on freeways, blocking government buildings, filling up emergency rooms by people needing care, a school boycott to turn D.C. children out into the streets.

King said the direct action must be "as dramatic, as dislocative, as disruptive, as attention-getting as the riots without destroying life or property." The plan would be for two or three hundred well-trained activists from each of a dozen cities and rural areas to converge on Washington in April to demand action. Larger contingents, some walking or riding mule trains for hundreds of miles, would reinforce them, camping out in D.C. parks and government offices. This would lead to a second March on Washington, not "to have a beautiful day" like the first, but to immobilize the city until the government changed its course at home and abroad. The protest would not aim directly at the war in Vietnam, but by disrupting the capital and raising the domestic cost of the war it would unite social justice with peace. King hoped also, perhaps naively, that new federal spending to end poverty would make it harder to continue funding the war.

Right after the staff retreat, overriding opposition from key advisers and staff, he announced the Poor People's Campaign to the world at an Atlanta press conference on December 4, 1967.

SCLC "will lead waves of the nation's poor and disinherited to Washington, D.C., next spring to demand redress of their grievances by the United States government.

"If this means forcible repression of our movement," he stated, "we will confront it, for we have done this before. If this means scorn or ridicule, we embrace it, for that is what America's poor now receive. If it means jail, we accept it willingly, for the millions of poor already are imprisoned by exploitation and discrimination." It would be a trek to the capital by "suffering and outraged citizens who will go to stay until some definite and positive action is taken to provide jobs and income for the poor."

Conveying his own anguish as much as the nation's, he said that those serving in the human rights movement were "keenly aware of the increasing bitterness and despair and frustration that threaten the worst chaos, hatred, and violence any nation has ever encountered. We are already at war with and among ourselves." All Americans could feel a "social insanity which could lead to national ruin."

Look at "the spectacle of cities burning while the national government speaks of repression instead of rehabilitation. Or think of children starving in Mississippi while prosperous farmers are rewarded for not producing food. Or Negro mothers leaving children in tenements to work in neighborhoods where people of color cannot live. Or the awesome bombardment, already greater than the munitions we exploded in World War II, against a small Asian land, while political brokers de-escalate and very nearly disarm a timid action against poverty."[83]

Showing off his newfound militancy, Young threw in that they had waited long enough. It might be necessary to tie up the country, or at least the capital.

"The way Washington is," he explained to the abashed reporters, "a few hundred people on each of those bridges would make it impossible to get in or out." But that would be a last resort that he hoped would not come to pass. "It would probably be much better to have a thousand people in need of health and medical care sitting in around Bethesda Naval Hospital, so that nobody could get in or out until they get treated."[84]

Playing the media with their usual virtuosity, King and Young had mustered the kind of credible threat that in diplomacy must be taken dead seriously. The White House, reeling still from the Pentagon siege and heightened antiwar protests, braced itself for a new front of civil disorder. Not doubting that King meant business, the FBI fired up a new operation to disable the Poor People's Campaign before it could spread its poison upon the land.

Whatever his occasional rhetoric to the contrary, by the end of 1967 King had swung away from his earlier resolve to go all out to stop the war. He had chosen justice at home over peace overseas. Both to his face and behind his back, most of his staff were in mutiny against the poverty push. Field staff assigned to get things going in northern cities were dragging their heals, alienating local supporters.

Having heard the voice of Jesus commanding him to crusade against the war, Bevel was fiercely opposed to the Poor People's Campaign. For one thing, he asserted at a December 27 staff meeting, "I do not know whether Johnson would give enough opposition for us to build up steam and momentum." LBJ was a master of co-optation. What Daley had done in Chicago would seem like kids' play compared to what the President could pull off with policy promises. After all, he had actually led a war on poverty, whatever its weaknesses. No one could claim that he didn't care about the poor, even if he had turned his back on them to chase demons in Vietnam.

Bevel believed it would be tragic to turn away from the war. He was convinced that no social progress was possible while the war was raging, eating up the nation's resources. A month earlier King had proclaimed young people to be the prime agents of change. Bevel felt that youth would never pour their passion into a fight for the poor. They could not see beyond the war, which overrode all other concerns. He believed that draft resistance, mounted on a massive scale, was the answer. "We need a movement to get the war machine to attack us rather than us attacking the war machine."

King was chagrined by his intransigence. "The thing you are talking about is much harder to mobilize around and takes much longer," he countered. "You have a lot of people agreeing with you but they are not willing to spend five years in jail over it. In addition, you have the national press against you." He was still scarred from his raking over the coals by the media.

"I see levels of struggle" in the Poor People's Campaign, with the war being the second level. "I see still another level behind that—the international level." He made clear that the meaning of the campaign went beyond people's livelihoods. Nonviolent struggle had to prove itself, redeem itself, in order to be able to fight on.[85]

KING HAD BEEN BUILDING up to his "go for broke" battle against poverty since SCLC had launched its Chicago campaign just after the Watts explosion. He had long known, intellectually, that economic deprivation was rooted in race as much as class. The Chicago stalemate had taught him that racism was more intractable than he had realized, implacable *because* of its malignant kinship with the class and power structures of the big cities, and of Washington.[86] Since fall 1966 he had been searching for a strategy to confront the symbiotic entwinement of class oppression and racial prejudice.

Partly because they did not tackle this symbiosis, partly because of Vietnam, none of the earlier movement economic strategies had borne fruit. Whether it was Whitney Young's domestic Marshall Plan, King's Bill of Rights for the Disadvantaged, or Randolph's Freedom Budget, Congress did not take them seriously; even with LBJ's war on poverty, its support was halfhearted. Nor did movement leaders mobilize grassroots armies behind economic reform as they had for civil rights. One grassroots initiative more than any other pushed King toward a poor people's movement that could fuse empowerment with economic justice, by means of a multiracial alliance of the poor and disadvantaged.

In fall 1965 social scientists Richard Cloward and Frances Fox Piven circulated a working paper among civil rights and antipoverty organizers later published in *Nation* magazine.[87] Responding to the black movement's search for new directions, they proposed organizing a mass movement of welfare recipients, who were mainly women. Given that for every recipient another was eligible, several million more could be recruited to the welfare rolls. And given that welfare agencies typically refused to grant clients full benefits, Cloward and Piven pointed to a huge untapped potential for expanded payments. Their goal was to disrupt the welfare system and foster such a grave bureaucratic, fiscal, and electoral crisis that Washington would be compelled to guarantee a livable income for all citizens.

With little leadership the urban poor already had been sweeping into welfare centers in much larger numbers, which resulted in a quadrupling of clients during the 1960s. The freedom movement had taught poor people that they had rights as citizens, even economic rights. Concurrently the idea of economic entitlements had begun to take hold in academic and policy circles. Liberal economist Robert Theobald had argued for the poor's "absolute constitutional right to an income."[88] Thirteen hundred economists petitioned Congress for a national system of income guarantees. Randolph's 1966 Freedom Budget also embraced a guaranteed income.

Many activists dismissed the Cloward-Piven strategy, either because they did not think the welfare poor could be organized, or because they felt that economic solutions required creation of jobs, not perpetuation of dependency. One seasoned organizer, however, seized upon their ideas as the answer to his frustration. George Wiley, great-grandson of slaves, had grown up in Rhode Island, conquered one racial barrier after another, including becoming the first black to earn a Ph.D. in chemistry from Cornell. In the early 1960s he had blossomed into a respected research chemist at Syracuse. But as with so many others, civil rights activism inexorably took over his life. He worked first as a local CORE leader, then with James Farmer as CORE's associate director. He came to realize that neither CORE nor any other existing rights group was prepared to build the grassroots movement of poor people he dreamed about.

As a first step, in June 1966 Wiley's Poverty/Rights Action Center coordinated protests for "welfare rights" in twenty-five cities. Marching 150 miles from Cleveland to Ohio's capital to present grievances to the governor, several hundred welfare women sang:

> We feed our children bread and beans
> While rich folks ride in limousines.
> After all, we're human beings,
> Marching down Columbus Road.[89]

Responding to such cries of need, Wiley created the National Welfare Rights Organization to fight for the lowest stratum of American citizenry—impoverished urban women of color. NWRO was led jointly by Wiley and a national board of dynamic, no-nonsense black welfare mothers including chair Johnnie Tillmon from Los Angeles. Calling for concrete reforms grounded in principles of adequate income, dignity, justice, and democracy, NWRO set forth its goal: "Jobs or income now! Decent jobs with adequate wages for those who can work; adequate income for those who can not work."[90]

Local groups multiplied in 1967 and 1968 and carried out the "street strategy" of creative direct action. Most effective were "basic need" campaigns to secure special grants for winter clothing, furniture, and school lunches. NWRO organizing spread throughout the country, even among poor whites in Appalachia and the South. It proved most successful in New York and Massachusetts. In New York City demonstrators camped out in welfare offices, generally without violence, but wreaking havoc on mountains of paperwork and throwing welfare services into chaos. More often than not they won their demands.

Whether practical or not, the right to a livable income had generated enough steam by 1967 that it did not seem wildly radical, especially in the turbulence of the times. It would have been surprising had King and his staff not chosen it as the basic aim of the Poor People's Campaign. It was a logical expression of radical moderation.

In speeches and in *Where Do We Go from Here* he followed NWRO in stressing the adequacy of income as well as its legal guarantee. Two conditions were indispensable, he wrote, "if we are to ensure that the guaranteed income operates as a consistently progressive measure. First, it must be pegged to the median income of society." Second, it "must be dynamic; it must automatically increase as the total social income grows."[91] In the wake of the July revolts he had called for the government to provide jobs for the jobless. That would still be the priority, but one way or another Washington would have to make sure that every American family had a decent income. They would abolish poverty in the world's wealthiest nation.

Well aware that staff members such as Bevel and Jackson were opposed to the Poor People's Campaign, that hardly any were excited about it, and that field workers in designated cities were ill informed, King held a mid-January staff workshop at Ebenezer for the several dozen PPC organizers. He concluded a lengthy speech to participants by reemphasizing the imperative of nonviolent conduct.

"We are the custodians of the philosophy of nonviolence," he asserted. "And it has worked." He was confident that it would succeed in Washington as well as it had in the South. It just had to be more creatively engineered. At a press conference he announced that they were pulling out all the stops, that the first wave of protesters would involve blacks, Puerto Ricans, Mexicans, American Indians, and poor whites; they would include welfare moms and kids; and they would build shantytowns to dramatize their plight. But unlike the Depression Bonus Marchers, World War I veterans fighting for their rightful benefits, they would not be run out of Washington. Tying up traffic would be a last resort.

Reporters seemed more curious about King's Vietnam doings, and whether he might be indicted for supporting draft refusal like Spock and Coffin. He replied that it was a definite possibility; he'd heard rumors of a bigger crackdown. Nevertheless, he would continue to make his Ebenezer altar a sanctuary for young men who chose to turn in their draft cards or refuse induction. This was two days after he had visited his friends at Santa Rita jail.

That night, while King was away, the staff held a stormy session in which they let loose their frustrations with the Poor People's Campaign as they could not have done with him present. Led by Bevel and

Jackson, the rebels ripped the proposed campaign for casting aside other pressing projects while being poorly thought through. "The winds of anger were blowing mighty hard," King gathered.

Sensing the seriousness of the staff rebellion, aware that his leadership was on the line as perhaps never before, he was determined to change the minds of his doubting disciples. He spoke to them next day in a masterful display of compassion mixed with firm resolve. He affirmed the "confusions" that they all shared in this "sick, neurotic nation," the schizophrenia of divided loyalties, of ambivalent passions: love vs. hate, integration vs. separatism, nonviolence vs. violence.

Much of the acrimony had been about the nature of the PPC's demands. He agreed that "jobs or income" would have to be spelled out in specifics. But for the purpose of mobilizing the masses of the poor, many of them unschooled, it was preferable to have a simple goal conveyed in a down-to-earth, straightforward slogan.

"My brothers and sisters," he said, "the people that we are going to be recruiting are not going to be fired up on the basis of a long list of demands. They wouldn't know what you're talking about, because of long years of denial and deprivation.

"Let's find something that is so possible, so achievable, so pure, so simple that even the backlash can't do much to deny it. Yet something so non-token and so basic to life that even the black nationalists can't disagree with it. Now that's jobs or income." He was talking about a reform that could not be co-opted by the establishment, by the canny politician in the White House. A reform that could be embraced by a broad liberal-left consensus across race and class lines. A reform that reflected basic American values of fairness and decency yet would bring about a radical result—getting rid of poverty. The politics of radical moderation had one more chance to prove its mettle. It was a middle path between unacceptable extremes of rioting and "timid supplication," which would shift the center to the left.

King could see his own doubts and despair reflected in the eyes of his colleagues. To bring them back he needed something more than rational persuasion. He needed to minister to them. He told them that going to Washington would be good for their souls. It would be a spiritual renewal or restoration, a resurrection of the Spirit. He reminded them how Jesus had faced the doubts and fears of his disciples, trying to get them to Jerusalem.

"It was that pull of expectation," he explained, "that caused Peter, on the day of Pentecost to go out fired up with that something he got from Jesus, and he preached until three thousand souls were converted. Aren't we talking about three thousand?" Jesus had exhorted Peter to turn from sand into rock, and he eventually did. "I'm expecting you to be like a rock," King said to his own staff.

No matter what their tribulations, they should never succumb to "give-up-itis." Hope was the final refusal to give up. "Genuine hope involves the recognition—I think this is very important in what we are about to do—that what is hoped for is already here. It is already present in the sense that it is a power which drives us to fulfill what we hope for.

"That is what Jesus meant when he looked at his disciples and said one day, 'You don't have to wait for some distant day for the kingdom of God to come.' Brethren"—King now speaking to those before him— "you've got to realize that the kingdom of God is in you, it's right now, as an inner power within you that drives you to fulfill the hope of a universal kingdom." Hope was personally and socially therapeutic, a force of survival, of immortality. Going to Washington, they were crossing to Jerusalem.

"I don't know if I'll see all of you before April." With faith "I send you forth," he instructed his staff in closing the retreat, "as Jesus said to his disciples: Be ye as strong and as tough as a serpent, and tender as a dove. And we will be able to do something that will give new meaning to our own lives and, I hope, new meaning to the life of the nation."[92]

II

_____

By the end of January 1968 the Pentagon was at war with itself. Inside its mighty, indefensible walls a cluster of civilian officials, following McNamara's timorous lead, had grown demoralized by the Vietnam stalemate. The rising public protests deepened their doubts. The clincher was the spectacular Tet offensive set off on the Vietnamese lunar new year, January 31. In a sudden blitz NLF guerrillas backed by North Vietnam invaded every major city and town in South Vietnam and even took over part of the U.S. embassy in Saigon.

"What the hell is going on?" newscaster Walter Cronkite yelped off camera in his CBS studio. "I thought we were winning this war."[93] He spoke for millions. A high-level source revealed that the brilliantly coordinated, all-out offensive caught the military and the White House by surprise, and "its strength, length, and intensity prolonged this shock."[94] Body counts on both sides soared. The bloody massacre of civilians by the NLF and Hanoi in the ancient city of Hue dwarfed all previous atrocities by either side. But all along U.S. forces had massacred South Vietnamese villagers, most sensationally (but not exceptionally) the slaughter of 350 men, women, and children in the hamlet of My Lai, March 1968. When GIs could not tell the difference between Vietcong fish and the sea of villagers, survival demanded that they drain the sea.

Command of the air and high-tech weaponry enabled the shaken

U.S. forces to repel the Tet offensive by mid-February in a debilitating military defeat for the NLF. "We lost our best people," an NLF leader ruefully admitted later.[95] Their once impregnable military, political, and social infrastructure never recovered. It was the beginning of the end for the Vietcong. From this point on they played a weakened role. Hanoi took control of both military command and provision of forces.

Nonetheless, in the age of color television, the Tet offensive proved in the short run a breathtaking political and psychological victory for the NLF, the kind that mattered in a guerrilla war. Tet shattered the die-hard illusion that the United States could win in Vietnam, at least on the ground, without nuclear weapons. It graphically showed that the war could never be other than a stalemate.

Unbeknownst to any at the time, except perhaps to Hanoi's strategists, the trauma of Tet represented the end of a largely guerrilla war and the onset of more conventional warfare. Just when the U.S. military was finally comprehending that it was fighting a guerrilla war, the adversary was changing its strategy—to fight the war by massing forces to hold territory. Washington was concluding that the United States could not prevail just when the North Vietnamese were beginning to turn the conflict into something more like wars that America had never lost.

But this unseen shift with its Sophoclean irony had little bearing on the immediate chaos.

THE COLD WAR WITHIN SCLC continued apace. Inefficiency and insubordination fed on each other. King grew so frustrated with his staff leaders' hubris that he delivered a sermon on it at Ebenezer, where some of his staff would hear him, and all of them would get the message. Oratory was ever his favored means to deal with conflict. But the sermon spoke more to himself than anyone else.

He started out with a story from the Gospel of Mark about two of Jesus' disciples, James and John, who asked him for privileged positions in the kingdom that he will rule. Text and context made it likely that he referred to his own James (Bevel) and Jesse Jackson (Jack being a variation of John)—but casting his eye on all staff members afflicted with hubris. Jesus told James and John that they must share his travail and sacrifice, but that it was not up to him who will sit on his right and left hands. But King was just as surely scolding himself for his own puffed-up pride and vanity.

Jesus explained that the favored disciples would be those who were the greatest servants. The greatest of all would be the servant of all.[96]

Before we judge ambitious disciples for their egotism, King said, let us realize that we all have the drum-major instinct, the drive for recognition, distinction, specialness, to lead the parade, to be first. But if unmanaged, undisciplined, the drum-major instinct was pernicious; it distorted and degraded one's personality, one's soul. Runaway egotism spawned a host of sins, including corruption, criminality, exploitation, dishonesty, and exclusion. On a larger scale it led to prejudice and racism, and to powerful nations' lust to rule the world. Their own country was the "supreme culprit." The nation's narcissism bore poisonous fruit in America's criminal conduct in Vietnam, and in the supreme arrogance of both superpowers threatening the planet with annihilation, holding the whole world ransom for their own rivalry.

But just as James and John, or James and Jesse, should not be condemned for their hubris, neither should the drum-major instinct be condemned out of hand. It was only the perversion of this instinct for self-aggrandizement that was dangerous, even deadly.

"The great issue of life," King told his home congregation, "is to harness the drum major instinct" for constructive purposes. He pointed out that Jesus did not scold James and John for being selfish. Jesus affirmed them for being ambitious. King paraphrased Jesus to make sure he was getting through.

"Oh, I see you want to be first," King said. "You want to be great. You want to be important. You want to be significant. Well you ought to be. If you're going to be my disciple, you must be. Keep feeling the need for being first. But I want you to be first in love. I want you to be first in moral excellence."

Jesus transformed the situation "by giving a new definition of greatness," a new norm of nobility. Jesus said to James and John, "You must earn it. True greatness comes not by favoritism, but by fitness." By defining greatness in terms of servanthood, Jesus and Martin were declaring that "everybody can be great. Because everybody can serve." All one needed was "a heart full of grace, a soul generated by love." Long before and after Jesus, prophets and philosophers have been trying to reconcile the fullest individuality with the most just community. Greatness of servanthood may have been as good an answer as any ever found. The best woman or man was the one who did the most for the community.

In his sermons, in his all-night chats, in his meditations, King was more than ever preoccupied, obsessed, with his own death. This was not the first sermon in which he preached his own eulogy—he had done so the past April—but it was his most complete, and his last. Here he would bring judgment back on himself. He would transubstantiate his own hubris into humility, his own sins into virtue.

"If any of you are around when I have to meet my day," he said in the sanctuary where it would inevitably come to pass, "I don't want a long funeral," nor a long eulogy. He didn't want the preacher to say that he'd won the Nobel Prize, or several hundred other awards.

No, "I'd like somebody to mention that day," that he had "tried to give his life serving others," that he had "tried to love somebody. I want you to say that day, that I tried to be right on the war question," that he tried to feed the hungry, clothe the naked, visit the imprisoned. "I want you to say that I tried to love and serve humanity.

"Yes, if you want to say that I was a drum major, say that I was a drum major for justice. Say that I was a drum major for peace. I was a drum major for righteousness. And all of the other shallow things will not matter." All of his weaknesses, his failures might be forgiven. All of his sins washed away.

"I just want to leave a committed life behind.

"Yes, Jesus, I want to be on your right side or your left side, not for any selfish reason. I want to be on your right or your left side, not in terms of some political kingdom or ambition, but I just want to be there in love and in justice and in truth and in commitment to others, so that we can make of this old world a new world."[97]

12

The Poor People's Campaign was cranking up its sticky gears. Even without fire in their bellies, SCLC organizers were hard at work in a dozen cities and the Deep South. Support came from various groups involved with empowering poor people, including labor unions. Cesar Chavez, founder of California's United Farm Workers, about to begin a fast that nearly killed him, sent a telegram of solidarity. One constituency that the PPC could not do without was welfare mothers; it had to bring in the burgeoning welfare rights movement.

But the leaders of NWRO, whose ten thousand members King coveted, were suspicious. He had not notably supported their efforts for welfare reform. Why should they divert resources to this quixotic Johnny-come-lately campaign? George Wiley insisted that King come to Chicago for a face-off with the NWRO leadership. He walked through an adoring crowd at the Chicago YMCA to the upstairs conference room, where NWRO board members greeted him cordially. They sat him on the dais with Wiley and the board, cut off from his aides placed in far corners. Community organizer Tim Sampson described Wiley's seating plan as "a grand piece of psychological warfare."[98]

The leaders were rankled that King's people had tried to seduce NWRO locals into joining the PPC. Wiley and the women leaders had built NWRO from scratch "with their blood, sweat, and tears," Sampson noted. "Not to be recognized was an attack on their very being." A collision with the drum-major instinct. "And to have it taken away was unthinkable."[99]

Board chair Johnnie Tillmon presided, an infant grandchild in her lap. After each board member had introduced herself, King gave a spiel about the PPC and asked for their support.

Board member Etta Horn began the inquisition. "How do you stand on P.L. 90-248?" Befuddled, King looked over to Andy Young for a cue.

Mrs. Tillmon broke in. "She means the anti-welfare bill," just passed by Congress and signed by the President, that would freeze benefits and require work. "Where were you last October," she asked, "when we were down in Washington trying to get support for Senator Kennedy's amendments?" The women fired one question after another that he fumbled.

"You know, Dr. King," Tillmon scolded him like a stern school-marm, "if you don't know about these questions, you should say you don't know, and then we could go on with the meeting."

"You're right, Mrs. Tillmon," he confessed. "We don't know any-thing about welfare. We are here to learn."[100] He should have listened before he spoke. He did not have the patience he once had. They proceeded to teach him about the plight of welfare recipients and the feds' crackdown. He was unaccustomed to being browbeaten. "They jumped on Martin," Young recalled, "like no one ever had before. I don't think he had ever been that insulted in a meeting. They were test-ing him."[101] His empathy allowed him to rise above his dismay. He promised that SCLC and the PPC would fully support their demands for fairer and more democratic welfare.

THE WELFARE RIGHTS SHOWDOWN touched off a week of con-frontations with black militants. King hated nothing more. He sched-uled an SCLC board meeting in Washington to coincide with a two-day antiwar mobilization organized by Clergy and Laity Concerned, which he served as cochair. Sixteen thousand clergy came to D.C. from all over the country. King headed up a march to Arlington National Ceme-tery, where he led a long prayer at the Tomb of the Unknown Soldier. His friend Rabbi Abraham Heschel closed the prayer by calling out in

Hebrew: *"Elohi, Elohi, lama sabachthani?"*—my God, my God, why has thou forsaken me?—the last words of Jesus on the cross.[102]

That silent protest contrasted with harassment of SCLC board members at Vermont Avenue Baptist Church by local black militants. In his speech, "In Search for a Sense of Direction," King reported progress in the Poor People's Campaign. He recounted his visits with "the least of these," who lived with "wall to wall rats and roaches." He pointed out portentous parallels between their nation's losing its soul and the Roman Empire's decline and fall.

"God's judgment is standing today on America." They will be coming to Washington to say, repent America, and to "demand that the nation grant us what is truly ours."

He concluded with words of encouragement, more to himself than anyone else.

"I can't lose hope," he said. "I can't lose hope because when you lose hope, you die. When you lose hope"—he was speaking also to the militants outside the church—"you become so nihilistic that you engage in disruption for disruption's sake rather than for justice' sake." He was especially wary fearing that somewhere, maybe right outside the door, militants were gunning for him.

"When you lose hope, you may still stand up and think you're a man physically, but you are dead psychologically and spiritually. We've lost a great deal, and we've had our disappointments, but we must develop something on the inside that causes us to go on anyway. If we give up, we are dead.

"If I can leave you with any message tonight," he closed, "I would say don't lose hope. Wait for the next morning. It may be dark now. It may look like we can't get out of this thing now. It may appear that nonviolence has failed, and the nation will not respond to it.

"Don't blow your brains out now. Don't give up hope. Wait until the next morning, for our check will surely come. And we will be a new people."[103]

His faithful board of directors, many of whom had known him since the bus boycott, had never seen him so down, so weary. His words may have girded up his loins a notch, but they didn't lift his colleagues' morale, or their once unshakable confidence in him.

Black militants' invective toward him and SCLC board members aggravated King's fear that they might cause trouble for the Poor People's Campaign. One evening he met with Carmichael, Rap Brown, and other SNCC-associated militants. They agreed not to oppose or criticize the campaign, to help calm the black community, and to march with him pledged to tactical nonviolence.[104] The mood of reconciliation was broken by a black woman accusing King of selling out the movement in Selma and being about to do it again. For the first time in public, King erupted in anger. His whole body quivered as he vociferously denied her accusation.

Next day King and staff colleagues met again with Carmichael, Brown, and company to firm up their peace pact. During the dialogue King reproved executive director William Rutherford for accommodating the militants' stance against nonviolence. He blew up at him after the meeting.

"You're wrong. You're absolutely wrong," he nearly shouted. "Violence begets violence, that's what it's all about."

"I would have been humiliated if I hadn't been so shocked," Rutherford recalled. "Dr. King never ever humiliated anyone in public in front of anyone else. But he was *shaking.* He went on for about ten minutes, and then I very quickly realized he wasn't talking to me anymore, he was talking to himself or he was speaking for history." Now that he and others such as his radical Catholic friends were taking nonviolent action to its outer limits, he felt it more critical than ever to draw a line between their ramped-up tactics and actual violence, in word or deed.

In hindsight Rutherford thought that his boss's fit reflected his utter exhaustion and his frustration with the Washington campaign's slow progress and his own staff's growing skepticism of nonviolence, which he felt as personal betrayal. "I think he was beginning to have self-doubts as well. Would this really work?"[105]

Next day he sought support for the PPC from the D.C. Chamber of Commerce, mainly black businessmen, as the best antidote to rioting. He worried out loud that one more explosive summer might bring fierce repression, even a rightwing regime.

"They'll throw us into concentration camps," he warned. "The Wallaces and the Birchites will take over. The sick people and the fascists will be strengthened. They'll cordon off the ghetto and issue passes for us to get in and out." To prevent this, "we're going to be militant. We're going to plague Congress."[106]

Practically as he spoke, his fearful premonition was being borne out in Orangeburg, South Carolina, a hotbed of rights activism since the Montgomery bus boycott year. Students at the two black colleges had been protesting segregation of Orangeburg's hospital and bowling alley that clearly violated the four-year-old Civil Rights Act. Over several days in early February police and protesters skirmished; students, some of whom broke windows, were arrested and beaten. Then on the night of February 8, state police and national guardsmen surrounded students around a bonfire at the state college. State troopers, apparently unprovoked, opened fire on the unarmed students with high-powered shotguns, killing three and wounding thirty, many shot in the back as they fled. SNCC leader Cleveland Sellers, whose marriage ceremony King had conducted over at Ebenezer the week before, was charged with inciting the riot. He had little to do with it and was never tried, but was sent to prison for draft resistance. Although the FBI was complicit in the police misconduct, allegedly falsifying evidence, nine state troopers were indicted on federal charges for the "Orangeburg massacre," but were predictably acquitted.

TOWARD THE END of February King hoped he might get a reprieve from the battlefield by escaping to Jamaica for a short vacation. His rest was broken by a painful jolt. In a one-liner Rustin, his close adviser for twelve years, publicly chastised the upcoming campaign. "I seriously question the efficacy of Dr. King's plans for the April march," he told a reporter.[107] As a longtime member of MLK's research committee, his key advisers, Rustin had written a memo a month earlier with constructive suggestions and criticisms. He supported the PPC's objectives (though he thought they should be clearer and more winnable), but he opposed the most publicized tactics.

Only a few years past, before becoming a true believer in electoral politics, he had promoted a strategy he called "social dislocation," militant, Birmingham-type direct action, as the route to social change.[108]

But he felt that the urban revolts had transformed the nation's climate. Now he wrote that "any effort to disrupt transportation, government buildings, etc., can only lead, in this atmosphere, to further backlash and repression." Such tactics will "fail to attract persons dedicated to nonviolence" but "attract elements that cannot be controlled." He hoped that the spring protest would be limited to "constitutional, non-violent protest," presumably allowing symbolic civil disobedience but not actual blockades. He did not want to risk alienating liberal-leaning voters in the 1968 elections.

But in concluding he expressed second thoughts about whether SCLC could maintain control even of tamer nonviolent tactics. "SCLC essentially lost control of the Mississippi march [June 1966] when the splintering and confusion was quite simple as compared to the current mood."[109]

In his cover letter to King accompanying the memo he explained that he was not able to finish it "because I haven't thought through two important problems: (1) What do we mean by the escalation of non-violence (particularly since the press is interpreting this to mean the inclusion of minimal violence). (2) What kind of commitment must individuals make," what discipline must they accept?[110]

Apparently his memo never received a response from King or senior staff. He felt rebuffed—worse, ignored. Rather than follow up with another memo, he went public with his concerns. King was hurt. Staff leaders felt that Rustin had betrayed trust. King adviser Harry Wachtel, a research committee member, was so angered that he broke off relations with his friend for seventeen years. In a letter of reconciliation Wachtel later wrote:

"I did know from Martin, first-hand, and from Coretta and others, second-hand," that he was "stung by your public views" about the PPC. "For you were on the inside when that was being planned and developed. It was this act on your part which made Martin feel so badly. He felt let down because he held you up so high."[111] King and Rustin never got a chance to reconcile.

RUSTIN HAD PUT HIS FINGER on momentous questions that King had been groping to answer. What did they mean by the escalation of nonviolent tactics? What commitment and discipline must practitioners adhere to? Activist writer Barbara Deming put forth the most cogent answer in that month's *Liberation* magazine—an article that King probably read and Rustin surely did. *Liberation* coeditor Deming, fifty, had been jailed for civil disobedience several times, notably in Albany, Georgia, during the Quebec to Guantanamo march for nuclear peace in 1962, the subject of her classic account, *Prison Notes*. No one was more responsible for the successful nonviolent communication between protesters and troops at the Pentagon the past October.

Her February 1968 essay, "On Revolution and Equilibrium," was the decade's most persuasive intellectual challenge to the violent call of the wild, deepening the understanding of nonviolent activists for years to come. Employing Frantz Fanon's own words to argue for nonviolence, she asserted that every time he called for violence, "radical and uncompromising action" that was nonviolent would work even better, at lesser cost. Like King and many radical pacifists, she suggested that nonviolent action must be more forceful, more aggressive; disruption was needed along with massive noncooperation. But, she pleaded, at the same time it escalated in militancy it had to escalate in humanity, in its compassion for adversaries mired in unjust institutions.

"'Do you want to remain pure? Is that it?' a black man asked me, during an argument on nonviolence," she began her essay. "It is not possible to act at all and to remain pure." What she wanted was, in Fanon's words, "to escape becoming dizzy"—to keep the movement from losing its equilibrium, its collective sanity—and thus be able to set afoot a new person, a new people. "What are the best means for changing our lives," she asked, "for really changing them?"

Establishing and preserving one's relationship with the adversary was crucial—in the first place, by not killing or harming him. Let us recall the young man in Selma hell-bent on praying with the hostile deputy sheriff who blocked his passage to the courthouse.

"We can put *more* pressure on the antagonist for whom we show human concern," Deming wrote in *Liberation*. "It is precisely solicitude for his person *in combination with* stubborn interference in his actions that can give us a very special degree of control. We put upon him two pressures—the pressure of our defiance of him and the pressure of our respect for his life—and it happens that in combination these two pressures are uniquely effective."[112] But they must be combined: neither worked without the other. The escalation of righteous action must be matched by the escalation of empathy.

This was where King was at, where his epic journey had brought him. The mad maelstrom of the times never gave the master of words a chance to explain his modus operandi as well as Deming did.

ONE REASON that black militants were upping the heat on King and SCLC was their own internal pressure to escalate tactics—the result not only of heightened repression but of infighting among Black Panthers, SNCC, Maulana Ron Karenga's US organization in Los Angeles, and other black liberation groups. After Huey Newton's capture in October 1967, journalist and ex-convict Eldridge Cleaver, author of the best-selling memoir *Soul on Ice,* eclipsed Bobby Seale as the BPP's major-domo.

In early 1968 the Panthers mounted an all-out campaign to "Free Huey," culminating in mammoth Oakland and Los Angeles rallies in mid-February. Cleaver recruited Carmichael to speak at the rallies, where Cleaver announced a "merger" of SNCC with the Panthers. Carmichael, no longer a SNCC leader, was chosen to be the BPP's prime minister. Although the Panthers depended upon Carmichael's fame and oratorical power to advance their goals, they were troubled by his public criticism of the party's ties with white leftists and adherence to Marxist socialism. He espoused a pan-Africanist philosophy that downplayed class struggle and insisted upon full black separatism. He might have thought that he was faithfully carrying Malcolm's torch; actually Malcolm departed from such racial exclusivism.

Over the next year animosity grew between the Panthers and SNCC, forcing Carmichael out as titular leader. FBI covert action exacerbated BPP's antagonism with Karenga's US, culminating in a gunfight on the UCLA campus in January 1969 that killed two Panthers. Conflicts among black liberationists were even more tempestuous than between them and SCLC. No black liberation group apparently ever threatened

King with violence, yet with the FBI's conniving they were slandering and murdering each other.

KING WAS NOT ALONE in his time of trial. The commander-in-chief, his onetime friend, was besieged as never before. One of LBJ's closest confidants, young special assistant Bill Moyers, confided to Arthur Schlesinger Jr. in early March that the White House was "impenetrable," sealed off from reality. The President dismissed all criticism as driven by political or personal enmity. Despite his admiration for his mentor, Moyers now believed that "four more years of Johnson would be ruinous for the country."[113]

The political damage of the Tet offensive was irreparable. This was just the kind of setback that Johnson's policy of incremental escalation had been designed to prevent. He was aware that McNamara was not the only Pentagon hawk who had transmogrified into dove. And protests were proliferating all over. He could not muffle the chants of demonstrators at the White House gates. One in particular got to him, according to his wife: "Hey, hey, LBJ, how many kids did you kill today?" In January black singer Eartha Kitt had marred a White House women's gathering hosted by Lady Bird Johnson with her comments blaming the war for problems of American youth. King was one of few public figures who lauded her "very proper gesture. I admire her for saying what needed to be said."[114]

In February a prominent liberal scholar was invited to have dinner with the Johnsons in the upstairs family quarters. LBJ had not given up hope that historians would redeem him. The scholar had visited the White House many times before, but this time it felt truly under siege, a palpable onslaught. After being greeted by the First Couple, he tried to lighten the deathly grim atmosphere.

"Well, Mr. President, I have to confess to you that all four of my children marched on the Pentagon last October, and one got arrested." Johnson did not even pretend to smile. The dinner conversation was "guarded and subdued, everyone avoiding the subject that lay over the White House like a shroud." Suddenly the President's elder daughter "flounced into the room in a housecoat, sat in her father's lap, then beside him on the floor." She started talking about Vietnam, where her marine captain husband was about to be sent, as was her younger sister Lucy's spouse. "Most of her friends and those of her husband were military men, she said, but she understood the feelings of young people who hated the war. She then presented those feelings, as simply and eloquently as I could remember having heard." Lynda Bird tried to explain to her father that the young protesters felt passionately about peace the way he had felt, as a young man, fighting poverty in the New Deal. Her father listened, but for once had no reply.

The scholar broke the stony silence with a story about how his son, the one who was jailed at the Pentagon, had nursed a passionate love for Texas as a young boy growing up in New England and dreamed about being a Texas rancher and politician. The President was transfixed—anything to get his mind off the war that had hog-tied him.[115]

HOW COULD IT HAVE HAPPENED that this political genius who had been elected by a historic landslide, commanded solid majorities in Congress, controlled the mightiest military the world had ever known, with hundreds of bases spanning the globe, felt paralyzed by the domestic forces opposing him? His fear and paranoia compelled him to escalate espionage against the peace and freedom movements and in particular against King. He could not tolerate any more shocks or surprises. By early 1968 he was less interested in discrediting King—the thrust of White House machinations against his Vietnam stand—than in keeping close watch on him, his organization, and his allies.

The FBI, however, was still obsessed with destroying him politically and psychologically. "We were operating an intensive vendetta against Dr. King in an effort to destroy him," former Atlanta FBI agent Arthur Murtagh testified to the House Select Committee on Assassinations.[116]

In August 1967, stunned by the massive multicity rioting that they had not foreseen, the FBI created a major new program: Counterintelligence—Black Hate Groups. Counterintelligence was a euphemism for counterinsurgency. The agency had set up a "Cointelpro" operation in 1964 targeting the Klan and white hate groups, and earlier against the Communist Party, Socialist Workers, and Puerto Rican nationalists, but this was a far grander enterprise. Its mission was to "expose, disrupt, misdirect, discredit, or otherwise neutralize the activities of black nationalist, hate-type organizations and groupings, their leadership, spokesmen, membership and supporters, and to counter their propensity for violence and civil disorder."[117] Shortly thereafter the "racial intelligence section" was established to oversee this new program. While King and SCLC were included in it—despite not fitting the profile—not much changed right away because they were already heavily targeted. It was likely, though, that the new Cointelpro was responsible for the more distasteful dirty tricks against King, such as the bogus death threats from black militants that roiled him so.

Then came the Pentagon siege in October, prompting an expanded Cointelpro against the New Left, followed by King's announcement of the Poor People's Campaign, which raised red flags all over Washington. The FBI reinforced their secret war against King with a full-bore campaign against the PPC of infiltration, red-baiting, disinformation, and disruption.

In early January 1968 Hoover instructed twenty-two field offices to coordinate intelligence gathering on the PPC with local and state police. It was the FBI's first opportunity to activate its Ghetto Informant Program, which utilized over three thousand ghetto residents as "listening posts." They were paid to report on and thwart SCLC recruitment efforts for the PPC. The new attorney general, Ramsey Clark, refused to approve renewed FBI wiretapping of SCLC headquarters in Atlanta, where agents wanted to tap all ten phone lines (they still had taps on Levison, Rustin, and other New York advisers).

It hardly mattered, though. Since fall 1964 the FBI had lodged a trusted informant at the heart of SCLC's executive staff: Jim Harrison, the controller, who managed SCLC's finances and payroll. He reported regularly to his FBI handler on all aspects of SCLC operations, paid ten thousand dollars per year. Harrison's duplicity was not revealed until much later. Undoubtedly other spies were secreted in SCLC at lower levels and in the field.

Recruiting of PPC participants in northern and southern cities was already slowed down by field organizers' lack of clarity and commitment. The FBI's espionage and disinformation took a further toll, especially in the South. In Birmingham the network of informants spread the lie that PPC participants would have their welfare benefits cut off. By March SCLC recruiters had signed up only forty Birmingham blacks. While the South was lagging, they did better in northern cities. In Philadelphia SCLC staff tripled their quota of two hundred. PPC coordinator Bernard Lafayette brought in seasoned organizers from the American Friends Service Committee (AFSC) and endorsement by a slew of religious and community associations in D.C. and an impressive roster of national groups.

Despite public words to the contrary, King was worried about the Poor People's Campaign, intensified by his underlying gloom. He feared that because of faltering progress, they would have to delay or even cancel the spring campaign.

"There's no masses in this mass movement," he complained. "We are not doing our homework," he chided staff leaders in a mid-February meeting recorded by FBI informant Harrison. "We have not gotten off the ground as far as engaging in the enormous job ahead. I am disturbed about the fact that our staff has not gotten to the people we are talking about, the hard-core poor people.

"If we cannot do it, I would rather pull out now. The embarrassment and criticism would be much less now than if we went to Washington with about three hundred people."[118] His colleagues tried to convince him that things were not so bleak. They debated what to do, whether to stop or go forward. They reached consensus on Lafayette's proposal that if they did not garner enough volunteers by April 1 they would postpone the campaign but not call it off. King barnstormed through Mississippi and Alabama to jazz things up at rallies and mass meetings.

The Poor People's Campaign got a timely lift at the end of February when the National Commission on Civil Disorders, chaired by Illinois governor Otto Kerner, issued its five-inch-thick, fourteen-hundred-page report. Johnson set up the commission immediately after the Detroit riot to investigate the causes and prevention of urban violence. After three months of hearings with 130 witnesses, including King, the commission concluded: "Our nation is moving toward two societies, one black, one white—separate and unequal. Reaction to last summer's disorders has quickened the movement and deepened the division. To pursue our present course will involve the continuing polarization of the American community and, ultimately, the destruction of basic democratic values.

"What white Americans have never fully understood—but what the Negro can never forget—is that white society is deeply implicated in the ghetto. White institutions created it, white institutions maintain it, and white society condones it."

Their proposed solution was nearly as blunt: a commitment to national action, "compassionate, massive and sustained. From every American it will require new attitudes, new understanding, and above all, new will. Hard choices must be made, and if necessary, new taxes enacted." The middle class would have to sacrifice in order to save the ghettos. Large-scale programs to meet the problem "will require unprecedented levels of funding and performance. There can be no higher priority for national action and no higher claim on the nation's conscience."[119]

The damning report delivered extra clout because the eleven commission members were moderate to conservative, with not a single community leader from the inner city. Black leaders across the board praised the document, especially the admission that white racism was the fundamental problem. King and Whitney Young pointed out that they had urged similar remedies for several years—the former's Bill of Rights for the Disadvantaged and the latter's domestic Marshall Plan. SNCC chief Rap Brown, in a New Orleans jail under high bail on a weapons charge, proclaimed that commission members "should be put in jail under one hundred thousand dollars' bail each, because they're saying essentially what I've been saying."

King stated that the report was "a physician's warning of the approaching death of American society, with a prescription to life." It showed how "the lives, the incomes, the well-being of poor people everywhere in America are plundered by our economic system," and proved "the absolute necessity of our spring campaign in Washington." He announced that the PPC would kick off in late April.

"We believe the highest patriotism demands the ending of the war and the opening of a bloodless war to final victory over racism and poverty," he said. "Flame throwers in Vietnam fan the flames in our cities. I don't think the two matters can be separated." While he and other leaders would lobby Washington officials, three thousand people of color in a mule train of wagons would start out for the capital from the Mississippi Delta, retracing paths famously trod by protesters.[120]

President Johnson ignored his own advisory commission's recommendations. He was unhappy that the Kerner commission failed to praise his war on poverty and refuted his conviction that the riots were caused by a black radical conspiracy, probably communist inspired. Funds that might have gone toward removing the causes went to arm local police forces with high-tech arsenals of tanks, personnel carriers, machine guns, nerve gas, and other weapons of mass suppression.

13

Despite the good news of the Kerner gospel, King continued to spiral downward. Abernathy accompanied him on a brief getaway to Acapulco, where, fraught with fear about the Washington campaign, he could not relax or sleep. While his staff was reluctantly following his marching orders, SCLC board members and other allies blasted him with confidential criticism. His toughest in-house critic was board officer Marian Logan from New York, who feared that the PPC would stiffen congressional resistance and help elect reactionary candidates, moving Congress and the presidency further to the right. Like others she worried about confused aims, poor planning, and the propensity for violence. Public attacks did not let up. In Michigan he suffered the worst heckling of his life by rightwing protesters, yelling "Commie!" and "Traitor!"

Traveling in Los Angeles, "he felt that his time was up," an aide recalled. He said he knew that they were going to get him. His inner circle felt that his depression was deeper and more serious than before, that his obsession with his dying amounted to a death wish, to escape his torments and tormentors.

"You think I'm paranoid, don't you?" he had asked Rustin, when they were still talking.

"Sometimes I do, Martin," his old friend replied. Young, Rutherford, and Dorothy Cotton believed that his free-falling depression was more spiritual than emotional. Clinging for dear life to his nonviolent faith, he was beginning to doubt that it could save his nation. Cotton thought the turning point was his vilification the year before for denouncing the war. "That whole last year I felt his weariness, just weariness of the struggle, that he had done all that he could do."

He appeared "a profoundly weary and wounded spirit," Justice Department official Roger Wilkins recalled. A "profound sadness" had engulfed him.[121] He also seemed, despite his caring extended family and many friends, a desperately lonely man.

MORE THAN EVER his best therapy was sermonizing, especially preaching to himself, about himself, confessing to God. Yet he was always, at the same time, preaching to the world, about the world, delivering the words of God. On March 3, 1968, shaky of soul, losing his equilibrium, he preached a sermon about shattered dreams.

"Approaching the darkness, living in the shadow, perhaps anticipating the elusive, eternal light," his friend Vincent Harding wrote years later, "our brother needed to share these words of self-reflection, confession, and hope. Where better than at Ebenezer, with the congregation that had known him before he knew himself, the extended family of faith whose love could provide a space for their internationally renowned son to come home and say things that only a compassionate family could receive? Where everyone could see the implacable opposition and the shadow of death that seemed to envelop him."[122]

King had seen his dream of beloved community turn into a nightmare of chaos, of nihilism. He was struggling now to transform the dream turned nightmare into a new dream, a bolder dream, powerful enough to recast the nightmare into a new morning. But was the temple he was trying to build, of justice and love, unbuildable? He took refuge in God's soothing words to King David: "Thou didst well that it was within thine heart."[123]

But what if one's heart was sick with sin? Would that pollute the dream? He pointed out in his sermon, as he had so many times before, that forces of good and evil were locked in a cosmic death dance, though good would ultimately prevail. Every human being internalized this struggle.

"And in every one of us this morning, there's a war going on. (*Yes, sir*) It's a civil war. (*Yes, sir*) There is a civil war going on in your life. Every time you set out to be good, there's something pulling on you, telling you to be evil. (*Preach it*) Every time you set out to love, something keeps pulling on you, trying to get you to hate. (*Yes. Yes, sir*) There is a schizophrenia. There are times that all of us know somehow that there is a Mr. Hyde and a Dr. Jekyll in us.

"I want you to know this morning that I'm a sinner like all of God's children. But I want to be a good man. (*Yes. Preach it*)"

In an earlier sermon he had probed the nature of one's lower self, one's devilish domain, first with sexual temptation.

"Sex is sacred," he had said. "It's beautiful, it's holy." But "if one becomes a slave to sex, you can never satisfy it! And then the long road of promiscuity comes along. And then you discover what hell is. Hell is God giving a man what he thought he wanted. When you get it, you discover you don't want it any longer, and you move on and you get something else. Whenever you become a slave to a drive, you can never satisfy it.

"It's a strange mixture in all of us, isn't it? You'll do what's right most of the time, but every now and then you'll do some wrong. You'll be faithful to that and those that you should be faithful to most of the time. But every now and then you'll be unfaithful to those you should be faithful to.

"Do you know that there is a bit of a coward in the bravest of us, and a bit of a hero in the meanest of us? There is much good in the worst of us, and so much bad in the best of us."

In this sermon he retold the parable of the prodigal son, hinting that he himself had been wastefully extravagant, especially in stockpiling acclaim and fame, accumulating glory. Even the extravagance of a perhaps unrealizable dream that raised false hopes for millions and dashed them.

But in his March 1968 homily he reassured his flock and himself that God judged all of them by "the total bent of our lives." God required that your heart was right. "Salvation isn't reaching the destination of absolute morality, but it's being in the process and on the right road."

One found salvation in the heartfelt struggle to keep one's higher self right side up.

For King the road to redemption was to return from the "far country," the dark places of physical and spiritual extravagance, to repent for his sins and come home—coming home to Ebenezer, his birthplace, his fount of baptism.

For America, the road to redemption was to come home from the "tragic far country" of racism, war, and poverty amid plenty.

"There's a famine in this country, a moral and spiritual famine, because somewhere America strayed away from home. I can hear the voice of God saying, 'America, it isn't too late if you will only come to yourself.'" Like his own country, King had to slough off the waste, empty himself of extravagance, of his overflow of ego, and find the courage to walk humbly with his God. King and his country had to follow the same road to salvation.[124]

14

On March 1, 1968, corporate lawyer Clark Clifford took over as secretary of defense. As we have seen, McNamara's mounting misgivings about Vietnam had estranged him from LBJ and his shrinking inner circle. No one had been a more loyal friend. The President had been utterly dependent upon him. In McNamara's words, they "loved and respected each other."[125] His disaffection from the war they had managed together was a grievous blow to the commander-in-chief.

The breaking point was a memo McNamara wrote to the President one week after October's Pentagon protest. "Continuation of our present course of action in Southeast Asia," he concluded, "would be dangerous, costly in lives, and unsatisfactory to the American people." He doubted that they could "maintain our efforts in South Vietnam for the time necessary to accomplish our objectives."[126] Johnson eased his departure by sending him off to run the World Bank. But McNamara's no less disgruntled lieutenants remained at their watches. These dissenters, led by assistant secretary Paul Warnke and his deputy Morton Halperin, saw Clifford's arrival as a crucial chance to rethink Vietnam policy.

Clifford was the quintessential cold warrior, a key Washington power broker who had advised Truman, Kennedy, and Johnson on foreign policy. Although little known to the public, he had been a kingpin of the national security elite, author of the Truman doctrine of communist containment in 1947. At that time, he reminisced later, he and other policy makers "had this feeling that we could control the future of the world."[127] LBJ respected him no less than he had McNamara.

In the aftermath of the Tet offensive General William Westmoreland, American commander in Vietnam, requested the President for two hundred thousand additional troops. Over half a million U.S. forces were already swamping South Vietnam. Westmoreland admitted later that he intended to use the infusion of troops for an invasion of North Vietnam he had been secretly planning; and he wanted to expand the ground war into Cambodia and Laos. The war's biggest troop request was the punch line of a report by General Earle Wheeler, chairman of the Joint Chiefs of Staff, after his latest Vietnam visit. It was the military's first pessimistic assessment of the war's progress.

President Johnson set up a task force under Clifford to advise him on the post-Tet crisis. The Pentagon doves felt that the portentous troop call, on the heels of the offensive, marked a watershed between all-out escalation and scaling down the war. They fought hard for a defensive strategy and negotiations. Making a clean start, Clifford might have the clout to begin the colossal job of turning the war around.

The Clifford task force agreed that further escalation of the ground war would mean activating at least 250,000 reserves and substantially upping draft calls. Air force secretary Townsend Hoopes and others pressed the view that mobilizing the nation for what was still officially a limited war, for dubious aims, would have disastrous effects on the country's economy, politics, and social fabric.

Assistant defense secretary Phil Goulding argued that if the troop requisition were granted, requiring bloated draft calls and mobilizing reserves, "the shock wave would run through the entire American body politic. The antiwar demonstrations and resistance to the draft would rise to new crescendos, reinforced by civil rights groups who would feel the President had once again revealed his inner conviction that the war in Vietnam was more important than the war on poverty."[128]

Hoopes fired a memo to Clifford titled "The Infeasibility of Military Victory," stating that the war was "eroding the moral fiber of the nation, demoralizing its politics, and paralyzing its foreign policy." More troops "would intensify the domestic disaffection, which would be reflected in increasing defiance of the draft and widespread unrest in the cities."[129]

Another element came into play—the specter of nuclear warfare. Five thousand U.S. marines were encircled by North Vietnamese forces at the mountain stronghold of Khe Sanh. In a White House luncheon Joint Chiefs chairman Wheeler was unable to reassure the commander-in-chief that the siege of Khe Sanh could be lifted without using tactical nuclear weapons. Wheeler reportedly told senators that he would recommend their use at Khe Sanh if needed. Senator J. William Fulbright and other war critics denounced this option.[130]

General Westmoreland had set up a secret group to examine using battlefield nukes, in particular at Khe Sanh, where "civilian casualties would be minimal." In his 1976 memoir he wrote that if Washington officials were determined to send a message to Hanoi, "surely small tactical nuclear weapons would be a way to tell Hanoi something. Use of a few small tactical nuclear weapons in Vietnam—or even the threat of them—might have quickly brought the war there to an end." Fearing a leak, his superiors told Westmoreland to can nuclear planning. "I felt at the time and even more so now that to fail to consider this alternative was a mistake."[131] During late winter 1968 anxiety about this frightful alternative inflamed war opposition both on the street and in official corridors. Would the Vietnam intervention deter the holocaust of World War III, or trigger it?

The Clifford task force ended up pushing another round of incremental escalation—more of the same. The blockbuster troop request did not win out, but Warnke's proposal for de-escalation was vetoed under heated pressure from the Joint Chiefs. Although the task force supported giving the military much of what it wanted, the painstaking efforts of Warnke and other dissenters paid off. By the strange logic of bureaucratic physics, defeat augured victory, or the illusion of victory. The rough-and-tumble debate convinced the new defense czar that the policy must change. He knew how to reach his embattled friend in the Oval Office.

Clifford convened a meeting of the "Wise Men"—pillars of the national security establishment such as Dean Acheson, McGeorge Bundy, and Cyrus Vance—who had counseled LBJ on Vietnam and had backed him to the hilt. Now they informed him that his war was bankrupt. The cost, political, fiscal, and moral, was too high. Vance, a future secretary of state, disclosed later that a key factor in their turnabout was the Wise Men's alarm that the "divisiveness in the country was growing with such acuteness that it was threatening to tear the United States apart."[132]

THE WINTER SAW a slackening in the antiwar movement's effort to raise the social cost of the war. Some of its volatile energy was absorbed by electoral challenges and other moderate peace activism, such as the clergy's Washington protest. Younger activists were furiously preparing for expected upheaval in the spring; the Student Mobilization Committee was organizing "ten days of resistance" for April on campuses nationwide. Some activists, like King, were struggling to choose between fighting against the war, and fighting against racial injustice at home.

In its national office and multitude of local chapters, Students for a Democratic Society was torn once again. Since summer and fall 1967 many members had begun to see SDS as a revolutionary vanguard. SDSers were rushing to adopt Marxist-Leninist mind-sets, partly to counter an invasion of disciplined cadres from the Maoist Progressive Labor Party intent on taking over. A majority of chapters had decided to work with constituencies other than white students, especially "third world" groups of color. After rancorous debate in Lexington, Kentucky, in late March, the SDS National Council voted for schizophrenia: letting chapters decide whether to focus on the war or racism, while committing the organization to support "the black struggle for liberation."

ON MARCH 12, two weeks before LBJ's fateful meeting with the Wise Men, Senator Eugene McCarthy came close to beating him in the New Hampshire presidential primary, garnering 42 percent of the vote and most delegates. The pious-sounding, poetry-writing Minnesota senator and his battalions of well-groomed student volunteers had campaigned for an end to "Johnson's War." The Tet offensive not only shook up the White House and Pentagon and vitalized the antiwar movement, but it transfigured the presidential race just taking off. Since the past summer, the "Dump Johnson" movement had been searching for a viable candidate to challenge LBJ in the spring primaries on a forthright antiwar platform. When dream candidate Kennedy demurred, Al Lowenstein and associates turned to McCarthy, who took the plunge in late fall 1967. But McCarthy's campaign was slow to catch fire; in January it seemed almost moribund. Tet turned it around. In the weeks leading up to the New Hampshire vote it became a young people's crusade. Scruffy antiwar protesters were even willing to cut their long locks and get "clean for Gene."

McCarthy's remarkable showing in the Granite State did not surprise Kennedy, who had been agonizing for weeks over whether to run. He knew how weak Johnson was on the war. Despite opposition from all of his close advisers, including younger brother and Senate colleague, Ted, he decided to go for it just before the March 12 primary and told McCarthy. His colleague's success strengthened RFK's belief that his own entry would not be seen as a vendetta against LBJ. His campaign would not divide the Democratic Party because it was already split.

Kennedy tried a last-ditch effort to sway LBJ from the inside. He met with Clifford to get him to urge Johnson to set up a presidential commission on Vietnam, like that on the summer riots, that would include RFK. Johnson refused, knowing that this would provide a potent platform for his arch-rival to attack him on Vietnam. He did not want to grease the rail for RFK to challenge his renomination and recapture the glory of Camelot. Four days after the first primary (after putting a call in to King), Kennedy threw his hat into the ring.

He seemed to feel real anguish about the war, strangely divorced from political calculations. It was partly driven by guilt. As JFK's closest adviser, he had been a cheerleader for the intervention and headed up the Special Group Counter-Insurgency that oversaw it. RFK had matured during the painful odyssey since his brother's death four years before. During a tumultuous time the "ruthless" tough-skinned attorney general had evolved into a conscientious, if still cautious, advocate of peace and racial justice, showing heartfelt compassion for the people of Indochina and for America's poor.

The multiracial, multiclass coalition that Kennedy sought to build could politically empower the bottom-up alliance of the disadvantaged that King envisioned. Through Marian Wright and other activists, the King and Kennedy staffs had already linked arms on the PPC. King felt hopeful about RFK's candidacy, which would not only bolster his crusade for the poor, putting it on the national agenda, but relieve pressure on him to push harder against the war, freeing him to concentrate on poverty. For better or worse RFK would become the messiah of the peace movement, the role King had reluctantly relinquished. The senator had the added asset of appealing to the white working class, King's nemesis in Chicago and the South. For the first time the preacher was ready to break his long-standing rule of not endorsing a presidential candidate. He had supported neither John Kennedy nor (formally) LBJ.

"We've got to get behind Bobby now that he's in," he told Washington SCLC leader Walter Fauntroy.[133]

What about the Republicans? Normally in a presidential election the opposition party made the biggest ruckus. This time they took a backseat to the Democrats' civil war. The GOP was handicapped by an oversupply of stars. Front-runner Richard Nixon was hotly pursued by New York governor Nelson Rockefeller, Hollywood emanation Ronald Reagan, Michigan governor George Romney, made famous by the Detroit riot, and Illinois senator Charles Percy.

George Wallace had been running for almost a year, under the banner of his one-man American Independent Party. He had challenged LBJ once before, in the Democratic primaries of 1964, and his anti–civil rights harangues had played well in the North. Barred from succeeding himself as Alabama governor in 1966, he got his wife, Lurleen, elected in his place. The trouble was that she had been secretly diagnosed with uterine cancer in late 1965. A physician had told him four years before that his wife had a cancerous condition; he opted not to tell her. She grew sicker during her ceremonial governorship run by him. Although he did not let her illness stymie his presidential ambition, her rapid deterioration in late winter 1968 forced him to pause until after her death in early May. He then revved up his campaign for "law and order" and Vietnam victory. In November, when Nixon beat Humphrey, Wallace took votes from both to capture the Deep South and 13 percent of the popular ballot, nearly making his goal of throwing the race into the House of Representatives. Despite his "party" being only paper, he was the most formidable third-party challenger since Teddy Roosevelt helped elect Woodrow Wilson in 1912.

ONE REASON that King's staff dragged their feet in organizing the Washington campaign, and that he chafed at them, was the irrepressible spirit of black nationalism that had taken hold within SCLC, especially among field organizers. When King lost his temper with Rutherford and others for questioning nonviolence, his chagrin was linked to the staff's flirtation with separatist black liberation, itself a violation of nonviolence as unifying and all-inclusive, as breaking down walls. While not separatist, SCLC had always been a black organization (with a handful of token white organizers), unlike SNCC and CORE, which had earlier been biracial, or the NAACP, which continued to be. King himself showed occasional black nationalist tendencies; he might be described as a minimal nationalist. Key staff leaders rationalized their involvement in multiracial coalition building—which included whites—only by stressing the vanguard role that black activists would play, first among equals.

In recruiting black participants, Hosea Williams, the campaign's field director, downplayed the multiracial aspect and stressed that the PPC was (as it surely was) a new front in the struggle for black freedom, to be led by black people.[134] Williams and other staff members were more interested in building a multiclass coalition of blacks than a multiracial coalition of the poor. He wrote to Atlanta activists that "some of us are defined as radicals, some as moderates and others as 'Uncle Toms.' But we are all inextricably bound—we are Black; each of us are flesh of one another's flesh and blood of one another's blood."[135] Unifying blacks across class lines might mean toning down the PPC's rhetoric and demands in order to attract the black middle class. This nationalist bias took a toll on the PPC's outreach and nonblack recruitment.

Because SCLC was organizing the campaign, and African Americans were the primary constituency, numbers alone would necessitate that black activists be dominant. Blacks were the majority of the organized poor, such as in the welfare rights movement. Switching their consciousness from a black-centered movement to a true poor people's movement was not easy for some SCLC staffers. One candidly confessed at a staff meeting: "I do not think I am at the point where a Mexican can sit in and call strategy on a steering committee."[136]

Pulling in poor whites might be especially tricky. An AFSC organizer in eastern Kentucky wrote Andy Young that the Appalachian poor "even less than the Mexican-Americans or the Indians see the reality of their common cause with the black poor." She argued that SCLC "will need to involve in some of the decision-making processes representatives of other poor groups if their cooperation is to be a reality."[137]

The United States in 1968 was still a nation of white and black. Other racial minorities (Latinos, Asians, and American Indians), which combined did not yet equal half of the black population of 22 million, were relatively invisible, along with poor whites, who were in fact the majority of poor people. So when King called an Atlanta meeting in which fifty-three nonblack organizations made a "declaration of unanimous support" for the PPC, it was a breakthrough of major proportions, the high point of the entire campaign. Seventy-eight leaders from seventeen states represented Chicano organizations from the Southwest, United Farm Workers (UFW), American Indian groups, Puerto Ricans, Appalachians, welfare rights, labor unions, tenant unions, inner-city community coalitions, and faith-based activists. Only Asian Americans seemed to be missing from the rainbow.[138]

The meeting was a dream come true for Myles Horton from Highlander in Tennessee. "I believe we caught a glimpse of the future," he wrote to Young, "the making of a bottom-up coalition." He counseled SCLC to break away from its centralized mode and encourage autonomous actions in Washington by Mexican Americans and others, sharing the limelight.[139]

King heralded "the beginning of a new cooperation, understanding, and a determination by poor people of all colors" to achieve economic security. "Delegates repeatedly pointed out that the established powers of rich America have deliberately exploited poor people by isolating them in ethnic, nationality, religious, and racial groups." A white delegate stated that it wasn't the poor people "who are responsible for hatred in our country, but the powerful economic and political managers who want to keep us down. We will no longer permit them to divide us."[140]

King hoped that participants' racial identity would buttress their identity as a class, the class of the poor—not to undermine the emerging identity politics but to raise it to a higher level, give it more reach and clout. This new coalition or "true alliance," both class and race based, would be a creative synthesis combining the strengths of the old civil rights coalition with those of the new politics of liberation.

Right after this meeting King embarked on what was planned as a nineteen-day, nineteen-city tour to hold grassroots hearings to learn about grievances, meet with community leaders, and push recruitment. The Deep South, heartland of poverty, would get special attention. Flying over Mississippi's hills and molehills by small plane, King fired up rallies in eight cities and towns, ending up in Jackson at 4 A.M. after a twenty-one-hour day pressing the flesh. He campaigned as hard as any presidential candidate.

He exhorted whole families of Delta blacks to descend on Washington to "plague Congress and the President until they do something." In the Delta town of Marks in Quitman County, poorest in the nation, he stood at a pulpit listening to locals' cries for help. In this county many survived on wild rabbits and berries. Children didn't know the feel of shoes. He listened to mothers plead for "shoes and a decent education" for their kids. "Johnson said when he come in he was going to wipe out poverty, ignorance and disease," one black woman shouted. "Now where's our money?"

"It's criminal for people to have to live in these conditions," he replied. "I am very deeply touched. God does not want you to live like you are living."[141] He and his entourage visited a day-care center.

"There was one apple," Abernathy remembered, "and they took this apple and cut it into four pieces for four hungry waiting students. And when Dr. King saw that is all they had for lunch," he cried. "The tears came streaming down his cheek. He had to leave the room."[142]

Before they left Marks, a rough-hewn white fellow handed King a crisp one-hundred-dollar bill to help with the campaign.

Several hundred black Mississippians and Alabamians filled out registration forms to join up for the long trek to Washington. Most were women; many had been involved in civil rights work, active in the Freedom Democratic Party, arrested in past protests. They spelled out their motives in plain English.

Virgia Mary Genes scribbled on her form: "i have 6 children no one to suport them But me and I don't have a job and they wont give me one. and i need a job Bad."

Mrs. Louella Wright: "for mony, better housing and more jobs and better streets and I want land."

Vonell Jamison, twenty-one: "So I can get what belong to me and my right to."

Mrs. Rose Kendrick of Marks, fifty-five, put it all together: "For jobs money decent house to live in and some land. poor people do not even get respect as human being. I dont have no job. I don't have any money. I am hungry. I need clouths. My house is falling in. Congressmen you have the job and you have the money. I want some of it so i can live to."[143]

THE CAMPAIGN'S ANTIPOVERTY GOALS were still not as clear as SCLC staff and board wanted, or as poor people expected. In early February the staff announced a set of legislative objectives with multibillion-dollar price tags to achieve full employment and a guaranteed income, but nothing that caught the public's imagination. King was not as concerned about specific reforms as he was about forging a national consensus behind what he conceived to be a universal right of citizenship, authorized by the Declaration of Independence with its inalienable right to pursue happiness, for a livable income for all citizens, provided directly by the government if someone could not work.[144]

Thus the PPC called for an "economic and social bill of rights" featuring a "meaningful job at a living wage" and "secure and adequate income for all who cannot find jobs or for whom employment is inappropriate."[145] He did not consider this human right a one-way street, a bureaucratic dole that would deepen dependence. He believed that entitlement to income support, for those who were not employed, entailed the responsibility of community service or some contribution to social betterment. Although he was a far cry from a feminist, and didn't think much about gender discrimination, his sensitivity to the unpaid labor of housewives (like his own wife's) caused him to consider that the right to an income might encompass child rearing and house-work.[146]

In his many speeches to build this true alliance of the poor, King harped on the fact that the government had granted such economic rights to white people for at least as long as slavery had been abolished. While the freed slaves were denied "forty acres and a mule," whites set-tling the West were given four times that acreage plus credit, technical services, land-grant colleges, and of course railroads. Since the New Deal white farmers were paid billions not to grow crops while their black and brown neighbors, some dependent on those fallow fields, went hungry. Taxpayers (including the working poor) paid for the free-ways that took middle-class whites from suburban homes to city jobs and pleasures. The tax system, notably the home-mortgage interest deduction, heavily favored property owners. It was socialism for the rich and middle class, King emphasized, cutthroat capitalism for the rest. Special preferences for the already advantaged. Poor people were com-ing to Washington to claim "what is ours," their fair share of the national harvest.

For twelve years King had been able to straddle the barbed wire between direct action and electoral politics. Now the tumult of 1968 and criticism by friends, private and public, were forcing him to make a painful choice. It might have been different had it not been a presiden-tial election year, which always tended to disrupt grassroots activism. But King could not wait until after the election. This dilemma partly reflected the ethic of immediacy so pervasive at the time, and the fric-tion between immediate results (freedom *now*, end the war *now*) and the realism to pursue a step-by-step, longer-term strategy. King's imme-diatism was driven not only by the still escalating war and urban explo-sions, but by the apocalyptic mood all around and by his steadily sinking depression and strong premonition that death was nearing. He knew he didn't have much time. He had to get results.

But something more was at stake that was the antithesis of immediacy. He was determined as well to strike a blow for the long haul. From his perspective it was presidential politics as much as rock throwing that was driven by short-run thinking. He felt acutely the urgency to dump Johnson. In fact he had come to see that this might be the quickest way to end the war. The McCarthy and Kennedy campaigns were bearing this out. But real change, fundamental change, would take more time. He wanted to send a message to posterity, a prophecy for the ages.

Nonviolent mass action, he believed, was the most fruitful means not only to end immediate evils but to bring about social regeneration, and not only in his own country. Replacing the president might bring peace for a season; it might even, for a time, still the troubled waters of racial strife. But electing a new president, even the prince of Camelot, was not more than a short-term expedient. It was militant mass action (with electoral politics playing an intermediate role) that would reshape history, that would make the revolution for human rights and economic justice, that would enable men and women to set foot as new people in a new land. Racked with doubts about so many things, he held fast to his faith that the fateful choice was between nonviolent revolution and barbarism, between nonviolence and nonexistence.

But none of this dialectical thinking made much sense to board secretary Marian Logan. King called her almost daily to get her to withdraw her criticisms of the PPC, which she had communicated to the SCLC board. His board members did not usually rock the boat. Andy Young wrote her that "we are too far gone to turn around. This is very much a faith venture."[147] Spending the night with Logan and her husband in their New York apartment, King argued with Marian until dawn, downing one tumbler after another until he was quite drunk and her husband told him to desist. They had drunk and argued before, but this time it was different, she recalled. King careened from anger to grave anxiety to icy calm as he sought to convince her that the Washington campaign was right, his certitude betrayed by his taut, nervous body language. His sense of humor was a shambles. She thought he was "losing hold."[148]

He canceled his morning events in New York because he was so exhausted and hung over. "I've been getting two hours' sleep a night for the last ten days," he told reporters when he lunched with a welfare mom in her shabby Harlem tenement.[149]

We should not forget that there were moments in the Birmingham movement and in Selma when things looked nearly as bleak. In fact, by the first day of spring, when King was most downhearted, the Poor People's Campaign was finally charging up. Most of the chosen cities had recruited their two hundred volunteers, and some had done much better. Backing and money continued to pour in from organizations all over. While the leaders at the top were having jitters and second thoughts, the field staff were pulling rabbits out of their hats.

By one measure it had already won—shaking up the higher circles. Washington officialdom was terrified that the PPC might ignite a spasm of rioting in the capital. Attorney General Ramsey Clark reported later that high officials were panic-stricken and paranoid. Congress members lashed King and the PPC and urged that the protests, though protected by the Constitution, be banned as a danger to national security. The FBI stepped up its maneuvers to sabotage the PPC. Hoover directed his field offices to go all out against "the most violent and radical groups," SCLC foremost. The agency's mission: to "prevent the rise of a 'messiah' who could unify, and electrify, the militant black nationalist movement." Preventive measures were left undefined. Hoover advised that King was the leading candidate for this position, along with Stokely Carmichael.[150]

Looking back, Andy Young was convinced that the White House and the FBI were determined to stop the Poor People's Campaign by any means necessary. "We had become the enemy."[151]

15

Now it was the disciples' turn to get mad at their messiah.

Amid the first swing of his "people to people" tour of the nation to drum up support for the PPC, King got a phone call from Rev. James Lawson, pastor of Centenary Methodist Church in Memphis, SCLC board member, and head of SCLC's Memphis affiliate. A decade before, he had been kicked out of Vanderbilt divinity school for teaching nonviolent methods to a new generation of young activists—Diane Nash, John Lewis, Jim Bevel, Bernard Lafayette, and other trailblazers—who built the Nashville movement and then SNCC. No one in the movement except Rustin had as much expertise in nonviolent techniques. Lawson asked King, who had also gotten pointers from him, if he would speak to a mass rally of striking sanitation workers in Memphis while traveling through the nearby Delta country.

Thirteen hundred black workers, members of an AFSCME public employees' local, had been striking for five weeks, since Lincoln's birthday, to win union recognition by the city. The strike was brought on by long-running discrimination and measly pay (with no benefits), but precipitated by two rainy-day incidents. Two workers were pulverized by their compactor when they took refuge from a storm in the back of their garbage truck; unlike white workers, they were not permitted to sit out rain in the cab. During another storm black sewer workers were sent home without pay; white workers were paid.

Despite their just grievances, the newly elected mayor, Henry Loeb, adamantly refused to recognize their union local and allow a dues checkoff to make it viable. A peaceful protest organized by Lawson and other community leaders was attacked by police, who sprayed Mace on workers and ministers alike. In response Lawson and colleagues created a support group, Community on the Move for Equality (COME), that organized rallies, marches, and a boycott of downtown businesses. The workers' slogan: "I am a man." They invited in nationally known black leaders such as Rustin and Roy Wilkins to build solidarity. King was the prize.

Lawson lured his friend in part by stressing how the Memphis strike reprised the southern movement at its best—huge rallies, wide community support, strict adherence to nonviolence. Nothing like it since the Montgomery bus boycott. The strike epitomized the interplay of racial and class oppression that was the whole point of the Poor People's Campaign. More important, it was a place where nonviolent struggle was still respected and still working—or so King thought. He agreed to speak at a rally the next day, March 18.

Andy Young and other SCLC leaders hit the roof. Here he had single-mindedly corralled all of them to throw in with the PPC, against their collective better judgment, insisting that they drop everything, put their cherished projects on hold. Now he was abandoning the PPC recruitment effort at a crucial juncture, just when momentum was finally hitting its stride.

"There was just a tremendous organizing job," Young recalled, "and I didn't know how you could take on anything else."

"Well, Jim Lawson has been around for so long," the chief replied, "and here are garbage workers on strike. He just wants me to come in and make a speech, and I'll be right back."[152] If the past was any guide, the staff well knew, going off to make a speech, as in Albany or St. Augustine, led to embroilment, often with an unhappy ending. Despite their angry pleading, they could not change his mind. For him it was win-win: the striking workers would get national attention, and he would dramatize the cruelty of race-based poverty. He saw it as not a diversion from the Poor People's Campaign but the blastoff.

King spoke to fifteen thousand excited people who packed prodigious Mason Temple church, the largest indoor crowd he had ever roused in the South. He felt right away the mood and makings of a great people's movement.

"One day our society will come to respect the sanitation worker if it is to survive, for the person who picks up our garbage is just as significant as the physician. For if he doesn't do his job, disease is rampant. And you are reminding not only Memphis but the nation that it is a crime for people to live in this rich nation and receive starvation wages." He and the assembly merged in call and response. Their cheers grew wilder as he swayed to his climax.

"You know what?" He talked as though fifteen thousand souls had gathered in his living room. "You may have to escalate the struggle a bit. If they keep refusing, I tell you what you ought to demand, and you're together here enough to do it. In a few days you ought to get together and just have a general work stoppage in the city of Memphis." He set off an explosion of human will, thunderous clapping and whooping sparked by the lightning vision of victory.

"You let that day come and not a Negro in this city will go to any job downtown, not a Negro in domestic service will go to anybody's kitchen, black students will not go to anybody's school."[153] He was inciting nonviolent insurrection.

Despite the jubilant mood, maybe because he felt so at home with these folk, he couldn't help but lift the veil on his inner self: "Sometimes I feel discouraged," he admitted, "having to live under the threat of death every day, having to take so much abuse and criticism, sometimes from my own people. Sometimes I feel discouraged." But he said he could always count on the holy spirit to resuscitate his soul.[154]

King's aides were frantically conferring with Lawson and other Memphis leaders behind the pulpit. After King sat down to roaring applause, Abernathy suggested that perhaps they might all march down to city hall that night. Then King came back and announced that he and SCLC would return in a few days to lead a march to turn the mayor around. The strikers had been steadily losing hope with one frustration after another. He had restored their hope.

AFSCME organizer Bill Lucy was astonished by King's ability, in the heat of oratorical passion, not only to connect intimately with the mammoth audience but to get what the conflict was about. "He had not been there before," Lucy recalled, "and he had had the most minimal of briefings. But he clearly understood that the struggle was really about a new kind of people, who worked forty hours a week and still lived in poverty."[155] He made their battle legitimate, just, and God-sent.

The first try for the march and work stoppage was called off because of a bizarre snowstorm that dumped record snow on a city that rarely saw any. "The Lord has done it again," COME leader Rev. Ralph Jackson quipped. "It's a white world!"[156]

Rescheduled for Thursday morning, March 28, the big march was delayed getting started because King's flight was late. Lawson insisted on waiting until he arrived. Earlier, violence had broken out at a black high school when teachers and police tried to keep students from leaving for the protest. The march, King and Abernathy up front, had been moving only a few minutes along Beale Street, where W. C. Handy had built the blues, when marchers heard the sound of shattering glass coming from the rear. Shouting "Black Power!" several dozen youths, some stoned on wine or drugs, darted out of the main body to smash store windows with poster sticks and grab armfuls of shoes, stereos, portable TVs, and musical instruments. Then they would hide back among the marchers.

Just before police moved in with shotguns and gas, Lawson ordered the march to turn around and for King to be spirited away. Abernathy, Bernard Lee, and others swept him up, commandeered a car from an agreeable black woman, and whisked him out of harm's way. A motorcycle cop led them to the Holiday Inn on the Mississippi River—too dangerous to stay downtown.

Although the march had turned back, cops arrested a few hundred, mostly peaceful protesters or bystanders. About two hundred stores had windows broken, but most had not been entered. At worst it was a mini-riot, lasting hardly more than an hour. Mayor Loeb nonetheless declared a state of emergency and called in four thousand national guard, who patrolled the streets in armored personnel carriers. Besides many injured, a cop killed a sixteen-year-old boy with a shotgun blast against his chest. His mother claimed he had his hands up. King and Abernathy glumly watched the denouement on TV in their plush hotel suite.

If ever King needed the holy spirit to rescue him, this was the time.

Abernathy had accompanied his friend through countless low ebbs, but he had never seen him so distressed, almost catatonic. King knew how the media would eat him alive, the eulogies for nonviolent protest, the warnings that the PPC would unleash greater violence, the denunciations of his inability to control a protest, the chorus of catcalls for the PPC to be canceled. When Lawson and other COME leaders arrived at the motel, King was in bed, fully clothed, covers pulled over him, metaphor of his fear and vulnerability, covering up his naked exposure.

Lawson and fellow leaders apologized for the debacle but blamed a militant black group called the Invaders, with whom they had had a stormy relationship. King had not been told about this group, nor of any significant black militancy in Memphis. He told the Memphis leaders that the Invaders could no longer be ostracized; they would have to be included and an understanding worked out.

He was devastated that, for the first time, a march he had led—for once it was actually his own idea—turned violent, even though less than 1 percent of participants had broken discipline. And that a boy, possibly innocent of wrongdoing, had been killed.

Many previous SCLC marches had provoked police or white mob violence, of course; they could not have succeeded without it. But this was not the first SCLC-led protest in which some participants engaged in riotous actions. The climactic Birmingham marches, during which King remained holed up at the Gaston Motel, were similar to what had just happened in Memphis. Black youths on the fringes who had not been "workshopped" caused the trouble. In Birmingham it worked to the movement's advantage. This time it had the opposite effect. It was ironic that in the less violent era of spring 1963, the Birmingham minirioting (because it was something new?) did not discredit King in the way that comparable violence did five years later.

The media hit him even harder than he had feared. They added insult to injury by accusing him of fleeing the scene in a cowardly manner to a luxury motel; actually he had no choice. As part of its PPC sabotage operation the FBI sent out derogatory disinformation that was published by many newspapers, even as editorials.

Despite Abernathy's and Lee's efforts to console him, King could not sleep till morning came. He told Levison in New York that he might have to call off the Poor People's Campaign.

"He was worried, worried," Abernathy recalled. "He didn't know what to do. It was then that he raised this question with me if those of us who advocated nonviolence should not step back and let the violent forces run their course."[157] Perhaps they would have to admit that the day of violence had arrived. The nation wasn't listening to them.

In late morning, as King dressed for a press conference, Abernathy heard a loud knock. Three young men were at the door, leaders of the Invaders. They had come to apologize, to set the record straight, and to get help. While waiting for King to come out, Abernathy angered the trio by blaming them for the violence. King walked in, wearing a shiny silk suit, surprised that he knew one of them. Charles Cabbage, a Morehouse student, had worked with Hosea Williams in the SCLC headquarters the past summer, and had been proposed for the field staff in Baltimore to recruit for the PPC. Calvin Taylor was the only black intern on the *Memphis Commercial Appeal,* the city's more conservative daily.

"For a man he had very soft looking skin," Taylor remembered of his first encounter with the heroic leader he had heard about most of his life. "His hands were very soft. He wasn't bitter. This man actually lived and believed nonviolence. This is one of the reasons he looked so soft to me. You talk about depressed! He looked as if he was about to cry. Not so much 'Why did you have a riot with me leading it?' but 'Why would you resort to violence anyway?' As if to say, 'You know that violence hasn't worked for white people. Why would you do that?'

"I have never seen a man that looked like peace, and that man looked like peace. I swear he did. I was kind of shocked. Dr. King wasn't raising his voice. There was no shouting. The only time Cab shouted was when Abernathy accused the Invaders of being responsible. Then Dr. King said, 'Well, it doesn't matter who was responsible. Lawson and them should have told us. We should have sat down and talked before we had this march. When I come back to the city, that's what we're gonna do—sit down and talk. You will not be left out.'"

Cabbage and colleagues explained that they had not been present at the march, because Lawson and COME had excluded them from the planning. They had tried to talk with King when he spoke at the March 18 rally, but they claimed Lawson wouldn't let them. They admitted that some of their members might have taken part in the disturbance but that it would not have happened if their group had been included in the leadership. They were sure that none of their members had started it. Cabbage then asked if SCLC could help them out financially, since the Invaders were involved in organizing poor people and could bring some of them to Washington. Taking it as a good-faith request, not an implied threat, King said he would see what he could arrange.

"What can I do to have a peaceful march?" he asked them. "Because you know that I have got to lead one. There is no other way." He wanted to meet with them before the next march and pledged that they would be part of the leadership.

The three young men, who had been ready for a rough face-off, were blown away by his disarming patience, compassion, and reason-ableness. "Nobody can be as peaceful as that man," Taylor concluded. "When he came into the room it seemed like all of a sudden there was a real rush of wind and everything just went out and peace and calm settled over everything. You could feel peace around that man. It was one of the few times in my life when I wasn't actually fighting some-thing." It felt to him like a psychotherapy session.[158]

King then conducted a press conference in an assertive manner that contrasted with his torpor of the night before. He explained to antago-nistic reporters that SCLC had not been involved in planning the failed march.

"We came in here cold," he said. "Our intelligence was nil. I wouldn't have come if I had known the outbreak of violence was possible." SCLC would organize a return engagement in a week. The sanitation workers' strike, he said, proved the necessity of the Poor People's Cam-paign. "We are fully determined to go to Washington."[159]

That was his brave public face. Behind it he was still forlorn. He instructed Abernathy to get him out of Memphis as fast as possible. He had a long phone conversation with Levison, recorded by the FBI, in which he poured out his true feelings. They were in serious trouble, he told his longtime confidant. "I think our Washington campaign is doomed." It would be much harder to get people there because they would fear the outbreak of violence that the media, with FBI feeding, was doing double time to make happen. Levison disagreed that the sit-uation was so dire.

"All I'm saying," King countered, "is that Roy Wilkins, Bayard Rustin and that stripe, and there are many of them, Adam Clayton Powell, their point is, 'Martin Luther King is dead. He's finished. His nonviolence is nothing, no one is listening to it.' Let's face it, we do have a great public relations setback where my image and my leadership are concerned." Levison stressed that only a tiny fraction had been violent. King agreed. "It was a failure of the leadership here." For one thing, there had been minimal training, usually Lawson's forte. He told Levison about the Invaders' visit.

"They came up here, they love me. They were fighting the leadership of Memphis. They were fighting Jim Lawson and the men who ignored them, who neglected them, who would not hear them, wouldn't give them any attention. I had no knowledge of all this. I know the fellows, and they really do love me. They were too sick to see that what they were doing yesterday was hurting me much more than it could hurt the local preachers.

"I was so upset about this thing and so shocked," he continued, "that I was just going to announce that I was going on a fast, and through this fast to appeal to the leadership of Memphis as well as those who participated in the violence to come to me in a united front and let's take up the cudgel and move on in this movement. I think that that kind of powerful spiritual move would be the kind of thing that would pull all the forces. It would be a way of unifying the movement and transforming a minus into a plus."[160] He might even bring back home his own prodigal staff.

He was looking to Gandhi, of course, who had fasted to atone for his own movement's violence and to discipline his people when they had erred. But he was no doubt inspired as much by the nearly fatal twenty-five-day fast by his ally United Farm Workers chief Cesar Chavez, in California's Central Valley. It had ended two weeks before, lasting longer than Gandhi's. Chavez, a longtime admirer of King, his own methods influenced by him, was sending a UFW delegation to the Poor People's Campaign. At a low point in his grape strike and boycott, Chavez fasted to keep farm workers nonviolent; some union members had allegedly destroyed growers' property. A week before he announced his presidential bid, Robert Kennedy had joined the frail Chavez in a massive UFW celebration in Delano when he broke his fast. The two leaders, both devout Catholics, shared a portion of bread broken and blessed by a priest. The fast proved a turning point in the union's fortunes.

King felt that the powerful act of fasting, which was excruciating for Chavez but would have been an even tougher sacrifice for this man who loved to eat, would help redeem the power of nonviolent action and counter his drubbing by the media. But he let go of the idea once convinced that SCLC would pull out all the stops to make the next Memphis march a triumphant vindication of soul force and of himself. He had married nonviolence back in November, after a long engagement, and had promised to stay with her till death them did part. He believed that the outcome in Memphis and Washington would determine whether nonviolent action would be "the dominant instrument for social change," or whether it would be cast aside by guerrilla warfare and armed struggle—or by the masses' timid supplication.[161] He could tell that the next few weeks would be the severest test of his abiding nonviolent faith.

AFTER FLYING HOME to Atlanta with Abernathy, King got his usual workout at the YMCA. Not wanting to be seen in public, he joined Coretta to spend the night at the Abernathys'. His head was pounding from a bad migraine headache. The two men, wiped out, fell asleep scrunched up on matching loveseats.

"Ralph," King joked as he drifted off, "I wish you'd had enough money to buy a whole sofa instead of just a half sofa."[162]

King was late for the executive staff meeting he had called the next morning at Ebenezer. When he walked into the conference room, Jesse Jackson, Bevel, and others were, one more time, marshaling arguments against the Poor People's Campaign. They criticized him for going into Memphis at such a precarious moment. Sitting in back in a wooden classroom seat, he listened agitatedly. Finally he strode to the front. He blasted them for not supporting him.

"He just jumped on everybody," Young recalled. "He said we'd let him down. That we all had our own agendas. Never before had I seen him so aggressive in dealing with us."[163] He demanded that everyone drop what they were doing and go back with him to Memphis. He mentioned the fast he might undertake, that they might have to call off the Poor People's Campaign if the staff would not rally round.

"I can't take all this on by myself," he protested. "I need you to take your share of the load. Everyone here wants to drag me into your particular projects. Now that there is a movement that originated basically from Mississippi-born folk, not from SCLC leadership, you don't want to get involved.

"Now that I want you to come back to Memphis to help *me,*" he charged, "everyone is too busy."[164] He had already instructed them to concentrate on the PPC, of course, and most had followed orders reluctantly.

"Succumbing to their own egomania," Young wrote later, some staff leaders "had begun to feel that they were more important to the movement than Martin. When they were really feeling their oats, Hosea, Bevel, and Jesse acted as if Martin was just a symbol under which they operated. Bevel was so arrogant as to think he was smarter than Martin." He was eager to send a peace delegation to the Mekong Delta to stand between American and North Vietnamese forces. Williams wanted SCLC to focus on running black candidates in the South. Meanwhile, "Jesse was busy building his own empire in Chicago," with Operation Breadbasket going full tilt.[165]

Eyes aflame, fury no longer hidden, King declared that each of them had to decide whether they would be part of the SCLC team, or if they were just using him and SCLC to glorify themselves.

"I'm getting out of here." He marched out of the room.

The dozen senior staff members, plus Levison, who had flown down from New York, were stunned. They had never seen him explode like that. They hoped that he had just gone off to pray, like so many times before. But he did not look like he was in a praying mood. Abernathy instinctively rushed after him, catching up with him on the stairs.

"Martin, what is wrong with you? Tell me."

"I'm going to the country. I need to go to the farm." He probably meant the biracial Koinonia Farm community in southern Georgia run by his friend Rev. Clarence Jordan.

"Tell me what is bugging you?"

"All I'll say is, Ralph, I'll snap out of it. Didn't I snap out of it yesterday? I'll pull through it."[166]

At that instant Jackson appeared at the top of the stairs. "Doc," he called out. "Don't worry, everything's going to be all right."

King swung around and glared at him with an icy stare, stabbing his finger at him.

"Jesse, everything's not going to be all right! If things keep going the way they're going now, it's not SCLC but the whole country that's in trouble. If you're so interested in doing your own thing, that you can't do what this organization is structured to do, go ahead. If you want to carve out your own niche in society, go ahead. But for God's sake, don't bother me!"[167]

Jackson was visibly wounded by the tirade. He must have felt like Peter rebuked by Jesus in the garden of Gethsemane. Or did he feel more like Judas?[168] One Judas was still sitting in the conference room meticulously taking notes to hand to the FBI.

Under Abernathy's and Young's direction, the staff managed to collect itself and get down to business. By his impulsive direct action King had closed the door on dissent. There was no longer any question of defying the boss's will. They had to pull together behind their leader, no matter how bad they felt about it, no matter how wrong they thought the course. Back to Memphis and on to D.C.

A few hours later, after they had finalized plans, Joe Lowery from Mobile said to the group: "The Lord has been in this room this afternoon. I know He's been here because we could not have deliberated the way we did without the holy spirit being here. And the holy spirit is going to be with us in Memphis and Washington."[169] He gave an Indian war whoop. Young did a little dance. All stood up and shook hands with each other like passing the peace of Christ. Abernathy managed to reach King and urged him to come back. A few more hours passed until he showed up. After taking twelve-year-old Yoki to her ballet lesson, he had visited a friend, then had a long talk with his father back at Ebenezer. He was gratified to hear what the staff had decided, that they would back him all the way. The meeting had lasted for ten hours. The staff were giddy with relief.

KING'S BLISTERING REBUKE was an emotional scourging that Jackson never let go of. Only thirteen years older, King was more his father than anyone had ever been. Jackson was born out of wedlock to a teenage mother in Greenville, South Carolina, in 1941, two months before Pearl Harbor. He had barely known his biological father, an older married man with a family of his own who abandoned him. As a young adult he would rebel against his adopted father, in an almost Oedipal sense challenging his movement leadership. But King had lifted him from obscurity, had trusted him to run the Breadbasket program, had raised this nobody into a somebody. Now this man he revered had shamed him in front of his movement siblings.

"I had never seen him under such a spiritual cloud before," Jackson remarked later with understatement.[170] The experience confirmed for him what a lot of King's staff and confidants were feeling. De Lawd was deliberately retreading the steps of Jesus as he arrived in Jerusalem with his languid disciples and struggled through his last days, especially the night of passion in the garden of Gethsemane below Mt. Calvary.

Like Jesus, King confronted the presumed disloyalty of his disciples, Jackson above all but also Bevel, Williams, and others, and tried to shape them up into worthy successors. While he had already anointed Abernathy to succeed him as SCLC president, he expected that all of these leaders he had cultivated would spread his gospel of justice and love. This was why he was so angered when Rutherford, Williams, and other close associates seemed to be questioning the worth of nonviolent principles. If his own senior staff were not committed to building the temple of nonviolence, what hope could there be that others would pick up his mantle?

And so, at this Saturday staff meeting and other crucial moments during that flood-tide spring, he was beseeching God, if possible, to lift the cup of destiny from his lips. Should he continue moving forward on his perilous path, or should he leave the movement and retire to an ivory tower, or to a farm in south Georgia—returning to his distant roots in the red clay soil? Should he stay in command, or hand over the reins to his own disciples? Which ones could he trust? Could he get Peter to keep faith with him? Would Judas betray him? Had he already?

If up to him, he wanted to be released from his suffering. But if not? He wanted to do God's will.[171]

King's passion ran deeper than whether he should continue to fight, who would carry on his work and how well, and how he could keep his disciples from denying him, betraying his principles and vision. It ran deep into his inner self, into the state of his wounded soul, into the dark shadows of his heart. He wanted to save his soul. If he could redeem his own soul, maybe he could redeem the soul of America, of humanity.

King had always been a glutton for guilt, ever since he had jumped out the upstairs window of his boyhood home blaming himself for his grandmother's death. By his fortieth year the guilt that he had accumulated was monumental. In one compartment of his conscience was guilt about the extravagance of praise and honor lavished upon him that he felt he did not deserve, that others, unsung, unknown, already dead, deserved far more than he. In another compartment was remorse about neglecting his wife and children. In another, one can imagine, was searing guilt about his alleged extramarital relationships. And in another whole edifice of contrition was the guilt that he felt for all the failures of the freedom movement, the peace movement, the human rights movement, movements that he both personified and internalized. He felt responsible for the endless war, the burned babies of Vietnam. He felt responsible for the emaciated kids of Marks, Mississippi, running around barefoot, living on trapped rabbits and apple slices.

He found it more and more difficult to disentangle his own failures of leadership from the collective failures of the movements he led. And then he would feel guilty as well for treating these movements as extensions of his cosmic self.

He may have smothered his personal guilt with his political—overlaying guilt about his family with guilt about the world—sometimes the other way around. But however these multiple layers of guilt coexisted uneasily in his overgrown conscience, his cosmic guilt inflicted torturous anguish at the same time that it offered hope of relief and release. It was perhaps the balancing tension of pain and promise that enabled him to keep going against overwhelming odds.

The more guilt he endured, the more anger he turned inward, the more self-destructive his behavior, the more debased he felt—the more he felt he was humbling himself in the eyes of God. The silver lining in all his sinning, personal and public, was that he was pulling himself down from his exalted status, reducing himself to the least of these, or at least to less than what he had been, or could have been. If, as he truly believed, the first would be last and the last would be first, he wanted to be last in order to be first, to make himself small enough to squeeze through the eye of a needle to the promised land. He believed that the path to his personal redemption passed through the deepest depths of personal sin, the deepest darkness of private evil.

King dealt with his prodigious guilt by extreme self-punishment. The more he suffered, the more he sacrificed, the more he felt he could transform this punishing perdition into a way out of no way, into an exorcism of the devil inside of him. On some primal level he knew that he could never be reborn until he hit rock bottom, that only in the deepest darkness would he be able to see the stars. And so he sank, his drowning the way of deliverance.

It was no wonder then that he fixated on his own death. Nothing redeemed like martyrdom. By sacrificing his life he believed that he might wash away more than his own sins.

As if he were following the road map of a fellow Christian martyr, sixteenth-century Spanish mystic St. John of the Cross, who talked of "the dark night of the soul," he seemed to believe that his soul could find union with the divine only if it were fully purged of all impurities and temptations. But in order to cleanse his sins he had to embrace them. For years he had tried to humble himself, to decrease himself, through acts of will. But it seemed that the more he humbled himself, the higher he was exalted. The more he strove to transcend his self, the more it was magnified, by others if not by himself. As he had preached so often, one could only merge with God if one were stripped naked. The lower one fell into darkness, the more completely could one be reborn and exalted. To rise up was to fall down; to fall was to rise.

The darkness was the abode of sin, but it was also the place where sin could be faced and exposed and overcome. It was only in the dark night of the soul that one could empty oneself of wickedness, one could annihilate one's ego, in order to be filled by divine light, light that could be blinding as it was to Saul of Tarsus, the persecutor of Christians. "When the spirit of good yields to the spirit of evil," wrote St. John of the Cross, "the soul is purified and prepared for the feast to come."[172] The darkness was a place of torment for the soul but also the forcing house of re-creation. It was in the deepest darkness of the soul that the divine fire forged life out of death. It was from the darkness of this womb that new life, new worlds, could be born.

Dedicated to the faith that personal and social rebirth were interwoven, King believed that his nation should follow the same course of naked exposure and moral cleansing. It was not that a person or a nation ought to strive to be evil in order to be purified and exalted. It was that each person and every nation, but especially his own, were already overwrought with evil, while also blessed with good. King's self-destructive actions were not to make him worse than he was—only to force him to face and come to terms with the evil in his being, to illuminate it like he had racial segregation, so that it could be transformed. He was not urging America to fall from grace, to seal its doom. He was not preaching, like millennialist doomsayers, that the nation had to be destroyed in order to be saved. He was doing his utmost to meliorate the society both short and long term.

What he was saying was that in order to be reborn, to be redeemed, the nation had to humble itself, eschew its arrogance. It had to burrow into the depths of its own soul to face the evil at its core—the evil of which a quarter millennium of slavery was metaphor as well as reality, as Lincoln had suggested in his Second Inaugural address. By cleansing itself of its triple evils of racism, human exploitation, and war making, the United States of America could return to the divine mission of enlightenment that was promised in the sacred covenant of the Declaration of Independence.

16

On Sunday morning, March 31, King flew to Washington to preach the Passion Sunday sermon at the National Cathedral. It would be his final Sunday service. Easter was two weeks away. He urged people not to be passive during this revolutionary era of robust transformation. It was time for a "national awakening."

"We are not coming to tear up Washington," he reassured the mainly white congregation that overflowed the huge Episcopal cathedral. "We are coming to demand that the government address itself to the problem of poverty. We are going to bring children and adults and old people. People who have never seen a doctor or a dentist in their lives.

"We read one day—We hold these truths to be self-evident, that all men are created equal, that they are endowed by their creator with certain inalienable rights. That among these are life, liberty, and the pursuit of happiness. But if a man doesn't have a job or an income, he has neither life nor liberty nor the possibility for the pursuit of happiness. He merely exists." He extolled the Poor People's Campaign as the harbinger of a new Jerusalem. They were Davids fighting the Goliath of injustice, determined to make America the truly great nation it was called to be.

"'Behold, I make all things new,'" he quoted from the New Testament's last book, Revelation, "'former things are passed away.'

"God grant that we be participants in this newness. If we will but do it, we will bring about a new day of justice and brotherhood and peace. And that day the morning stars will sing together and the sons of God will shout for joy."[173]

After the service he told reporters that they would show in Washington that the real issue "is not violence or nonviolence, but poverty and neglect." He said that because of the campaign he would not be able to fly to West Africa in mid-April to mediate the barbaric civil war in Nigeria. He noted that if they did not make hay in Washington, they might take poor people to the party conventions in Miami and Chicago. "They will have a real awakening in Chicago." He disclosed that he was willing to negotiate with the government to call off the PPC—his mentor Randolph had been successful with FDR in 1941—but only if Johnson agreed to substantive demands, "with a positive timetable," including implementation of his own commission's recommendations on urban disorder. He was not optimistic that this would happen.

Then his words took an ominous turn. "We cannot stand two more summers like last summer," he warned, "without leading inevitably to a rightwing takeover and a fascist state" that would "destroy the soul of the nation."[174]

Whatever happened, it would not be more of the same. That night from the Oval Office President Johnson delivered a long, nationally televised speech dealing mostly with Vietnam. He announced that he had cut back the bombing of North Vietnam in the hope that it would lead to peace talks with Hanoi. He did not mention that he had approved the small troop increase favored by the Clifford task force. Nor that he had rejected Westmoreland's big request and removed him as U.S. commander. Moving to conclude, he astounded the nation. After a glance at his wife, he stared dead on into the Teleprompter and declared that he would not run for reelection nor accept his party's nomination.

Although slightly skeptical, King was thrilled with the bombshell. Vice President Humphrey would no doubt jump in, but RFK would no longer face the long odds (historically unprecedented) of unseating the incumbent president.

"He's doing just like a Baptist preacher," King observed to SCLC organizer Walter Fauntroy in Washington, "you know, trying to get a vote of confidence. He'll pull back in later. But this country's through with him."[175]

Johnson seemed finally to realize that his fellow Americans—more than a disloyal fringe of elite intellectuals and students—were turning against the war.

"I felt that I was being chased on all sides by a giant stampede coming at me from all directions," he confided to a biographer. "On one side, the American people were stampeding me to do something about Vietnam. On another side, the inflationary economy was booming out of control. Up ahead were dozens of danger signs pointing to another summer of riots in the cities. I was being forced over the edge by rioting blacks, demonstrating students, marching welfare mothers, squawking professors, and hysterical reporters. And then the final straw. The thing I feared from the first day of my presidency was actually coming true. Robert Kennedy had openly announced his intention to reclaim the throne in the memory of his brother. And the American people were dancing in the streets. The whole situation was unbearable for me. After thirty-seven years of public service, I deserved something more than being left alone in the middle of the plain, chased by stampedes on every side."[176]

BACK IN ATLANTA on Monday, King took part in an SCLC strategy meeting for the Poor People's Campaign. They considered whether Johnson's good news might alter their plans, but resolved to forge ahead. He had dispatched Young, Bevel, Williams, Jackson, and other leaders to hit the ground running in Memphis, organizing the march set for Monday of Holy Week. They met with a wide swath of community leaders, giving special attention to the Invaders as King had promised. He and Abernathy were supposed to arrive in Memphis on Tuesday, but he begged off to get more rest, to Abernathy's chagrin. He was in no hurry to get back to Golgotha.

On Wednesday morning, April 3, King's Eastern Airlines flight was held up for over an hour on the Atlanta runway. Just before takeoff the pilot announced that there had been a bomb threat because of Dr. King's being on board. The plane had been guarded all night, but all the bags had to be examined. King chuckled.

"Well, it looks like they won't kill me this flight."[177] When he, Abernathy, Young, Lee, and Dorothy Cotton arrived late in Memphis, ahead of a big storm, they were greeted by several Memphis detectives who, in light of mushrooming threats, offered police security for King. The police top brass were worried: the police commissioner told another official that "we've gotten some threats that he is going to be killed if he comes back to Memphis." The local organizers declined the offer, suspecting correctly that Memphis police, in cahoots with the FBI, were more interested in surveillance than protection. SCLC staff knew that their boss was the FBI's enemy number one. They knew how intimately FBI agents colluded with southern police departments.

King had accepted police protection in other cities, but bad blood between the strike movement and police, aggravated by the March 28 police overkill, made such protection here politically unwise as well as of dubious value: the proverbial fox guarding the chicken coop. "He wasn't the kind just to play and flirt with death," a Memphis friend, minister Samuel (Billy) Kyles, noted. "By the same token, he wouldn't try to live secretively. There were always threats. He lived with it."[178]

King's regular Memphis chauffeur, Solomon Jones, a funeral-home driver, took them in a white Cadillac downtown to the Lorraine Motel, where King usually stayed. For years the black-owned motel had been a second home for blues and jazz musicians, church leaders, and other notable black visitors. The husband and wife proprietors treated King and his staff like family and cooked food he liked. After checking in, King and staff rushed to a meeting with black ministers at Lawson's Methodist church. They got the bad news that a local federal judge had blocked their march. King was dismayed, but knew that this could play into their hands.

Back at the Lorraine, King politely greeted federal marshals who handed him the injunction order. A battery of lawyers was preparing to contest the injunction at a hearing the next day. He had informed them that the march would not be stopped.

Late afternoon, he and his staff held a frank discussion with Cabbage and other Invader leaders. He told them that if they would not help to make the next march nonviolent, he didn't want anything to do with them. They said they would do everything they could, but that they could not guarantee no violence. They could only control their own members. This rankled SCLC leaders, who expected them to rein in their followers, the street people they served. The Invaders agreed to serve as parade marshals, which would have prevented the earlier violence since the marshals on that day were few and weak. The staff reiterated that SCLC would try to help them get funding; there was even casual talk of the Invaders' youth project coming under SCLC's umbrella. While SCLC staffers did not fully trust the peace pact, they were now less concerned that violence might break out the following Monday, April 8.

KING FELT TOO TIRED to speak at the rally that night at Mason Temple, national headquarters of the Church of God in Christ, largest black Pentecostal denomination. The gathering storm, with tornado warnings, portended a small turnout. He sent Abernathy in his place. But when the second-in-command arrived, he sensed that the people who had braved the howling rain had come for one reason. Rather than fire up a speech, he found a phone in the vestibule.

"Your people are here and you ought to come on and talk to them," he told his weary friend. "They didn't come tonight just to hear Abernathy. They came tonight in this storm to hear King."[179]

He dressed up quickly. When he walked onstage the assembly of about three thousand, one-fifth the number who had heard him there two weeks before, greeted him with applause so loud it drowned out the thunder outside. The stained-glass windows high in the rafters shuddered. Abernathy took half an hour to introduce him, elaborately telling his life story, from cradle to this day. As King started speaking in the hot, humid hall, large fans banged, scaring him. They were turned off. Civil defense sirens blared as heavy rain and tornados swept across Tennessee and Kentucky, smashing houses and barns, killing twelve people. Lightning lit up the hall. King's words were punctuated by blasts of thunder.

He thanked Abernathy, "the best friend that I have in the world," for his long-winded introduction that annoyed the other preachers. "But I wondered who he was talking about."

In his first public address in Montgomery twelve years before, he had stressed the cosmic significance of the time they were living in, and how they were collectively agents of God's will. Now he asserted that their time was as pregnant as any in human history.

If he could have asked God to live in any historical period, starting with the Israelites crossing the Red Sea toward the Promised Land, and Plato, Aristotle, and other Greek sages pondering eternal thoughts up on the Parthenon, "strangely enough, I would turn to the Almighty, and say, 'If you allow me to live just a few years in the second half of the twentieth century, I will be happy.'" He knew this sounded strange, "because the world is all messed up. The nation is sick. Trouble is in the land. Confusion all around."

Just as he came to accept that his own redemption would happen only after he hit bottom, so he believed that their nation would be redeemed and regenerated when doom thundered across the sky. God was working in the world, and people were joining in, doing his will, actualizing his plan. A new covenant was taking shape. People had no choice now but to grapple with crisis problems that had come to a head. If the human rights revolution did not move forward, across the globe, the whole of humanity was in peril. It was time to act.

"Let us rise up tonight with a greater readiness," he belled. "Let us move on in these powerful days, these days of challenge, to make America what it ought to be." He was grateful for the gift of being alive during this promising era, these days of miracle and grace.

He told them he was glad to be with them on this stormy night, despite the Memphis death threats, despite the fear of a bomb on his plane that morning. He knew that their "sick white brothers" were out to get him. Sweat was streaking down his brow and cheeks. His eyes danced, drawing in and reflecting back the unloosed passion of the resolute garbage workers, their families and friends.

"Well, I don't know what will happen now," he said. "We've got some difficult days ahead. But it doesn't matter with me now. Because I've been to the mountaintop. And I don't mind. Like anybody, I would like to live a long life. Longevity has its place. But I'm not concerned about that now. I just want to do God's will.

"And He's allowed me to go up to the mountain. And I've looked over. And I've *seen* the promised land. I may not get there with you. But

I want you to know tonight, that we, as a people will get to the promised land. And I'm happy, tonight. I'm not worried about anything. I'm not fearing any man." Sweat and tears commingled on his glowing brown face.

"Mine eyes have seen the glory of the coming of the Lord!"[180]

The applause was unearthly. He swiveled around and fell back into Abernathy's arms. A minister asked if he wanted water. Standing in the rear, Lawson felt "a great feeling of oneness" in the hall. "I was basking in this feeling of kinship and warmth."[181] Ministers were wailing all through the sanctuary. Jackson, who had hoped he could speak that night, told his wife that King "was lifted up and had some mysterious aura around him."[182]

Once recovered, King was visibly elated. Normally he would have left right after such an oration. Tonight he stayed around to shake hands and mingle. He did not want to leave. It was like the best of the movement days. Perhaps the best of all.

While the COME strategy committee deliberated, King and Abernathy enjoyed a late dinner at the home of his old friend Benjamin Hooks, a Memphis judge and pastor. They returned to the Lorraine Motel in the middle of the night, where King was happy to find his younger brother. A. D. had driven over spontaneously from Louisville, where he pastored a Baptist church. He brought with him a Kentucky politician, the state's first black woman senator, who was close to his brother. King relaxed with A. D. and spent time with his Kentucky friend.[183] He slept till nearly noon on Thursday, April 4.

17

While King was sleeping, meetings were taking place all over Memphis—some black, some white, some mixed—to deal with the upcoming march and to resolve the labor struggle. It was day fifty-three of the strike. Young rose early to accompany Lawson to the federal court hearing, where they testified about the nature of the planned march and SCLC's history of nonviolent protest. Late in the afternoon the judge told the lawyers in his chamber that he would permit the march with restrictions that King had approved (such as more parade marshals) to make the protest more manageable.

Soon after waking King joined Abernathy for a catfish lunch at the Lorraine café. They ate off the same plate, since the waitress brought only one and King didn't want to trouble her. Then he presided over a staff meeting that focused on the necessity of nonviolent discipline, reaffirming their commitment to it, and whether they could trust the Invaders to keep their word. A few staff members still worried about the prospect of violence, from whites if not from blacks.

"I'd rather be dead than afraid," he chided them. "You've got to get over being afraid of death."[184]

Williams suggested that SCLC hire a couple of the Invaders as a way to teach them nonviolence. King rebuked him. "Dr. King had gotten onto me," Williams told a reporter later that day, "because we have a few people on our staff who question nonviolence. He said, 'Hosea, no one should be on our payroll that accepts violence as a means of social change.'" Williams had wondered out loud whether protective violence might be acceptable in certain situations, such as in self-defense against police attack. In an angry tone King insisted that violent action by protesters would not be permitted under any circumstances, and that he did not respect a man who would not be publicly nonviolent. He paced the floor, preaching about soul force one more time to his staff.

"The only hope for mankind upon this globe is the true fostering—not only speaking, but living—the kind of life Jesus Christ lived, nonviolently."[185]

They did not know, but would hardly have been surprised, that one or two of the Invader members were informants for the FBI, another for the Memphis police.

Just as they were adjourning in laughter and high spirits, Andy Young walked in the door. King had been irritated because he hadn't heard from him about the court hearing that everything depended on. Young had not been able to get to a phone.

"L'il nigger, just where you been?" King barked at him, half in jest. Of course he knew where he had spent the long day. "You ought to stay in touch with me. You're always running off doing something without me knowing about it."

Like a big kid he leapt from the bed and clobbered his executive vice president with a pillow. Abernathy beat him with another. "After all the tension we had been through," Young wrote later, "this kind of child-like play was exhilarating. I dodged and ducked my way over to the other bed, grabbed a pillow, and fought them off."[186] The other staffers joined in a raucous free-for-all. FBI eavesdroppers would have thought these nonviolent soldiers were slaughtering each other. When their nervous energy was spent, Young delivered the good news from the federal court. King grinned as others cheered. After more jiving and backslapping they headed for their rooms to dress for an elaborate soul-food dinner at the Reverend Kyles's home.

SINCE KING'S ARRIVAL at the Lorraine the day before, Memphis detectives, FBI agents, and army intelligence had been watching his party closely from a fire station across the street. Cops had papered over the window facing the motel and kept binoculars trained through holes they had snipped. Two army special forces sharpshooters were reportedly stationed on the roof. Tactical squad police patrolled the area in cars and on foot. The police and military presence increased the next day. They were there not only to spy on King but to be positioned for anticipated rioting during the coming march, or sooner.

Late afternoon on Thursday a well-dressed white man about forty registered for a room at a run-down rooming house a block away. He signed in as John Willard. His real name was James Earl Ray, a career criminal who had recently escaped from the Missouri penitentiary. In his bare room he took out of his bag a .30-06 caliber rifle with scope, bought four days before. He could see the Lorraine from his window, a hundred yards away. He found a clearer view from the bathroom down the hall.[187]

ABOUT THIS TIME King was joking with proprietor Lorraine Bailey outside his room.

"I'm getting ready to go to Dr. Kyles," he said. "If he don't have good food out there, like that catfish we had, I'm going to come back and eat here."

"All right, Doctor," she laughed.[188] King and his brother talked with their mother on the phone, joking around and impersonating each other. He called Ebenezer to give his secretary the title of his sermon for Palm Sunday: "Why America May Go to Hell."

Billy Kyles showed up to hurry them along, knowing his friend's habitual tardiness and that they had a mass meeting to get to after dinner. King was dressing.

"All right now, Billy," Abernathy ribbed him, "I don't want you kidding me tonight. Are we going to have soul food?" King had already asked Abernathy to call Gwen Kyles to find out what was in store for them. She reeled off: roast beef, chitlins, neck bones, potatoes, ham, macaroni and cheese, spaghetti, greens, candied sweet potatoes, tossed salad, potato salad, coleslaw, corn bread, corn muffins, corn pone, rolls, cakes, pies, ice cream, lemonade, iced tea, coffee. Mrs. Kyles had recruited the best chefs from their church to help her out. "We had the mood set where they could just relax," she recalled.

Abernathy did not let up on her husband. "Now if we go over there and get some filet mignon or T-bone," he teased, "you're going to flunk. We don't want no filet mignon."

"Yeah," King joined in, "we don't want it to be like that preacher's house we went to in Atlanta, that great big house. We went over there for dinner and had some ham—a ham bone—and there wasn't no meat on it. We had Kool Aid and it wasn't even sweet. If that's the kind of dinner we're going to, we'll stay here."

"You just get ready," Kyles deadpanned. "You're late. I told my wife six o'clock. Hurry up, let's go."

"You know, your wife is real pretty," Abernathy came back. "I'm gonna put some cologne and stuff on."

"Yes, she's so pretty," King said. "Can she really cook soul food? Course, she'd have to be pretty to be married to a fashion plate like you." The threesome talked preacher's talk while King shaved, an arduous process. His skin was too tender for a razor, so he rubbed on a foul-smelling paste called Magic Shave that burned off his whiskers, which he scraped off with a knife. It was one reason he was always late. They talked about Daddy King.

"He's got lots of spunk left in him," his son said. "You know, Dad is really something. When he was courting Mama, not only did Dad get the daughter, but he got the church, too." They laughed. He seemed in a good mood, relaxed. He had put on his shirt but couldn't find his tie. He thought someone was playing a trick on him, but they found it in a drawer. His shirt was so tight he couldn't button the collar.

"Oh, Doctor, you're getting fat," Kyles threw in.

"Yeah, I'm doing that." He put on a bigger shirt and noosed his tie.

"Billy," he asked his friend, "what do you think brought the Negroes together in Memphis?" Kyles replied that the black community empathized with the sanitation workers' plight.

"This is like the old movement days, isn't it?" King gloated. "This really is the old movement spirit."

"I better put some more of this good-smelling stuff on me," Abernathy said.

King stepped outside on the balcony in the approaching twilight. Staff members were milling around in the courtyard below with the driver, Solomon Jones, and his Cadillac limousine. Young and Bevel were clowning and shadowboxing with a much taller staff member, James Orange. King greeted his colleagues warmly.

"All right, load up," he called down. "We're getting ready to go."[189] Jackson looked up at King admiringly: "Our leader!" he shouted. Someone asked him why he was not wearing a tie. He quipped that all one needed to wear to dinner was a hearty appetite. Jackson reintroduced King to Ben Branch, a singer and saxophonist with the Operation Breadbasket band. They would be performing at the rally that evening.

"Oh yeah, he's my man," King said, both hands gripping the balcony railing. He seemed pleased that he and his wayward disciple were getting along.

"Ben," King said slowly, "I want you to sing 'Precious Lord' for me tonight like you never sung it before."

"Dr. King," Branch replied, "you know I do that all the time."

"But tonight, especially for me. I want you to sing it real pretty."[190]

Jones told King it was getting cool and he should get his overcoat. The sun was about to set.

"I don't know whether I need a coat."[191]

At that moment, about six o'clock, his staff heard a loud clap that sounded like a car backfiring or a firecracker. Their leader was no longer standing. An eyewitness saw him flying backward, his arms out to his sides. He lay on his back, knees raised, feet pressed against the railing. Blood gushed out of his throat and neck. The high-powered bullet had exploded in his right cheek and jaw, tearing off his tie. It passed through his neck and severed his spinal cord. The first to reach him was Marrell McCollough, an undercover Memphis cop who had infiltrated the Invaders. He tried to stanch the bleeding with a towel. Kyles put a blanket over him. Abernathy cradled him in his arms. People were screaming and moaning in the courtyard. Young sprinted up the stairs.

"Oh God!" he cried. "Oh God, Ralph. It's over."

"Don't you say that, Andy. It's not over. He'll be all right." Kyles bolted into King's room to call an ambulance, but the office switchboard did not answer. He howled in frustration. Lorraine Bailey suffered a stroke that evening; she died four days later.

Dozens of heavily armed, riot-clad police, on alert around the firehouse, burst into the courtyard. Staff members felt at first under attack. Young and others pointed across the street to the rooming house. Jones saw a shadowy figure with white skin moving through bushes above the retaining wall and running down the street. He jumped in his Cadillac to chase after him, but the driveway was blocked.

King's eyes were wide open, gazing at Abernathy, who was stroking his left cheek.

"Martin, this is Ralph. Can you hear me? Can you hear me? Don't be afraid. Don't be afraid. This is Ralph. Everything will be all right."[192] At one point Abernathy scooped up King's pool of blood into a jar. Jackson came up and bathed both his arms in the blood, soaking his shirt-sleeves.

An ambulance took King, accompanied by Abernathy, to St. Joseph's Hospital. He breathed his last breath an hour later, his closest friend caressing him in his arms. Abernathy called Coretta, who had already heard about the shooting. She would come in the morning.

"It hit me hard—not surprise, but shock," she wrote in her memoir, "that the call I seemed subconsciously to have been waiting for all our lives had come."[193]

When the shocked and grieving staff leaders returned to the Lorraine from the hospital, they gathered for a meeting. Abernathy grimly declared that they had to keep going, that their fallen leader would not want them to pause. Bevel stood up.

"Our leader is dead," he said. "In many respects I loved Dr. King more than Jesus."[194] But now he was gone, and they had to choose a new leader. The band of brothers reaffirmed Abernathy as his chosen heir. They prayed and sang "We Shall Overcome."

THAT DAY ROBERT KENNEDY had begun his campaign for the Indiana primary. John Lewis, former SNCC chair and bloodied freedom rider, had thrown in with the Kennedy campaign and set up a gig for him that night in a poor black neighborhood of Indianapolis. On his plane the candidate learned that King had been shot; upon landing, that he had died. He "seemed to shrink back," a reporter recalled, "as though struck physically." The mayor, police chief, and his own aides thought it would be suicidal to appear in the ghetto, but RFK insisted. The police refused to escort him. Because they had been waiting for him outside on this cold night, the black audience had not heard. Kennedy clambered onto a flatbed truck in a parking lot, "hunched in his black overcoat," a TV man reported, "his face gaunt and distressed and full of anguish."

"I have bad news for you, for all of our fellow citizens," the senator said sadly, "and people who love peace all over the world, and that is that Martin Luther King was shot and killed tonight." The crowd gulped and moaned in the wind.

"For those of you who are black and are tempted to be filled with hatred and distrust at the injustice of such an act, against all white people, I can only say that I feel in my own heart the same kind of feeling. I had a member of my family killed." Then, speaking as much about his own journey to healing as that of black Americans, he recited from memory "my favorite poet," Aeschylus:

"In our sleep, pain which cannot forget falls drop by drop upon the heart until, in our own despair, against our will, comes wisdom through the awful grace of God."[195]

Later in the evening he reached Coretta King in Atlanta and then sent a jet to take her to Memphis to bring home her husband's body.

MAYOR LOEB WAS DRIVING down to Mississippi for a law school reunion when he heard that King had been shot and turned around. Back at city hall the mayor and some city council members, white and black, cried when they heard the final bulletin. He composed himself to request several thousand national guardsmen from the Tennessee governor and reimposed the dusk-to-dawn curfew he had ordered during the last week's disorder. Memphis black leaders struggled past their horror to urge calm. SCLC staff scrambled to the Mason Temple rally, defying police warnings, to grieve with the strikers and to make-believe hope. Lawson, who had enticed King to Memphis, spoke over and over on the radio, beseeching people to stay faithful to their slain hero's non-violent creed. He "died on behalf of all of us."[196]

That evening theologian Howard Thurman, one of King's spiritual mentors, delivered a eulogy for his friend on Pacifica radio in Los Angeles.

"Tonight there is a vast temptation to strike out in pain, horror, and anger," he said. "Riding just under the surface are all the pent up furies, the accumulation of generations of cruelty and brutality. A way must be found to honor our feelings without dishonoring him whose sudden and meaningless end has called them forth. May we harness the energy of our bitterness and make it available to the unfinished work which Martin has left behind. It may be, it just may be that what he was unable to bring to pass in his life can be achieved by the act of his dying. For this there is eloquent precedence in human history. He was killed in one sense because mankind is not quite human yet. May he live because all of us in America are closer to becoming human than we ever were before."[197]

Largely because the black leadership rallied to keep the peace, Memphis did not explode in vengeful violence. There was some vandalism, looting, and burning, and a hostile atmosphere for the white majority, but many who might have blown stayed cool out of respect for Dr. King.

Not so in the rest of the nation. While Americans of all colors grieved quietly, black and brown youth (over half under sixteen) in more than a hundred cities released their rage in the most widespread urban violence America had ever seen. Twenty thousand soldiers and four times that many national guardsmen assisted local police to battle looters, snipers, and arsonists. At least forty people were killed, mostly black as usual; many thousands were arrested. Fires gutted thirty blocks of downtown Chicago, looting reached the Loop, and Mayor Daley gave police orders to shoot to kill. In Oakland a police assault killed Black Panther treasurer Bobby Hutton, a teenager, and wounded Eldridge Cleaver and chief of staff David Hilliard.

Washington, burning, looked to be hardest hit. Smoke billowed over the Capitol and the White House. Some of the worst rioting was but blocks away. Johnson ordered several thousand army paratroopers to defend the city, the first military deployment inside the district since the Bonus Marchers were ousted in 1932.

It appeared during the long weekend, at least to foreign eyes, that the urban devastation Europe and Japan had suffered during World War II was now ravaging American cities—not bombs from the skies but blasts from the ground up. A West German newspaper witnessed "the world's mightiest country in tragic conflict with itself." *Le Monde* of Paris saw "the disintegration of everything that makes up the life of a civilized collectivity."[198]

But the combined force of black remonstration, tanks in the streets, better-trained and -led law enforcers, and King's battered spirit of non-violence managed to douse America's broadest insurrection on the brink of civil war.

OVER THE WEEKEND in Memphis, ministers led somber memorial services, sanitation workers kept up their daily marches, and a large interracial gathering took place on Sunday, a national day of mourning, seeking to reconcile the divided city. On Monday, April 8, the great march that King had died for, a march both to redeem nonviolence and to win the two-month strike, took over the town. Forty thousand people, many from labor unions around the country, marched quietly to city hall behind Coretta Scott King, her three oldest children, entertainment stars, and national labor and religious leaders including Walter Reuther and Rabbi Abraham Heschel, who had trekked with King from Selma to Montgomery. Like a replay of that famous march, five thousand national guardsmen patrolled the streets. Nonviolence ruled. Mrs. King spoke to the huge rally at city hall.

"I would challenge you today to see that his spirit never dies," the long-prepared widow sang out, "and that we will go forward from this experience, which to me represents the Crucifixion, on toward the resurrection and the redemption of the spirit.

"How many times have I heard him say that with every Good Friday there comes Easter. When Good Friday comes, these are the moments in life when we feel that all is lost, and there is no hope. But then Easter comes as a time of resurrection, of rebirth.

"But then I ask the question: how many men must die before we can really have a free and true and peaceful society? How long will it take? If we can catch the spirit and the true meaning of this experience," she concluded, "I believe that this nation can be transformed into a society of love, of justice, peace and brotherhood."[199]

With pressure snowballing on Mayor Loeb from city fathers, national unions, President Johnson (who sent an assistant labor secretary as mediator), and his own shaken conscience, the city agreed to recognize the AFSCME public works local a week later, acceding to a dues checkoff and pay raise. Although it had taken the martyr's death to bring it off, the hard-pressed strikers had won. And in Washington the 1968 Civil Rights Act, outlawing most housing discrimination, finally passed Congress after being bottled up in the House.

CORETTA KING WAS SHROUDED in a dark veil as she viewed her husband's body at Ebenezer, and as she sat with her four children and A. D. King in the front pew of the funeral on Tuesday. Daddy and Mama King sat with unspeakable sorrow next to the children. Before them the casket was coated with a cross of white carnations. Mrs. King cradled in her bosom her youngest child, Bernice, just turned five, as the little girl's eyes begged an answer from her brave, bereaved mother.

The assembled congregation, which included a sprinkling of white faces—political figures and presidential candidates like Hubert Humphrey, Robert Kennedy, and Richard Nixon—heard the dead prophet deliver his own eulogy over the loudspeakers, from his "Drum Major" sermon at Ebenezer two months earlier. The gospel choir sang like it had never sung before.

After this service in King's own church, tens of thousands of mourners from all over the country followed behind an old farm wagon drawn by two mules carrying the shiny mahogany coffin bereft of its flowered cross. The multitude trekked up Sweet Auburn to a final memorial service at Morehouse College before burial. Wearing their blue denim uniforms, Young, Bevel, Williams, Jackson, and other SCLC leaders held the mules' reins and clasped the wooden sides as the old wagon creaked and clip-clopped forward bearing their beloved.

Precious Lord, take my hand, lead me on, let me stand,
I am tired, I am weak, I am worn.
Through the storm, through the night, lead me on to the light.
Take my hand, precious Lord, lead me home.
When the shadows appear and the night draws near,
And the day is past and gone,
At the river I stand, guide my feet, hold my hand.
Take my hand, precious Lord, lead me home.[200]

Building the Beloved Community

Dr. Martin Luther King Jr. was never more of a moral warrior, and never more deeply committed to nonviolence, than when he was approaching the end of his life. He did not see these stances as inconsistent, but as prerequisites for each other. Some claimed that nonviolence died with Dr. King. Quite the contrary. In the United States and around the world, from Eastern Europe to the Philippines to South Africa, nonviolent direct action flexed its muscle during the last third of the twentieth century.[1]

King was convinced that assertive nonviolent action, which he liked to call soul force, was not only more ethical than violence but more effective, especially long-term. He did not think that violent methods had ever been truly effective, whether in the Civil War, which left its legacy of wretched white supremacy, in global warfare, or in ghetto riots. In just six decades since its "invention" by Gandhi in 1906, mass nonviolent action in King's view had proven more successful than six millennia of human violence. This was partly because it did not leave bitterness behind to haunt future generations. It stymied the law of the multiplication of evil. He aspired to create the moral equivalent of civil war, whose just reconciliation would not give lie to Lincoln's malice toward none, charity for all.

King believed that soul force—the synthesis of justice and compassion, of faith and understanding, of social and personal rebirth—was rooted in ancient wisdom but geared to the future of human evolution. Soul force required the fire of faith and moral passion not only to break down the walls of inhumanity, but to forge the new person: a free person whose emotional capacity would be as mature as her intellect, whose mental and emotional being, rather than sabotaging each other, would coalesce into a more enlightened creature who more truly reflected the image of God. Soul force would deliver as well the beloved community, knit together by compassionate understanding, heartfelt communication, bonds of human intimacy.

But however strong his faith, King had grave concerns about what was to come. He believed that the Poor People's Campaign—he somehow knew it was to be his last—would demonstrate whether creative nonviolent action would prove to be the dominant instrument of social change for the future.[2] Or, would it be thrust aside by armed struggle on one side, and people's anomie and "timid supplication" on the other?

Let us transplant King's anguish onto the uncertain terrain of our new century. Will we inherit a future brokered by self-righteous terrorists, official or unofficial, and by masses of disempowered consumers alienated from the world and their own souls, terrified to their bones?

We who claim the legacy of Martin Luther King Jr. must cling to the life raft of nonviolence, in word and deed, in passion and compassion, as determinedly as he did during the last years of his life.

The alternative is unspeakable.

Notes

Many quotations in Book One are cited to the author's previous work, *Daybreak of Freedom* (University of North Carolina Press, 1997), a documentary history of the Montgomery bus boycott; see this volume for fuller text and documentation of sources.

Excerpts from King sermons and addresses sometimes contain italicized words in parentheses that express audience response. Dialogue was drawn from recollections by one or more participant, or an observer, in each conversation. Misspellings in quotations are not corrected.

Bible references are from the New King James version, which King generally used. King's and others' references to God or divinity using masculine nouns and pronouns have been preserved.

Book One

Prologue

1. Quoted in Richard Willing, "Civil Rights' Untold Story," *USA Today,* 28 November 1995.

2. Quoted in "Civil Rights' Untold Story."

3. Ellen Levine, ed., *Freedom's Children* (New York: Putnam, 1993), 20–22.

4. Quoted in Paul Hendrickson, "The Ladies Before Rosa," *Washington Post,* 12 April 1998.

5. Ruth Hamilton testimony, quoted in Lamont H. Yeakey, "The Montgomery, Alabama Bus Boycott, 1955–56" (Ph.D. diss., Columbia Univ., 1979), 234–35.

6. Colvin's accounts of her arrest, in Levine, *Freedom's Children,* 23–25; Colvin testimony in *Browder v. Gayle* in Stewart Burns, *Daybreak of Freedom* (Chapel Hill: Univ. of North Carolina Press, 1997), 74–76.

7. Claudette Colvin testimony, quoted in Yeakey, "The Montgomery, Alabama Bus Boycott," 236.

8. Quoted in Yeakey, "The Montgomery, Alabama Bus Boycott," 238–39.

9. Jo Ann Gibson Robinson, *The Montgomery Bus Boycott and the Women Who Started It*, ed. David J. Garrow (Knoxville: Univ. of Tennessee Press, 1987), 41.

10. Police Report on Arrest of Claudette Colvin, 2 March 1955, Police Dept., Montgomery, AL; *Montgomery Advertiser*, 19 March 1955; *Alabama Tribune*, 25 March 1955.

11. Robinson, *Montgomery Bus Boycott*, 42.

12. *Montgomery Bus Boycott*, 42.

13. Martin Luther King Jr., *Stride Toward Freedom* (New York: Harper & Row, 1958), 42.

14. J. Mills Thornton III, letter to author, 10 June 1998.

15. Quoted in Willing, "Civil Rights' Untold Story."

16. Quoted in Hendrickson, "The Ladies Before Rosa."

17. Quoted in Stephen B. Oates, *Let the Trumpet Sound* (New York: New American Library/Mentor, 1982), 58.

18. Mary Louise Smith testimony, in *Browder v. Gayle* hearing, Montgomery, AL, 11 May 1956.

Chapter 1

19. Burns, *Daybreak of Freedom*, 131–32.

20. *Daybreak of Freedom*, 132.

21. King, *Stride Toward Freedom*, 135–36.

22. *Stride Toward Freedom*, 136.

23. Coretta Scott King, interview by author, Atlanta, 6 June 1994.

24. Quoted in King, *Stride Toward Freedom*, 136.

25. Quoted in Coretta Scott King, *My Life with Martin Luther King, Jr.* (New York: Penguin, 1969, 1993), 119.

26. This paragraph from Burns, *Daybreak of Freedom*, 135 ("The Bombing Episode," by Willie M. Lee, 31 January 1956).

27. Quoted in David J. Garrow, *Bearing the Cross* (New York: Vintage, 1988), 60.

28. *Montgomery Advertiser*, 31 January 1956.

29. Quoted in Burns, *Daybreak of Freedom*, 135.

30. Coretta Scott King, *My Life*, 120.

31. *My Life*, 120.

32. King, *Stride Toward Freedom*, 138.

33. Coretta Scott King, interview by author.

Chapter 2

34. Quoted in Burns, *Daybreak of Freedom*, 9.

35. Quoted in *Daybreak of Freedom*, 9.

36. Quoted in Douglas Brinkley, *Rosa Parks* (New York: Viking Penguin, 2000), 13, 6.

37. Little known by posterity, Montgomery blacks had organized a two-year boycott of public transport half a century before. In August 1900, four years after the Supreme Court's *Plessy v. Ferguson* decision that sanctified racially segregated public conveyances, the city of Montgomery, like other southern cities at the time, enacted an ordinance requiring segregated seating on its electric trolleys. In response many of the city's African-American ministers urged their congregations to walk instead of ride. The protest forced the streetcar firm to suspend segregation, though Jim Crow seating resumed after the boycott died down.

38. Mary Fair Burks, "Trailblazers: Women in the Montgomery Bus Boycott," in *Women in the Civil Rights Movement: Trailblazers and Torchbearers, 1941–1965*, ed. Vicki L. Crawford et al. (Brooklyn: Carlson Publishing, 1990), 78.

39. Quoted in Lewis V. Baldwin and Aprille V. Woodson, *Freedom Is Never Free: A Biographical Portrait of Edgar Daniel Nixon* (Atlanta: United Parcel Service, 1992), 10.

40. Quoted in Burns, *Daybreak of Freedom,* 82.

41. Virginia Foster Durr, *Outside the Magic Circle* (New York: Simon & Schuster/Touchstone, 1987), 280.

42. Quoted in Burns, *Daybreak of Freedom,* 86.

43. Quoted in Howell Raines, *My Soul Is Rested* (New York: Penguin, 1983), 44.

44. Quoted in *My Soul Is Rested,* 45.

45. King, *Stride Toward Freedom,* 61.

46. Ps. 34, New King James Bible.

47. King, *Stride Toward Freedom,* 59–60.

48. *Stride Toward Freedom,* 59.

49. Clayborne Carson, Stewart Burns, and Susan Carson, eds., *Birth of a New Age: December 1955–December 1956,* vol. 3 of *The Papers of Martin Luther King, Jr.* (Berkeley: Univ. of California Press, 1997), 73–74, 79. (Hereafter *King Papers,* vol. 3.)

50. *King Papers,* 74.

Chapter 3

51. King, *Stride Toward Freedom,* 111, 112.

52. Virginia Durr to Clark Foreman, 7 December 1955, in Burns, *Daybreak of Freedom,* 96.

53. Juliette Morgan to *Montgomery Advertiser,* 12 December 1955, in Burns, *Daybreak of Freedom,* 101–3.

54. Quoted in King, *Stride Toward Freedom,* 77, 78; quoted in Raines, *My Soul Is Rested,* 61.

55. *Montgomery Advertiser,* 4, 13, 5 January 1956.

56. Carl T. Rowan, *Breaking Barriers* (New York: Harper Perennial, 1992), 140.

57. Burns, *Daybreak of Freedom,* 122.

58. Quoted in Garrow, *Bearing the Cross,* 55.

59. King, *Stride Toward Freedom,* 128–29.

60. *Stride Toward Freedom,* 131.

61. Burns, *Daybreak of Freedom,* 125–27.

62. Martin Luther King Jr., *Strength to Love* (Philadelphia: Fortress Press, 1963, 1981), 125.

63. Quoted in King, *Stride Toward Freedom,* 133.

64. Quoted in King, *Strength to Love,* 125–26; Clayborne Carson and Peter Holloran, eds., *A Knock at Midnight* (New York: Warner Books, 1998), 137.

65. Carson and Holloran, *A Knock at Midnight,* 161–62; King, *Stride Toward Freedom,* 134–35.

66. Isa. 11:1–2, 42:1–4; Matt. 3:16–17.

Chapter 4

67. *King Papers,* 3:115–16.

68. Fred Gray, interview by David J. Garrow, Tuskegee, AL, 20 August 1985 (courtesy of Garrow).

69. Burns, *Daybreak of Freedom,* 128–30.

70. Quoted in Garrow, *Bearing the Cross,* 62.

71. Heb. 10:39.

72. *Montgomery Advertiser,* 7, 8, 9 February 1956; *Time,* 20 February 1956; Tiya Miles, "Autherine Juanita Lucy Foster," in *Black Women in the United States,* ed. Darlene Clark Hine (Brooklyn: Carlson Publishing, 1993), 446–49.

Chapter 5

73. R. B. Edmonds, "Shiloh Baptist Church minutes," 15 October 1848, quoted in Clayborne Carson, Ralph E. Luker, and Penny A. Russell, eds., *Called to Serve: January*

1929–June 1951, vol. 1 of *The Papers of Martin Luther King, Jr.* (Berkeley: Univ. of California Press, 1992), 2. (Hereafter *King Papers*, vol. 1.)

74. G. S. Ellington, "A Short Sketch of the Life and Work of Rev. A. D. Williams, D.D.," 16 March 1924, quoted in *King Papers* 1:4.

75. Michael and Alberta King's son was first given the name Michael after his father, who then changed his name to Martin Luther King. His son followed suit. King Jr. formally changed his birth certificate to Martin Luther King Jr. on July 23, 1957.

76. Quoted in Lawrence Levine, *Black Culture and Black Consciousness* (New York: Oxford Univ. Press, 1977), 36.

77. Quoted in James H. Cone, *The Spirituals and the Blues: An Interpretation* (New York: Seabury Press, 1972), 55.

78. W. E. B. Du Bois, *The Souls of Black Folk* (Chicago: A. C. McClurg & Co., 1903), 190–91.

79. Quoted in Albert J. Raboteau, *Slave Religion* (New York: Oxford Univ. Press, 1978), 260.

80. Mircea Eliade, *The Sacred and the Profane* (New York: Harcourt Brace, 1959), quoted in Levine, *Black Culture*, 31–32.

81. Gayraud S. Wilmore, *Black Religion and Black Radicalism* (Garden City, NY: Doubleday Anchor, 1973), 19–20. A person must "in some prescribed way, enter into communion with it in order to receive its benefits and avoid its condemnation. The Supreme Being, departed ancestors, spirits resident in or associated with certain lakes, trees, and animals, and living human beings who possessed mysterious gifts of healing or of making mischief, were all united in one overarching, invisible world that has its own laws and conventions which sustain and order the visible world" (20).

82. "An Autobiography of Religious Development," in *King Papers* 1:361, 363.

83. *King Papers*, 361.

84. Clayborne Carson, Ralph E. Luker, Penny A. Russell, and Peter Holloran, eds., *Rediscovering Precious Values: July 1951–November 1955*, vol. 2 of *The Papers of Martin Luther King, Jr.* (Berkeley: Univ. of California Press, 1992), 495, 494. (Hereafter *King Papers*, vol. 2.)

Chapter 6

85. Burns, *Daybreak of Freedom*, 184–93.

86. *Montgomery Advertiser*, 11 February 1956.

87. Quoted in Virginia Foster Durr, *Outside the Magic Circle* (Tuscaloosa: Univ. of Alabama Press, 1985, 1990), 171–72.

88. Quoted in Durr, *Outside the Magic Circle*, 263–64.

89. *Montgomery Advertiser*, 11 February 1956.

90. Durrs to George Eddy, 21 February 1956, in Burns, *Daybreak of Freedom*, 158.

Chapter 7

91. Quoted in Jervis Anderson, *Bayard Rustin: Troubles I've Seen* (New York: Harper Collins, 1997), 171.

92. Rustin, "Montgomery Diary," in Burns, *Daybreak of Freedom*, 164–65.

93. Quoted in David J. Garrow, ed., *The Walking City* (Brooklyn: Carlson Publishing, 1989), 263.

94. Quoted in Taylor Branch, *Parting the Waters* (New York: Simon & Schuster, 1988), 177.

95. Quoted in Rustin, "Montgomery Diary," in Burns, *Daybreak of Freedom*, 166.

96. *Baltimore Afro-American*, 11 February 1956.

97. Quoted in Garrow, *Bearing the Cross*, 64.

98. Quoted in Garrow, *Bearing the Cross*, 64.

99. Quoted in *Montgomery Advertiser*, 21 February 1956.

100. Quoted in Branch, *Parting the Waters*, 173.

101. King, *Stride Toward Freedom*, 143–44.

102. *Stride Toward Freedom*, 144.

103. Quoted in Rustin, "Montgomery Diary," in Burns, *Daybreak of Freedom*, 165.

104. Rustin, "Montgomery Diary," in *Daybreak of Freedom*, 165.

105. Quoted in Garrow, *Bearing the Cross*, 65.

106. Quoted in Branch, *Parting the Waters*, 177.

107. Quoted in King, *Stride Toward Freedom*, 145.

108. Quoted in Garrow, *Bearing the Cross*, 65.

109. Rustin, "Montgomery Diary," in *Daybreak of Freedom*, 166.

110. 1 Cor. 13.

111. Quoted in Burns, *Daybreak of Freedom*, 162–63, 166.

112. Quoted in *Daybreak of Freedom*, 163, 166.

113. Quoted in Anderson, *Bayard Rustin*, 187.

114. Quoted in Rustin, "Montgomery Diary," in Burns, *Daybreak of Freedom*, 167.

115. Quoted in Anderson, *Bayard Rustin*, 189.

116. Quoted in Rustin, "Montgomery Diary," in Burns, *Daybreak of Freedom*, 167.

Chapter 8

117. Bayard Rustin, "Reminiscences of Bayard Rustin" (Oral History Research Office, Columbia Univ., 1988), 137–40.

118. Bayard Rustin, interview, 13 February 1970, Moorland-Spingarn Library, Howard Univ., Washington, DC.

119. *King Papers*, 3:125. King actually made the comment in this paragraph in an interview with Fisk University researcher Donald T. Ferron, Montgomery, 4 February 1956.

120. Quoted in Rustin, "Montgomery Diary," in *Daybreak of Freedom*, 169.

121. Quoted in Raines, *My Soul is Rested*, 55.

122. Bayard Rustin, "Report on Montgomery, Alabama," 21 March 1956, American Civil Liberties Union Archives, Mudd Manuscript Library, Princeton University, hereafter referred to as ACLUA-NJP.

123. "Report on Mass Meeting," in Burns, *Daybreak of Freedom*, 173–75.

124. Rustin, "Montgomery Diary," in Burns, *Daybreak of Freedom*, 170.

125. Quoted in Anderson, *Bayard Rustin*, 190.

126. See Bayard Rustin to Martin Luther King Jr., 8 March 1956, *King Papers*, 3:164.

127. Quoted in Garrow, *Bearing the Cross*, 67.

128. Quoted in Anderson, *Bayard Rustin*, 122.

129. John M. Swomley Jr. to Glenn E. Smiley, 29 February 1956, Fellowship of Reconciliation Papers, Swarthmore Peace Collection, Swarthmore College, hereafter FORP-PSC-P, in Burns, *Daybreak of Freedom*, 171–72.

130. Quoted in Garrow, *Bearing the Cross*, 69.

Chapter 9

131. John M. Swomley Jr. to Wilson Riles, 21 February 1956, FORP-PSC-P, in Burns, *Daybreak of Freedom*, 160.

132. Glenn Smiley, interview by author, Los Angeles, 14 June 1991; Glenn Smiley, interview by David J. Garrow, North Hollywood, CA, 6 April 1984 (courtesy of Garrow); Glenn Smiley, *Nonviolence: The Gentle Persuader* (Nyack, NY: Fellowship Publications, 1991), 5.

133. Smiley, interview by author.

134. Smiley, interview by author.

135. Smiley, interview by author.

136. Glenn Smiley to John M. Swomley Jr. and Alfred Hassler, 29 February 1956, FORP-PSC-P, in Burns, *Daybreak of Freedom,* 22–23.

137. Glenn Smiley to Neil Salinger et al., 29 February 1956, FORP-PSC-P, in Burns, *Daybreak of Freedom,* 163–64.

138. Quoted in Garrow, *Bearing the Cross,* 68.

139. Donald T. Ferron, "Report on MIA Mass Meeting, March 1," in Burns, *Daybreak of Freedom,* 197.

140. Quoted in Garrow, *Bearing the Cross,* 70.

141. Glenn Smiley interview by author, Los Angeles, 14 June 1991, author's archive.

142. King, *Stride Toward Freedom,* 85.

143. Martin Luther King Jr., interview by Glenn Smiley, Montgomery, 28 February 1956, FORP-PSC-P.

144. Lillian Smith to MLK, 10 March 1956, King Papers, Mugar Library, Boston University, hereafter MLKP-MBU: box 65.

145. Norman Thomas to Homer Jack, 12 March 1956, Norman Thomas Papers, New York Public Library, hereafter NTP-NN.

146. Homer Jack to Norman Thomas, 15 March 1956, NTP-NN.

147. *Montgomery Advertiser,* 7 March 1956.

148. Ella J. Baker to MLK, 24 February 1956, MLKP-MBU: box 14A.

Chapter 10

149. *State of Alabama v. M. L. King, Jr.,* 19 March 1956, Circuit Court, Montgomery County Records, Montgomery, hereafter CMCR-AMC.

150. *State of Alabama v. M. L. King, Jr.,* 22 March 1956.

151. Gladys Moore testimony in *State of Alabama v. King,* in Burns, *Daybreak of Freedom,* 70–72.

152. Henrietta Brinson testimony in *State of Alabama v. King,* in Burns, *Daybreak of Freedom,* 68–70.

153. Martha K. Walker testimony in *State of Alabama v. King,* in Burns, *Daybreak of Freedom,* 65–66.

154. Georgia Jordan testimony in *State of Alabama v. King,* in Burns, *Daybreak of Freedom,* 62–64.

155. Anna Holden, "Report on MIA Mass Meeting, March 22," in Burns, *Daybreak of Freedom,* 212–19; *King Papers,* 3:200–201.

Chapter 11

156. Martin Buber, *I and Thou* (Edinburgh: Clark, 1937). Buber lived from 1878 to 1965.

157. "A Realistic Look at Race Relations," 17 May 1956, in *King Papers,* 3:282–83; Martin Luther King Jr., "Our Struggle," in Burns, *Daybreak of Freedom,* 244–45.

158. Rom. 12:2, in "Paul's Letter to American Christians," 4 November 1956, *King Papers,* 3:416.

159. Bernice Johnson Reagan, interview by Bill Moyers, *We Shall Overcome,* PBS video.

160. Martin Luther King Jr., "The Birth of a New Age," 11 August 1956, in *King Papers,* 3:340.

161. "Tract for the Times," *Liberation,* March 1956, in Burns, *Daybreak of Freedom,* 237–42.

162. Eleanor Roosevelt, "My Day," 14 May 1956, in Burns, *Daybreak of Freedom,* 267.

163. Juanita Moore to MLK, 3 June 1956, in Burns, *Daybreak of Freedom,* 260–61.

164. Quoted in Randall Kennedy, "Martin Luther King's Constitution: A Legal History of the Montgomery Bus Boycott," *Yale Law Journal* 98:6 (April 1989), 1046.

165. Transcript of Record and Proceedings, *Browder v. Gayle*, 11 May 1956, in Burns, *Daybreak of Freedom*, 267–77.

166. *Montgomery Advertiser*, 9 December 1956. The editorial actually referred to the Supreme Court decision of 13 November upholding the June *Browder* ruling.

167. See J. Mills Thornton III, *Dividing Lines* (Tuscaloosa: Univ. of Alabama Press, 2002), 84–88. While Thornton suggested in his thoroughly researched study that the boycott did not influence the *Browder* ruling, though setting the stage for it, he offered evidence and argument that might support a different view.

168. MLK to Joffre Stewart, 21 October 1956, in *King Papers*, 3:352.

169. *Montgomery Advertiser*, 5 May 1956, 12 June 1956.

170. *Stride Toward Freedom*, 154–57; "Reverend Fields's Retraction," 18 June 1956, in Burns, *Daybreak of Freedom*, 276.

171. E. D. Nixon, interview by Steven M. Millner, in *The Walking City*, ed. David J. Garrow (Brooklyn: Carlson Publishing, 1989), 496, 550.

172. "Reverend Fields's Retraction," from *Daybreak of Freedom*, 276.

173. Quoted in Burns, *Daybreak of Freedom*, 274–75.

174. Erna Dungee, interview by Steven M. Millner, in Garrow, *The Walking City*, 524–25.

Chapter 12

175. King, *Stride Toward Freedom*, 157.

176. Martin Luther King Jr., "Pilgrimage to Nonviolence," April 1960, in *A Testament of Hope*, ed. James M. Washington (San Francisco: HarperSanFrancisco, 1991), 39.

177. Martin Luther King Jr., "An Experiment in Love," September 1958, in Washington, *Testament of Hope*, 20.

178. Martin Luther King Jr., "Walk for Freedom," in Washington, *Testament of Hope*, 83.

179. "MIA Mass Meeting at Holt Street Baptist Church," 5 December 1955, *King Papers*, 3:73.

180. Matt. 7:1.

181. Martin Luther King Jr., "Love, Law, and Civil Disobedience," 16 November 1961, in Washington, *Testament of Hope*, 45.

182. Martin Luther King Jr., "We Are Still Walking," *Liberation*, December 1956, in Burns, *Daybreak of Freedom*, 323.

183. Martin Luther King Jr., "An Experiment in Love," in Washington, *Testament of Hope*, 20.

Chapter 13

184. J. Pius Barbour, *National Baptist Voice*, September 1956, quoted in *King Papers*, 3:28, 366.

185. C. W. Kelly to MLK, 8 September 1956, *King Papers*, 3:366. In a letter of 18 July Kelly lauded King's work as a "missionary journey akin to Paul's of old," and stated that Paul "never did it more effectively" (quoted at 365).

Chapter 14

186. *Montgomery Advertiser*, 26 August 1956.

187. Thornton, *Dividing Lines*, 91.

188. Minutes of MIA special committee, 25 September 1956, in Burns, *Daybreak of Freedom*, 291.

189. Dialogue taken from report by Robert Cannon to Alfred Hassler and Glenn Smiley, 3 October 1956, FORP-PSC-P, in Burns, *Daybreak of Freedom*, 292–94.

190. Thornton, *Dividing Lines*, 91–93.

Chapter 15

191. Quoted in Garrow, *Bearing the Cross,* 80.

192. *U.S. Reports* (Supreme Court), 352 U.S. 903 (1956).

193. King, *Stride Toward Freedom,* 160.

194. John 3:2–7; MLK comments, 14 November 1956, in Burns, *Daybreak of Freedom,* 301.

195. Martin Luther King Jr., "Address to MIA Mass Meeting at Holt Street Baptist Church," 14 November 1956, in *King Papers,* 3:428–29, 433.

196. *Montgomery Advertiser,* 14 November 1956.

197. King, "We Are Still Walking," in Burns, *Daybreak of Freedom,* 318.

198. Martin Luther King Jr., "Facing the Challenge of a New Age," 3 December 1956, MLKP-MBU: box 10.

199. Quoted by Inez J. Baskin, *Norfolk Journal and Guide,* 15 December 1956.

200. "Montgomery Board of Commissioners Statement on Supreme Court Decision," 17 December 1956, in Burns, *Daybreak of Freedom,* 323–25.

201. King, *Stride Toward Freedom,* 171.

202. "Integrated Bus Suggestions," MLKP-MBU: box 3, in Burns, *Daybreak of Freedom,* 326–27.

203. Thornton, *Dividing Lines,* 93–94.

204. Eugene P. Walker, "A History of the Southern Christian Leadership Conference, 1955–1965" (Ph.D. diss., Duke Univ., 1978), 31.

205. Joseph Lowery, interview with Aldon D. Morris, Atlanta, 21 September 1978, quoted in Morris, *The Origins of the Civil Rights Movement* (New York: Free Press, 1984), 82.

206. Rustin to MLK, 23 December 1956, Bayard Rustin Papers, Library of Congress.

207. Moore wrote to King on Oct. 3: "A group of this nature would solidify our efforts and give a coherent philosophy behind what we are attempting to do. As you probably know there are not many Negroes or Whites who have a firm spiritual or intellectual grasp upon this whole idea of love and nonviolence. This power has been in the Negro Church for generations.

"I feel that we can not let this get cold on us for the work that you have done in Montgomery is but the starting of a work that needs to be done throughout the South. [To do this job that needs to be done] there must be direction that is systematic, consistent and above all coherent and Christ like." Moore also wrote that "when a man is afraid to die for what he believes to be true his concept of what is ultimately real is shallow." Douglas Moore to MLK, 3 October 1956, *King Papers,* 3:394–97.

208. Rustin, "Reminiscences," 151.

209. Stanley Levison, interview, Moorland-Spingarn Research Center, Howard Univ., 9–10.

210. Bayard Rustin, "Working Paper #1," in Burns, *Daybreak of Freedom,* 337.

211. "A Statement to the South and Nation," 11 January 1957, in Burns, *Daybreak of Freedom,* 345–46.

212. King, *Stride Toward Freedom,* 178; *Montgomery Advertiser,* 15, 16 January 1957.

213. Coretta Scott King told the author that she herself did not know about her husband's kitchen experience until she read a manuscript draft of *Stride Toward Freedom* sometime in 1957 (Coretta Scott King, interview by author).

214. *New York Times,* 28 January 1957.

215. Thornton, *Dividing Lines,* 94–95.

216. Although King and his colleagues largely followed Rustin's design for SCLC, Rustin did not want the group to be as dominated by preachers or so overtly Christian. He feared it would exclude Jews, Muslims, and nonreligious people. He tried to recruit southern black labor leaders, for example, drawing several to the founding meetings, but they never played a major role. The founders added "Christian" to the name for practical

reasons: to distinguish it from the besieged NAACP and to provide cover against expected white supremacist attacks for leftist influence and "un-American" activities.

217. Quoted in Ted Poston, *New York Post*, 14 April 1957, in *King Papers*, 3:33.

Book Two

Prologue

1. Quoted in Ken Burns, *The Civil War*, PBS television documentary, episode 5 (Florentine Films, 1989).

2. Quoted in Garry Wills, *Lincoln at Gettysburg* (New York: Simon & Schuster, 1992), 21.

3. This interpretation of the Gettysburg Address is indebted to Wills, *Lincoln at Gettysburg*.

4. Quoted in Merrill D. Peterson, *Lincoln in American Memory* (New York: Oxford Univ. Press, 1994), 225.

5. *Portable Walt Whitman* (New York: Viking, 1945), 530.

6. Quoted in David S. Reynolds, *Walt Whitman's America* (New York: Knopf, 1995), 424.

7. *Portable Walt Whitman*, 287.

8. Quoted in Ronald C. White Jr., *Lincoln's Greatest Speech* (New York: Simon & Schuster, 2002), 182, 199.

9. Quoted in Leon F. Litwack, *Been in the Storm So Long* (New York: Vintage, 1980), 172.

10. Martin Luther King Jr., interview, *Playboy*, January 1965, in Washington, *Testament of Hope*, 343.

11. Martin Luther King Jr., "The Negro and the Constitution," May 1944, in *King Papers*, 1:109–11.

Chapter 1

12. Police memo, 10 April 1963, mass meeting, quoted in Diane McWhorter, *Carry Me Home* (New York: Simon & Schuster, 2001), 341.

13. Quoted in *New York Times*, 12 April 1963.

14. Martin Luther King Jr., *Why We Can't Wait* (New York: Harper & Row, 1963, 1964), 70, 71; Andrew Young, *An Easy Burden* (New York: Harper Collins, 1996), 214.

15. King, *Why We Can't Wait*, 72.

16. Quoted in Taylor Branch, *Parting the Waters* (New York: Simon & Schuster, 1988), 730.

17. King, *Why We Can't Wait*, 73.

18. Quoted in James Farmer, *Lay Bare the Heart* (New York: Arbor House, 1985), 207.

19. *Eyes on the Prize*, episode 4, "No Easy Walk (1962–66)" (Blackside, Inc., PBS Video, 1986).

Chapter 2

20. *Jet*, 26 October 1961, 4; Martin Luther King Jr., "It's a Difficult Thing to Teach a President," *Look*, November 1964, 61; SCLC news release, 18 October 1961 (MLKP-MBU); quoted in Branch, *Parting the Waters*, 518.

21. Martin Luther King Jr., interview by Berl Bernhard, Atlanta, 9 March 1964, JFK Library, Boston, quoted in Taylor Branch, *Pillar of Fire* (New York: Simon & Schuster, 1998), 248.

22. Quoted in Farmer, *Lay Bare the Heart*, 205–6.

23. Robert Kennedy, *In His Own Words* (New York: Bantam, 1988), 89.

24. Quoted in Andrew M. Manis, *A Fire You Can't Put Out* (Tuscaloosa: Univ. of Alabama Press, 1999), 332.

25. Quoted in Garrow, *Bearing the Cross*, 229; Young, *An Easy Burden*, 194.

26. Mary McKinney Edmonds, interview by author, Stanford University, 16 April 1993.

Chapter 3

27. *Time*, 19 April 1963; *Newsweek*, 4 April 1963; Graham quoted in *New York Times*, 18 April 1963.

28. *Birmingham Post Herald*, 14 April 1963.

29. Martin Luther King Jr., "Paul's Letter to American Christians," Dexter Avenue Baptist Church, Montgomery, 4 November 1956, MLKP-MBU.

30. See Malinda Snow, "Martin Luther King's 'Letter from Birmingham Jail' as Pauline Epistle," *Quarterly Journal of Speech* 17 (1985): 318–34, in *Martin Luther King, Jr.: Civil Rights Leader, Theologian, Orator*, vol. 3, ed. David J. Garrow (Brooklyn: Carlson, 1989), 857–73.

31. Quotations from "Letter from Birmingham Jail" are from King, *Why We Can't Wait*, 77 ff.

32. Lillian Smith, "The Right Way Is Not a Moderate Way," 5 December 1956, in Burns, *Daybreak of Freedom*, 308–13.

33. Stewart Burns, "James Baldwin's Rainbow Sign" (1963, typescript).

34. James Baldwin, *The Fire Next Time* (New York: Dial Press, 1963), 111, 119, 120.

Chapter 4

35. King, *Why We Can't Wait*, 74.

36. Quoted in Branch, *Parting the Waters*, 735.

37. Police report, 18 April 1963, on mass meeting of 12 April 1963, Connor Papers, Alabama Dept. of Archives and History, Montgomery, box 13; *Birmingham Post Herald*, 23 April 1963; quoted in Glenn T. Eskew, *But for Birmingham* (Chapel Hill: Univ. of North Carolina Press, 1997), 242–43.

38. Quoted in Young, *An Easy Burden*, 221.

39. Quoted in Garrow, *Bearing the Cross*, 246.

40. Quoted in Joan Baez, *And a Voice to Sing With* (New York: Summit Books, 1987), 104.

41. Police memo, 5 May 1963, mass meeting, quoted in McWhorter, *Carry Me Home*, 386.

42. Quoted in McWhorter, *Carry Me Home*, 387.

43. *Carry Me Home*, 154.

44. Dave Dellinger, "The Negroes of Birmingham," *Liberation*, summer 1963, 19.

45. King, *Playboy* interview, in Washington, *Testament of Hope*, 347.

46. Quoted in Eskew, *But for Birmingham*, 266.

47. Raines, *My Soul Is Rested*, 157–60; Henry Hampton, Steve Fayer, and Sarah Flynn, eds., *Voices of Freedom* (New York: Bantam, 1990), 136; quoted in McWhorter, *Carry Me Home*, 414–15; Manis, *A Fire You Can't Put Out*, 381–83; Eskew, *But for Birmingham*, 287–88; Garrow, *Bearing the Cross*, 256–57.

48. Young, *An Easy Burden*, 247.

49. *Eyes on the Prize*, episode 4, "No Easy Walk."

50. King, *Voices of Freedom*, 130.

51. Quoted in Eskew, *But for Birmingham*, 222.

Chapter 5

52. Robert Kennedy, *In His Own Words* (New York: Bantam, 1988), 223–26; quoted in Arthur Schlesinger Jr., *Robert Kennedy and His Times* (Boston: Houghton Mifflin, 1978), 331–35; Arthur Schlesinger Jr., *A Thousand Days* (Boston: Houghton Mifflin, 1965), 962–63.

53. Quoted in Branch, *Pillar of Fire*, 92.

54. White House meeting, 20 May 1963, audiotape 88.4, Kennedy Library, quoted in Branch, *Pillar of Fire*, 88–89.

55. John F. Kennedy, 11 June 1963, *Public Papers* (Washington, DC: U.S. Government Printing Office, 1962–64), 3:468–71.

56. Theodore C. Sorensen, *Kennedy* (New York: Harper & Row, 1965), 506.

Chapter 6

57. *We Shall Overcome!*, authorized audio recording of the March on Washington (Council for United Civil Rights Leadership, 1963); Washington, *Testament of Hope*, 217–20.

58. Quoted in Clayborne Carson, *In Struggle* (Cambridge: Harvard Univ. Press, 1981), 94.

59. Anne Moody, *Coming of Age in Mississippi* (New York: Dell, 1968), 307.

60. Quoted in McWhorter, *Carry Me Home*, 510.

61. Quoted in *Carry Me Home*, 525.

62. Quoted in Garrow, *Bearing the Cross*, 292.

63. Washington, *Testament of Hope*, 221–22.

Chapter 7

64. Martin Luther King Jr., address to SCLC, 27 September 1963, quoted in Branch, *Pillar of Fire*, 145.

65. W. E. B. Du Bois, *The Souls of Black Folk* (New York: Dodd, Mead, 1979), 3.

66. "The wisdom tradition of black North American folk culture dissents from the predominant Western form of disjunctive thinking—that conventional 'either/or' in which rationalism insists on unambiguous, univocal meanings for things. Instead this tradition prefers the conjunctive 'both/and' of archaic and oral cultures, in which ambiguity and multivocity are taken for granted (even promoted). . . . In conventional dialectical approaches (for example, Hegel's), 'opposites are conceptualized as coexistent, but only antagonistically.' Rather than the thesis-antithesis disjunction of such formulations, conjunctive approaches are able to affirm both elements in a dyad. This dual affirmation of opposites is the crucial aspect of wisdom traditions that feature conjunctive forms of cognition." Theophus H. Smith, *Conjuring Culture* (New York: Oxford Univ. Press, 1994), 143.

67. Ken Burns, *The Civil War*, PBS television documentary, 1989, episode 9, "1865."

68. Bayard Rustin, *Strategies for Freedom* (New York: Columbia Univ. Press, 1976), 49.

69. *Strategies for Freedom*, 49–50.

70. Whitney M. Young Jr., *To Be Equal* (New York: McGraw-Hill, 1964), 27–28.

71. *New York Times*, 1 July 1963; *St. Louis Post-Dispatch*, 21 September 1963.

72. Quoted in Branch, *Pillar of Fire*, 248.

73. David J. Garrow, "The FBI and Martin Luther King," *Atlantic Monthly*, July/August 2002, 80–88.

74. Quoted in Branch, *Pillar of Fire*, 27.

75. King, interview by Bernhard, quoted in Branch, *Pillar of Fire*, 248.

76. Coretta Scott King, *My Life*, 227.

Chapter 8

77. Quoted in James H. Cone, *Martin & Malcolm & America* (Maryknoll, NY: Orbis Books, 1991), 184.

78. Quoted in Cone, *Martin & Malcolm & America*, 158–59, 182–83.

79. "A Declaration of Independence," 12 March 1964, in *Malcolm X Speaks* (New York: Grove Press, 1965), 18–22.

80. "The Ballot or the Bullet," 3 April 1964, in *Malcolm X Speaks*, 34–35.

81. "The Ballot or the Bullet," 58–60; Malcolm X Collection, Schomburg Center, New York Public Library, quoted in *New York Times*, 8 January 2003.

82. Kenneth Clark and Jeannette Hopkins, *A Relevant War Against Poverty* (New York: Harper Torchbooks, 1970), 248–49.

83. Marshall Frady, *Martin Luther King, Jr.* (New York: Viking Penguin, 2002), 136.

84. Quoted in Garrow, *Bearing the Cross*, 330.

85. Quoted in Frady, *Martin Luther King, Jr.*, 138.

86. Quoted in Garrow, *Bearing the Cross*, 331.

87. Quoted in Frady, *Martin Luther King, Jr.*, 138–39

88. *New York Times*, 26 June 1964.

89. Frady, *Martin Luther King, Jr.*, 138. This description of the June 25 battle is indebted to Frady's eyewitness account.

90. *Martin Luther King, Jr.*, 142.

91. *Martin Luther King, Jr.*, 142.

92. Quoted in Garrow, *Bearing the Cross*, 337.

93. C. Vann Woodward, *The Strange Career of Jim Crow* (New York: Oxford Univ. Press, 1974), 186.

94. CORE Legal Dept., "The 1964 Civil Rights Act—A Hard Look" (CORE pamphlet, 1964).

95. Malcolm X, "Prospects for Freedom in 1965," in *Malcolm X Speaks* (New York: Grove Press, 1966), 151.

Chapter 9

96. Ella Baker, interview by Clayborne Carson, New York, 5 May 1972, unpublished transcript.

97. Ella Baker, "Developing Community Leadership," in *Black Women in White America*, ed. Gerda Lerner (New York: Pantheon, 1972), 352.

98. Matt. 16; quoted in Charles Marsh, *God's Long Summer* (Princeton: Princeton Univ. Press, 1997), 10–11; Fannie Lou Hamer, *To Praise Our Bridges* (Jackson, MS: Kipco, 1967), 12.

99. Raines, *My Soul Is Rested*, 249.

100. *My Soul Is Rested*, 250; Hamer, *To Praise Our Bridges*, 12, 13; quoted in Howard Zinn, *SNCC: The New Abolitionists* (Boston: Beacon Press, 1965), 94.

101. Quoted in Raines, *My Soul Is Rested*, 240.

102. Quoted in Sally Belfrage, *Freedom Summer* (Greenwich, CT: Fawcett, 1966), 65.

103. Quoted in *Freedom Summer*, 186.

104. *Freedom Summer*, 209–10.

105. Quoted in Doris Kearns, *Lyndon Johnson and the American Dream* (New York: Harper & Row, 1976), 198.

106. "Life of Fannie Lou Hamer," Pacifica radio program, 1983 (Pacifica Radio Archive, Los Angeles).

107. Quoted in Branch, *Pillar of Fire*, 470.

108. Quoted in Chana Kai Lee, *For Freedom's Sake: The Life of Fannie Lou Hamer* (Urbana: Univ. of Illinois Press, 1999), 89.

109. Michael R. Beschloss, ed., *Taking Charge: The Johnson White House Tapes, 1963–1964* (New York: Simon & Schuster, 1997), 526, 528–29, 531–32.

110. Quoted in Kay Mills, *This Little Light of Mine* (New York: Penguin/Plume, 1994), 125.

111. Quoted in *New York Times*, 13 December 2002.

112. Quoted in Branch, *Pillar of Fire*, 469.

113. Quoted in Garrow, *Bearing the Cross*, 347.

114. Quoted in James Forman, *The Making of Black Revolutionaries* (Washington, D.C.: Open Hand, 1985), 392.

115. Quoted in Branch, *Pillar of Fire*, 471, 473.

116. Quoted in Marsh, *God's Long Summer*, 31, 33, 45.

Chapter 10

117. Farmer, *Lay Bare the Heart*, 215–19, 298–99.

118. Quoted in Garrow, *Bearing the Cross*, 343.

119. Quoted in Garrow, ibid., 343.

120. King, "President's Annual Report," quoted in Garrow, *Bearing the Cross*, 353.

121. Coretta Scott King, *My Life*, 1–4.

122. *My Life*, 1–4.

123. Quoted in Garrow, *Bearing the Cross*, 355.

124. Quoted in Garrow, *Bearing the Cross*, 363.

125. Quoted in Branch, *Pillar of Fire*, 533.

126. Quoted in Garrow, *Bearing the Cross*, 366.

Chapter 11

127. Quoted in Garrow, *Bearing the Cross*, 368.

128. Quoted in Charles E. Fager, *Selma, 1965* (Boston: Beacon Press, 1985), 9–10.

129. Quoted in Branch, *Pillar of Fire*, 528.

130. Quoted in Fager, *Selma, 1965*, 44–45.

131. Quoted in Branch, *Pillar of Fire*, 566.

132. Quoted in Fager, *Selma, 1965*, 52.

133. Quoted in Charles Fager, *In These Times*, 9 February 1983.

134. Quoted in Branch, *Pillar of Fire*, 578.

135. Quoted in Fager, *Selma, 1965*, 57; Branch, *Pillar of Fire*, 579.

136. Coretta Scott King, *My Life*, 256.

137. Numbers 13–14; Arnold Sternberg, interview by author, Sacramento, CA, 26 January 2002.

138. Quoted in Branch, *Pillar of Fire*, 599; Acts 12:2–3, Est. 4:8.

139. Hampton, Fayer, and Flynn, *Voices of Freedom*, 226.

140. Quoted in Garrow, *Bearing the Cross*, 394.

141. Quoted in Fager, *Selma, 1965*, 93, 94.

142. Maria Varela, "Crumpled Notes (found in a raincoat) on Selma," in Fager, *Selma, 1965*, 91, 99.

143. Quoted in Garrow, *Bearing the Cross*, 400.

144. Quoted in Garrow, *Bearing the Cross*, 405.

145. Quoted in Dan T. Carter, *The Politics of Rage* (New York: Simon & Schuster, 1995), 253–54; Michael R. Beschloss, ed., *Reaching for Glory: Lyndon Johnson's Secret White House Tapes, 1964–1965* (New York: Simon & Schuster, 2002), 231.

146. Quoted in Eric F. Goldman, *The Tragedy of Lyndon Johnson* (New York: Dell, 1974), 372.

147. Johnson, *Public Papers* (Washington, DC: U. S. Government Printing Office, 1965–70), vol. 2, pt. 1, 281, 284.

148. Quoted in Fager, *Selma, 1965,* 146.

149. Quoted in Susannah Heschel, "Theological Affinities in the Writings of Abraham Joshua Heschel and Martin Luther King, Jr.," in *Black Zion,* ed. Yvonne Chireau and Nathaniel Deutsch (New York: Oxford Univ. Press, 2000), 177, 175.

150. Quoted in Garrow, *Bearing the Cross,* 412.

151. Martin Luther King Jr., "Our God Is Marching On!" 25 March 1965, in Washington, *Testament of Hope,* 229–30.

Chapter 12

152. Scott B. Smith Jr., interview by author, Philo, CA, 28 February 2002.

153. Quoted in Clayborne Carson, *In Struggle* (Cambridge: Harvard Univ. Press, 1981), 166.

154. Cleveland Sellers, *The River of No Return* (New York: William Morrow, 1973), 151.

155. Quoted in *The River of No Return,* 153; quoted in Stokely Carmichael and Charles V. Hamilton, *Black Power* (New York: Vintage, 1967), 115.

156. *New York Times,* 1 May 1965; SCLC Newsletter, April/May 1965.

157. *New York Times,* 3, 5 July 1965.

158. Quoted in Garrow, *Bearing the Cross,* 430.

159. MLK/LBJ telephone conversation, 7 July 1965, in Beschloss, *Reaching for Glory,* 388–89.

160. Quoted in David J. Garrow, *Protest at Selma* (New Haven: Yale Univ. Press, 1978), 113.

161. Quoted in Garrow, *Bearing the Cross,* 439, 440.

162. Quoted in Martin Luther King Jr., *Where Do We Go from Here: Chaos or Community?* (Boston: Beacon Press, 1968), 30–31.

163. Sellers, *The River of No Return,* 164, 169.

Book Three

Chapter 1

1. Martin Luther King Jr., "A Time to Break Silence," in Washington, *A Testament of Hope,* 231–44.

2. Thich Nhat Hanh, "Letter to Martin Luther King from a Buddhist Monk," 1 June 1965, published in *Dialogue* (Saigon: La Boi, June 1965), reprinted in *Liberation,* December 1965, 18–19.

3. Quoted in Garrow, *Bearing the Cross,* 445; Adam Fairclough, *To Redeem the Soul of America* (Athens: Univ. of Georgia Press, 1987), 273–74; King, "To Chart Our Course for the Future," address to SCLC staff retreat, Frogmore, SC, 29–31 May 1967, MLKP-GAMK.

4. "SNCC Position Paper: Vietnam," *The Movement,* January 1966, in Judith C. Albert and Stewart E. Albert, eds., *The Sixties Papers* (New York: Praeger, 1984), 117–18.

5. Quoted in Mark Lane and Dick Gregory, *Code Name "Zorro": The Murder of Martin Luther King, Jr.* (Englewood Cliffs, NJ: Prentice Hall, 1977), 53–54.

6. Robert S. McNamara, *In Retrospect* (New York: Times Books, 1995), 216–17.

7. Quoted in Nancy Zaroulis and Gerald Sullivan, *Who Spoke Up?* (New York: Holt, Rinehart & Winston, 1985), 3.

8. Quoted in David Halberstam, *The Best and the Brightest* (Greenwich, CT: Fawcett/Crest, 1973), 779.

9. Daniel Ellsberg, *Papers on the War* (New York: Simon & Schuster, 1972), 42.

Chapter 2

10. Martin Luther King Jr., "The Casualties of the War in Vietnam," Los Angeles, 25 February 1967; Martin Luther King Jr., "Address to the Peace Parade and Rally," Chicago, 25 March 1967; both in Martin Luther King Jr. Papers, King Center, Atlanta, hereafter MLKP-GAMK.

11. Young to Bevel and Dellinger, 14 March 1967, MLKP-GAMK.

12. MLK to Levison, 25, 27 March 1967, quoted in Garrow, *Bearing the Cross,* 550.

13. David Dellinger, *From Yale to Jail* (New York: Pantheon, 1993), 285; quoted in Zaroulis and Sullivan, *Who Spoke Up?,* 112.

14. Martin Luther King Jr., address, New York, 15 April 1967, MLKP-GAMK.

15. *Face the Nation,* 16 April 1967, CBS News.

16. Quoted in Michael Ferber and Staughton Lynd, *The Resistance* (Boston: Beacon Press, 1971), 81; Staughton Lynd, "The Movement: A New Beginning," *Liberation,* May 1969.

17. Quoted in Alice Lynd, ed., *We Won't Go* (Boston: Beacon Press, 1968), 206.

18. Paul Rupert, interview by author, San Francisco, 5 January 1975.

19. *Washington Post,* 6 April 1967.

20. *Life,* 21 April 1967.

21. *Pittsburgh Courier,* 15 April 1967; the black newspaper headlined its editorial, "Dr. King's Tragic Doctrine."

22. Quoted in Young, *An Easy Burden,* 431; Garrow, *Bearing the Cross,* 546.

23. Quoted in Garrow, *Bearing the Cross,* 554–55.

24. Quoted in Young, *An Easy Burden,* 434.

25. Martin Luther King Jr., "Three Dimensions of a Complete Life," Chicago, 9 April 1967, MLKP-GAMK.

Chapter 3

26. *Pittsburgh Courier,* 29 April 1967; also 8 April and 6 May 1967.

27. Martin Luther King Jr., "Why I Am Opposed to the War in Vietnam," Atlanta, 30 April 1967, MLKP-GAMK. Ali never served time in prison. He appealed his conviction for draft refusal, and the Supreme Court overturned it in June 1970 because of an illegal FBI wiretap on his telephone. He spoke widely against the war and regained the world heavyweight title in 1974.

28. Quoted in Garrow, *Bearing the Cross,* 561.

29. Patricia Williams, "Alchemical Notes: Reconstructing Ideals from Deconstructed Rights," in *A Less Than Perfect Union,* ed. Jules Lobel (New York: Monthly Review Press, 1988), 64.

30. Quoted in King, *Where Do We Go from Here,* 130. Although this might have sounded like a sweeping rights claim, it did not go beyond the Universal Declaration of Human Rights approved by the U.N. General Assembly in December 1948.

31. John 3:1–21. Martin Luther King Jr., "To Chart Our Course for the Future," Frogmore, SC, 29–31 May 1967, MLKP-GAMK.

32. Quoted in Fairclough, *To Redeem the Soul of America,* 343.

33. "Martin Luther King on the Middle East," *San Francisco Chronicle,* 23 February 2003.

Chapter 4

34. Chapter 5 typescript draft, MLKP-GAMK, box 12.

Chapter 5

35. Quoted in Garrow, *Bearing the Cross*, 565.

36. Quoted in *Bearing the Cross*, 565.

37. *Report of the National Advisory Commission on Civil Disorders* (Kerner Commission) (New York: E. P. Dutton, 1968), 10.

38. Bob Clark, "Nightmare Journey," *Ebony*, October 1967.

39. Jimmy Breslin, "Breslin on Riot: Death, Laughter, but No Sanity," *Detroit News*, 25 July 1967.

40. Quoted in *Report of the National Advisory Commission*, 91, 92.

41. Quoted in Hampton, Fayer, and Flynn, *Voices of Freedom*, 384.

42. Quoted in Garrow, *Bearing the Cross*, 569, 570.

43. Martin Luther King Jr., "Telegram to the President," press conference, Atlanta, 24 July 1967, MLKP-GAMK.

44. Martin Luther King Jr., "Standing by the Best in an Evil Time," Ebenezer, 6 August 1967, MLKP-GAMK.

45. Norman Mailer, *The White Negro* (San Francisco: City Lights Books, 1957), n.p.

46. Theodore Roszak, *The Making of a Counter Culture* (Garden City, NY: Doubleday, 1968, 1969), 50–51.

47. Martin Luther King Jr., testimony to U.S. Senate Subcommittee on Executive Reorganization, 15 December 1966.

48. David Riesman, *The Lonely Crowd* (New Haven: Yale Univ. Press, 1950), 11.

49. Martin Luther King Jr., "A Realistic Look at Race Relations," New York, 17 May 1956, MLKP-MBU.

50. Frady, *Martin Luther King Jr.*, 191–92.

51. Testimony to Senate Subcommittee on Executive Reorganization, 15 December 1966.

Chapter 6

52. Martin Luther King Jr., "Great, but," audiotape recording, Ebenezer, 2 July 1967, MLKP-GAMK.

53. Quotations and dialogue from Coretta Scott King, interview by Charlotte Mayerson, Manchester, NH, 15 July–5 August 1968, pt. 27, quoted in Garrow, *Bearing the Cross*, 571.

54. Martin Luther King Jr., "A Knock at Midnight," Los Angeles, 25 June 1967, MLKP-GAMK.

55. *America*, 22 July 1967; *Commonweal*, 17 November 1967.

56. Martin Luther King Jr., "The Crisis in America's Cities," address to SCLC convention, Atlanta, 15 August 1967, MLKP-GAMK.

Chapter 7

57. Martin Luther King Jr., "Why Jesus Called a Man a Fool," Chicago, 27 August 1967, in Carson and Holloran, *A Knock at Midnight*, 160, 163–64.

58. Peter Edelman, interview by L. J. Hackman, 5 August 1969, RFK Oral History Program, quoted in Schlesinger, *Robert Kennedy and His Times*, 873.

59. Hampton, Fayer, and Flynn, *Voices of Freedom*, 453–54.

60. Quoted in Garrow, *Bearing the Cross*, 577, 578.

61. Martin Luther King Jr., keynote address, Conference for New Politics, Chicago, 31 August 1967, MLKP-GAMK.

62. Quoted in Zaroulis and Sullivan, *Who Spoke Up?*, 128–29.

Chapter 8

63. Carl T. Rowan, "Martin Luther King's Tragic Decision," *Reader's Digest,* September 1967.

64. "Good Company," ABC News, 11 October 1967.

65. Quoted in Michael Ferber and Staughton Lynd, *The Resistance* (Boston: Beacon Press, 1971), 91.

66. *East Village Other,* New York, 1 November 1967.

67. Dellinger, *From Yale to Jail,* 307.

68. McNamara, *In Retrospect,* 303, 305.

69. Gregory Nevala Calvert, *Democracy from the Heart* (Eugene, OR: Communitas Press, 1991), 250–51.

70. *Democracy from the Heart,* 254.

71. Martin Luther King Jr., "What Are Your New Year's Resolutions?," Ebenezer, 7 January 1968, MLKP-GAMK.

Chapter 9

72. Martin Luther King Jr., remarks to Birmingham mass meeting, 4 November 1967, MLKP-GAMK.

73. Martin Luther King Jr., "The State of the Movement," address to SCLC staff retreat, Frogmore, SC, 28 November 1967, MLKP-GAMK.

74. Martin Luther King Jr., "Why a Movement," Frogmore, SC, 28 November 1967, MLKP-GAMK.

75. Quoted in Ferber and Lynd, *The Resistance,* 209.

76. Charlotte Bunch, *Passionate Politics* (New York: St. Martin's Press, 1987), 4, 6.

77. Quoted in Sara Evans, *Personal Politics* (New York: Vintage, 1980), 211.

Chapter 10

78. Joan Baez Sr., *Inside Santa Rita* (Santa Barbara: John Daniel, 1994), 83; Joan Baez, interview by Amy Goodman, 19 November 2002, "Democracy Now," Pacifica Radio; Joan Baez, *And a Voice to Sing With,* 111–12.

79. Ira Sandperl, interview by author, audiotape recording, Stanford University, 2 February 1995, author's archive.

80. Sandperl interview.

81. Martin Luther King Jr., "See You in Washington," address to SCLC staff retreat, Atlanta, 17 January 1968, MLKP-GAMK.

82. Martin Luther King Jr., speech and press conference, Santa Rita, CA, 14 January 1968, Pacifica Radio Archive.

83. Martin Luther King Jr., press conference, Atlanta, 4 December 1967, MLKP-GAMK.

84. Quoted in Garrow, *Bearing the Cross,* 583.

85. Minutes of SCLC executive staff meeting, 27 December 1967, SCLC Papers, box 49, GAMK.

86. Thomas F. Jackson, "Recasting the Dream" (Ph.D. diss., Stanford Univ., 1993), 424.

87. Richard A. Cloward and Frances Fox Piven, "A Strategy to End Poverty," *Nation,* 2 March 1966.

88. Quoted in James T. Patterson, *America's Struggle Against Poverty, 1900–1980* (Cambridge: Harvard Univ. Press, 1981), 188.

89. Quoted in Nick Kotz and Mary Lynn Kotz, *A Passion for Equality* (New York: Norton, 1977), 190.

90. Quoted in *A Passion for Equality*, 200.

91. King, *Where Do We Go from Here*, 164.

92. Martin Luther King Jr., "See You in Washington," address to SCLC staff retreat, Atlanta, 17 January 1968, MLKP-GAMK.

Chapter 11

93. Quoted in Michael Maclear, *The Ten Thousand Day War* (New York: St. Martin's Press, 1981), 195.

94. *Pentagon Papers* (New York: Bantam, 1971), 592.

95. Quoted in Stanley Karnow, *Vietnam* (New York: Viking Press, 1983), 534.

96. Mark 10:35–45.

97. Martin Luther King Jr., "The Drum Major Instinct," Ebenezer, 4 February 1968, in Washington, *Testament of Hope*, 259–67.

Chapter 12

98. Quoted in Kotz and Kotz, *A Passion for Equality*, 249.

99. Quoted in *A Passion for Equality*, 249.

100. Quoted in *A Passion for Equality*, 249.

101. Quoted in *A Passion for Equality*, 252.

102. Quoted in Zaroulis and Sullivan, *Who Spoke Up?*, 153.

103. Martin Luther King Jr., "In Search for a Sense of Direction," address to SCLC board meeting, 7 February 1968, MLKP-GAMK.

104. *New York Times*, 2 February 1968.

105. Quoted in Garrow, *Bearing the Cross*, 596.

106. Quoted in *Bearing the Cross*, 596–97.

107. *Washington Post* and *New York Post*, 26 February 1968, quoted in Anderson, *Bayard Rustin*, 305.

108. Bayard Rustin, "Social Dislocation and the Civil Rights Revolution," 1964, Bayard Rustin Papers, Library of Congress.

109. Rustin to MLK, "Memo on Spring Protest in Washington, D.C.," 29 January 1968, Bayard Rustin Papers, Library of Congress; also in Bayard Rustin, *Down the Line* (Chicago: Quadrangle, 1971), 202–5.

110. Rustin to MLK, 5 February 1968, Bayard Rustin Papers, Library of Congress.

111. Wachtel to Rustin, 25 September 1985, Bayard Rustin Papers, Library of Congress, quoted in Anderson, *Bayard Rustin*, 306.

112. Barbara Deming, "On Revolution and Equilibrium," *Liberation*, February 1968.

113. Schlesinger, *Robert Kennedy and His Times*, 848.

114. Quoted in Garrow, *Bearing the Cross*, 594.

115. James MacGregor Burns, *Leadership* (New York: Harper & Row, 1978, 1979), 422; J. M. Burns, interview by author, audiotape recording, Chilmark, MA, July 1979, author's archive.

116. Quoted in Harris Wofford, *Of Kennedys and Kings* (New York: Farrar Straus Giroux, 1980), 205.

117. Quoted in David J. Garrow, *The FBI and Martin Luther King, Jr.* (New York: Norton, 1981), 182–83.

118. Quoted in Young, *An Uneasy Burden*, 444; Garrow, *Bearing the Cross*, 597.

119. *Report of the National Advisory Commission on Civil Disorders* (Kerner Commission) (New York: Dutton, 1968), 1–2, 107.

120. *New York Times*, 2, 5 March 1968.

Chapter 13

121. Quoted in Garrow, *Bearing the Cross*, 602, 599.

122. Carson and Holloran, *A Knock at Midnight*, 187, 188.

123. 1 Kings 8.

124. Martin Luther King Jr., "Unfulfilled Dreams," Ebenezer, 3 March 1968, in Carson and Holloran, *A Knock at Midnight*, 191–200; Martin Luther King Jr., "Prodigal Son," audiotape recording, Ebenezer, 1966, MLKP-GAMK.

Chapter 14

125. McNamara, *In Retrospect*, 311.

126. McNamara, memo to Johnson, 1 November 1967, quoted in ibid., 307, 308.

127. Clifford comment in *Hearts and Minds*, documentary film, 1976.

128. Quoted in Townsend Hoopes, *The Limits of Intervention* (New York: David McKay, 1969), 179–80.

129. Quoted in *The Limits of Intervention*, 192.

130. Daniel Ellsberg, *Secrets* (New York: Viking, 2002), 201–2.

131. William C. Westmoreland, *A Soldier Reports* (Garden City, NY: Doubleday, 1976), 338.

132. Quoted in Hoopes, *The Limits of Intervention*, 216.

133. Walter Fauntroy, interview by Jean Stein, 11 November 1969, Stein Papers, quoted in Schlesinger, *Robert Kennedy and His Times*, 873.

134. Albert Turner and Hosea Williams to Organizations in Alabama, 2 February 1968, SCLC Papers, box 177, GAMK.

135. Hosea Williams and Fred Bennette to Officers, Members and Friends, 9 March 1968, SCLC Papers, box 179, GAMK.

136. Quoted in Garrow, *Bearing the Cross*, 607.

137. Eleanor Eaton, American Friends Service Committee, to Andy Young et al., 29 February 1968, SCLC Papers, box 49, GAMK.

138. *New York Times*, 15 March 1968.

139. Horton to Andrew Young, 15 March 1968, quoted in Frank Adams with Myles Horton, *Unearthing Seeds of Fire* (Winston-Salem, NC: Blair, 1975), 180.

140. Martin Luther King Jr., "Poor People's Campaign News," 15 March 1968, SCLC Papers, box 179, GAMK; Jackson, "Recasting the Dream," 521–23.

141. *New York Times*, 20 March 1968.

142. Hampton, Fayer, and Flynn, *Voices of Freedom*, 456.

143. PPC registration forms, SCLC Papers, box 181, GAMK; Jackson, "Recasting the Dream," 507–8.

144. If he had been leading at a time when immigrants (resident aliens) comprised a larger social force, he might have extended this right to resident noncitizens as well.

145. "Statement of Demands by the Poor People's Campaign," MLKP-GAMK.

146. Martin Luther King Jr., testimony to U.S. Senate Subcommittee on Executive Reorganization, Committee on Government Operations, 15 December 1966.

147. Andrew Young to Arthur and Marian Logan, 21 March 1968, MLKP-GAMK, quoted in Garrow, *Bearing the Cross*, 601.

148. Marian Logan, interview by David J. Garrow, New York, 6 August 1980, quoted in Garrow, *Bearing the Cross*, 609.

149. *New York Times*, 27 March 1968.

150. Director to FBI field offices, "Counterintelligence Program, Black Nationalist Hate Groups," 4 March 1968, quoted in Fairclough, *To Redeem the Soul*, 368.

151. Young, *An Easy Burden*, 446.

Chapter 15

152. Hampton, Fayer, and Flynn, *Voices of Freedom,* 459.

153. Martin Luther King Jr., address at Mason Temple, Memphis, 18 March 1968, MLKP-GAMK; Joan Turner Beifuss, *At the River I Stand* (Brooklyn: Carlson Publishing, 1989), 194–95.

154. King, address at Mason Temple.

155. Hampton, Fayer, and Flynn, *Voices of Freedom,* 459–60.

156. Quoted in Beifuss, *At the River I Stand,* 203.

157. Raines, *My Soul Is Rested,* 465.

158. Calvin Taylor comments quoted in Beifuss, *At the River I Stand,* 253–54.

159. *Atlanta Constitution,* 30 March 1968; *New York Times,* 29, 30 March 1968.

160. MLK, telephone conversation with Levison, 29 March 1968, quoted in Garrow, *Bearing the Cross,* 614–15.

161. *New York Times,* 1 April 1968.

162. Quoted in Abernathy, *And the Walls Came Tumbling Down* (New York: Harper & Row, 1989), 424.

163. Quoted in Marshall Frady, *Jesse* (New York: Random House, 1996), 224–25; quoted in Young, *An Easy Burden,* 457.

164. Quoted in Frady, *Jesse,* 224–25; quoted in Young, *An Easy Burden,* 458.

165. Quoted in Young, *An Easy Burden,* 458.

166. Raines, *My Soul Is Rested,* 467.

167. Quoted in Frady, *Jesse,* 225.

168. Jesse Jackson, conversation with author, Stanford University, 12 May 1992, author's archive.

169. Levison, telephone conversation, 31 March 1968, quoted in Fairclough, *To Redeem the Soul,* 379.

170. Quoted in Garrow, *Bearing the Cross,* 616.

171. Jackson, conversation with author.

172. St. John of the Cross, *Dark Night of the Soul,* trans. Mirabai Starr (New York: Riverhead Books, 2003), 178.

Chapter 16

173. Rev. 21:4–5. Martin Luther King Jr., "Remaining Awake Through a Great Revolution," Washington, DC, 31 March 1968, in Washington, *Testament of Hope,* 274, 277, 278.

174. *New York Times,* 1 April 1968; *Atlanta Constitution,* 1 April 1968; *Washington Post,* 1 April 1968.

175. Fauntroy, interview by Jean Stein, quoted in Schlesinger, *Robert Kennedy and His Times,* 873.

176. Quoted in Doris Kearns, *Lyndon Johnson and the American Dream* (New York: Harper & Row, 1976), 343.

177. Quoted in Abernathy, *And the Walls Came Tumbling Down,* 428.

178. Quoted in Beifuss, *At the River I Stand,* 269.

179. Quoted in *At the River I Stand,* 276; Hampton, Fayer, and Flynn, *Voices of Freedom,* 464.

180. Martin Luther King Jr., "I've Been to the Mountaintop," Memphis, 3 April 1968, in Washington, *Testament of Hope,* 279–86.

181. Quoted in Beifuss, *At the River I Stand,* 279.

182. Quoted in Frady, *Jesse,* 226.

183. Georgia Davis Powers, *I Shared the Dream* (Far Hills, NJ: New Horizon Press, 1995), 227–36.

Chapter 17

184. *Atlanta Constitution*, 5 April 1968.

185. *Atlanta Constitution*, 5 April 1968.

186. Young, *An Easy Burden*, 463–64.

187. The fact that Ray was staying in a second-floor room in the rooming house on April 4, 1968, and carried the rifle into his room was indisputable. The King family and their attorney, William F. Pepper, have contended that Ray did not actually shoot Martin King, and that he disposed of his rifle a short while before the killing. They have not claimed that Ray was uninvolved, but that he was set up as a "fall guy" for the murder by a conspiracy that included the Mafia, members of the Memphis Police Dept., and even Tennessee and U.S. government officials. The *King v. Jowers* civil case for wrongful death that the King family brought to trial in 1999 in a Memphis state court was decided by the jury in favor of the conspiracy claim by Pepper and the King plaintiffs. The truth about whether Ray killed King, and about the nature and extent of a possible conspiracy, are beyond the scope of this book. See William F. Pepper, *An Act of State* (London: Verso, 2003) and the *King v. Jowers* trial transcript (www.thekingcenter.org/news/trial). For an alternative view, see Gerald Posner, *Killing the Dream* (New York: Random House, 1998).

188. Quoted in Beifuss, *At the River I Stand*, 290.

189. Quotations (and dinner menu) from *At the River I Stand*, 290–92.

190. Quoted in Frady, *Jesse*, 227.

191. Andrew Young recollection in *Voices of Freedom*, 467.

192. Abernathy recollection in *Voices of Freedom*, 467.

193. Coretta Scott King, *My Life*, 293.

194. Quoted in Abernathy, *And the Walls Came Tumbling Down*, 446.

195. Quoted in Schlesinger, *Robert Kennedy and His Times*, 874–75.

196. Quoted in Beifuss, *At the River I Stand*, 314.

197. Howard Thurman, "Memorial Tribute to Martin Luther King, Jr.," 4 April 1968, KPFK-FM, Los Angeles, author's archive.

198. Quoted in *Life*, 19 April 1968, 4.

199. Coretta Scott King, "How Many Men Must Die?" Memphis, 8 April 1968, *Life*, 19 April 1968, 34–35.

200. Thomas A. Dorsey, "Precious Lord," 1932.

Conclusion

1. Although the media spotlighted the minority who turned to violence, a growing number of American activists firmly embraced nonviolent action. During its most successful phase (1969–72), the antiwar movement, which broadened into the mainstream, engaged in exemplary nonviolent protest on a large scale. As President Nixon confessed in his memoir, these actions forced him to bring the troops home and move toward serious negotiations, which eventually ended the decade-long conflict. In the late 1970s and 1980s mass nonviolent action reached new heights with the campaigns against nuclear energy and weapons, marches for women's rights and gay and lesbian liberation, and in the 1990s with "million man" and "million woman" marches in Washington. Environmental activism and the movement for global justice appeared to be carrying on this tradition into the twenty-first century.

On the world stage, nonviolent action looked even more promising. The relatively nonviolent French revolt of May 1968 was accompanied by the peacefully explosive "Prague spring," that despite being crushed by Soviet tanks in August presaged the velvet revolutions and the Cold War's end twenty years later. Western Europeans mounted colossal protests against U.S. and Soviet first-strike nuclear missiles in the 1980s.

Nonviolent direct action inspired by King and the American movements swept through Eastern Europe and into the Philippines, China, Tibet, Burma, and (ultimately) South Africa, and other countries less noticed.

2. Determined to fulfill their slain leader's will, the mule-train army of the poor arrived at the Washington Mall in mid-May 1968. Hundreds of many-hued souls set up a shantytown of canvas and plywood on the south side of the reflecting pool between the Lincoln Memorial and the Washington Monument. They christened their new community Resurrection City. SCLC leaders hammered out a comprehensive manifesto of demands for economic justice. PPC activists led by SCLC lobbied Congress and Cabinet departments week after week for their Bill of Economic and Social Rights to end poverty. None blocked streets or bridges, as had been feared; occasional acts of civil disobedience were carefully controlled. There was no violence.

Bayard Rustin agreed to take charge of organizing a massive march on Washington for late June, hoping it to be an encore of his masterpiece of August 1963. But everything had changed in that epic half decade. Rustin resigned in a tiff with the tense new SCLC hierarchy over the demands, and the march was underwhelming. Racial tensions surfaced in Resurrection City, compounded by inadequate provisions. Punishing rains conspired with human foibles to make the flooded encampment inhospitable, the beleaguered residents soaked with mud. Police forcibly evicted them in early July. The poor, who always seemed to lose, were routed once again.

Acknowledgments

I have spent a decade researching and developing this book and two years writing it. During that journey and before, many people have helped me in many ways, some perhaps unknowingly. I want to express heartfelt appreciation to my intellectual mentors: Robert McAfee Brown, John H. Schaar, Dick Flacks, Marge Frantz, James MacGregor Burns, and (though we haven't met) Garry Wills, whose writing has inspired me for thirty years. David Garrow, dean of civil rights historians, reviewed the manuscript carefully and was generous as usual with advice and suggestions. I have benefited from groundbreaking research by Clay Carson and the staff of the King Papers Project at Stanford University, where I served as associate editor. I have benefited also from Mills Thornton's expertise on the Montgomery bus boycott. Writer and editor Suzanne Lipsett, who died of breast cancer, steered me toward writing a deeper biography of King. Janet Keep, Deborah Schneer, Ann Manheimer, Randy Schutt, and Tamara Watts gave me cogent criticisms of the manuscript. Randy and Tamara have been my cherished colleagues for many years. Any errors or misinterpretations in the book are my own.

Helen Schrader's guidance and support have nourished my soul. Ira Sandperl, Arnold Sternberg, Lee Beckom, Jamie Godfrey, Rabbi Margaret Holub, Rev. Dr. Karen Lebacqz, and Jane Benson have helped me in important ways. The fellowship of Evergreen United Methodist Church in Fort Bragg, Calif., has sustained my heart.

I thank the staffs of Stanford's Green Library, Williams College Library, and Fort Bragg Public Library, as well as the resourceful staff of

Gallery Bookshop and Ian Mayeno of Zo Office Supply, both stores in Mendocino, Calif. David Russell creatively designed my Web site.

I am grateful to my agents, Peter Sawyer and Fifi Oscard in New York, for their confidence in my work and for making arrangements with my fine publisher. My editors and others at HarperSanFrancisco have done a remarkable job preparing the manuscript for publication. Executive editor John Loudon's support has been a Godsend. His skillful assistant, Kris Ashley, performed editorial miracles of all kinds. Managing editor Terri Leonard has been both efficient and patient. I want to thank associate publisher Mark Tauber for his support, as well as marketing director Margery Buchanan, copy editor Carl Walesa, indexer Charlee Trantino, and proofreader Carol Lastrucci. Harper-Collins attorney Mark Jackson expertly handled legal issues.

I am grateful for the loving support and creative guidance of Deborah Schneer, who has been my anchor and beacon during this voyage. Her writing wisdom and editing expertise made vital contributions to the book. Janet Thompson Keep, my mother, has been my intellectual and spiritual companion through the years of preparing this work. She has helped deepen my understanding of the Bible, has offered valuable insights on many subjects, and has given me steadfast support when I most needed it.

Index

Note: The abbreviation JFK refers to John F. Kennedy; LBJ to Lyndon Baines Johnson; MLK to Martin Luther King Jr.; RFK to Robert F. Kennedy

117, 135–36, 460n. 37; bus, Tallahassee, FL, 115, 139–40, 144, 146, 149; South Carolina State College, Orangeburg, 114; stores, Birmingham, 177, 178; violence and threats of violence, 30, 43, 135–36, 141–42

Boynton, Amelia, 263, 274, 283

Brady, Tom, 58

Branch, Ben, 449

Brightman, Edgar, 53

Brinson, Henrietta, 102–3

Brock, Jack, 140

Brockwood Labor College, 66

Brooks, Hilliard, 19, 21, 102

Brotherhood of Sleeping Car Porters, 20, 66

Browder, Aurelia, 116–19

Browder v. Gayle, 7–9, 41, 43–44, 70, 115, 116–19, 141, 465n. 167

Brown, H. Rap, 349, 395, 404

Brown Chapel AME Church, Selma, AL, 264, 272, 274, 275

Brown v. Board of Education of Topeka, 6, 10, 41, 99, 202; "all deliberate speed" and enforcement problems, 234; Eastland's condemnation of, 64; governors vow to resist through "interposition," 45; grassroots campaign of "massive resistance," 58; State of the Race Conference, Washington, DC and call for school de-segregation campaign, 115

Buber, Martin, 50, 110, 340, 464n. 156

Bunch, Charlotte, 372–73

Bundy, McGeorge, 412–13

Burks, Mary Fair, 19, 20, 21

Burroughs, Nannie, 144

Butler, Mac, 74, 279

Cabbage, Charles, 428

Calvert, Greg, 365

Campbell, Will, 149

Capetown, South Africa, 115

Carawan, Candie, 193–94

Carawan, Guy, 169, 193–94

Carmichael, Oliver Cromwell, 45

Carmichael, Stokely, 284, 291–93; antiwar activity, 304, 310, 311, 312, 395; Black Panthers and, 399; MLK disapproval of, 349

Carter, Eugene, 9, 98–106, 140, 141

Carter, Robert, 99

Castro, Fidel, 228

Catonsville Nine, 371–72

Cellar, Emanuel, 289

Chambliss, Robert "Dynamite Bob," 41, 46, 213

Chaney, James, 246–47, 248

Chavez, Cesar, 392, 430–31

Cherry, Bobby, 214

Chicago, IL: Breadbasket campaign, 334; MLK,

NWRO meeting, 392–93; SCLC campaign, 291, 308, 322, 327–28, 381; urban rioting, post MLK death, 452; urban rioting, threat of, 337

Chomsky, Noam, 363

CIA, "Operation Chaos," 366

Civil Rights Act of 1964, 206–8, 210, 238, 250; compliance, public-accommodations, 258; implementation problems, 241

Civil Rights Act of 1968, 454

Civil rights movement: African American women as driving force of, 28, 104–5, 152; Albany, GA, 171, 176,178, 185, 197, 221; analysis "state of the movement," by MLK, St. Helena Island, 1967, 369–71; arrest and beating of Fannie Lou Hamer and group, Mississippi, 205–6; assassination of Medgar Evers, 208; Birmingham campaign, "Project Confrontation," 177–79, 189–201, 221; black militancy in, 221, 259, 291–93, 310, 356–57, 372, 393–95, 416–17; black student movement, 205 (*see also* SNCC); boycotts, 8, 23–39, 31, 42–44, 70–80, 99–107, 115, 149, 150; broadening of Montgomery movement, 80, 84, 97, 130–34; bus desegregation campaigns, 150; Chicago campaign, 291, 308, 322, 327–28; as church-based protest, 29, 76–78, 90, 152–55; civil disobedience and, 149; Cleveland campaign, 334–35; college campuses, 114–15; Communism and communist charges, 65, 69, 132, 147, 210, 226, 288; deaths, desegregation of U. of Miss. and, 174; dispute about role of northern activists, 96–97; dissension within, 119–22, 123–25; division in, 1967, 356–57; electoral politics, focus on, 246–55, 256, 257–59, 289–90, 396; federal intervention requested, 149, 150; freedom riders, 1961, 174–76, 221; Freedom Summer, 237–38, 246, 247, 255, 257; fund-raising and finances, 120–22, 131, 133, 188; Greenwood campaign, 189–90; informants and spies, 43, 100, 433; killing of James Reeb, 277–78; killing of Jimmie Lee Jackson, 272; killing of Jonathan Daniels, 285; killing of Schwerner, Goodman, and Chaney, 246–47, 248; killing of Viola Liuzzo, 281–82; LBJ and halting of civil rights demonstrations before 1964 election, 257; lessons of Montgomery bus boycott, 28, 155; mass nonviolent action, tactic, 201; mass "turn-in," Montgomery, as first act of civil disobedience of era, 74–75; MLK arrest and jailing, Birmingham, 167–71, 180–85, 188, 189; MLK called to leadership, 90, 97, 154; MLK emergence as national leader, 130–34, 170–71, 199–200; MLK as mediator,

Howe, Julia Ward, 161–62
Hubbard, Rev. H. H., 72, 84
Hugo, Victor, 348
Hulett, John, 284, 285
Humphrey, Hubert, 250, 251–52, 254, 255, 256, 416
Hungarian uprising, 136
Hutton, Bobby, 452
Huxley, Aldous, 89

Indianola, MS, 244
In Friendship, 97
Ingalls, Luther, 58–63, 68, 137
interracial relationships and marriage: 61, 63, 150–51; Nazi party member assault on King and, 177; White House and Sammy Davis Jr., incident, 174
Isaiah (prophet), 325, 345
Israel, state of: Arab-Israeli conflict, 325–26; MLK and, 325–26
"I've Got the Light of Freedom" (song), 112
"I Want to Be Near the Cross Where They Crucified My Lord" (hymn), 106
"I Want Jesus to Walk with Me" (hymn), 194

Jack, Homer, 96
Jackson, Emory, 85, 199
Jackson, J. H., 131, 144
Jackson, Jesse, 334; conflict with MLK, 433; funeral of MLK and, 454; in Memphis, 440; opposition to PPC, 385–87, 389–91, 431–34
Jackson, Jimmie Lee, 272, 273
Jackson, Mahalia, 210, 212
Jackson, MS, 176; freedom riders and arrests, 176, 190
Jackson, Rev. Ralph, 426
Jakes, Wilhelmina, 115
Jefferson, Thomas, 184, 351
Jemison, T. J., 32, 144, 146
Jenkins, Walter, 251
Jeremiah (prophet), 230, 345
Jesus: black Christianity and intimate relationship with, 49–50, 76; cross and crucifixion, MLK and, 125–26, 449–50, 452, 453; as extremist, 184; invoked by MLK, as model for protest, 26, 28; MLK parallel, 302, 387, 434, 450; Spirit of God, descending on, 39
Jim Crow apartheid, 19, 96; bus segregation, Montgomery, 19; church segregation, Birmingham, 193–94; Civil Rights Act of 1964 and death of, 241; in the courts, 8; states identified with, 53; See also segregation
Johns, Vernon, 21
Johnson, Frank M., Jr., 117–18, 140, 275, 278
Johnson, June, 205–6
Johnson, Lady Bird, 400

Johnson, Lynda Bird, 400–401
Johnson, Lyndon B. (LBJ): announces will not run for reelection, 439–40; antiwar movement and, 366, 400–401; assassination of MLK and, 452–53, 454; Atlantic City National Convention and MFDP, 249–55, 262; Civil Rights Act of 1964 and, 233, 238, 240, 250, 256; civil rights leaders and, 233, 240, 256; Detroit and Newark riots and, 336, 337; Dominican Republic invasion, 287, 288; doubts, ego, neurosis of, 250–51, 255; election, 259; finest hour of, 278; Gettysburg speech, 204; "Great Society," 259, 262, 264, 332; halting of civil rights demonstrations before elections and, 257; Kerner Report and, 405; liberal support for, 311; master of co-optation, 381; MLK and, 252, 253, 254, 261, 262, 288–89, 301, 302, 304, 317–18, 337, 350; MLK's "disloyalty" and, 318; Poor People's Campaign, fear of, 422; reelection challenged, 355–56, 413–16; speech to Congress, evoking Lincoln, 227; State of the Union address, 1965, 264–65; Vietnam War, 248–49, 274, 288–89, 302, 304, 306–7, 316, 317–18, 332, 410–13, 439; Voting Rights Act, 277, 278, 289–90, 302; Wallace meeting on Selma, 277–78; "war on poverty," 233–35, 256
Jones, Clarence, 188, 288
Jones, Moses, 106, 107
Jones, Solomon, 441, 449
Jones, Walter B., 116
Joplin, Janis, 344
Jordan, Clarence, 432
Jordan, Georgia, 104, 105
Jordan, Rosa, 146

Kant, Immanuel, 53
Karenga, Maulana Ron, 399
Katzenbach, Nicholas, 277
Kennedy, Jacqueline, 172
Kennedy, John F. (JFK), 147; assassination of, 227; Birmingham and, 195, 213, 214; calls to Coretta King, 172, 189; Civil Rights Act, 206–8; inaugural address, 173; March on Washington and, 210; MLK and, 172–74, 189, 204, 217, 225; national address on Civil Rights Act, 207–8; national guard deployed to integrate U. of Alabama, 205; New Frontier, 173; poverty issues, 224; racial issues and, 173–74, 175, 176, 177–78; second Emancipation Proclamation and, 172, 173, 204, 208; troops sent to Birmingham, 199
Kennedy, Robert F. (RFK): antiwar movement and, 415; assistant attorney generals sent to Birmingham, 195; Birmingham use of children in protests and, 196–97; Chavez and,

King, Martin Luther, Jr. (MLK) *(continued)*
movement aimed for, 209; Negro Revolution of 1963, 205, 217, 235; radical moderation of, 221–23; radicalizing of and breach with liberals, 285–86, 290; RFK and, 175–76, 188–89; risk and personal danger, 267; St. Augustine, FL, arrest, 238–39; St. Augustine, FL, campaign, 238–40; SCLC and, 167–71, 176–79, 216–17, 233, 237–38, 257–58, 262–63, 275, 285–88, 292–93, 302, 310, 327–28, 331, 431–37, 466n. 216 *(see also specific campaigns; specific individuals)*; Selma, AL, 263–82 *(see also Selma, AL)*; SNCC and, 171, 175–76, 185, 270, 276, 283, 287–88, 303–4, 331; social programs envisioned by, 235–36; telegram to LBJ, 337; urban rioting and, 290, 336–38, 349; voting rights, focus on, 258; war on poverty and, 233–34
philosophy and theology: black social gospel tradition and, 92–93; Buber's *I and Thou*, 50, 110, 340; civil disobedience and, 320, 349–50; communism and, 89–90, 225–226, 260; conversion experience ("kitchen conversion," 1956), 39, 56–57, 73, 151, 170, 181, 308, 352–53, 466n. 213; creative extremism, radical moderation, 184–85, 220–23, 235–36, 315, 349; creative maladjustment, 341–42; "derivative bondage," 236; dialectics, Hegel, synthesis, and divided consciousness, 217–19, 469n. 66; in doctoral dissertation, 54–56; early, intellectual and rational view of God, 52; Easter and Easter as metaphor, 108–10, 125, 145; end is "preexistent in the means," 129; evil, Niebuhr's conception of and problem of, 91, 92–93, 94, 330; forgiveness, 120–21; on freedom, 344–45; Gandhi and Gandhian soul force, 89, 226, 457–58; good and evil, 38, 89, 91–93, 106, 126; goodwill, 93; healing through public witness, 341; Hebrew prophets and, 345; Hebrew Scriptures and, 91, 92, 270–71, 325; "Letter from Birmingham Jail," ideas expressed in, 181–85, 188, 222; love, as *agape*, 127; love and justice as co-joined, 27, 28, 91, 93–94, 126, 298, 343; love and power, 330; moral militancy, 27–28, 457; nonviolence, 15–16, 34, 37–38, 78, 81–83, 89–93, 124, 217, 226, 326, 395, 426–29, 428–29, 457–58; "passive resistance," 124–25, 127–29; Paul of Tarsus and, 181, 184–85, 436, 465n. 185; personalism, 53–56; personal redemption, personal salvation, 109–10; personal relationship with Jesus, 352–53; pivotal speech, prefiguring moral quest that defined his ministry (Dec. 5, 1955), 26–28; Plato's *Republic*, 237; redemptive power of suffering, 125–26; revolution driven by power of love and, 300; socialism and, 267; the soul, 109–10, 128; synthesis of rational and emotional theology, 57; technology, alienation, and depersonalization, 340–43, 344; Tillich and, 54–55, 56, 298, 330, 340; transformation of society through transformation of individuals, 110–12; Wieman and, 55–56
sermons and speeches: address to SCLC, "To Chart Our Course for the Future," 1967, 322–25; Alpha Phi Alpha address 1956, 112, 464n. 160; analysis, "state of the movement," St. Helena Island 1967, 369–71; boycott end address, Holt St. Baptist Chruch, Montgomery, 142–43; Democratic National Convention 1956, 134; "I Have a Dream," March on Washington, 211–12; "In Search of a Sense of Direction" 1967, 394; Institute on Nonviolence and Social Change, MLK opening, 143; March on Montgomery address, 281; Memphis sanitation workers strike address, 425–26; Memphis strike rally ("Mountaintop" speech), 3 April 1968, 442–44; NAACP dinner, 17 May 1956, 110–11, 464n. 157; NBC convention, Sept. 1956, "Paul's Letter to American Christians," 131–32, 181; NCNP convention, Chicago, 1967, 356–57; "The Negro and the Constitution," debate contest speech, 1944, 164–65; Nobel Prize acceptance, 261; Poor People's Campaign, announcement to press, 380–81; Poor People's Campaign, workshop speech, on healing dissension, 386–87; "Prayer Pilgrimage," Washington, 17 May 1957, speech at Lincoln Memorial, 154; Rev. Fields's Retraction, 18 June 1956, 120; Riverside Church, NYC, address against the Vietnam War, 297–300, 317; SCLC convention, Richmond, address, 216–17; SCLC convention, Savannah, address, 257–58; SCLC tenth anniversary convention, Ebenezer Baptist, call for mass civil disobedience, 348–51; Senate testimony, 1966, on welfare, 343; sermon, "Death of Evil upon the Seashore," May 1956, 93; sermon, Dexter Baptist Church, "Paul's Letter to American Christians," 4 Nov. 1956, 111, 181, 464n. 158; sermon, Ebenezer Baptist Church, Atlanta, 1967, 320–21; sermon, Ebenezer Baptist Church, Atlanta, Christmas 1967, 374–75; sermon, Ebenezer Baptist Church, Atlanta, July 1967, 345; sermon, Ebenezer Baptist Church, Atlanta, drum major (eulogy), 389–91, 454; sermon, Ebenezer Baptist Church, Atlanta, on shattered dreams,

March 1968, 407–9; sermon, First Baptist Church, Montgomery, AL, 23 Feb. 1956, 78; sermon, First Baptist Church, Montgomery, AL, 30 Jan. 1956, 12–13; sermon, Holt Street Baptist Church, Montgomery, AL, 5 Dec. 1955, 26–28; sermon, Holt Street Baptist Church, Montgomery, AL, March 1956, 106–7; sermon, Mount Pisgah Missionary Baptist Church, Chicago, August 1967, 352–53; sermon, National Cathedral, 31 March 1968, 438–39; Spring Mobilization Against the War address, 15 April 1967, 312, 359

Vietnam War: avoids Pentagon March, Oct. 1967, 360; black press and, 316; Clergy and Laity Concerned mobilization, Washington, DC, 393–94; combining peace movement and civil rights, 309–10; critics of antiwar position, 316–18, 360, 429–30; draft resistance, position on, 314–15, 320–21, 366–67, 378–79, 385; *Face the Nation*, MLK on, 314–15; first peace march, 309–10; first public criticism of, 273–74; letter from Thich Nhat Hanh and, 301–2; Los Angeles speech, first full criticism of war, 309; Louisville, struck by rock, 321; march, 15 April 1967, NYC, and speech, 311–13, 359; opposition to the war, 288, 297–307, 308–18; peacemaking mission, 302; point of no return on, 304–5; reluctant involvement, reasons for, 301, 303; risk of sedition charges and, 367, 385; sermon at Ebenezer, 320–21; Vietnam Summer, 320; visit to Santa Rita jail, 376–77; White House and MLK, 302

writings: "Autobiography of Religious Development," 51–52, 462n. 82; "An Experiment in Love," 125, 465n. 177; "Letter from Birmingham Jail," 180–85, 188, 235; "Our Struggle," 111, 464n. 157; *Stride Toward Freedom*, 235; *Where Do We Go From Here*, 304–5, 327–31, 348, 384, 473n. 30; *Why We Can't Wait*, 185, 235–37, 324, 348, 473n. 30

King, Martin Luther, Sr. (Daddy King), 48; in Birmingham campaign, 168, 169; fear for son's life, 72, 75, 169; name change, 48, 462n. 75; opposition to MLK's activism, 72–73, 75–76; Southern Negro Leaders Conference on Transportation and Nonviolent Integration hosting, 148–49; support of MLK's activism, 76, 131–32, 433; vocation choice of MLK and, 51, 52

King, Yolanda (Yoki, daughter), 13, 71, 170, 433

King v. Jowers, 479n. 187

Kitt, Eartha, 400

Koinonia Farm, GA, 432

Knabe, Walter, 140

Ku Klux Klan (KKK): assassination of Medgar Evers, 208; Birmingham bombings, 40–41, 148, 166–67, 199, 212–15; bombings, arrest and acquittal in, Montgomery, 151; fear of, 195; firebombing of buses, 175; Hugo Black in, 22; killing of Schwerner, Goodman, and Chaney, 246–47, 248; killing Viola Liuzzo, 282; leadership failure, 152; Montgomery bombings, arrests and acquittal, 151; Montgomery Klan caravan through black neighborhood, 141–42; Montgomery klavern formed, 137; rebirth, 1920s, 95; St. Augustine, FL, 238–40; threats against MLK, 199; Tuscaloosa violence against U. of Alabama desegregation, 46; white supremacy and, 42

Kyles, Gwen, 447–48

Kyles, Rev. Samuel (Billy), 441, 447–48

labor, organized: leaders, 6; Brockwood Labor College, 66; Brotherhood of Sleeping Car Porters and A. Philip Randolph, 20, 66, 133; CIO organizers, 22, 66; civil rights and, 210; civil rights opposition and, 140; democratic socialism and, 224; Red Scare and, 70; sit-down strike, 66; Wobbly (Industrial Workers of the World) indictment, Chicago, 71. *See also* Muste, A. J.

Lafayette, Bernard, 403, 423

Langston, John Mercer, 323

law and lawsuits: Alabama defense of segregation policies, states' rights, 116; Claudette Colvin case, 7–9; Emmett Till murder case, 10; Jim Crow and, 8; MLK's conspiracy trial, Montgomery, March 1956, 98–106, 130–31; South Carolina bus segregation case (*Flemming*), 115–16, 119; southern courts, racism in, 3, 10, 206, 208

Supreme Court decisions: *Browder v. Gayle* (Montgomery bus segregation challenge), 7–9, 41, 43–44, 70, 115, 116–19, 141, 465n. 167; *Brown v. Board of Education of Topeka*, 6, 10, 41, 45, 58, 202; desegregation of bus terminals, 174–76; *Plessy v. Ferguson* (separate but equal doctrine), 41, 117, 141; "white only" southern primaries, abolishing (1944), 20. *See also specific cases and Supreme Court decisions*

Lawford, Peter, 174

Lawrence, Charles, 68, 88

Lawson, James, 423–28, 430, 444, 451–52

leadership: African-American, Communism and, 132; African-American, elite, 131; Birmingham, conservative black clergy, 178, 180–81, 183, 191; collective, 114, 117; CUCRL, 209; mass "turn-in," Montgomery, 73–75; MLK, emergence as national, 130–34,

Memphis, TN: assassination of MLK, 445–50, 453–54, 479n. 187; MLK "Mountaintop" address, 442–44; Community on the Move for Equality (COME), 424, 428; FBI and police collusion, 441, 446–47; injunction against march, 441–42, 445; Invaders, 427–29, 445–46; Lorraine Motel, 441, 444, 446–50; MLK's march, violence and, 426–29; MLK and SCLC in, 440–44; sanitation workers strike, 423–28, 453

Men of Montgomery, 71

Meredith, James, 174, 290–91

Miles College, 45, 177, 221

Mississippi: Democratic Party in, 247–48, 249–55, 256; desegregation of U. of Miss., 174; Emmett Till murder, 9–11; freedom riders, arrest in, 176, 190; hunger in, 353–54; march through, after Meredith shooting, 291–93; MLK's visit to Marks, 418–19, 435; murders of Schwerner, Goodman, and Chaney, 246–47, 248; Parchman Penitentiary, 176, 190, 284; RFK and politicians of, 176; RFK visit to poor of, 353–54; shooting of James Meredith, 290–91; voting rights and registration, 244–46, 247; White Citizens Council formed in, 58–59, 244; white violence and terrorism, 244, 245

Mississippi Freedom Democratic Party (MFDP), 246–55, 256

Mississippi Freedom Summer, 237–38, 246, 247, 255, 257

Mobile, AL, 146; bus policy in, 8, 30

Montgomery, AL: arrest of car pool drivers, 79; black lawyers in, 6 (see also Gray, Fred); black organizations, 7; bombings, 13–16, 41, 42, 135–36, 148; bombings, arrest and acquittal in, 151; Browder v. Gayle (bus desegregation lawsuit), 7–9, 41, 43–44, 70, 115, 116–19, 135, 141, 465n. 167; bus boycott, 8, 23–39, 42–44, 70–80, 99–107, 117, 135–36, 460n. 37; bus boycott end, 142–46; bus company ends Jim Crow seating, city refuses to comply, 116; bus protest, Claudette Colvin, 4–9; bus protest, Mary Louise Smith, 10–11; bus protest, Rosa Parks, 17–19, 21, 22–23, 69 (see also bus boycott); civil rights movement in, as church-based protest, 29; clergy, as civil rights activists, 12–13, 15–16, 21, 24, 25–26, 28, 42–44, 73–75, 76–78, 80, 119–21, 146; code of nonviolent conduct, 145; Confederacy and, 17, 45; County Courthouse, 73–74; elections, black issues and political power, 6–7; freedom riders in, 175; Hilliard Brooks shooting, 19; indictment of bus boycott leaders, 70–72; informants, 43, 100; injunction to end MIA carpool, 140, 142; Jeremiah Reeves case, 3, 73;

King Hill neighborhood, 4; Ku Klux Klan in, 137, 141–42; mayor, Gayle, 8, 13, 14–15, 20, 30–31, 35, 45, 64, 116, 136; MLK's conspiracy trial, March 1956, 98–106, 130–31; NAACP in, 3, 6; nonviolent training workshops and preparation for boycott end, 137–40, 143–44, 145; police brutality, 19, 20, 21; police commissioner, Sellers, 8, 13, 14–15, 30, 43, 64, 116, 146; prayer vigils, 74; legal defenses to bus segregation, 1899 Alabama court ruling, 116, 138, 145; racial tensions, 1955–1957, 8, 146; Rustin in, 69–72, 74, 78–80, 81–87; segregation in, 4, 6, 7, 17, 19, 20, 21, 41–42; "separate but equal" bus law, 4, 6, 7, 19, 41–42; slavery in, 5, 17; prosecution of bus boycott leaders, 98–99; violence and repression, response to boycott, 30, 43, 135–36, 141–42, 145–46, 150–51; voter registration, 20, 21; white repression and official responses, 15, 30, 31, 33, 34, 61–62, 64–65, 135, 140, 145–46, 151–52; white supporters of desegregation, 9, 21–22, 31, 131, 135–36; white supremacy rally, 59, 63–65. See also specific churches; specific organizations

Montgomery Advertiser, 24, 85, 99, 117, 140, 465n. 166; code of nonviolent conduct published, 145; Fields' letter, 119; letters to, 33–34; letters to, by Juliette Morgan, 31–32

Montgomery Improvement Association (MIA), 24–25, 26, 30–31, 33; affiliations and partnerships, 153; boycott end, 142–44; call for nationwide day of prayer, 80; dissension within movement, Fields and, 119–22; indictments and, 71–72; funds misuse charges, 119–22; injunction to end carpool, 140, 142; Institute on Nonviolence and Social Change, 143, 183; mass "turn-in" and, 74; meeting of 30 Jan. 1956, 42–44; meeting of 1 March 1956, 90–91; meeting of Sept. 1956, to prepare for returning to buses, 137–38; MLK conspiracy trial and, 100–101; NAACP and, 42, 85; nonviolent training workshops for boycott end, 137–40, 143–44, 145; prayer meetings and, 74, 76; Smith, Lillian, address by, 183; outsiders and, 96

Montgomery Voters League, 21

Moody, Anne, 212

Moore, Alice, 285

Moore, Amzie, 245

Moore, Doug, 147, 466n. 207

Moore, Gladys, 102, 105

Moore, Juanita, 115

Morehouse College, 75, 131, 428, 454

Morgan, Juliette, 31–32, 135

Morgan, Robin, 374

Moses, Robert, 189, 243, 244, 245, 252, 253, 303, 348

"Prayer Pilgrimage," Washington, May 1957, 154

"Precious Lord, Take My Hand" (hymn), 49, 449, 455

Presley, Elvis, 137, 193

Prison Notes (Deming), 398

Pritchett, Laurie, 178, 192

Progressive Democrats, Montgomery, AL, 24

Progressive Labor Party, 413

Prosser, Gabriel, 323

racism: African-American anger and response, 35–36; alienation and, 341; American society, collapse of and, 345; black-white couples and, 3, 10; depersonalization and, 340–41; economic issues and, 382–83; housing discrimination, 174; interview with Luther Ingalls, 58–63; King refused service at Atlanta airport restaurant, 136; Lincoln's White House and, 163; Montgomery, AL, 3–9, 17–18, 20, 101–5; "Negro mass parliaments" to fight, 67; poll tax, 22, 64. *See also* Jim Crow apartheid; Ku Klux Klan; segregation; white supremacy; *specific issues*

Raisin in the Sun, A (Hansberry), 203

Rand, Ayn, 113

Randolph, Asa Philip, 20, 66, 67, 88, 173, 174; AFL-CIO and, 133; as "American Gandhi," 67; as architect of "nonviolent goodwill direct action," 67–68, 92, 128, 153; desegregation of armed forces and, 67; Freedom Budget, 382, 383; hope for Negro mass movement, 69, 224; LBJ's antipoverty program and, 234; March on Washington, 1963, 210–12, 224; march on Washington, 1941, 67; MLK and, 133, 153; Montgomery bus boycott and, 69, 80, 87; Rustin and, 68, 69, 80, 86; State of the Race Conference, Washington, DC, 115, 133–34

Rankin, Jeannette, 372

rape: charges against black men, 3, 23; by police, against black women, 21, 73

Rauh, Joseph, 249, 252–53

Rauschenbusch, Walter, 92

Ray, James Earl, 447, 479n. 187

Reagan, Bernice Johnson, 112, 171

Reconstruction, 235, 254, 256, 293

Redding, Otis, 340

Reeb, Rev. James, 277–78

Reedy, George, 251

Reese, Frederick, 283

Reese, Jeanetta, 70, 119

Reeves, Jeremiah, 3, 73

Riesman, David, 341

religion. *See* philosophy and theology

Republican Party: Nixon election, 416; presidential election, 1964, 248; primaries, 1968, 415. *See also* Eisenhower, Dwight D.; Goldwater, Barry; Nixon, Richard M.

Resistance (draft resistance group), 315, 360–61

Resurrection City, 480n. 2

Reuther, Walter, 250–51, 252, 254, 453

Rice, Condoleezza, 214

Rice, Rev. John, 214

Riverside Church, NYC, MLK address against the Vietnam War, 297–300, 317

Rives, Richard T., 117–18

Robertson, Carole, 213

Robeson, Paul, 132, 292

Robinson, Jackie, 316

Robinson, Jo Ann, 7, 8, 17, 19–20, 23, 24, 30, 44, 149, 154, 374

Robinson, Ruby Doris, 291

Roche, John, 317–18

Rockefeller, Nelson, 415

Rockwell, George Lincoln, 265–66

Romney, George, 336, 415

Roodenko, Igal, 68, 86

Roosevelt, Eleanor, 64, 67, 115, 166

Roosevelt, Franklin D., 9, 233; banning of racial discrimination in war industry, 67, 210

Rowan, Carl, 34, 360

Rowe, Gary Thomas, 282

Rubin, Jerry, 365

Rupert, Paul, 315–16

Rusk, Dean, 371

Rustin, Bayard: Abernathy and, 71, 78–79; arrogance criticized, 85, 86; California arrest, 68; Committee for Nonviolent Integration, 96–97; Communist and left-wing affiliations, 85, 132, 147, 210; Coretta King and, 79, 146; desegregation of interstate buses and, 69, 79; draft resistance and imprisonment, 79, 313; economic concerns, 342; electoral politics and, 252, 253, 350, 396; FBI surveillance, 402; FOR and, 68, 69; Gandhian principles and, 69, 91, 96; homosexuality of, 68, 87, 96, 210; jailing, North Carolina, and chain gang article, 79, 86; LBJ's antipoverty program and, 234; leads first freedom ride, 79, 86, 138; mentoring of, 245; mentors, Randolph and Muste, 68, 86; March on Washington, 1963, 210–12, 223, 224; mass "turn-in," Montgomery, 74; MLK and, 79–80, 81–83, 96, 133, 139, 146, 224, 257, 286, 406, 466n. 216; Montgomery protest and, 69–72, 74, 78–80, 81–87, 94; nonviolence, teaching of to Montgomery leaders, 80, 138; nonviolent philosophy and pacifism of, 79, 113; PPC and breach with MLK, 396–97, 429; as Quaker, 69, 79; radical pragmatism, 114; representing himself as foreign journal-

498   To The Mountaintop

ist, 70, 85; Smiley and, 88–89; southern regional organization plan, 146–49; surveillance and persecution of, Montgomery, 84–87, 96–97; vulnerability of, 68, 87, 96; Washington march, 1968, 480n. 2; WRL and, 68, 83, 85, 86

Rutherford, William, 395, 406, 416, 434

St. Augustine, FL, campaign, 238–40; MLK doubts and, 240

Saint John of the Cross, 436

Sampson, Tim, 392

Samstein, Mendy, 253

Sanders, Carl, 254

Sandperl, Ira, 376, 377–78

San Francisco: counterculture, Haight-Ashbury, and Gathering of the Tribes festival, 338–39; desegregation of, 205; Vietnam War protests, 312, 315

Santa Rita jail, CA, 376–77

Schlesinger, Arthur, Jr., 400

Schwerner, Michael, 246–47, 248

Scott, C. A., 75

Scripture: African-American tradition of prophetic criticism, 230; 1 Corinthians 13, 77, 93; Hebrews 10:39, 44; Isaiah 11:1–2, 42: 1–4, 30; Mark, 389–90; Matthew 3:16–17, 39; Psalm 27, 267; Psalm 34, 25, 28; Romans 12:2, 111

Scott, John B., 24

Seay, Rev. Solomon S., 13, 21, 43, 72, 78

Seeger, Pete, 169

segregation: alienation and, 341; armed forces, 67; Baptist Church, 47; Birmingham, 168; bus, 4–9, 10–11, 17–18, 19, 69, 115–16, 138, 150, 174–76; churches, 193–94; Civil Rights Act of 1964, prohibiting, 241; Claudette Colvin's childhood experiences, 4 ; fear and resignation by African Americans, 4, 11, 21, 22, 119; legal challenges, 6, 7–9, 41, 43–44, 70, 115, 116–19, 141, 174–76; MLK conspiracy trial, March 1956, and, 101–5; in Montgomery, AL, 4–9, 41, 70; psychological impact, 4, 186; school, 6, 15, 21, 45–46 115, 136, 138, 152 (*see also Brown v. Board of Education of Topeka*); University of Alabama, expulsion of first black student, Autherine Lucy, 45–46; University of Mississippi, federal troops to desegregate, 174; violence and desegregation attempts, 46, 135–36, 137; in Washington, DC, 67

Sellers, Cleveland, 285, 293, 396

Sellers, Clyde, 8, 13, 14–15, 30, 43, 64, 116, 146

Selma, AL, 263–85; American Nazi Party in, 265–66; arrests, 215, 267–68; Bloody Sunday, 274–75; children join protests, 268; conflict over strategy, 268, 279, 283; courthouse marches, 276–77, 278; demonstrations banned in, 263, 264; desegregation in, 283; director of public safety Baker and, 264, 266, 267; disenfranchisement of blacks in Dallas County, 263; electoral politics and black majority, 283–84; impact of, on Voting Rights Act, 289–90; Jimmy Webb dialogue, 276–77, 398; killing of Rev. James Reeb, 277–78; Malcolm X in, 268–69; March to Montgomery, 273, 275–76, 278–82; mayor, Smitherman, 263; MLK and, 264, 265–66, 268, 273, 279–80; MLK address, March to Montgomery, 281; MLK arrest, 267–68; MLK compromise, 275–76; night marches, 271; SCLC and, 263, 265, 270; Sheriff Jim Clark, 263, 266–67, 274; SNCC and, 263, 276; teachers' march in, 266; violence in, 266–67, 271, 274–75, 277, 279; Voters League, 265–66. *See also* Boynton, Amelia

Shelton, Robert, 199

Sherrod, Charles, 202

Shiloh Baptist Church, Penfield, GA, 47

Shores, Arthur, 99

Shridharani, Krishnalal, 89

Shuttlesworth, Fred, 135, 144, 146, 148, 154, 168, 177, 178, 179, 185, 204; ACMHR and, 177, 178; bombing of home, 148–49; civil disobedience of, 149; conflict over protest settlement, 196–99, 200; Good Friday arrest, 169–70, 368; injury, V-Day, 195; in St. Augustine, 240

Siegenthaler, John, 175

Sixteenth Street Baptist Church, Birmingham, AL; bombing and death of four girls, 40, 212–15, 223; kid's army and, 191–92

slavery: African spiritual beliefs and practices, 48, 51; black Christianity and, 48–49; "derivative bondage," 236; dissembling, tactic of, 101; Ella Baker's ancestors, 242; Lincoln and, 161, 162–63; in Montgomery, AL, 5; "ring shout," 48; scarring of the soul and personal transformation, 110–11

Smiley, C. T., 15

Smiley, Glenn, 88–91, 94, 138, 145, 146, 153, 313

Smith, Jerome, 202–3

Smith, Lillian, 68, 94–95; "The Right Way Is Not a Moderate Way," 183

Smith, Mary Louise, 10–11, 18, 116–19

Smith, Scott B., Jr., 284

Smitherman, Joe, 263

socialism (democratic socialism), 66, 224–25, 267

Sorensen, Ted, 208

soul, concept of, 109; *Atman* or Oversoul, 128; *satyagraha* (truth force, soul force), 91, 128–29, 367, 457–58; in MLK's preaching, 109–10